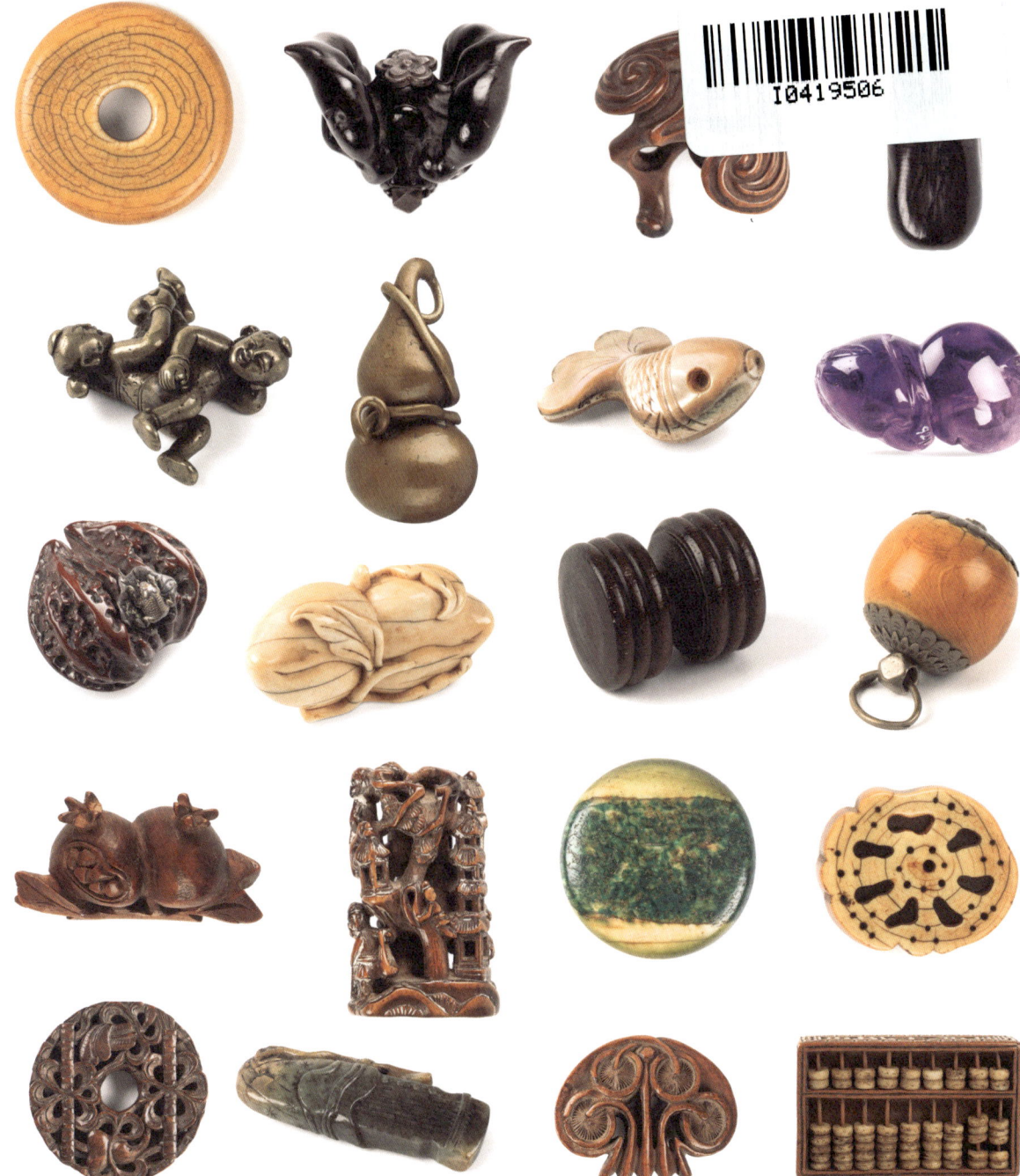

中国坠子

CHINESE TOGGLES

中国坠子

CHINESE
TOGGLES

Culture in Miniature
方寸见乾坤

Edited by Chen Shuxia and Min-Jung Kim

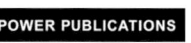 POWER PUBLICATIONS

THE UNIVERSITY OF SYDNEY

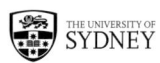 CHAU CHAK WING MUSEUM

POWERHOUSE

Note to reader
Chinese names and terms have been transliterated using Pinyin Romanisation. Chinese characters, including individuals' names, are written using the simplified system practised in the People's Republic of China. For Korean terms, Revised Romanisation of Korean is used, and Hepburn Romanisation is employed for Japanese terms. In accordance with Chinese, Japanese, and Korean systems, surnames precede given names, except for those individuals more widely published or known under alternative names. Birth and death dates are provided at first mention.

Forewords

Forewords

Michael Dagostino
Director, Chau Chak Wing Museum

The Chau Chak Wing Museum opened in 2020 at The University of Sydney, bringing together the collections of the Macleay Museum, the Nicholson Museum and the University Art Gallery. This new museum has transformed the profile, access and relevance of the university's diverse collections spanning arts, antiquity, humanity, natural history and the sciences. In contributing to Sydney's rich cultural life, the museum provides state-of-the-art facilities for the enjoyment, teaching and research of objects. Set in the heart of The University of Sydney's historic precinct, the museum is open seven days a week, free of charge, to students, staff and the broader Australian and international public.

The inclusion of a China Gallery was a significant new direction for the Chau Chak Wing Museum, providing impetus for widening collection development and programming focused on China and beyond, reflecting Australia's diverse cultures and place in the region. The China Gallery has also been a welcome opportunity to collaborate with neighbouring and international cultural institutions, most notably Powerhouse Museum—home to the Hedda and Alastair Morrison collection of toggles in the exhibition and publication — *Chinese Toggles: Culture in Miniature*. This is the third exhibition in the China Gallery in as many years, with Powerhouse also making a significant contribution to the previous exhibitions, *Auspicious* and *Sentient Paper*. These earlier exhibitions have also benefitted

from the generosity of significant loans from the Art Gallery of New South Wales and White Rabbit Gallery in Sydney, making the Chau Chak Wing Museum's China Gallery a showcase for local collections.

This insightful and comprehensive book, exploring the context, function, cultural appreciation and materiality of Chinese toggles, is the China Gallery's first focused publication, engaging with broader multifaceted discussions in museology, art history and scientific analysis.

I would like to thank the many contributors to this book and the numerous generous individuals who have made it, and the exhibition, possible. The exhibition and publication are co-curated and co-edited by Chau Chak Wing Museum Curator Dr Chen Shuxia and Powerhouse Curator Min-Jung Kim. Thanks to Dr Paul Donnelly, Chau Chak Wing Museum Deputy Director, and Dr Jacqui Strecker, Powerhouse Head of Collection Curatorial, for establishing the memorandum of understanding that was the origin and framework for this collaboration, and for driving it to completion.

The Toggles exhibition and publication have benefitted from the support and material analysis expertise of Professor Margaret Sunde and Dr Elizabeth Carter and her team at the university's core research facility, Sydney Analytical. Congratulations to exhibition designers Bel Youssofzay and David Hart for their elegant display, and to Matt Nix, graphic designer of both the exhibition and this book. In realising this publication, we are most grateful to Power Publications' Professor Mark Ledbury, Marni Williams, Dr Naomi Riddle and Lachlan Thompson for their support and expert input. We are also grateful to the anonymous peer reviewers whose comments have given additional rigour to the research.

The exhibition has been made possible thanks to the generous financial support of the Pauline and Tim Harding Asian Collection Fund, and David Anstice, AO, and Ana-Maria Zaugg. We are also grateful to the Gordon Darling Foundation for a publication grant in support of this book.

Chinese Toggles: Culture in Miniature is a lasting celebration of intriguing, beautiful objects, new research and institutional collaboration. I hope you enjoy the result.

Lisa Havilah
Chief Executive, Powerhouse Museum

For hundreds of years, it was a popular Chinese custom for people to carve and wear miniature ornaments as belt toggles. Yet no major collection of these beautiful and practical objects is known to exist in China today, because they have been considered by most as too ordinary to warrant study.

But these objects of traditional Chinese culture, colloquially known as *zhuizi* (坠子), captured the fascination of foreign travellers visiting China in the early-to mid-1900s, some of whom collected them as souvenirs. The two most significant collections of zhuizi known to exist today are the C. F. Bieber Collection held by the Field Museum, Chicago, USA, and the collection held by Powerhouse Museum, Sydney, Australia.

The Powerhouse Collection includes a total of 279 zhuizi, the majority drawn from a remarkable personal collection amassed by Hedda and Alastair Morrison from the 1940s to the 1960s that was donated to Powerhouse in 1992. They are part of the larger Morrison Collection, which includes over 500 photographic prints and slides that the German-born documentary photographer Hedda Morrison took over decades spent living in China and Sarawak (Malaysia), and travelling across Asia.

The exhibition *Chinese Toggles: Culture in Miniature* (April 2023 to August 2024, Chau Chak Wing Museum, Sydney) was developed under the exemplary curatorship of Chau Chak Wing Museum curator Dr Chen Shuxia and Powerhouse curator Min-Jung Kim. It includes a total of 110 objects from the Powerhouse Collection, including 80 Chinese toggles and nine Japanese toggles. This publication, edited by the exhibition's curators, allows a larger audience to engage with these unique objects, which combine form and function to embody Chinese folk traditions, beliefs and symbolism, while demonstrating material culture and craft skills.

Sincere thanks to Chau Chak Wing Director, Michael Dagostino, and Deputy Director, Dr Paul Donnelly, as well as Powerhouse Head of Collection Curatorial, Dr Jacqui Strecker, for their support not only of this project but also our ongoing collaboration. Thanks also to Professor Claire Roberts, Power Publications, and Sydney Analytical, The University of Sydney's core research facility dedicated to material, chemical and biological analysis, for conducting scientific analyses that improved our understanding of the materiality of the toggles.

Chinese Toggles: Culture in Miniature is the third exhibition for Chau Chak Wing Museum's China Gallery, realised in collaboration with Powerhouse Museum, since our two institutions signed a memorandum of understanding in November 2020. We are thrilled to have the opportunity to collaborate with the Chau Chak Wing Museum on this important project and look forward to many more collaborations that connect our communities with our collections.

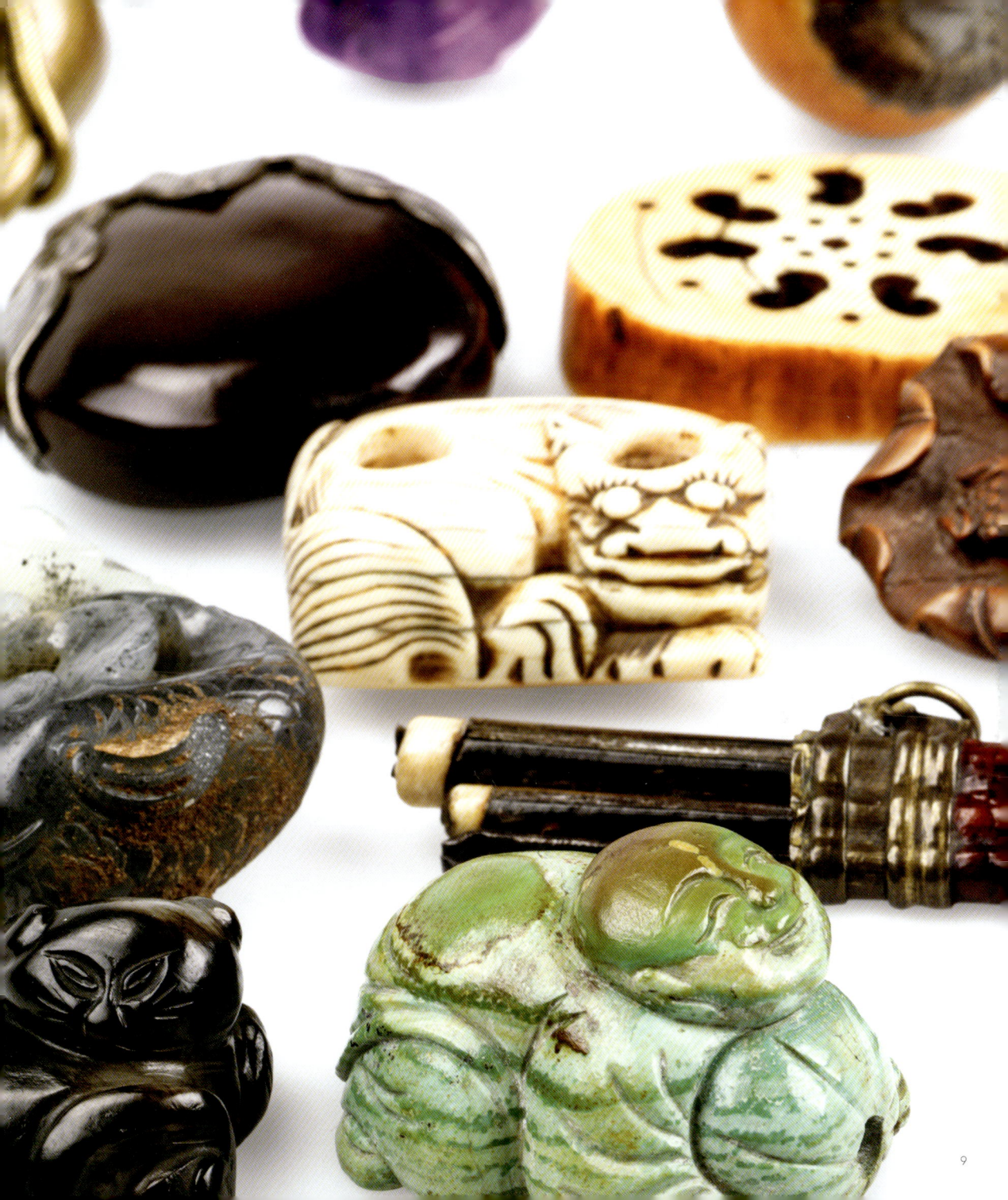

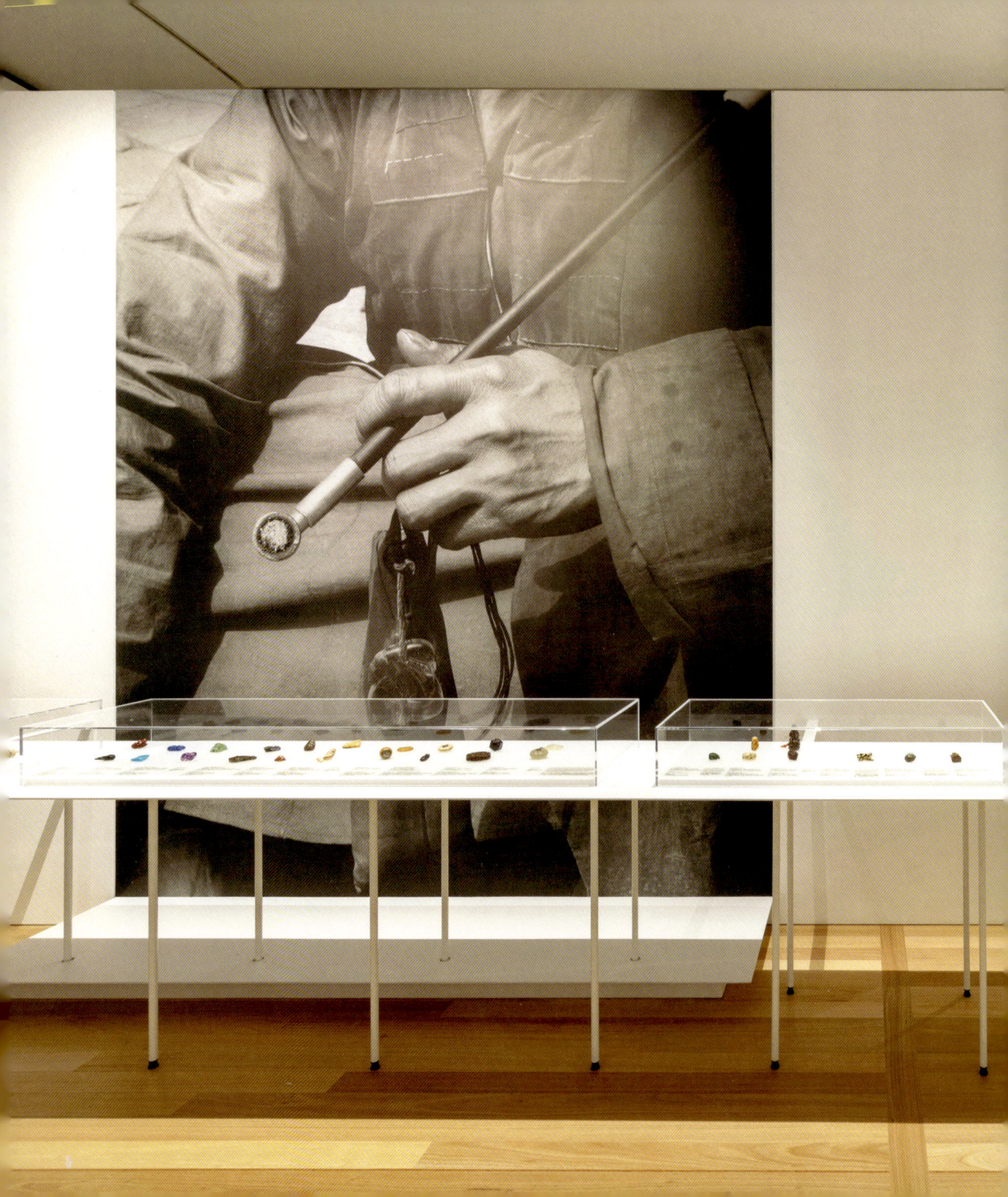

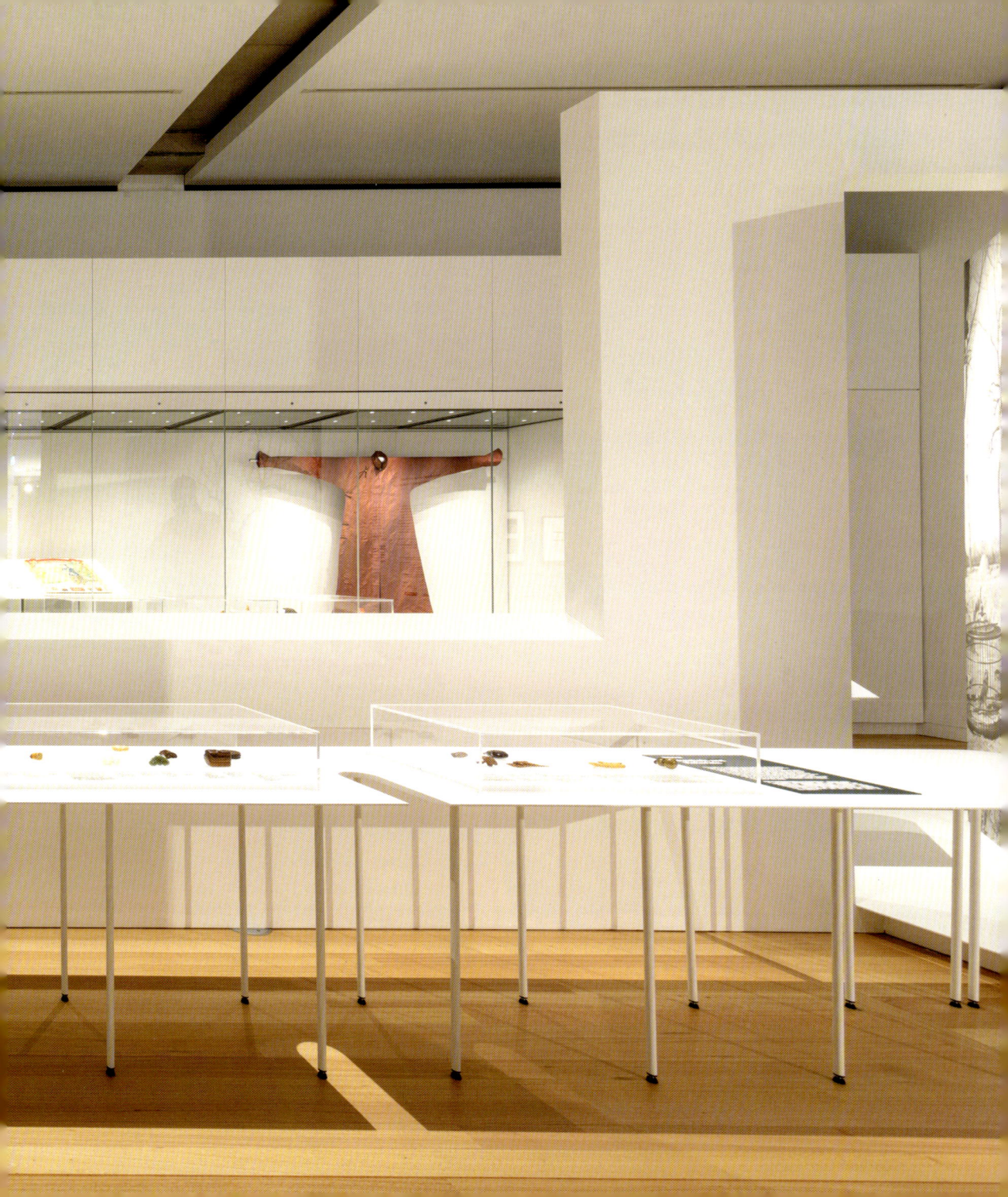

Introducing Chinese culture in miniature: a multifaceted examination of the toggle

Chen Shuxia and Paul Donnelly

Bright red jasper boys tumbling in miniature play, paired pomegranates of light green jade, pale amethyst peaches, a creased walnut in brown patinated ivory—these are just four examples of the incredible variety of forms and materials to be discovered among Chinese toggles, or *zhuizi* (坠子). Small but essential parts of everyday dress, toggles functioned as a counterbalance for a pouch used to carry portable items such as tobacco, which, from the seventeenth century, was increasingly used across all social classes in China. Hanging at the waist, toggles were practical and ubiquitous. Their broad range of artistic quality and materials meant that these delightful items were in the main unappreciated or overlooked in the realm of Chinese art.

This publication seeks to redress this through a multi-disciplinary approach to the research and interpretation of these little-known, wearable objects, popular between the eighteenth and early twentieth centuries. There are currently two publications in English dedicated to Chinese toggles. The first is *Substance and Symbol in Chinese Toggles* (1962) by anthropologist Schuyler Cammann. A relatively recent addition is *Traditional Chinese Toggles: Counterweights and Charms* (2011), by writer Margaret Duda. Cammann's pioneering work on Chinese toggles, based on the C. F. Bieber Collection in Chicago's Field Museum, laid the groundwork for the subject. His extensive knowledge of the material history of China and dissection of the symbolism used in Chinese toggles has been an excellent reference for researchers, including some of the authors in this volume. Nearly half a century later, and continuing Cammann's framework based on materials and signs, Duda offered a more comprehensive account for the general reader.

Departing from Cammann's and Duda's writings on materials and symbols, *Chinese Toggles: Culture in Miniature* offers an object-focused art historical and material-culture-based inquiry into Powerhouse's Chinese toggle collection. Here, contributions engage with recent discussions on relational approaches, prioritising the tactile and the user, and focus on carving techniques and scientific analysis to scrutinise materiality of these toggles. Such a multifaceted approach also informs the tripartite organisation of this book into the following sections:

I. Collecting the quotidian

II. Miniature, the user and tactile appreciation

III. Materiality

IV. Displaying culture in miniature

The fourth section is an illustrated overview of the bilingual exhibition of the Powerhouse Museum's Morrison collection held at the Chau Chak Wing Museum.

I: Collecting the quotidian

Considering how to engage with, revive and energise expanding collections, especially historic collections, has become an important task for museums and their curators.[1] Permanent collections can be 'the museum's greatest weapon'[2] to connect to the past, relate to the present and point towards the future. Powerhouse's Chinese toggles collection, arguably the world's largest known collection, embodies in everyday objects a disappeared sartorial and functional practice. The toggles provide solid context for and knowledge of cultural practice in a vernacular past, one that is often ignored by historians and curators, being outside the traditional artistic canon.

Min-Jung Kim provides insights into the institutional significance of toggles and the role of the Western perspective in chapter 1, 'Reflections on Chinese Belt Toggles from the Powerhouse Collection'. The toggles are defined by their social origins and functional attributes, in contrast to their Japanese descendants, *netsuke*. Netsuke, when referenced in early Japanese texts, are described as 'Chinese things',[3] but they diverged from their toggle predecessors when Western market demand increased artistic quality, and diminished functionality. This celebration by and responding production of netsuke for Western collectors contrasts to the incidental survival of Chinese toggles and their occasional appreciation by collectors such as Hedda and Alastair Morrison or Caroline F. Bieber. Bieber's collection was largely gathered for her in the 1930s by Hedda Morrison.[4]

Kim explores the ancient functional origins of toggles dating as early as the Yuan dynasty (1271–1368) as well as portable eating utensils attached at the belt that evolved during the Tang dynasty (618–907) which echo through the familiar form of zhuizi we see in the Collection, attached initially to fans. While some Powerhouse toggles may date as far back as the Ming dynasty (1368–1644), Kim suggests that most are from the eighteenth and nineteenth centuries, corresponding with increasing use of tobacco in that era.

The most common toggle material was wood, the simplest being naturally occurring root burls which were appreciated for their beauty and tactility. But toggles were made from many materials, from ivory and horn to jade and crystal. Kim discusses the objects' medicinal and apotropaic qualities, outlining their often multi-layered significance in materiality, form, Buddhist and Daoist symbolism, and etymological associations.

Claire Roberts, in addition to having been senior curator at Powerhouse when the toggles were donated, was a close friend of Hedda and Alastair Morrison. Roberts recalls with warmth and personal insight the serendipitous meeting of Hedda and Alastair in Beijing, when Alastair was living in the house of Caroline Bieber. Both of the world's best collections of Chinese toggles, and this book by extension, are the result of this chance arrangement of accommodation. Toggles had caught the eye of Bieber in the late 1920s to early 1930s, and Morrison's knowledge of Mandarin meant that she was able to negotiate with sellers on Bieber's behalf.

Discoveries, mainly in the jade market, were made among a diverse range of other miniature items. After Bieber left Beijing, the Morrisons continued collecting for themselves into the 1940s. Roberts (aided by oral recordings she made while at Powerhouse) notes Alastair Morrison fondly recalling that before their marriage he and Hedda playfully competed for toggles among the myriad antiques on the stalls. Their collections merged after their marriage in 1946, including examples Alastair had acquired while in military service at Shanghai during World War II. Roberts makes the observation that the coming together of Hedda and Alastair through collecting these objects was a happy coincidence, as toggles frequently symbolised happiness and good fortune in marriage. Their collection eventually found its home at Powerhouse, and Roberts' recounting of the circumstances of discovery of individual toggles, and Alastair Morrison's reminiscences of his and Hedda's haptic pleasures, ensure that the very personal origins and enjoyment of this collection lives on.

II: Miniature, the user, and tactile appreciation

While some disciplines in the humanities (in particular art history and history) have embraced the 'material turn' in the last few decades,[5] the focus on material mainly lies in physicality, the visual and the maker. In recent years, notions of trajectories, an object's 'life history',[6] the connected global network of objects,[7] or the networks between artefacts and people[8] have gradually caught the attention of scholars.

In this volume, Chen Shuxia echoes these interests by taking a relational approach to the cultural and social networks of Chinese toggles. Highlighting the often neglected role of the user through in-depth studies of selected objects, Chen characterises their 'objectness' as a sensuous or metaphysical presence.[9] In chapter 3, Chen further connects the toggles to the lives of their users, drawing from sources on Chinese literature, art, social customs and religious beliefs. She argues that the scale of these miniature wearable things manifests different 'metaphoric spaces'. By articulating these spaces, channelled by the toggles, she richly contextualises social and cultural life in early modern China, when toggles were popular everyday accessories carried by both elite and common folk alike.

Continuing her relational perspective in chapter 4, Chen emphasises the reciprocal relations between the toggles and their users brought about by tactile experience. Arguing that tactile appreciation has been a significant aesthetic in Chinese culture for centuries, Chen demonstrates that both human (the user) and non-human (the toggle) are active participants in such reciprocal relations. Breaking from the Western art history canon that often prioritises the visual, Chen delves into Chinese classical texts on the notion of *bawan* (把玩), to hold and play, and the sensory, Western modern theories on the haptic, as well as current debates on material culture, making the case that through our hands, we create the object, while the object in addition cultivates us.

III: Materiality

If the previous section embraces the 'material turn' by prioritising the reciprocity between the user and the objects in philosophical terms, Part III focuses on the elements of materiality—from the techniques that create form to the new insights into raw material now possible through scientific analysis. In chapter 5, Gu Fang and Chen Shuxia explore the traditional jade-carving procedure practised during the Qing dynasty (1644–1911), when most of these toggles were made. They construct a detailed illustration of the craftmanship and production of jade toggles by drawing on a Qing-period jade-carving manual, historic photographs of jade workshops in the late Qing and early Republican (1912–49) periods, as well as a major Chinese documentary film from 1976 on Qing-era jade carving produced by the Beijing Jade Factory and the Institute of Archaeology, Department of Philosophy and Social Sciences (now the Chinese Academy of Social Sciences in Beijing).

Chapter 6 presents the scientific analysis conducted on the toggles using X-ray fluorescence (XRF), and the vibrational spectroscopic techniques of near-infrared (NIR) and Raman spectroscopy. Led by Elizabeth Carter at Sydney Analytical, The University of Sydney's core research facility, this multi-authored chapter shows how the data from these methods enables the toggles to be separated into distinctive clusters that provide fresh insights into their materiality. The scientific testing detailed in this chapter focuses on ivory and jade—the two most nuanced materials, which have the greatest potential to authenticate or refute original curatorial assumptions. The analyses also interrogate and identify species or subcategories within these two material categories. Ivory has much to divulge with regard to the natural environment, broadly encompassing teeth and tusks of marine and terrestrial mammals. Similarly, jade is a general term potentially comprising many categories of rocks and minerals, but this study focuses on three main groups, ranging from the most prestigious to the less prized. Analytical distinctions between these qualitative types provide the opportunity to evaluate the availability of materials, test original attributions, and more accurately observe the status and use of toggles across classes.

IV: Displaying culture in miniature

The exhibition *Chinese Toggles: Culture in Miniature* was open to the public between April 2023 and August 2024 in the China Gallery of the Chau Chak Wing Museum at The University of Sydney. It stands as the most comprehensive presentation in Australia of these little-known everyday objects, with 80 toggles selected for display from the total collection of 279. The toggles were displayed and interpreted within the context of objects relevant to their use or inspiration, including robes, belt accessories, porcelains, paintings, daily necessities and games, enriching our understanding of a lost Chinese sartorial tradition. In this section at the end of this book, in addition to the beautifully photographed exhibited toggles, installation images are arranged together with bilingual (Chinese and English) exhibition didactic texts.

Exhibiting culturally diverse objects curated by culturally diverse curators (co-curators Chen and Kim are, respectively, of Chinese and Korean ethnic backgrounds) in bilingual exhibition texts highlights the significant role of the China Gallery at the Chau Chak Wing Museum, and its status as the only English/Chinese bilingual public gallery in Australia. Such sensitivity to a diversity of cultures, representations, objects, curators and visitors is not new to museum studies.[10] However, it is still highly relevant and even pressing to the development of the cultural sector in Australia to present and represent plurality and multiculturalism. In this publication, detailed photographic documentation of the exhibition display, accompanying bilingual exhibition texts and individual toggles provide a more visually comprehensive and accessible presentation of the collection, acting as the exhibition archive for future curators and researchers on Chinese toggles.

By looking from the perspectives of their different disciplines, the authors and curators have dissected these miniatures into multiple aspects, culturally and materially. This publication seeks to reposition and reimagine the history of toggles in Asia through such multi-layered research and provide a lasting visual record of an exhibition devoted to one of the largest toggle collections in the world. By engaging rigorously with non-canonical quotidian objects, that themselves speak of a diversity of cultural experiences,

Chinese Toggles: Culture in Miniature stresses the significance and benefits of energising historic collections in contemporary, multicultural Australia, and highlighting museums as instruments of cultural advocacy.[11]

Inevitably, there is still much to learn. The exhibition and this book benefit greatly from Hedda Morrison's photographs of toggles being used in everyday life. Toggles are captured in monochromatic detail, hanging from the hand when used or dangling to the ground in fleeting moments of people's individual lives. Where did they get them? Did they make the toggles themselves? Had they been handed down as heirlooms? These and more questions remain to be answered by future research. It is hoped that *Chinese Toggles: Culture in Miniature* has sparked new curiosity around this under-studied art form and that it will continue to spread and further our knowledge of these delightful reminders of lives and times past.

1. See Rachel Esner and Fieke Konijn, 'Curating the Collection', *Stedelijk Studies*, no. 5, 2017. https://stedelijkstudies.com/journal/curating-the-collection/ (viewed January 2022).

2. See Claire Bishop, *Radical Museology: Or, What's 'Contemporary' in Museums of Contemporary Art?*, Koenig Books, New York, 2013.

3. See chapter one, 'Reflections on Chinese Belt Toggles from the Powerhouse Collection' by Min-Jung Kim, p. 38.

4. Hedda Morrison is referred to throughout this book by her maiden and married names, Hedda Hammer, according to the historical context.

5. See Orianna Cacchione and Wei-Cheng Lin, 'Introduction', in Orianna Cacchione and Wei-Cheng Lin (eds), *The Allure of Matter: Materiality across Chinese Art*, The University of Chicago Press and Smart Museum of Art, Chicago, 2021, pp. 16–29.

6. See Francis Allard, Yan Sun and Katheryn M. Linduff (eds), *Memory and Agency in Ancient China: Shaping the Life History of Objects*, Cambridge University Press, Cambridge, 2018.

7. See Edward S. Cooke Jr., *Global Objects: Toward a Connected Art History*, Princeton University Press, Princeton, 2022.

8. See Hanna B. Holling, Francesca G. Brewer and Katharina Ammann, 'Material Encounters', in Hanna B. Holling, Francesca G. Brewer, and Katharina Ammann (eds), *The Explicit Material*, Brill, Leiden, 2019, p. 5.

9. This methodology draws from the work of Bill Brown. See Bill Brown, 'Thing Theory', *Critical Inquiry*, vol. 28, no. 1, 2001, p. 5.

10. Steven D. Lavine and Ivan Karp argued such concern in their 1991 edited volume *Exhibiting Cultures: The Poetics and Politics of Museum Display*. See Steven D. Lavine and Ivan Karp (eds), *Exhibiting Cultures: The Poetics and Politics of Museum Display*, Smithsonian Books, Washington, 1991.

11. Our approach has been informed by the work of Valentina Gamberi. See Valentina Gamberi, *Experiencing Materiality: Museum Perspectives*, Berghahn Books, New York and Oxford, 2021, p. 6.

Part I
Collecting the quotidian

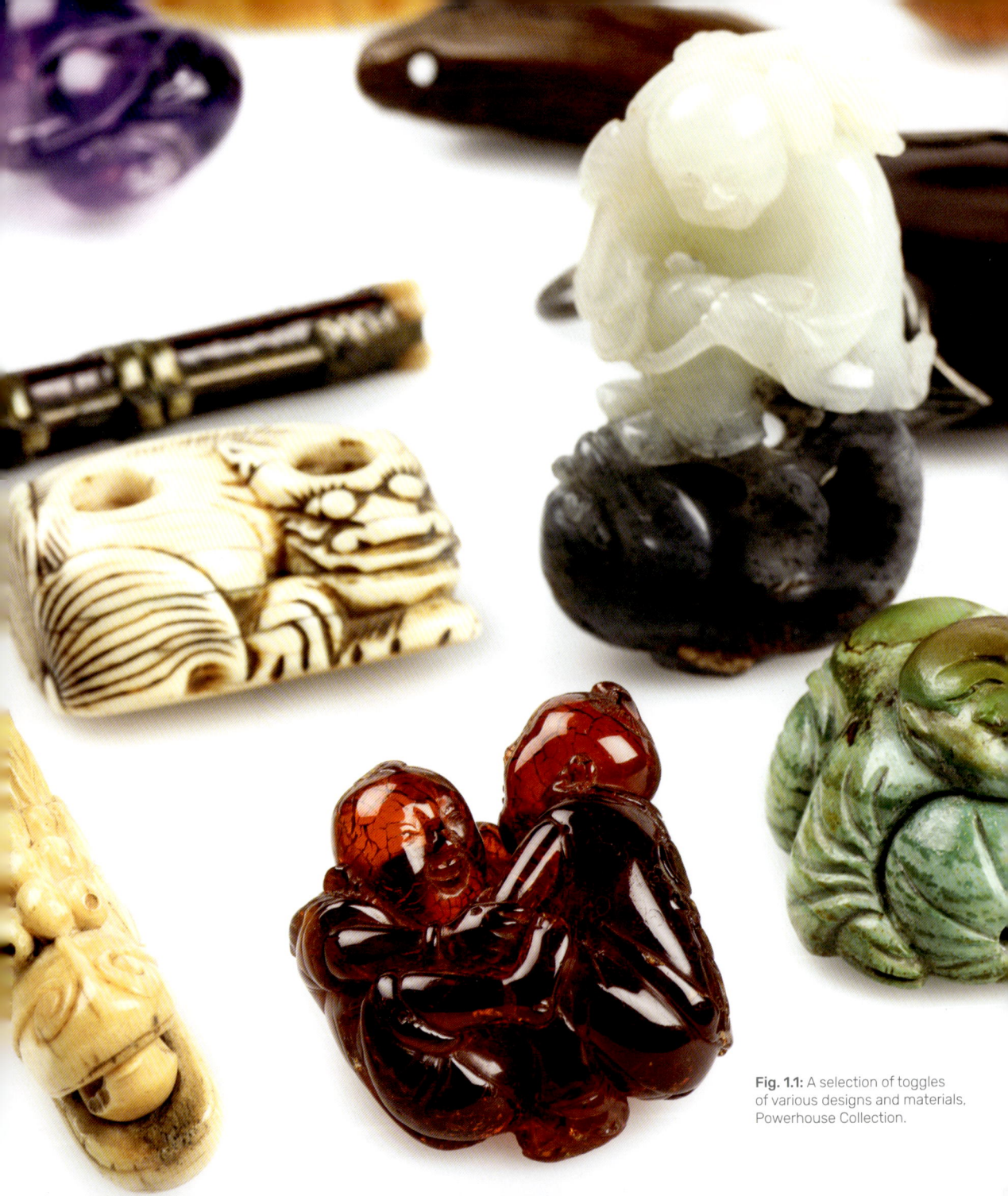

Fig. 1.1: A selection of toggles of various designs and materials, Powerhouse Collection.

1. Reflections on Chinese belt toggles from the Powerhouse Collection

Min-Jung Kim

Chinese belt toggles (fig. 1.1) are small carved ornaments that for more than three centuries could be seen hung at the belt as a counter-weight for pouches or cases. Traditional Chinese dress did not have the same types of pockets as Western garments and so pouches were used to carry such items as tobacco, pipes, knife and chopstick sets, flint and steel sets, fans, snuff bottles, spectacles, seals, needles, perfumes, medicine and money. In addition to their purpose as counter-weights, toggles could be worn on top of the belt and placed as a stopper to secure the pouches or cases. The Chinese custom of wearing toggles disappeared as Western-style dress became standard in the early twentieth century.

These enchanting carvings are functional objects: their production reflects Chinese artisanship and materialities, and their subjects and symbols provide a lens through which to appreciate Chinese beliefs and folk culture. Drawing from a collection of 279 of these diverse objects, amassed by Hedda Morrison (1908–91) and Alastair Morrison (1915–2009) from the 1940s onwards and donated to Powerhouse Museum following Hedda's death, this essay explores the materials, designs and symbols of Chinese belt toggles. It also touches on commonalities and differences in toggle culture in other Asian countries, most notably in Korea and Japan.

Origins

Little is understood today about the origins of Chinese belt toggles, and the production dates of surviving examples are often difficult to establish. The wearing of a belt and toggle as a high-status object occurred in ancient China. Some art historians claim that such toggles existed from as early as the Eastern Han dynasty (25–220). These suggestions of the toggle's origins can also be seen through a silver *kua* (銙), or belt with rings to attach toggles, that was discovered in an Eastern Han tomb in Ding county, Hebei province. The object indicates that people wore belts with pendants attached to the kua by a ring.[1] Different from this tradition, however, was the use of belt toggles as everyday objects. The Chinese term by which they are generally known in the West is *zhuizi* (坠子). This Chinese custom may initially have been impacted by the nomadic culture of Mongolia, with one theory suggesting that the practice arrived in China during the Yuan dynasty (1271–1368), when the country was under Mongolian rule.[2]

Mongolian belt toggles, particularly the button-shaped toggle, commonly accompanied knife and chopstick sets, as well as flint and tobacco pouches. The influence of this tradition in China is seen in a button-shaped toggle attached to a flint pouch from the Powerhouse

Collection (fig. 1.2). The custom of carrying a knife set at the belt would subsequently become a regular feature of toggle wearing. The comparison of a Chinese toggle in the form of a miniature knife set, which also functioned as a small knife and tweezer, with a full-sized Mongolian-style knife and chopstick set, offers further compelling evidence of this use (fig. 1.3 and plate 56, p. 218). Moreover, the fashion for these button-shaped toggles appears in both China and Japan, demonstrating aesthetic exchanges between the two cultures (fig. 1.4).

My research indicates that fan toggles may have played an important role in the evolution of belt toggle design and, in some cases, fan toggles may have been repurposed as belt toggles. Fan toggles were already known in China during the Song dynasty (960–1279). For instance, in volume 2 of his *Wu Za Zu* (五杂俎, date unknown), *Five Assorted Offerings*, the Ming-dynasty writer Xie Zhaozhe (谢肇淛, 1567–1624) relates that toggles on fans were not mentioned before the Tang dynasty (618–907). Further, he notes that when the Song-dynasty emperor Gaozong (宋高宗, 1107–87) hosted a banquet for his ministers, the emperor saw that Zhang Dunwang (张循王, 1086–1154) had a jade fan zhuizi in the shape of a child.[3] This might mark one of the earliest recorded uses of the term zhuizi for toggles.

It is possible that later, during the Yuan dynasty, the design of fan toggles was combined with that of Mongolian-style belt toggles. This can be seen in a Chinese fan from the Powerhouse Collection (figs 1.5 and 1.6) that has an ivory toggle from the 1800s depicting two human figures in a natural setting. In terms of materials, construction techniques, design motifs and size, it is strikingly similar to later Chinese belt toggles.

Some belt toggles in the Powerhouse Collection may date back to the Ming dynasty (1368–1644), although this is difficult to substantiate conclusively.[4] The majority of the toggles probably date to the eighteenth and nineteenth centuries, corresponding to the increased use of tobacco at this time.[5] Pipe smoking was introduced to China in the mid-sixteenth century and became

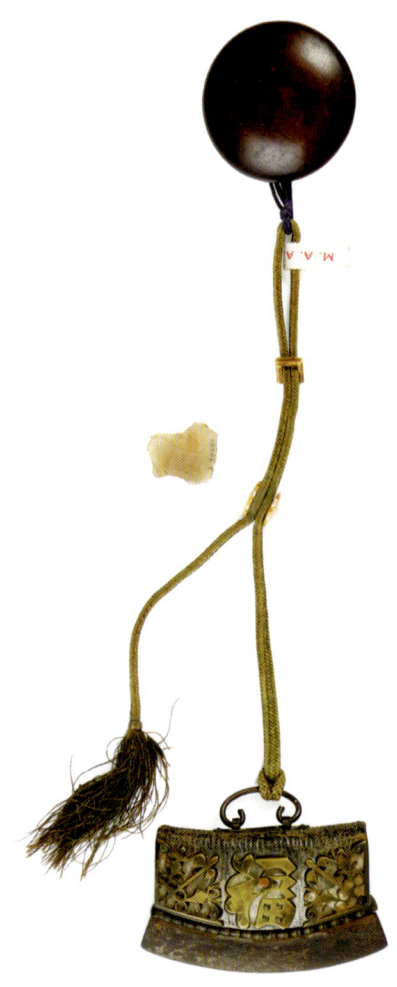

Fig. 1.2: Flint pouch with flint and button-shaped toggle, China, circa 1800–99. Leather, wood, metal, silk, ivory, flint, 310 x 85 x 20 mm, Powerhouse Collection. Gift of Miss E. A. Macdonald, 1979. Object A7247.

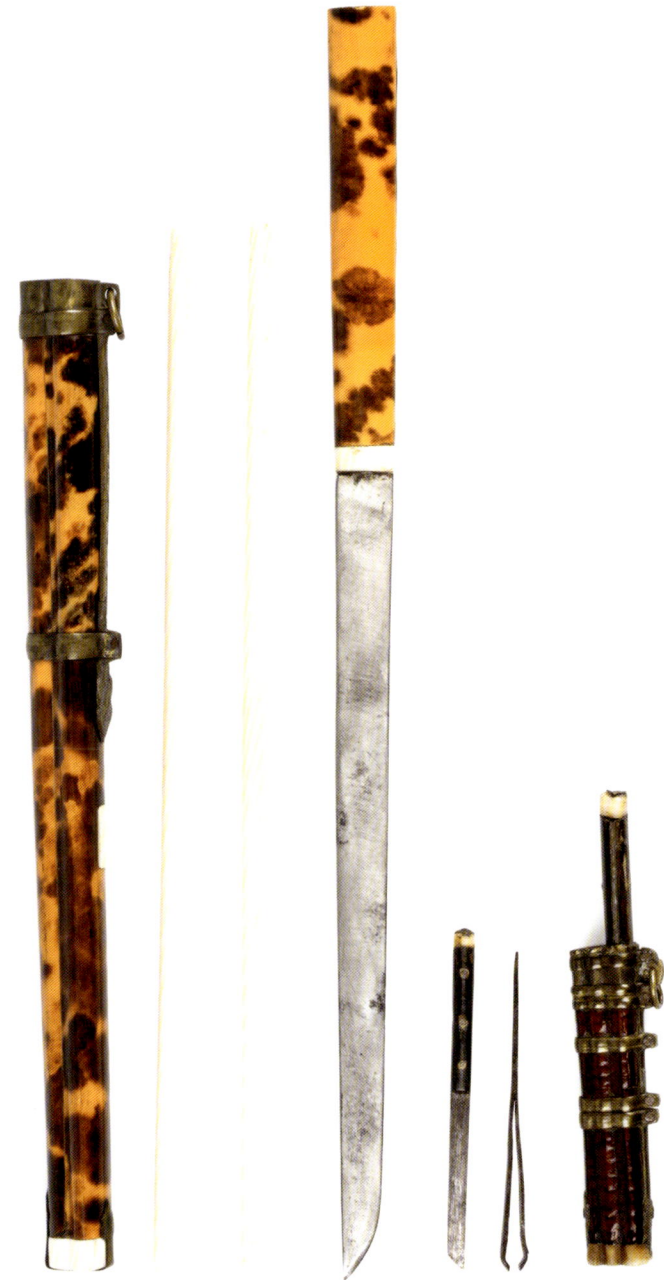

Left to right:

Fig. 1.3: Mongolian-style knife and chopstick set, China, 1800s. 11 x 29 x 295 mm, Powerhouse Collection. Gift of Mrs Smith, 1886. Object 11121;

Toggle in the form of a knife set, China, c.1700–1940. Wood, bone, metal. 10 x 20 x 95 mm, Powerhouse Collection, Gift of Alastair Morrison, 1992. Object 92/484.

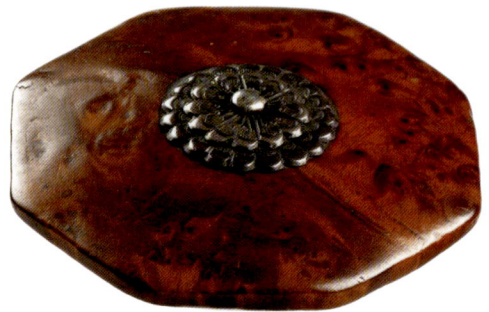
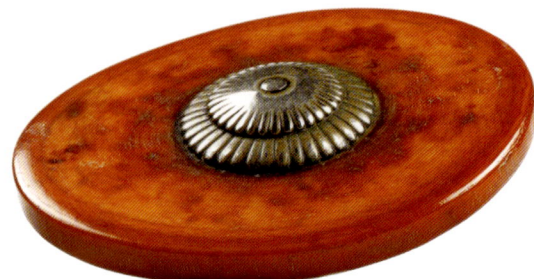

widespread early in the seventeenth century among the working classes and among merchants and the military.[6] During the eighteenth and nineteenth centuries, pipe smoking spread to other segments of society—even the elite, although tobacco pouches and pipes were mostly carried by their servants.[7]

Early visual historical records of belt-toggle wear are sparse, since traditional paintings generally showed the elite in formal attire. The representation of the middle and lower classes, who typically wore toggles, was unusual in Chinese art. There is rare pictorial evidence of how these members of society wore belt toggles in *The Costume of China, Illustrated in Forty-eight Coloured Engravings* (1805) by the English draftsman and watercolourist William Alexander (1767–1816). *The Portrait of the Purveyor*, for instance, depicts a flint pouch, a knife sheath and purses for tobacco or snuff (fig. 1.7).[8] In a number of the images in Alexander's publication, the toggles would have been hidden under the jacket, although in one, the '*Examination of a Culprit before a Mandarin*' (fig. 1.8), the secretary of the magistrate dons a knife-and-chopsticks set, handkerchief and pouch. Here, the toggle is placed on the top of the belt and is intended to secure the pouch preventing it from falling through the belt, rather than acting as a counterweight. Surviving photographs by Western photographers from the nineteenth and first half of the twentieth century portray Chinese people handling toggles, as seen in a photograph by Hedda Morrison dating from between 1933 and 1946 (fig. 1.9).

Fig. 1.4: Chinese and Japanese button-shaped toggles. Left : Toggle, China, 1700–1940. Wood, metal, 22 x 59 x 59 mm, Powerhouse Collection. Gift of Alastair Morrison, 1992. Object 92/475. Right: Netsuke, Japan, Edo/Meiji periods, (1700–1900). Wood, metal, 10 x 54 x 65 mm, Powerhouse Collection. Gift of Alastair Morrison, 1996. Object 96/61/31.

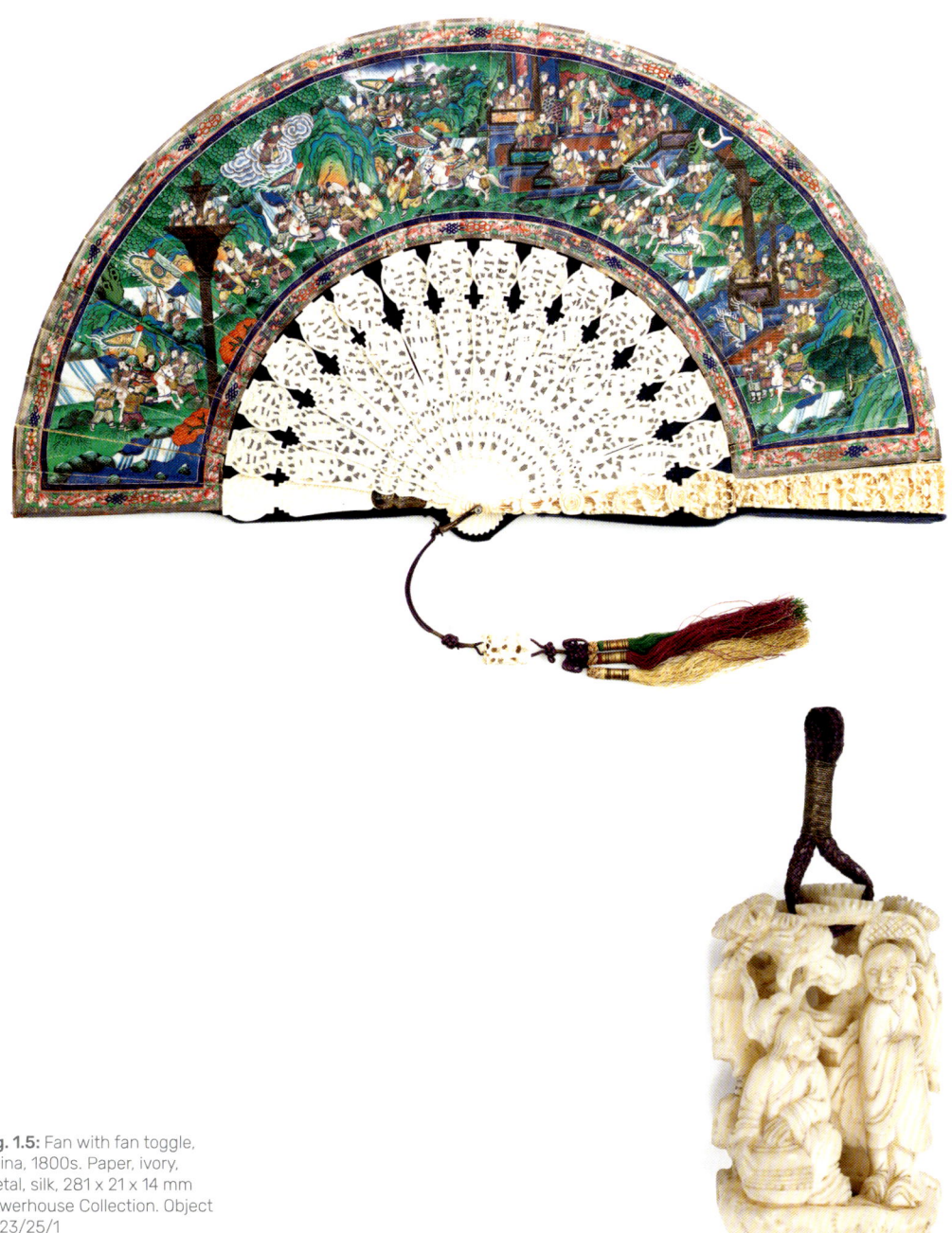

Fig. 1.5: Fan with fan toggle, China, 1800s. Paper, ivory, metal, silk, 281 x 21 x 14 mm Powerhouse Collection. Object 2023/25/1

Fig. 1.6: Detail of fan toggle

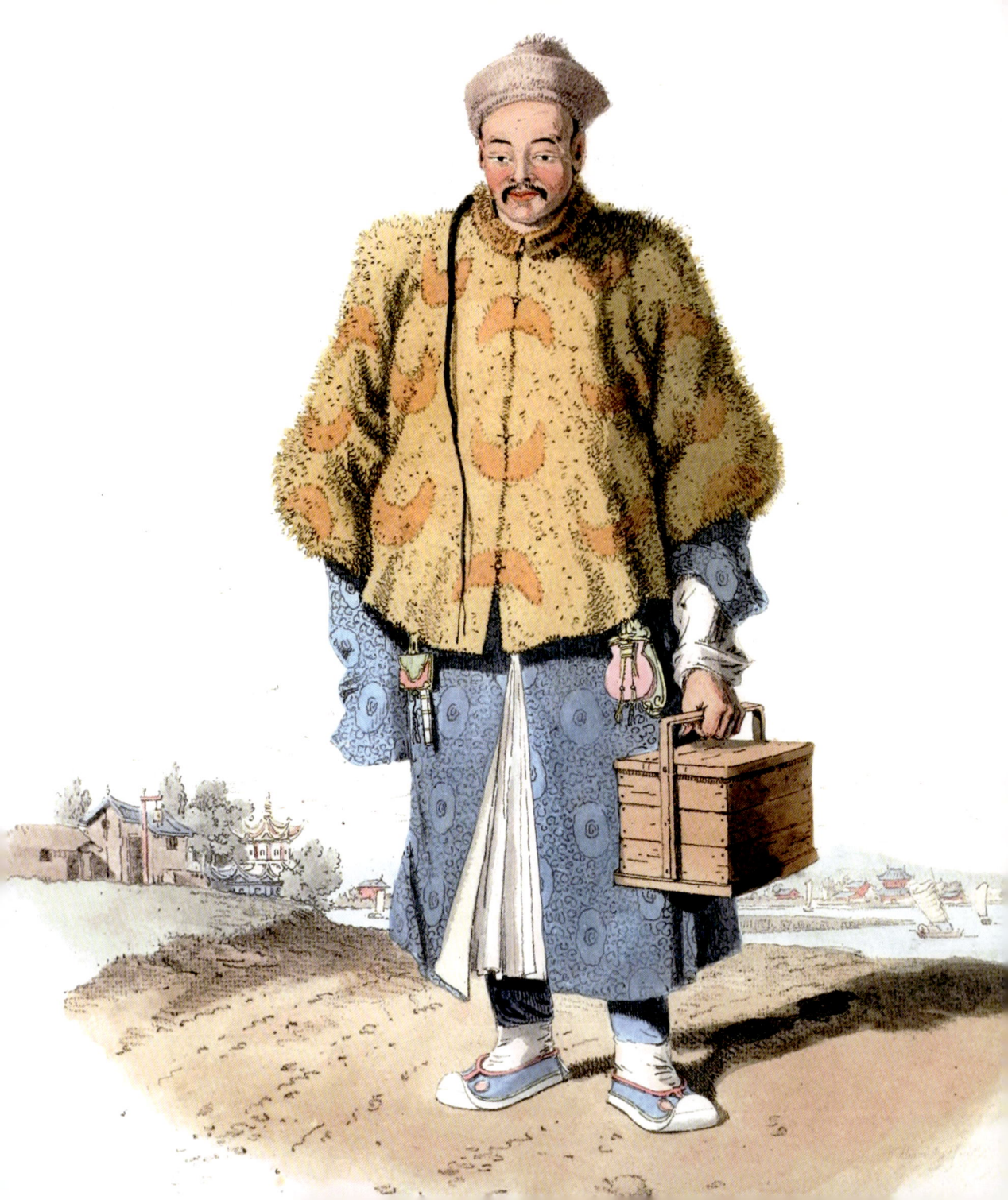

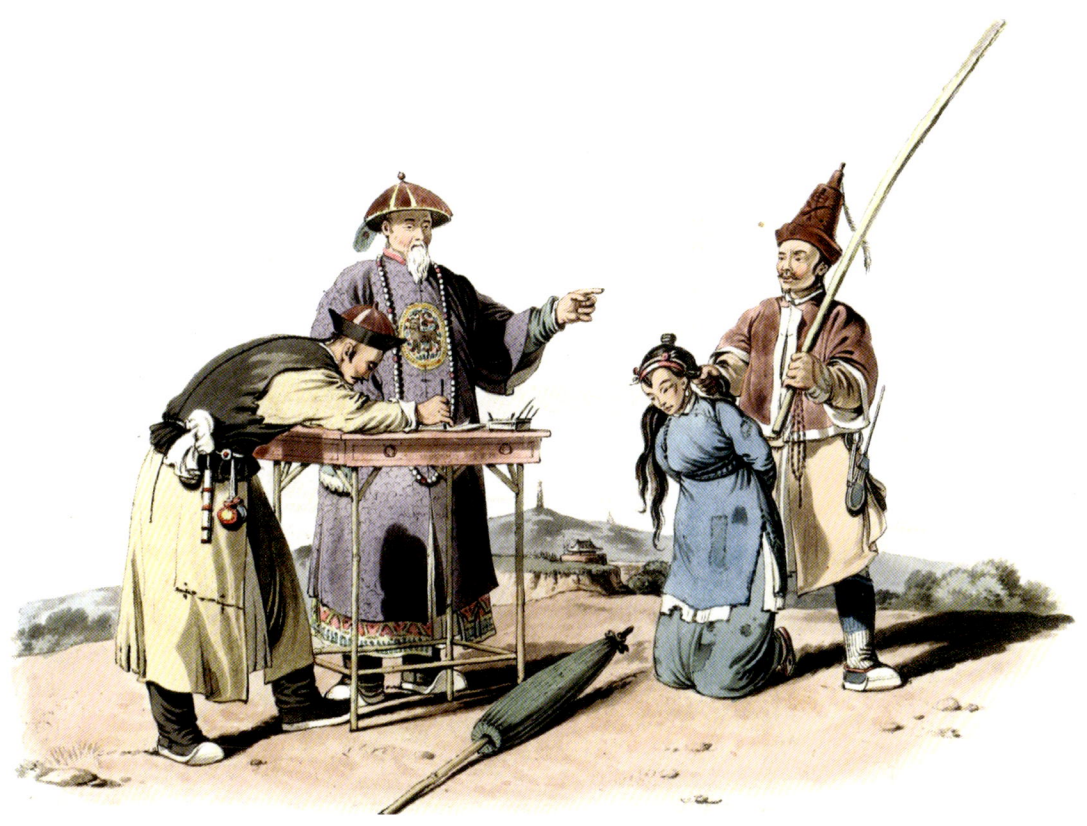

Opposite:

Fig. 1.7: *Portrait of the Purveyor*, William Alexander (1767–1816), published in *The Costume of China, Illustrated in Forty-eight Coloured Engravings*, William Miller, London, 1805;

Above:

Fig. 1.8: *Examination of a Culprit before a Mandarin*, William Alexander (1767–1816), published in *The Costume of China, Illustrated in Forty-eight Coloured Engravings*, William Miller, London, 1805.

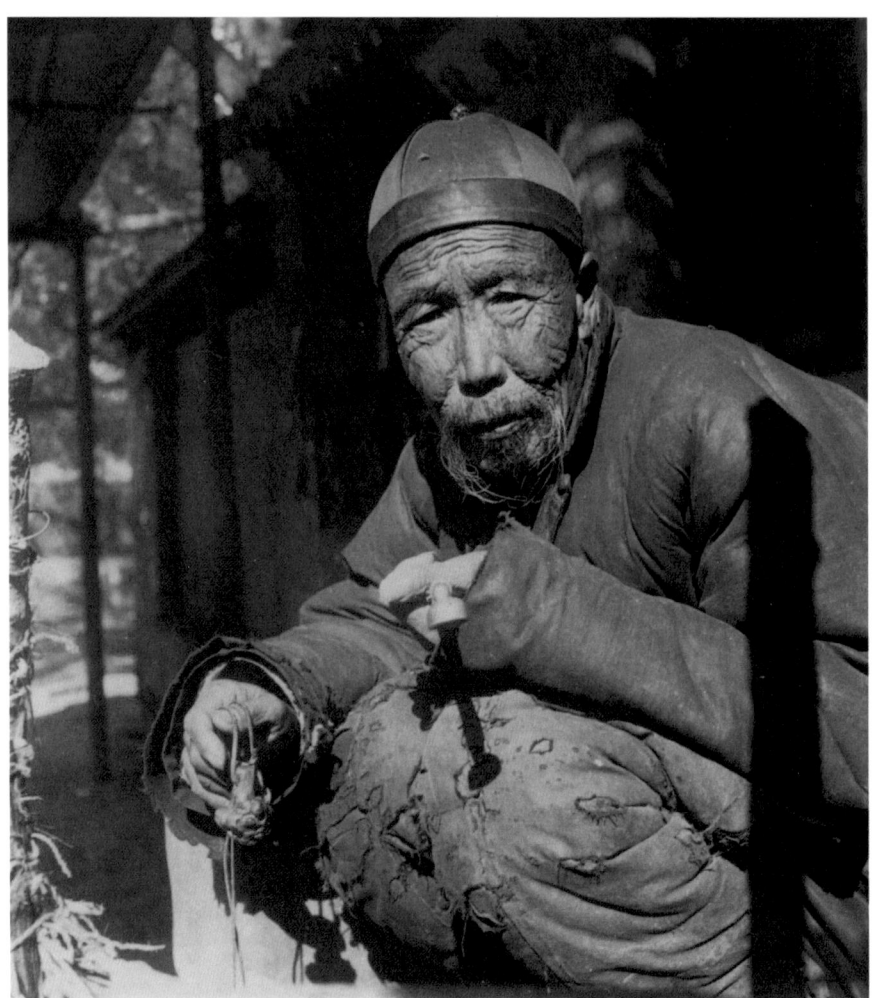

Fig. 1.9: Man holding a toggle and pipe, photograph by Hedda Morrison, China, 1933–46. Image: Harvard Yenching Library. Hv22-143.

Materiality

While the term zhuizi, or 'hanging thing', is commonly used in the West for belt toggles, it has in fact a broader application in China, subsuming any kind of dangling pendant. But belt toggles have characteristics that are different from other pendants or carvings. They were designed with smooth surfaces, without sharp edges or corners that might damage clothing. Most have holes or some form of ring to which a cord would be fastened, and as they were meant to be hung, every side is decorated. They would also have a certain weight, size and shape, in keeping with their function as counterweights. This distinguishes them from other types of miniature carvings, evidenced by an ivory carving of a lion or foo dog (fig.1.11) in the Powerhouse Collection, which, although strikingly similar in size and subject to a belt toggle, is clearly a decorative object.

Chinese belt toggles were, above all, practical objects produced for everyday use. Almost every natural material was employed in their manufacture, including wood, ivory, jade, brass, agate, jet, glass, crystal, amber, turquoise, amethyst, porcelain, shell, nuts and seed pods. There were certainly toggles of more precious materials, such as jade, that were made for wealthier patrons by artisans who typically produced other decorative objects. These differ, however, from the toggles fashioned by farmers, who often carved toggles during the winter months for themselves or as gifts for friends and family. Hunters, too, carved toggles from bone, horn, or antler in their spare time, and woodworkers created toggles from wood scraps.[9]

Carvers profited from the range of colours in the original materials. One example shows two meticulously crafted white jade cicadas nestled inside a leaf made from brown jade (plate 14, p. 175). In another, a toggle of mother-of-pearl in the shape of a woman on a banana leaf, the natural colour of the shell is used to distinguish between the woman and leaf (plate 26, p. 188), while a toggle in the form of jujubes and peanuts has different coloured bands of brown agate (plate 60, p. 223).

Among the materials used for Chinese belt toggles, wood is the most frequently encountered. This could be as rudimentary as tree roots or burls that were found in nature and adapted by carving out a cord hole. (The name of Japanese belt toggles known as netsuke (根付), literally 'fastened root', probably refers to the origin of this tradition.) The most commonly used wood was boxwood, or huangyangmu (黄杨木) 'yellow yang tree', as its fine grain made it a suitable material for printing blocks, combs, seals and toggles. The popularity of boxwood may also be due to the Chinese belief that boxwood contains the essence of yang, the active force in nature, versus yin, the more receptive force. Not only a symbol of longevity, boxwood was also employed in Eastern traditional medicine to cure pain, fever and inflammation.[11]

Medicinal associations

There is convincing proof that Chinese toggles had connections to therapeutic treatments, and the objects themselves could be used as portable medicine. Wearers believed that toggles made from materials with medicinal associations, or in shapes and subjects with auspicious connotations, could function as amulets.

Like boxwood, other materials adopted for belt toggles, such as antler horn, nuts and seeds, were recognised for their health benefits.

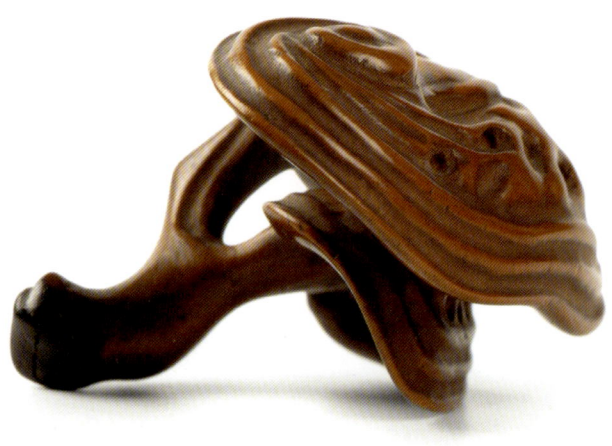

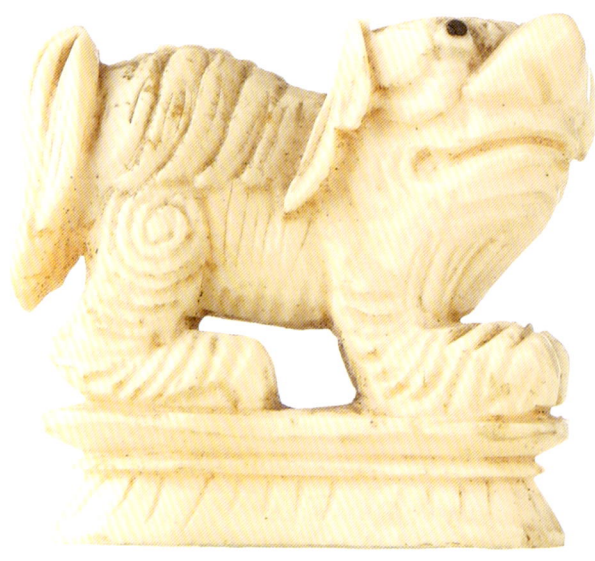

Fig. 1.10: Toggle in the shape of lingzhi, China, c 1700–1940. Wood, 43 x 44 x 32 mm. Powerhouse Collection. Gift of Alastair Morrison, 1992. Object 92/522;

Fig. 1.11: Ornament in the shape of lion or 'foo dog', China, date unknown. Ivory, 35 x 40 mm. Powerhouse Collection. Gift of E. Fraser Clark, 1946. Object A4036-4.

Ground deer antler, much prized in traditional Chinese medicine, was thought to improve stamina, fertility and blood pressure. (Even in contemporary Asia, antler is still added to herbal soups or consumed as a powder.) The carrying of such substances as a toggle thus had practical considerations such as in case of a medical emergency, as in the dragon-shaped toggle made of deer antler in the Powerhouse Collection (plate 37, p. 200). Nuts and seeds are generally viewed as symbols of fertility and the renewal of life and were a popular material for toggles. This is exemplified by the perfectly sized and beautifully coloured toggle made from a gila bean with a silver mount weight (plate 68, p. 230). The gila bean is credited with the power of relieving fever and pains.[12]

One of the most recurrent toggle shapes in the Powerhouse Collection is the bottle gourd (plate 77, p. 238). Alastair Morrison noted that an ivory bottle gourd toggle with a metal ring knob at the top was probably the oldest toggle in their collection (plate 78, p. 239). The cap-like silver mount on the top of this work is an emblem of wealth and of career accomplishment as a state official.

The bottle gourd was traditionally used as a container for medicine and as such was a symbol of good health and longevity. Moreover, it was associated with the popular Daoist figure, Li Tieguai (李铁拐), one of *Ba xian* (八仙), the Eight Daoist Immortals, who carried a bottle gourd containing a magic potion.[14] The design of this piece, in which the vine beautifully encircles the brass gourd, not only serves a decorative purpose but also invites the viewer to partake in a clever wordplay. The Chinese for bottle gourd vine is *man* (蔓), and the stem which holds the fruit is called *dai* (带). Together they would read *man dai*, which can imply the similarly sounding *wan dai* (万代), 'for ten thousand generations',

a phrase that often expresses wishes for long life, success and being blessed with many children. The bottle gourd also has other symbolic meanings—notably, its shape resembles the Chinese character *ji* (吉), 'auspiciousness'. These brass gourd toggles are heavier than other toggles and were perhaps used by doctors to grind medicine, a further indication that these toggles functioned as ornamental, symbolic and medicinal objects (plate 69, p. 231).[15]

Historically, the Chinese believed that a root toggle could be a healing charm, particularly if it was from a species of tree possessing special qualities, since the root was understood to be the repository of a tree's powers. It is not surprising, then, that the root toggle was a common belt-toggle type. Carvers would sometimes exploit the shape of a root, seen, for instance, in a toggle imitating a coiled snake (plate 23, p. 185).

Another popular belt toggle type with connections to medicine is the *linghzi* (灵芝), 'Mushroom of Immortality' (fig. 1.10). The bitter-tasting lingzhi mushroom, usually dark with a lacquer-like sheen, is used in Chinese herbal medicine as an effective relief for lung disease and high blood pressure. Moreover, it has connotations of long life and a flourishing career.

Perhaps one of the more unusual examples of the bond between belt toggles and medical practice are 'doctor toggles', which depict female figures, usually portrayed recumbent on leaves. A wooden piece in the Powerhouse Collection shows a woman stretched out on a leaf (plate 76, p. 237).[16] This piece points to the traditional Chinese method whereby physicians would consult a larger ivory carving in the shape of a nude woman lying on a leaf in order to diagnose female patients, who were otherwise forbidden to meet male doctors face to face. The female patient usually remained in bed concealed behind a curtain; the doctor would hand her the figure so that she could indicate where her illness was.[17] The wooden toggle in the Powerhouse Collection is not an actual doctor's tool, rather a miniature toggle replica.

Design and symbols

The discussion above demonstrates that Chinese belt toggles not only had a practical function as fasteners or counterweights for pouches and cases, but were equally valued as portable forms of medicine. Toggle-makers frequently employed materials believed to have magic, medicinal or auspicious connotations. The subjects and shapes of belt toggles could also represent belief systems and possess a cultural significance that reinforced societal notions of happiness, prosperity and family, as well as regarding longevity—in traditional China, the symbols of longevity were considered to be as potent as actual medicine. Many such symbolic toggles illustrate plants, animals and human figures derived from Chinese legend, and other auspicious images drawn from daily life. Fruits and plants with special meanings were likewise incorporated into designs, such as the citron; known as the Buddha's hand (plate 29, p. 192). The name, which is an emblem of wealth and longevity, derives from the citron's finger-like growths. Another wooden toggle, a beautifully carved grouping of plum blossom, bamboo and pine is identified as *Suihan sanyou* (岁寒三友), the 'Three Friends of Winter'—the faithful companions loyal even in times of hardship (plate 22, p. 184).

Many of the belt toggles draw from plants that would have had particular importance in Chinese culture. One of the most iconic motifs is the lotus, a Buddhist emblem of purity because of its ability to rise unsoiled and untainted from the depths of muddy waters. However, a single

motif can denote different things in different contexts. Many lotus toggles, for example, were created as personal charms; one such work, which depicts a large lotus leaf, animals and a seed pod, contains seven mobile seeds (plate 21, p. 183). Even when the pod is turned upside down, the seeds do not fall out. This ingenious use of seeds highlights the carver's expertise, the underlying design conceit being to call attention to *lian zi* (莲子), the lotus seeds. Here, lian zi is a word play on the expression 'successive children' that can be read *lian zi* but with variant characters (连子). A further distinctive toggle from the collection is a slice of lotus root carved from elephant tusk. The artisan skillfully utilised the schreger point from an elephant tusk, incorporating it into the design of the lotus root's hole.

The peach is associated with the ancient Daoist goddess Xi Wangmu, the 'Queen Mother of the West', who ruled over immortals and fed them a unique type of peach. Believed to only ripen every 6000 years; the fruit's link with longevity is clear. An ivory toggle with two peaches (plate 6, p. 168) is a particularly apt example of how toggles often possessed a beauty beyond the visual in their tactility, with surfaces that are very smooth and pleasurable to touch. The warm patina on some toggles might be the result of repeated handling (plate 73, p. 235). The handling of toggles not only had a sensory, tactile purpose, but it was believed that it carried health benefits such as the improvement of blood circulation. (For more on this notion of tactility, its enjoyment and benefits, see chapter 4.)

The repertory of belt-toggle imagery also extended to the depiction of real and mythical animals. Mythical creatures, whose representation in the Powerhouse Collection far outweighs those of animals from the natural world, including the three-legged *jin chan* (金蟾), 'money toad' (plate 33, p. 196 and plate 34, p. 197), a much-loved feng shui charm for prosperity. According to Chinese folk belief, the three-legged toad appears every full moon at the front door of houses or businesses whose owners will soon be the recipients of good news and wealth.[19]

Lions, though not native to China and often only imagined through travellers' tales, were displayed in pairs as gate guardians undertaking their roles as protectors (plate 57, p. 220).[20] Other creatures were the twelve animals of the zodiac; the most popular for belt toggles being the monkey (plate 18, p. 179). An ivory toggle in the shape of a seated monkey holding its baby is undoubtedly one of the most endearing belt toggles in the Powerhouse Collection: the faces of both mother and baby are delightful. The image also showcases a homonymic wordplay between the Chinese for monkey, *hou* (猴) and marquis, *hou* (侯), the latter a reference to nobility or a high rank obtained by passing the imperial examinations. A monkey cradling a baby therefore has associations with having successful children, and the wearer of this toggle could hope, too, that their children would be prosperous.[21] As everyday items, belt toggles did not normally include the dragon as a subject; because of its imperial associations it was typically forbidden. Although the illustration of the dragon is uncommon in toggles, the aforementioned example made of antler (plate 37, p. 200) has been reappropriated as one of the twelve zodiac animals. The pearl in the dragon's mouth is movable —again testament to the carver's talents.

In Chinese folk tradition, the act of symbolising a wish was believed to assist in its realisation. A shell toggle in the design of a goldfish, for instance (plate 12, p. 174), signifies the hope for affluence. Shells were seen as precious—in ancient China they were used as money—but a witty wordplay is also evident in this piece. The Chinese word for goldfish, *jin yu* (金鱼) puns on the meaning 'overflowing abundance of gold', making the goldfish a cherished metaphor for wealth. A clever feature of this design is the eyes of the fish, which serve as holes for the cord.

These examples exhibit how belt toggle designs embody wishes for good health and longevity, prosperity, and the hope for countless children. Toggles depicting boys were highly prized, as they represent the desire for many sons. One intriguing toggle is the aforementioned jade piece showing a boy holding a lotus as he rides a dragonfish (plate 47, p. 210). This subject of the boy and lotus is rooted in the Chinese folktale of Qixi (七夕). Once a year, on the seventh day of the seventh month of the lunar calendar, the cowherd Niulang (牛郎), appearing as the star Altair, and the weaver girl Zhinü (织女), appearing as the star Vega, are reunited in the sky. On this day, children would pick a lotus flower to carry on their shoulder, thus symbolising numerous children and blessings. The boy's mount—the dragonfish—is linked to achievement in the imperial examinations. The toggle combines the two subjects to express the owner's aspirations for successful children.

The amber toggle of two intertwined boys at play is a beautiful translucent deep crimson (plate 28, p. 190), and we can imagine that this object was appreciated for its colour and its warm, smooth texture. Another work, a brass toggle with boys (plate 1, p. 163), features a design that is frequently found on Chinese objects. At first glance it looks like two boys, but closer inspection reveals that there are actually four boys: two lying down and two sitting up. This representation is known as *Sixi tongzi* (四喜童子), the 'Four Happy Boys', illustrating the four blessings of happiness, high official position, longevity and good luck. Other figural toggles in the Powerhouse Collection include the Daoist immortals Shou Xing (寿星), also the God of Longevity, and Dongfang Shuo (东方朔, 154 BCE–93 BCE), a Han dynasty (206 BCE–220 CE) scholar-official. More powerful spiritual beings, such as buddhas and bodhisattvas, were avoided, since toggles were functional objects, and the portrayal of such high-status religious figures would have been considered disrespectful.[22]

Objects from daily life also provided inspiration for toggle designs. An abacus toggle made of wood and bone demonstrates detailed craftsmanship (plate 75, p. 236). Although seemingly an everyday item, its relation to money points to its place as a symbol of wealth. A toggle depicting a pair of shoes (plate 48, p. 212) might appear as a miniature model, but this image, too, has an embedded meaning. In Chinese, the word for shoe, *xie* (鞋), is a homonym with the term 'harmony', *xie* (谐), and the design of a pair of shoes is a metaphor for harmony in married life. The relief inscription of the *shou* (寿) character, meaning 'longevity', on the toe of the shoe further reinforces the idea of a prosperous, long-lasting conjugal union.

Toggle culture in Korea and Japan

In Korea, the mention of fan toggles, or *seonchu* (선추), frequently appears in historical records from as early as the Goryeo dynasty (918–1392), and a later portrait of Jo Yeong-bok (조영복, 1672–1728) shows the scholar-official wearing a fan and fan toggle in a style similar to Chinese practice (fig. 1.12). Korean fan toggles were made from wood, ivory, jade, bone and amber, all materials that were also employed for Chinese belt toggles. Their designs were indistinguishable from their Chinese counterparts in auguring longevity and prosperity.

Other Korean objects related to the Chinese belt toggle are the belt ornaments known as *norigae* (노리개) and *ttidon* (띠돈). Women hung norigae around the belt or underneath or over the jacket. With time, the jackets became shorter, and the skirt was fastened around the chest with a sash attached; the norigae were attached to this sash. An early twentieth-century photograph of women wearing traditional dress called hanbok, (한복) reveals that norigae were worn on their own or hung from the ttidon (a kind of belt toggle) through the use of a top ring hooked onto the belt sash (fig. 1.13). The design of norigae is analogous to the Chinese belt toggle, fashioned from more treasured materials such as jade, metal, amber and coral. The norigae was used for needle cases, perfume or medicine containers, small knives and earpicks. The design motifs were usually animals and plants that symbolised a long, healthy life, as well as the wish for wealth and fertility. During the Joseon dynasty (1392–1879), it was customary for women to possess a dagger norigae, a tradition related to the Mongolian practice of having a knife set. The carrying of a dagger became popular among women during the Goryeo dynasty, when Korea was subject to frequent Mongolian invasions.[24] One of the most interesting aspects of norigae is the origin of the name, which means an 'object to play with' or an 'object to handle'. This has immediate associations with the two walnut toggles called *son norigae*, or 'hand norigae' (fig. 1.14) which are similar to Chinese toggles made from materials chosen for tactile appreciation. Moreover, like Chinese belt toggles, norigae served dual functions as seals, perfume or medicine containers, needle containers and knife sets. A shared characteristic of Chinese toggles and norigae was their use as charms;

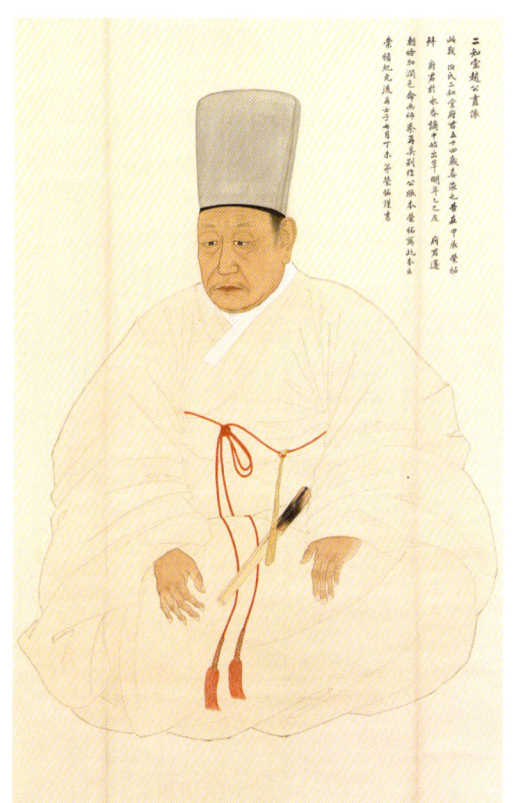

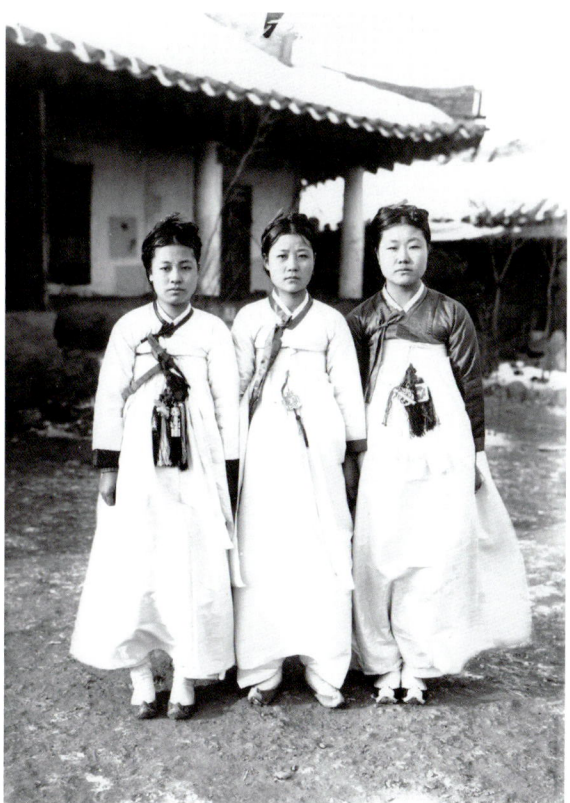

Left to right;
Fig. 1.12: Portrait of the Korean scholar Jo Yeong-bok (1672–1728), Jo Yeong-seok, Korea. Ink on silk, 1725. 1250 x 760 mm, Gyeonggi-do Museum Collection. Image: Academy of Korean Studies;
Fig. 1.13: Women in full traditional dress, Jaseong-gun, Pyeonganbuk-do province, North Korea, 1912–13. Image: National Museum of Korea.

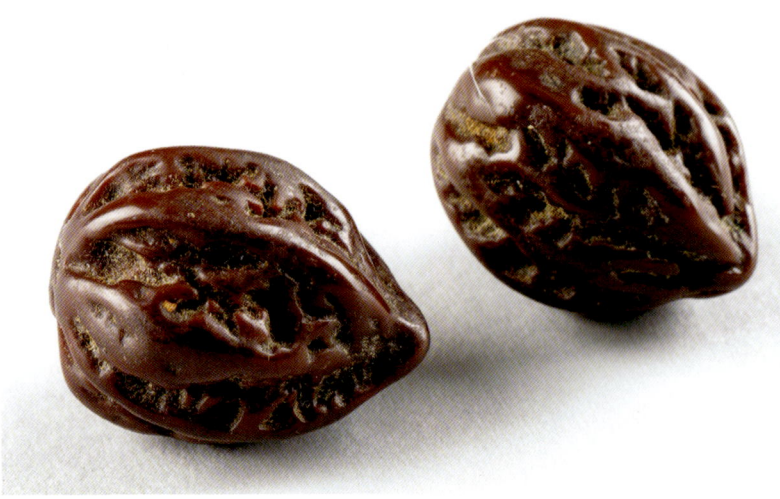

Fig. 1.14: Hand norigae, a pair of walnuts, Korea, 1800s. Collection of National Folk Museum of Korea. Image: National Folk Museum of Korea.

their designs espouse the wish for long, healthy lives blessed with many children, and for future wealth and prosperity. In Korea, it appears that silk knots called *maedeup* (매듭) were commonly used as belt toggles instead of carved objects.[25]

The custom of wearing belt toggles probably reached Japan from China around the end of the sixteenth century, although exactly how or when they were introduced is not known.[26] Scholars agree, however, that the earliest type of netsuke—as these toggles are called in Japanese—may have been Chinese seals utilised in lieu of signatures, pierced such that they could be threaded with a cord to double as a toggle.[27] A netsuke in the Powerhouse Collection in the shape of Gama Sennin (蝦蟇仙人), an Immortal who is knowledgeable in the magical medicinal arts, has a seal on the base (fig. 1.15). Numerous early netsuke designs were of Chinese origin, called *karamono* (唐物), 'Chinese things', while early figurative netsuke were called *tobori* (唐彫), 'Chinese-style carving'.[28]

Despite the shared origins of Chinese and Japanese belt toggles, belt-toggle production had a different historical trajectory in Japan. Unlike Chinese belt toggles, the production and collecting of Japanese netsuke evolved to reflect standards of connoisseurship, hierarches of achievement and genealogies of style. The most conspicuous distinction is that many netsuke are signed by the artisans who made them. Like the Chinese, Japanese men used netsuke as belt toggles to suspend various small objects, such as medicine cases called *inro* (印籠), tobacco sets, knives, purses and more. Furthermore, the subjects of netsuke were taken from nature, legends, religion, and literary and cultural history. After the introduction of tobacco by the Portuguese in 1542, netsuke were widely used to hang smoking sets; their popularity peaked during the Bunka to Bunsei eras (1804–1830).[29] With the introduction of the cigarette at this time, the fashion of wearing

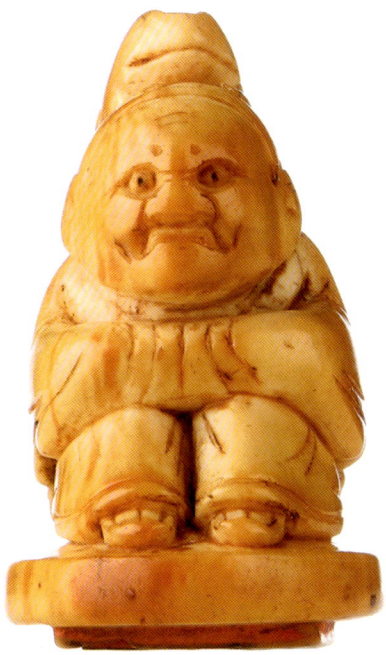

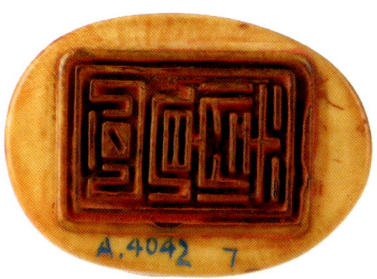

Fig. 1.15: Netsuke in the shape of Gama Sennin with toad, Japan, Meiji period, late 1800s. Ivory, 40 x 35 mm. Powerhouse Collection, Gift of E. Fraser Clark, 1946. Object A4042-7.

Detailed view of underside of Netsuke in the shape of Gama Sennin with toad, Japan, Meji Period, late 1800s. Powerhouse Collection object A4042-7 (fig. 1.15), showing seal on the base of the netsuke.

tobacco pouches and netsuke gradually disappeared. Before this time—in Japan as in China—toggle-carving had been a side industry for artisans, including the makers of musical instruments and wooden dolls, as well as for joiners, dentists and artists.[30]

After Japan opened up to broader international trade in the 1850s, netsuke became a favourite souvenir for Western visitors. Japanese carvers produced large quantities of netsuke to meet this collecting craze, leading to its development as an art form. Netsuke became very elaborate and eventually were unsuitable as a clothing accessory. Nonetheless, the economic viability of netsuke led a number of carvers to devote themselves entirely to their production, and international interest encouraged Japanese makers to craft finely detailed netsuke that could stand as artworks in their own right. Some netsuke-carvers also adopted subjects that reflected contact with the West, as seen in the figure of a Dutchman holding a flywhisk (fig. 1.16).[31]

Chinese culture and artisanship gave rise to a range of ornamental designs that influenced both Korea and Japan, but toggles evolved differently according to the needs, beliefs, sartorial customs, aesthetics and materials of these countries. Japanese netsuke have become more celebrated and more collectable due to the collecting habits of Westerners in the nineteenth century and, more recently, as a result of publications such as the 2010 memoir *The Hare with Amber Eyes: A Hidden Inheritance* by the British ceramic artist Edmund de Waal.[32] This netsuke tradition continues to the present day, continually evolving and reaching out to artists across the globe. In Australia, for example, Susan Wraight creates netsuke that imbue this carving tradition with an Australian sensibility (fig. 1.17).

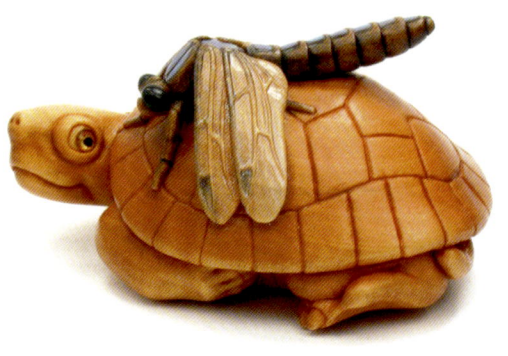

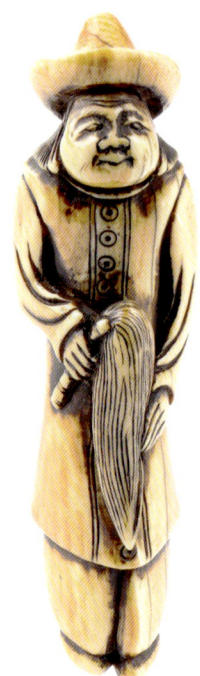

Left to right:

Fig. 1.17: Susan Wraight, *Brendan's Island,* Netsuke in the shape of a dragonfly atop a turtle, stained European boxwood with amber eyes inset over gold leaf, Melbourne, Australia, 2012. 50 x 35 x 28mm. Image: courtesy Susan Wraight.

Fig. 1.16: Netsuke Dutchman with a flywhisk, Japan, Edo /Meiji periods, 1700–1900. 80 x 22 x 19 mm, Powerhouse Collection, Gift of Alastair Morrison, 1996. Object 96/61/4.

Towards an appreciation of belt toggles

Belt toggles were ubiquitous, utilitarian objects, and few efforts were made to record their history. Even today, there is limited research into toggle collections and limited engagement between scholars working in the field. Scholars and curators in China, for instance, have remarked that such ordinary items would have been taken largely for granted and not recognised as a category of objects meriting dedicated research. In fact, the classification of toggles as zhuizi and their subsequent collection can be credited to the interest of Western collectors. According to Wang Yuegong at the Palace Museum in Beijing, 'In China, museums would classify such items [toggles] according to materiality and as objects of archaeological or art historical study, such as jewellery, jade-carving, stationary items, folk objects and so on.'[33]

The use and manufacture of belt toggles in China has long disappeared. Today, there are no unified collections in China similar to the Morrison collection at Powerhouse. Like many other Asian objects in Western museums, collections of Chinese belt toggles can be understood as the result of the longstanding Western fascination with Asian culture in the nineteenth century and of belt toggles as sought-after travel souvenirs.

For Western travellers, these easily portable small ornaments were emblematic of Chinese culture.

Caroline F. Bieber was one of the first to collect Chinese belt toggles in a systematic manner; her collection is at the Field Museum in Chicago, USA. Bieber's holdings served as the basis for Schuyler Cammann's 1962 publication, *Substance and Symbol in Chinese Toggles: Chinese Belt Toggles from the C. F. Bieber Collection*. With its in-depth treatment of the culture, symbolism and materials of belt toggles, Cammann's book remains a pivotal source on the topic. During his research, Cammann discovered that zhuizi was a common term for belt toggles. *Substance and Symbol* is thus acknowledged as the first non-Chinese source to use the term, which has become the standard nomenclature for these objects.[34]

Cammann notes that a small number of toggles were acquired by the Brooklyn Museum and Columbia University in New York, with Bieber's assistance. The latter collection was amassed by Dr George N. Kates in Beijing and Mrs William Gleysteen in Pennsylvania, who also acquired objects in Beijing.[35] Another work on Chinese toggles is the 2011 publication *Traditional Chinese Toggles: Counterweights and Charms* by Margaret Duda, a writer and photographer, and her husband Larry Duda, who visited China and purchased Chinese toggles from 1999 onwards. In her book, Duda classifies toggles according to materials and thoroughly documents the various types, drawing on examples from almost all Chinese toggle collections in the United States, including private collections, the Brooklyn Museum and the Royal Ontario Museum, in addition to toggles from the Field Museum's Bieber collection.[36]

The 279 toggles at the Powerhouse slightly outnumber the 237 in the Bieber collection. (For the Morrisons, their collecting, and their connections to Bieber, see chapter 2.) The two collections are comparable in terms of materials and designs, due to Hedda Morrison's key role in the development of the Bieber collection. Hedda aided Bieber in acquiring toggles in Beijing in the 1930s; her local knowledge and her ability to negotiate with Chinese vendors and craftspeople were invaluable.[37] Bieber left China in 1933, and Hedda and Alastair Morrison would later write about how they proceeded to amass their own collection (fig. 1.18).[38] The couple acquired 249 toggles in Beijing between 1940 and 1942, before leaving China in 1946, and thirty more in Shanghai, Chongqing and Singapore.[39] Today, the Bieber holdings at the Field Museum in Chicago and the Morrison donation at Powerhouse are recognised as the most significant Chinese belt toggle collections in the world. They offer a rare glimpse into a little known aspect of everyday sartorial culture in traditional China, one that celebrates skilfull artisanship, diverse materialities, and deep connections to the real and symbolic worlds.

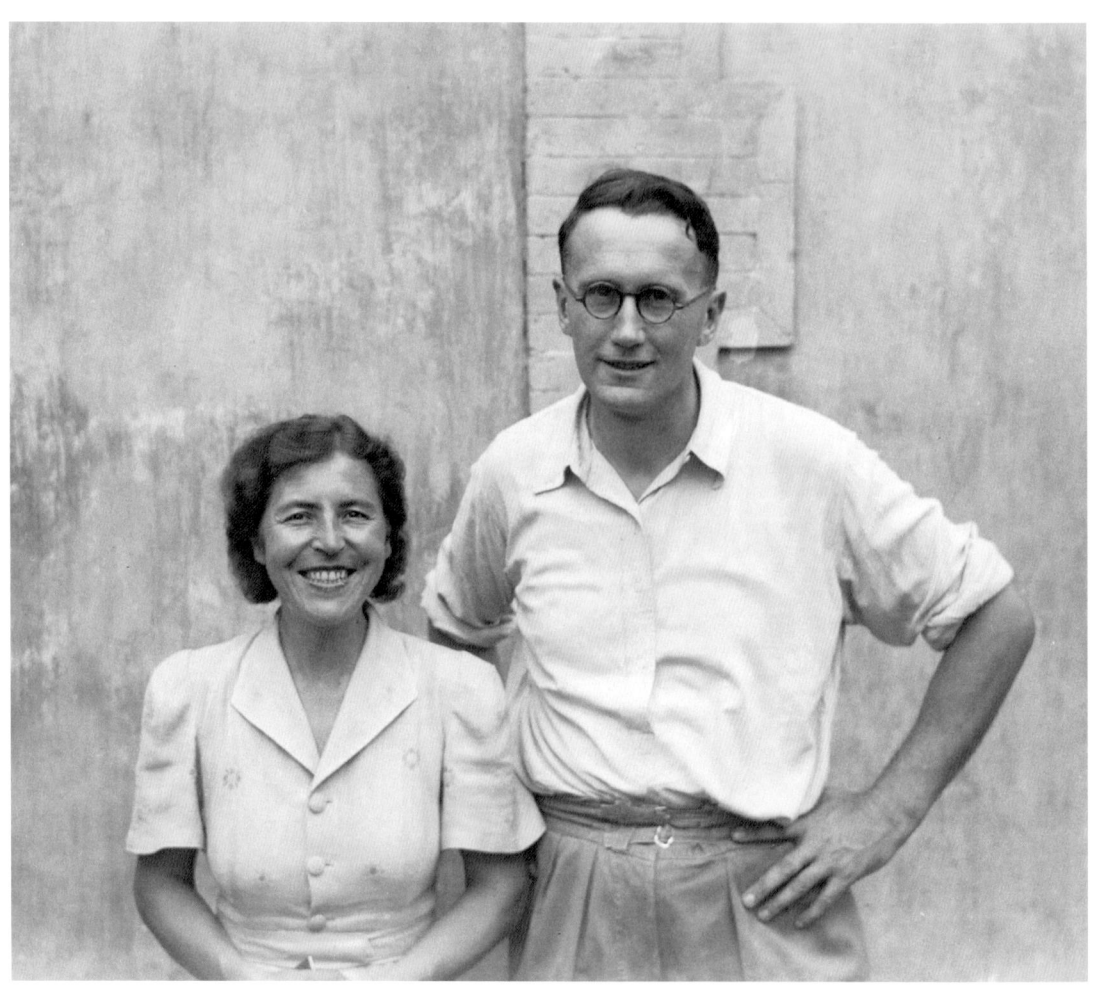

Fig. 1.18: Alastair and Hedda Morrison, Beijing, China, 1933–46. Photographer unknown. Powerhouse Collection. Object 2021/57/1-1.

1. Sun Ji 孙机, 汉代物质文化资料图说 [*Illustrated Explanations of the Material Culture of the Han Dynasty*], Shanghai Classics Publishing House 上海古籍出版社, Shanghai, 2008, p. 293.
2. Schuyler Cammann, *Substance and Symbol in Chinese Toggles: Chinese Belt Toggles from the C.F. Bieber Collection*, University of Pennsylvania Press, Philadelphia, 1962, p. 18.
3. Xie Zhaozhe 谢肇淛 (1567–1624) is well-known for his sixteen-volume *Wu Za Zu* (五杂俎), which includes book reviews, reflections on current affairs, local customs and the ethos of his time. The relevant passage here is '扇之有坠，唐前未闻，宋高宗宴大臣，见张循王扇有玉孩儿坠子，则当时有之矣'. [Toggles on fans were not heard of before the Tang Dynasty. When Emperor Gaozong of Song hosted a banquet for his ministers, the emperor saw that Zhang Dunwang had a jade fan toggle [zhuizi] in the shape of a child, so then zhuizi must have existed at that time.] Zhang Dunwang 张循王 was a poet-scholar.
4. Powerhouse Collection files 92/681 (plate 78, p. 239). See also Alastair Morrison, 'Toggle and Netsuke: A Minor Art from China and Japan', a lecture presented to the Asian Society Council, September 1979, Powerhouse Collection Masterfile 92/429-92/520, p. 5.
5. Morrison, 'Toggle and Netsuke', p. 2.
6. Carol Benedict, *Golden-Silk Smoke: A History of Tobacco in China, 1550–2010*, University of California Press, Berkeley, 2011, p. 18.

7. ibid., p. 61.
8. William Alexander, *The Costume of China, Illustrated in Forty-eight Coloured Engravings*, William Miller, London, 1805.
9. Cammann, *Substance and Symbol in Chinese Toggles*, p. 20.
10. ibid., p. 51.
11. Bae Kiwhan 배기환, *Hangukui yakyong sikmul* 한국의 약용 식물 [Bibliography of Medicinal Plants in Korea], Kyohaksa 교학사, Daegu, 2000, p. 320.
12. Cammann, *Substance and Symbol in Chinese Toggles*, pp. 43–4.
13. Powerhouse Collection files, 92/681 (plate 78, p. 239).
14. Wolffram Eberhard, *A Dictionary of Chinese Symbols: Hidden Symbols in Chinese Life and Thought*, Routledge and Kegan Paul, London, 1986, p. 45.
15. Cammann, *Substance and Symbol in Chinese Toggles*, p. 84.
16. ibid., p. 144.
17. ibid., p. 145.
18. Ibid., p. 111.
19. ibid., pp. 292–3.
20. Eberhard, *A Dictionary of Chinese Symbols*, p. 164. I would like to thank the anonymous reviewer pointed out that a lion was brought to Chang'an, the capital of Western Han Dynasty (202 BCE–8 CE) via the Silk Road as a gift for the emperor and therefore was not an animal that the majority of Chinese would have ever seen.
21. Beppe Berna, 'The Monkey as a Toggle: Discovering the Unknown World of the Primitive Art of China', *The Journal of Tribal Arts*, vol. 6, No 3, 2000, pp. 96–9.
22. Cammann, *Substance and Symbol in Chinese Toggles*, p. 150.

23. The most extensive Korean scholarly source on dress and accessories is Seok Ju-Seon 석주선, *Hangukboksiksa [The History of Korean Costumes]*, Bojinjae 보진재, Seoul, 1971. Here reference to pp. 575–84.
24. Sunny Yang, *Hanbok: The Art of Korean Clothing*, Hollym, Seoul, 1997, p. 118.
25. Ju-Seon 석주선, *Hankukboksiksa [The History of Korean Costumes]*, pp. 575–84. This publication contains images of different pouches for tobacco, perfume and money, cases for fans, glasses, knife and chopstick sets, and flints. Carved toggles are not listed, however, even though fans and *norigae* are amply represented.
26. Schuyler Cammann, 'Toggles and Toggle-wearing', *Southwestern Journal of Anthropology*, vol. 16, no.4, 1960, p. 466.
27. See Fredrick Maurice Jonas, *Netsuke*, Charles E. Tuttle, London and Kobe, 1928, later published, Tokyo, 1960, p. 22. See also Cammann, 'Toggles and Toggle-wearing', p. 466.
28. Jonas, *Netsuke*, p. 20.
29. Cammann, 'Toggles and Toggle-wearing', p. 466. See also Jonas, *Netsuke*, p. 22.
30. Jonas, *Netsuke*, p. 21.
31. Adrienne Barbanson, *Fables in Ivory: Japanese Netsuke and Their Legends*, Charles E. Tuttle, Tokyo, 1961, p. 74. Earlier sources on netsuke in Japan include the seven-volume *Sōken kishō* 装剣奇賞 [Strange and Wonderful Sword Fittings] 1781 by Inaba Tsūryū 稲葉通龍 (1736–1786), which lists over fifty *netsuke* masters in the last volume. The first

European study was published in 1905 by Albert Brockhaus (1855–1921), followed by Fredrick Maurice Jonas, *Netsuke*, 1928 (see note 27 above). In Japan, the International Netsuke Society, originally founded as Japanese Netsuke Kenkyūkai 根付研究會, has been producing quarterly journals since 1975.
32. Edmund de Waal, *The Hare with the Amber Eyes: A Hidden Inheritance*, Vintage Books, London, 2010.
33. Email correspondence with Dr Yin Cao, Curator of Chinese Art, Art Gallery of New South Wales, 23 September 2022.
34. See Cammann, 'Chinese Belt Toggles', *Oriental Art*, vol. 8, no. 2, Summer 1962, p. 72. Here Cammann notes that in 上田萬年, 大字典, [Ueda's Daijiten : a Japanese dictionary of Chinese characters and compounds], (Kazutoshi Ueda 上田萬年 (ed.), Keiseisha, Tokyo, 1924). The term netsuke equates with zhuizi.
35. Cammann, *Substance and Symbol in Chinese Toggles*, p. 9.
36. Margaret Duda, *Traditional Chinese Toggles: Counterweights and Charms*, Editions Didier Millet, Singapore, 2011, p. 7.
37. Claire Roberts, *In Her View: The Photographs of Hedda Morrison in China and Sarawak 1933–67*, Powerhouse Publishing, Sydney, 1993, p. 7.
38. Letter from Hedda Morrison to Charles Allen, 12 September 1983, Powerhouse Archives, 2021/57/1
39. Hedda and Alastair Morrison, 'Chinese Toggles: A Little Known Folk Art', *Arts of Asia*,

1986, vol. 16, no. 2, pp. 68–75, and Morrison, 'Toggle and Netsuke'. Of the 279 Chinese toggles in the Powerhouse Collection, three have been identified as netsuke. They may have been purchased by Morrison in Singapore.

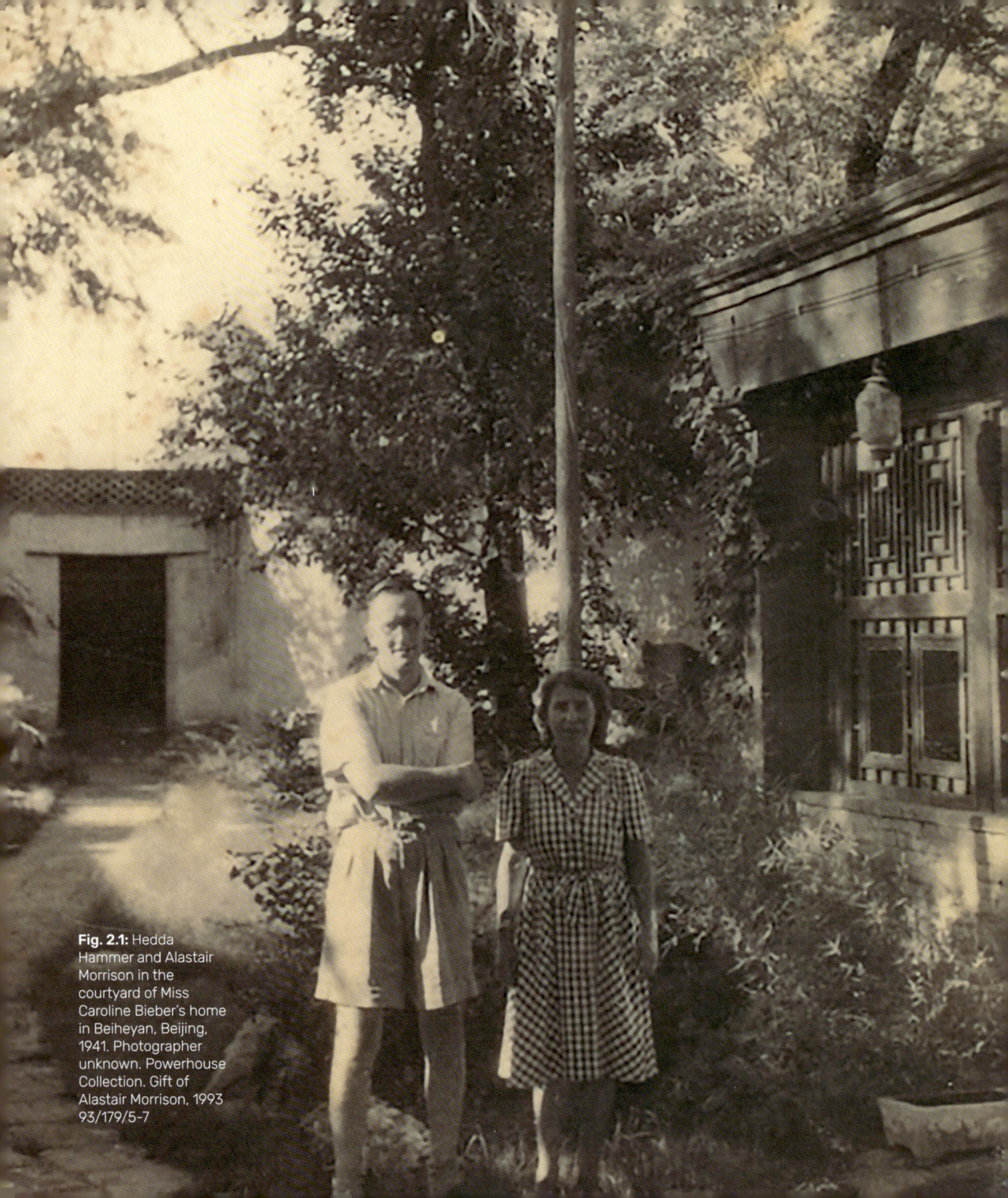

Fig. 2.1: Hedda Hammer and Alastair Morrison in the courtyard of Miss Caroline Bieber's home in Beiheyan, Beijing, 1941. Photographer unknown. Powerhouse Collection. Gift of Alastair Morrison, 1993 93/179/5-7

2. A shared passion: the Hedda and Alastair Morrison collection of Chinese belt toggles

Claire Roberts

The meeting of Hedda Hammer (1908–91) and Alastair Morrison (1915–2009) in Japanese-occupied Beijing in 1940 was serendipitous. After graduating from the University of Cambridge, Alastair, who was 'always an avid collector' and had kept birds as a child, travelled to South America to collect bird specimens. His desire was to become a naturalist and, following practices of acquiring knowledge that were current at the time, create a 'first class private collection of South American birds'.[1] Suffering from persistent knee and stomach ailments, he decided to take time out to recuperate, and at the urging of his elder brother, Ian, joined him in Shanghai.[2]

Ian and Alastair, the eldest of George Ernest Morrison's (1862–1920) and Jenny Wark Robin's (1889–1923) three sons, had been born in Beijing.[3] Their father was the political advisor to Yuan Shikai (袁世凯, 1859–1916), President of the Republic of China. Prior to that, he had been the Beijing-based correspondent for *The Times* newspaper from 1897 to 1912. Their New Zealand-born mother, who had been educated in Germany and spoke fluent German and French, had applied for a job to become Morrison's secretary. The parents met in Beijing in 1910 and married two years later.

Not long after Alastair's arrival in Shanghai, he followed his brother to Beijing. Entranced by the city, he decided to undertake a period of rest and recuperation there. Through his brother's network of contacts, he was offered a 'little furnished Chinese-style house' rented by well-to-do Englishwoman Caroline Francis Bieber. Bieber, who had lived in Beijing since the late 1920s, was preparing to travel to the United States.[4] The residence at 53B Beiheyan (北河沿), a street running parallel to the eastern wall of the Forbidden City, was one of the courtyards in a large house, 'a central courtyard around which lay the various single-storey rooms which communicated with one another'. In his memoir, Alastair describes the residence and the colonial-style living conditions that he inherited, which were typical of the privileged life enjoyed by many foreign nationals living in China, where the relative cost of living was cheap. 'Miss Bieber's house had a fine sitting room, a dining room and two bedrooms with adjoining bathrooms and running water. Her staff, whom I took over, consisted of a boy, a good cook, a coolie, a rickshaw puller and a wash *amah*.'[5] Also associated with the house was Bieber's 'German secretary' Hedda Hammer, who was to keep an eye on the house in her employer's absence.

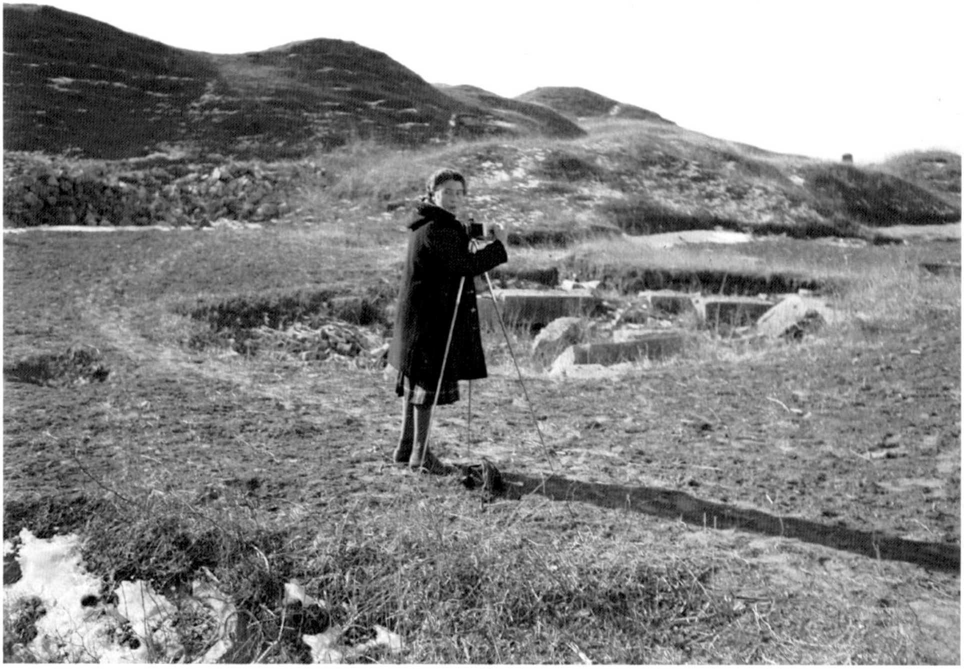

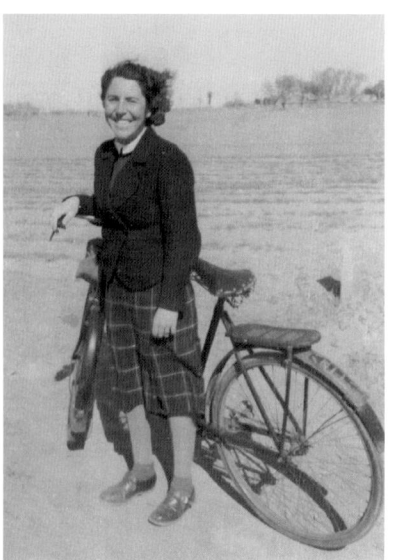

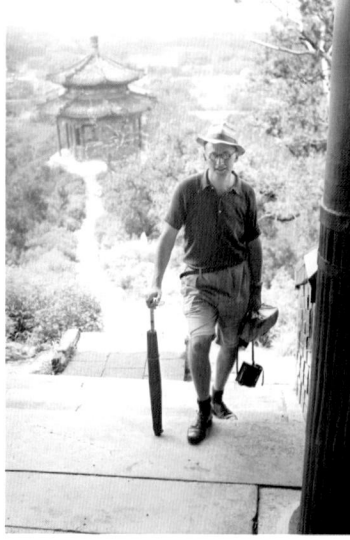

Top:
Fig. 2.2:
Hedda Hammer photographing
outside Beijing, 1930s.
Photographer unknown. Printed
by Jean-François Lanzarone from
a negative. Powerhouse Collection.
Gift of Alastair Morrison.
Object 2021/57/1.

Left to right:
Fig. 2.3: Hedda Hammer with her
bicycle outside Beijing, China,
1933–1946. Photographer unknown.
Photomechanical processes on
paper. Harvard-Yenching Library,
HM00.0010;

Fig. 2.4: Hedda Hammer, Alastair
Morrison sightseeing in Jingshan
Park, Beijing, early 1940s. Printed
by Jean-François Lanzarone from
a negative. Powerhouse Collection.
Gift of Alastair Morrison.

A photograph of Alastair and Hedda standing together in the leafy courtyard at Beiheyan shows the low-lying residence, with its lattice windows wrapping around the courtyard (fig. 2.1). 'Perhaps the most delightful thing about these houses' Alastair wrote, 'was the presence of fine trees in the courtyard. The Chinese were great tree lovers, and nearly every courtyard had trees growing in it'.[6] The photograph was taken in 1941, after Caroline Bieber had left Beijing. Alastair, who had no Chinese language, would often call upon Hedda for help communicating with Bieber's Chinese staff and to make arrangements. Perhaps one of the Chinese staff took the photograph.

Hedda lived in a section of a courtyard house in Nanchang jie (南长街), Nanchang Street, which ran between the Forbidden City and Nan Hai (南海), the Southern Lake of the Imperial city, a short bicycle ride from Beiheyan.[7] Recalling with fondness the early days of their friendship, Alastair described Hedda as a 'solitary European lady on a bicycle … a unique figure in some ways'[8] (fig 2.3). Hedda introduced Alastair to the city of his birth, which had been her home since 1933. Beijing was a city that he came to love like no other place. 'As a city it was magnificent—broad and spacious and built in beautiful surroundings as a capital for a great empire.'[9] A photograph of Alastair sightseeing at Jingshan Park, also known as Coal Hill, immediately north of the Forbidden City, suggests how through circumstances he and Hedda gradually became close friends (fig 2.4). Taken on a hot and hazy summer day from within the Wanchun ting (万春亭), Everlasting Spring Pavilion, Alastair smiles as he approaches her, umbrella and camera in hand, having made the steep ascent from the Guanmiao ting (观妙亭), Fine View Pavilion, below.

Hedda had been employed by Bieber since 1938, after her five-year contract as manager of the German-owned Hartung's Photo Shop in Beijing had expired. She had trained as a photographer in Munich at the Staatliche Fachakademie für Fotodesign München (State Academy of Photographic Design) and then worked in a commercial studio in Stuttgart. With the rise of Nazism, she was keen to leave Germany and successfully applied for the job in Beijing.[10] At Hartung's she managed an established studio overseeing some seventeen Chinese photographers.[11] The studio was located in the Legation Quarter and catered to the needs of resident foreigners and travellers. Her own photographs, taken in China during her years of residence in Beijing between 1933 and 1946, are among the most striking and significant photographs to record aspects of life and cultural practices in the ancient capital at that time (fig 2.2).[12]

With her working knowledge of the Chinese language, Hedda Hammer provided invaluable assistance to Bieber, who was interested in Chinese arts and design and involved herself in various arts and craft-related activities. Bieber developed a small business transforming Chinese jewellery and silverwork into costume jewellery that appealed to Western tastes. She is also said to have worked with Dr Yamei Kin (金韵梅, 1864–1934) on a charitable business employing poor women in Beijing to create embroidered table linens for sale to a foreign clientele.[13] Earlier, Bieber had assisted the Brooklyn Museum of Art to acquire a collection of Chinese arts and crafts, including a small but representative collection of toggles.[14] An important aspect of Hedda's work was liaising with locals and accompanying Bieber and her friends to markets, translating for them as they haggled over prices. Bieber's extensive collection of Chinese textiles and dress, dress accessories and other objects was later acquired by the Field Museum in Chicago, USA, including 237 belt toggles. Most of the toggles were acquired at the Jade Market in Beijing during the late 1920s and 1930s, but some were purchased directly from their wearers.[15] The collection was published by Schuyler Camman in 1962, who had himself collected a number of toggles during his residence in China from 1935 to 1938, and 1945. Camman, who describes Chinese toggles as 'miniature works of art', refers to two other collections that were formed in Beijing around the same time, one by the American scholar and writer George N. Kates, and another by the missionary Theodora Gleysteen, wife of Reverend William Gleysteen, who worked at the Presbyterian Mission in Beijing. The first black-and-white photographs for the publication were taken by Hedda Hammer in Beijing, with later photographs taken in the USA by Laura Gilpin.[16]

Sightseeing with Hedda, Alastair familiarised himself with the city. Together they roamed within and beyond the great walled city, visiting lakes, parks and temples. Alastair, too, became fascinated by the markets of Beijing. They frequented the Dong'an shichang (东安市场): 'a warren of little booths' off Wangfujing (王府井), then known to many expatriates as 'Morrison Street', where the family used to live, and the early morning Jade Market outside Hadamen Gate (哈达门) in the south, close to the Legation Quarter. Hedda described the Jade Market as:

'a miniature antique dealers' fair, where representative dealers from all over the city would congregate to trade with each other and with other customers who were early risers. Most of the objects for sale were small and easily transported, and the turnover was rapid. You never knew what you might see there and you could be quite sure that you would be unlikely to see it again.'

They also frequented the monthly temple markets at Longfu si (隆福寺), which Alastair described as a 'never-failing source of interest',

as well as antique shops hear the Drum Tower and in Liulichang (琉璃厂) in the southern part of the city (fig. 2.5).[17]

Almost everyone who spends time in China comes home with souvenirs, and Hedda and Alastair were no exception. At markets there is always the prospect of finding something special that is not too expensive, and it becomes a treasured keepsake, partly through the excitement of having found it and haggled over the price, successfully or unsuccessfully. For Hedda and Alastair, portability was paramount. With the Pacific War raging, the future was uncertain. Inspired by Bieber and her collection, they developed a keen interest in toggles, and each began to form their own collection. Visiting markets and 'toggle hunting' became a shared passion. 'Collecting toggles', Alastair later recalled, 'was always interesting, indeed it was exciting.'[18] The thrill of discovering a toggle and the art of securing its purchase—the art of negotiation being an important skill and a memorable cultural experience—could only be perfected over time. At the end of his life Alastair recalled the formation of their collection, explaining, 'We started both collecting toggles, which presented problems because if you went to a market the problem was *who saw the toggle first*, so eventually we decided that the simplest thing was to merge the two collections, and that was great fun.'[19]

Toggles, like their better-known Japanese cousin the *netsuke* (根付), are practical fastening devices. They generally incorporate two holes into the design to attach a cord, allowing the toggle to function as a counterweight to whatever is suspended on the other end. Created by unknown makers from a wide variety of materials, ranging from wood and ivory to semi-precious and precious stones such as amethyst and jade, they are worn against the body and may be as simple as a cuboid or disc shape or, in contrast,

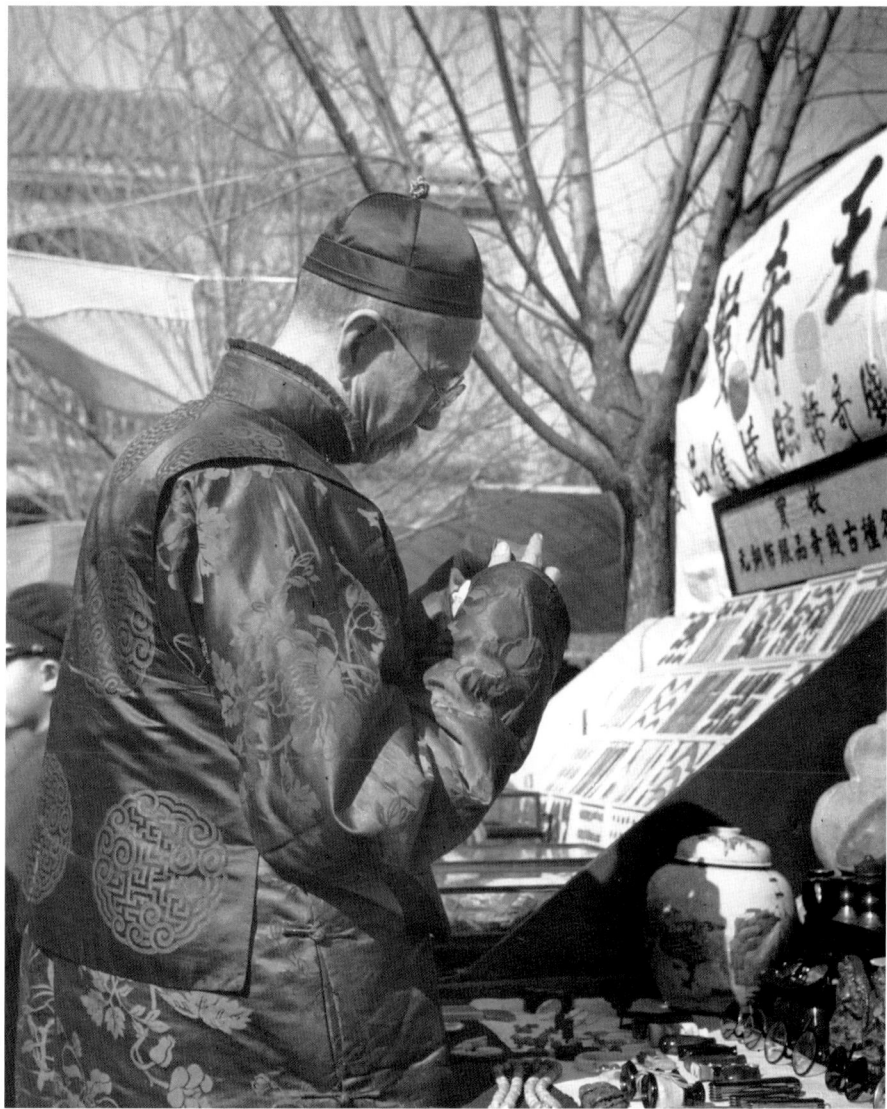

Fig. 2.5: Hedda Hammer, A man at a stall in Liulichang, 1933–1946. Powerhouse Collection. Gift of Alastair Morrison, 1993. Object 92/1414-290.

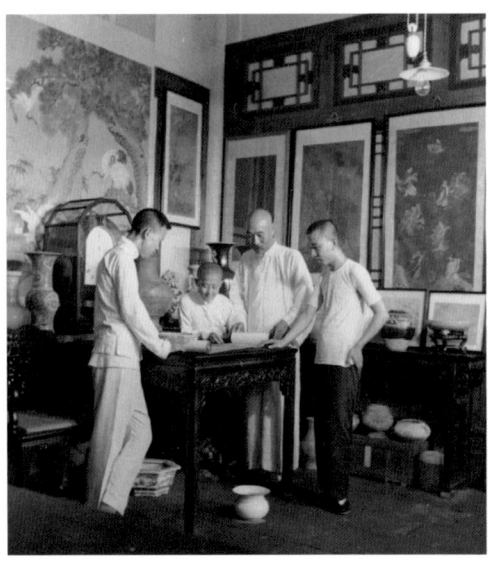

Fig. 2.6: Hedda Hammer, Mr Huang in his antique shop with his staff, Beijing, 1933-1946. Gelatin silver process. Harvard-Yenching Library, HM08.4474.

an elaborately carved motif that is designed to bring good luck. With practicality foremost in the minds of the makers, toggles need to have scale and substance in order to function as effective belt fasteners and counterweights and be comfortable against the body of the wearer. Sharp edges and angular forms were generally avoided. Making use of material offcuts for which there would be little other purpose, toggles represent the ingenious craft of making do, the shape of the scrap often suggesting the decorative form of the finished article. For example, a curly piece of root wood might be transformed into a snake, one of the animals of the Chinese zodiac (plate 23, p. 185); a section of ivory could be easily fashioned to appear like a slice of lotus root, a favoured culinary food also used in Chinese herbal medicine, referencing the plant that is associated with Buddhism and related ideas of purity and transcendence (plate 64, p. 227); or a knob of amethyst might become a pair of peaches, associated with

longevity (plate 7, p. 170). Each decorative toggle therefore represented a microcosm of Chinese cultural beliefs and aspirations. For the foreign collector, the task of decoding the meaning or significance of the imagery was fascinating.

Within the collection there are a number of toggles that held a particular significance for Hedda and Alastair.[20] The three-legged toad made from white and beige banded agate was a favourite of Hedda, the dappled colouration of the stone suggesting the texture of a toad's skin (plate 33, p. 196). It was purchased from the antique dealer Mr Huang, who was photographed by Hedda in his shop (fig. 2.6). The three-legged toad is associated with the Daoist immortal Liu Hai, who is popularly regarded as a god of wealth. A turquoise toggle of a three-legged toad with star-like incisions carved on its body was another favourite of Hedda (plate 34, p. 197). The toad's large eyes, humorous expression and pleasing

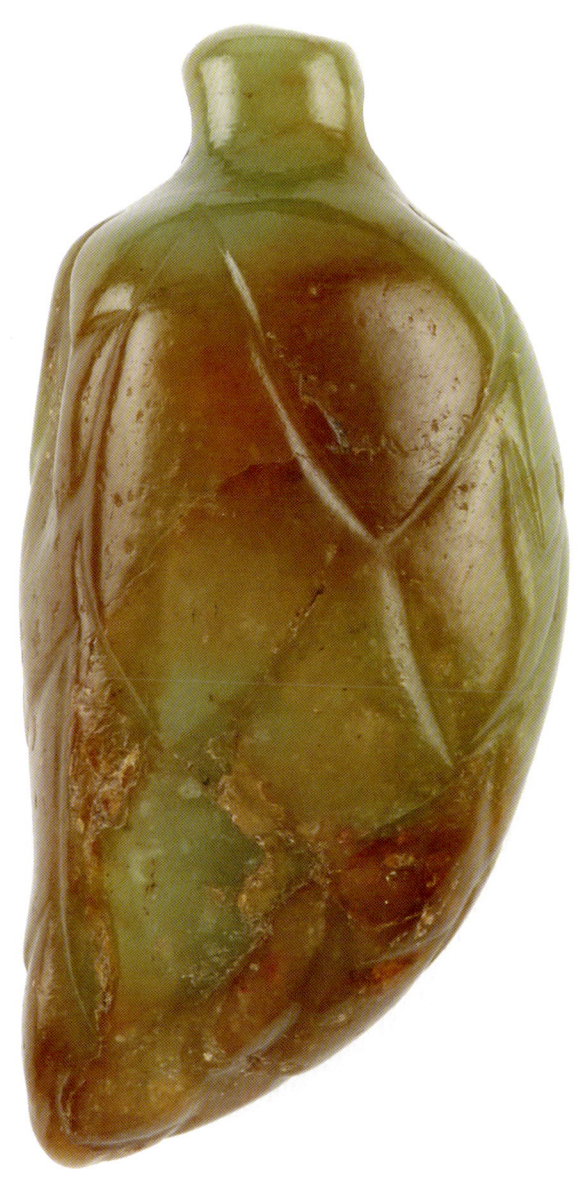

Fig. 2.7: Toggle in the shape of a lotus bud, China, c.1700–1940. Jade, 25 x 70 x 35 mm, Powerhouse Collection. Gift of Alastair Morrison, 1992. Object 92/440.

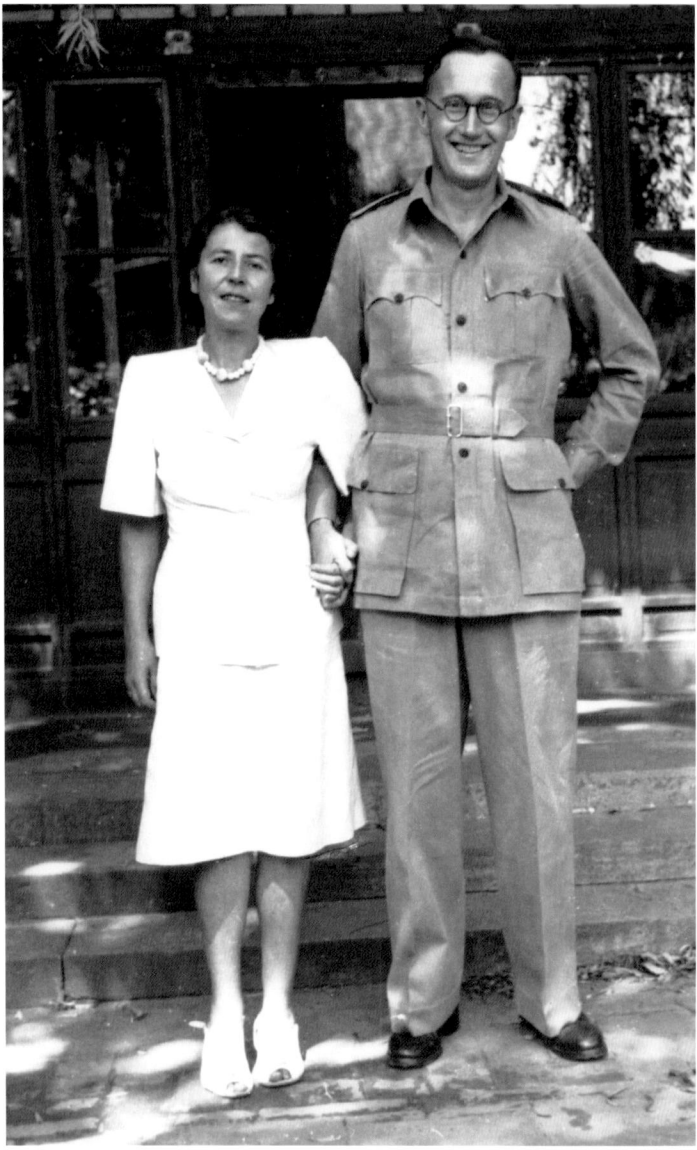

Fig. 2.8: Hedda and Alastair Morrison on their
wedding day, Beijing, 1946. Photographer
unknown. Printed by Jean-François Lanzarone
from a negative. Powerhouse Collection.
Gift of Alastair Morrison, 1993

rounded form, which makes good use of the two-tone dark green and turquoise colour of the stone, was probably part of its appeal. Other favourites include the black cat purchased in an antique shop at the end of Wangfujing (plate 42, p. 205) and the white jade piglet, another animal of the Chinese zodiac, associated with kind heartedness and loyalty (plate 58, p. 221).

Alastair prized the white semi-translucent jade toggle of two silkworms on a mulberry fruit and leaves (plate 25, p. 187) and a grey-white jade piece carved in the form of the fruit commonly known as *fo shou* (佛手), Buddha's hand citron, which was used as an altar offering at New Year, symbolic of good fortune, *fu/fo* (福), and longevity, *shou* (寿).

While the majority of Hedda and Alastair's toggles were collected in Beijing between 1940 and 1941, they continued to add to their collections. Not long after the declaration of the outbreak of the Pacific War on 8 December 1941, Alastair, who had been working as a cypher officer in an intelligence unit at the British Embassy, was moved to Shanghai. Before he left, he entrusted his 'treasured possessions', which included his 'collection of toggles, camera and field glasses' used for bird watching, to Hedda for safe keeping. Once in Shanghai, Alastair purchased 'a number of magnificent toggles for ridiculous prices' that he located in small markets off Canton Road.[21] After enlisting to join the war effort, Alastair worked in intelligence and joined the 2nd Ghurkhas, serving in India and later in China. In Chongqing, he acquired a mottled brown and pale green jade toggle simply carved in the form of a lotus bud (fig. 2.7) and a dark green jade toggle of a *guzheng*, or Chinese zither, in a silk case (plate 63, p. 226), purchases that indicate how he chose to spend his leisure time in China's wartime capital.

At the end of the war, Alastair returned to Beijing with the objective of being reunited with Hedda. Once there he hurriedly visited a number of antique and curio shops, anxious to try and trace and recover some 'treasured ivory toggles' that had recently been stolen from Hedda's compound. The quest was successful in that about half of the stolen toggles were located, but Alastair had no option but to buy them back at what, under the circumstances, he considered to be 'quite reasonable prices'.[22]

Alastair and Hedda were married in Beijing in 1946 (fig. 2.8), and the two collections that had been in Hedda's care during the war were formally merged. Their union in marriage was in many ways prefigured in the collection and in the passion they shared for toggle hunting. Within the collection there are many toggles that are symbolic of happiness and good fortune in marriage, which would have originally doubled as lucky charms or talismans. Among them are pairs of mandarin ducks (fig. 2.9), fish (fig. 2.10 and plate 13, p. 174), persimmons (fig. 2.11), peaches (plates 6 and 7, pp. 168–70), playing cats (plate 41, p. 204), baby boys (plates 1 and 28, p. 163, 190), entwined tigers (plate 11, p. 173) and bean pods (plate 39, p. 202), the seeds of which refer to the wish for progeny.

For Hedda and Alastair, the collecting of toggles played an important role in the development of their friendship. To them the objects were alive, imbued with the cultural significance created by their unknown makers, who designed them for practical use and to bring good luck. They carry the touch of the users whose traces of enjoyment and affection remain in the warm patina on their surfaces, having been worn and handled over decades and, in some cases, centuries. And they tell Hedda's and Alastair's own stories of collecting and connection. In their hands the toggles became transcultural objects signifying the

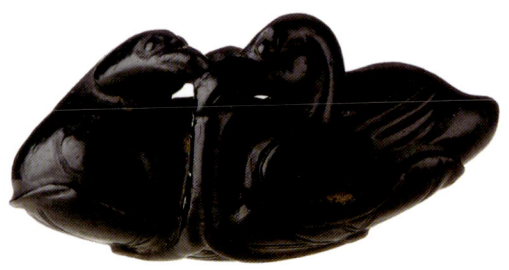

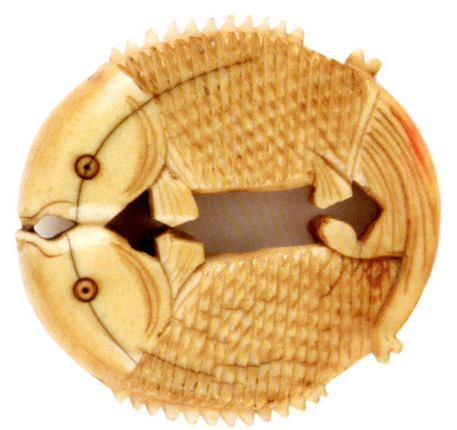

Fig. 2.9: Toggle in the shape of paired mandarin ducks, China, c.1700–1940. Hardstone, 20 x 20 x 55 mm, Powerhouse Collection. Gift of Alastair Morrison, 1992. Object 92/496.

Fig. 2.10: Toggle in the shape of paired fish, China, c.1700–1940. Ivory, 50 x 45 x 12 mm, Powerhouse Collection. Gift of Alastair Morrison, 1992. Object 92/615.

appreciation of Chinese culture that can occur far beyond China's borders.

As custodians of this collection of small, everyday items, the decorative and collectible parts of once functional objects, Hedda and Alastair maintained a practice of active handling and appreciation. They kept them alive as objects. While their original function had changed, their capacity to bring sensory delight continued. Fortunate visitors to the Morrisons' home would not only be encouraged to look at items in their bespoke wooden cabinet with multiple drawers, but also to pick them up, turn them over and appreciate them in the round as objects of weight, beauty and creative ingenuity (fig. 2.12). This haptic dimension of the objects, central to their original form and function, was also central to Hedda and Alastair's appreciation of them. Donating his collection of Chinese toggles and a smaller comparison collection of Japanese netsuke to Powerhouse Museum, Alastair recognised that his term as custodian of the items was part of a continuum. He wished the collection to remain together for the appreciation and enjoyment of generations to come. In letting go of the collection, full of personal memories and significances, his greatest concern was how to keep the objects alive. This is the challenge that he put to the museum, the new permanent home of the collection, a challenge that is now being addressed through storytelling and public display.

Alastair, like his father, George Ernest Morrison, was an avid collector.[23] He loved to be surrounded by the objects he had acquired, which he modestly referred to as *dongxi* (东西) in Chinese, which literally means 'east and west' in English but which is best understood as 'things'. Hedda and Alastair's collection of Chinese *dongxi*, including their collection of toggles, were important objects through which they understood their own lives, lived between East and West, and through which we can appreciate their deep-lived connections to China.

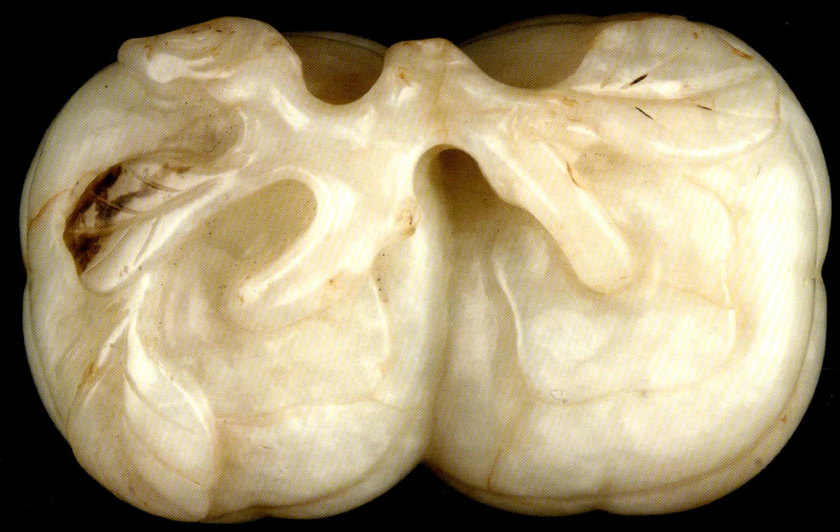

Fig. 2.11: Toggle in the shape of paired persimmons, China, c.1700–1940. Jade, 12 x 44 x 26 mm, Powerhouse Collection. Gift of Alastair Morrison, 1992. Object 92/513.

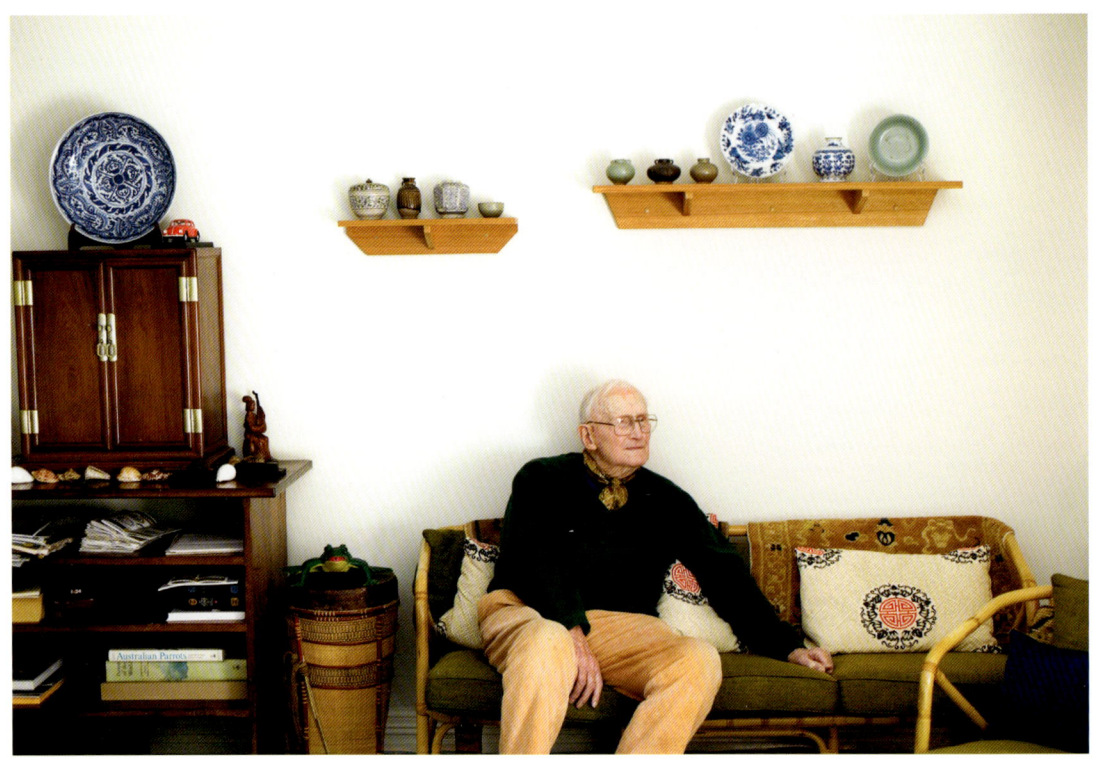

Fig. 2.12: Jean-François Lanzarone, Alastair Morrison at home in Hughes, Canberra, 2006.

1. Alastair Morrison, *The Bird Fancier: A Journey to Peking*, Pandanus Books, Canberra, 2001, p. 54, 110.

2. ibid., p. 123.

3. For a brief overview of Alastair Morrison's life see Claire Roberts, 'Alastair Morrison (1915–2009)', *China Heritage Quarterly*, no. 9, 2009.

4. Morrison, *The Bird Fancier*, p. 128. See also Hedda and Alastair Morrison, 'Chinese Toggles: A Little Known Folk Art', *Arts of Asia*, vol. 16, no. 2, 1986, p. 68.

5. Morrison, *The Bird Fancier*, p. 132.

6. ibid.

7. The courtyard house where Hedda lived from 1938 was in the precinct where the French Consul and art collector Jean-Pierre Dubosc and his wife Janine (daughter of the Paris-based art dealer C. T. Loo) lived.

8. *Interview with Alastair Morrison by Claire Roberts*, 2006, film, Powerhouse Museum, Canberra. Filmed by Jean-françois Lanzarone, part of collection of oral history interviews for the Powerhouse Museum. Powerhouse Museum Record Series (Item), MRS/278-218.

9. Morrison, *The Bird Fancier*, pp. 132–3.

10. Claire Roberts, 'China Bound: Hedda Hammer', in Amanda Bowen and Robert Sennett (eds.), *Harvard Library Bulletin: The Fine Arts Library at 50*, vol. 23, no. 3, Fall 2012, pp. 50-1.

11. Morrison, *The Bird Fancier*, p. 134.

12. After her death, Hedda Hammer Morrison's personal archive and a collection of exhibition prints were donated to the Powerhouse Museum. Her archive of negatives relating to her time living in China and Hong Kong and a series of thematic photograph albums that she assembled while living in Beijing were donated to the Harvard-Yenching Library, Harvard University.

13. Hedda Morrison, *A Photographer in Old Peking*, Oxford University Press, Oxford, 1985, p. 13. See also letter from Bennet Bronson, Curator, Asian Archaeology and Ethnology, Field Museum of Natural History, to the author, 17 November 1992. Powerhouse Museum curatorial file Exhibitions-Temporary-Hedda Morrison-Content Development F/92/135. Examples were gifted by Bieber to the Field Museum. The embroidered table linens donated by Alastair Morrison to the Powerhouse Museum relate to this activity.

14. Letter from Deborah Wythe, Archivist and Manager of Special Library Collections, The Brooklyn Museum, to the author, 21 December 1992, The Brooklyn Museum, Records of the Asian Art Department: file 263. See also letter from Elizabeth P. Weiland, Assistant Curator, Asian Art, The Brooklyn Museum, to the author, 14 December 1992, and copies of accession cards for objects, some of which include the statement: 'One of a large collection of Chinese objects purchased in Peking by Miss C. F. Bieber with $400 from the Frank L. Babbott Fund and delivered to the Museum in Dec. 1937'.

15. See Kenneth Starr, Curator, 'The Miss C. F. Bieber Collection of Chinese Folk and Minor Arts – Preliminary Report' to Mr E. Leland Webber, Director, Field Museum of Natural History, Chicago IL, Museum Accession File 2786. In Powerhouse Museum curatorial file Exhibitions-Temporary-Hedda Morrison-Content Development F/92/135. See also '237 Toggles Boggle Museum Imagination', *Chicago Tribune*, 25 October 1962, Field Museum of Natural History, Chicago IL, Museum File 2780. See also Schuyler Cammann, *Substance and Symbol in Chinese Toggles: Chinese Belt Toggles from the C. F. Bieber Collection*, University of Pennsylvania Press, Philadelphia, 1962, p. 175.

16. Cammann, *Substance and Symbol in Chinese Toggles*, pp. 9–10. A more recent, less scholarly publication that brings together six major toggle collections in addition to the author's own is Margaret Duda, *Traditional Chinese Toggles: Counterweights and Charms*, Editions Didier Millet, Singapore, 2012.

17. Hedda Morrison, *A Photographer in Old Peking*, p. 93.

18. Alastair Morrison, 'Toggle and Netsuke: A Minor Art from China and Japan', a lecture presented to the Asian Society Council, September 1979, Powerhouse Collection Masterfile 92/429–92/520.

19. *Interview with Alastair Morrison by Claire Roberts*, Powerhouse Museum.

20. The following observations were noted by the author during a conversation with Alastair Morrison on 29 April 1992.

21. Morrison, *The Bird Fancier*, p. 153, 161.

22. ibid., p. 253.

23. A collection of Chinese objects acquired by George Ernest Morrison in China is in the collection of the National Gallery of Victoria. G. E. Morrison's extensive library of books and works on paper relating to China was acquired by the Toyo Bunko, Tokyo, which also houses Alastair Morrison's collection of books relating to Southeast Asia. G. E. Morrison's personal archive is in the State Library of New South Wales.

Part II
Miniature, the user and tactile appreciation

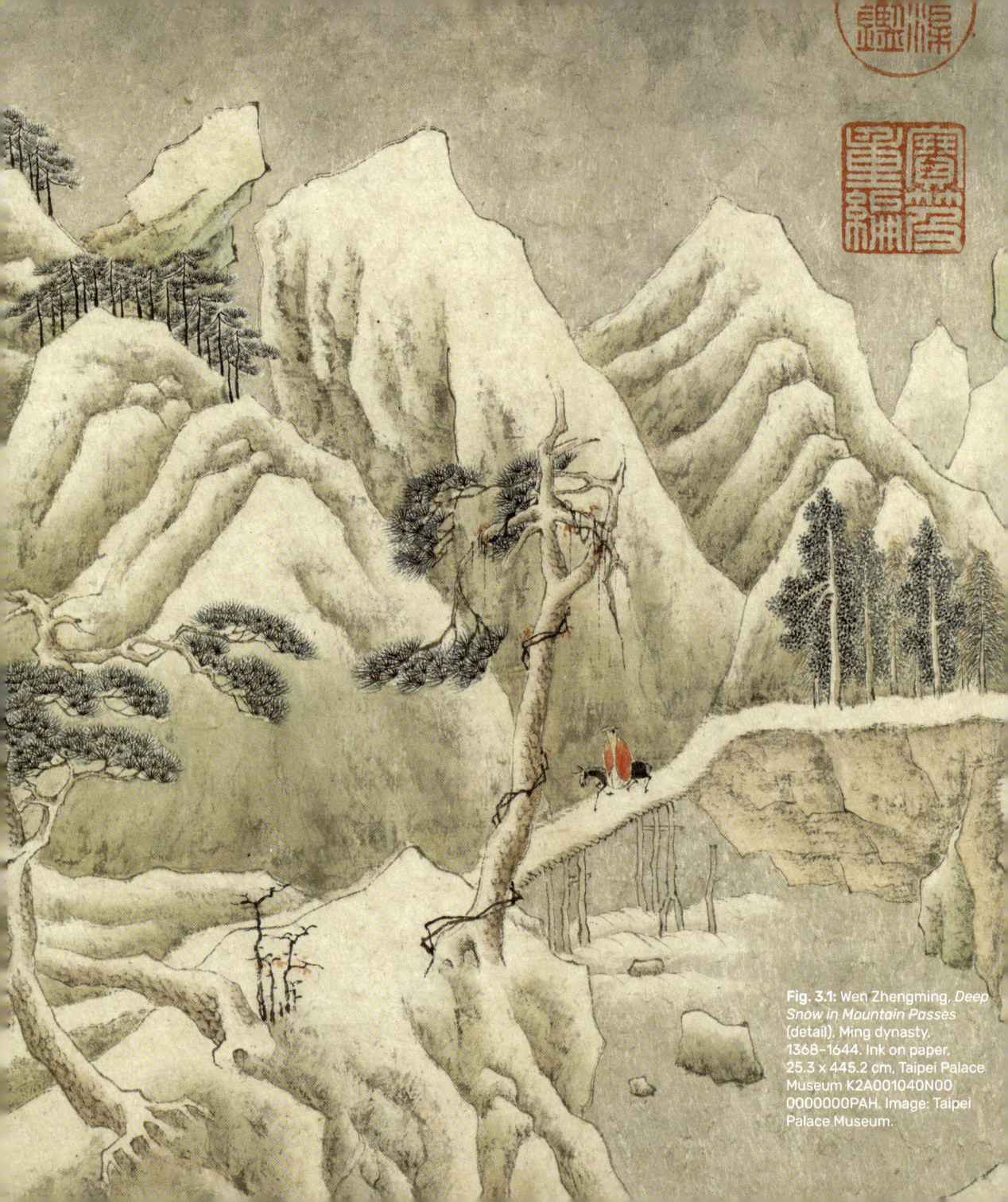

Fig. 3.1: Wen Zhengming, *Deep Snow in Mountain Passes* (detail), Ming dynasty, 1368–1644. Ink on paper, 25.3 x 445.2 cm, Taipei Palace Museum K2A001040N00 0000000PAH. Image: Taipei Palace Museum.

3. Chinese toggles at scale: miniatures and metaphoric spaces

Chen Shuxia

The bodhisattvas can see Mount Sumeru within a grain of mustard seed.

—*Vimalakīrti Sūtra*

In addition to their function as counterweights, traditionally worn about the waist, Chinese toggles are miniature sculptures that held multiple versions of the world for their wearers. In China, miniature objects have a remarkably long history in cultural rituals and artistic production. The earliest known examples, which can be traced back to the late Western Zhou dynasty (c.1046–771 BCE), are burial objects such as human figurines and domestic animals made of bronze and clay that probably had ritual significance.[1] Much research has focused on such ritual miniatures from archaeological sites or later decorative objects from imperial collections, as well as the more extravagant *wanhaozhiwu* (玩好之物), 'pleasurable things', collected by cultural elites.[2] In contrast, scholars (and collectors) have given very little attention to less precious forms of miniature sculpture such as toggles, which originate in the more functional context of everyday sartorial needs.

As poet and literary critic Susan Stewart argues, despite their discreet size, miniatures (in her case miniature books or doll houses) are significant for revealing social space and hence embodying desire, belief, fantasy, knowledge, social histories and narratives.[3] In this way, the miniature goes beyond the physical appearance or even the materiality of the object. Chinese toggles similarly mediated different cultural narratives, memories and emotions for their carriers and the world they lived in or sought to fashion. Through a selection of toggles from the Powerhouse Collection, this chapter considers what it might mean to see the toggle as opening a metaphoric space in which culture, personal aspiration and fashion were condensed in miniature as something more akin to a culture of accessory and sartorial presentation.

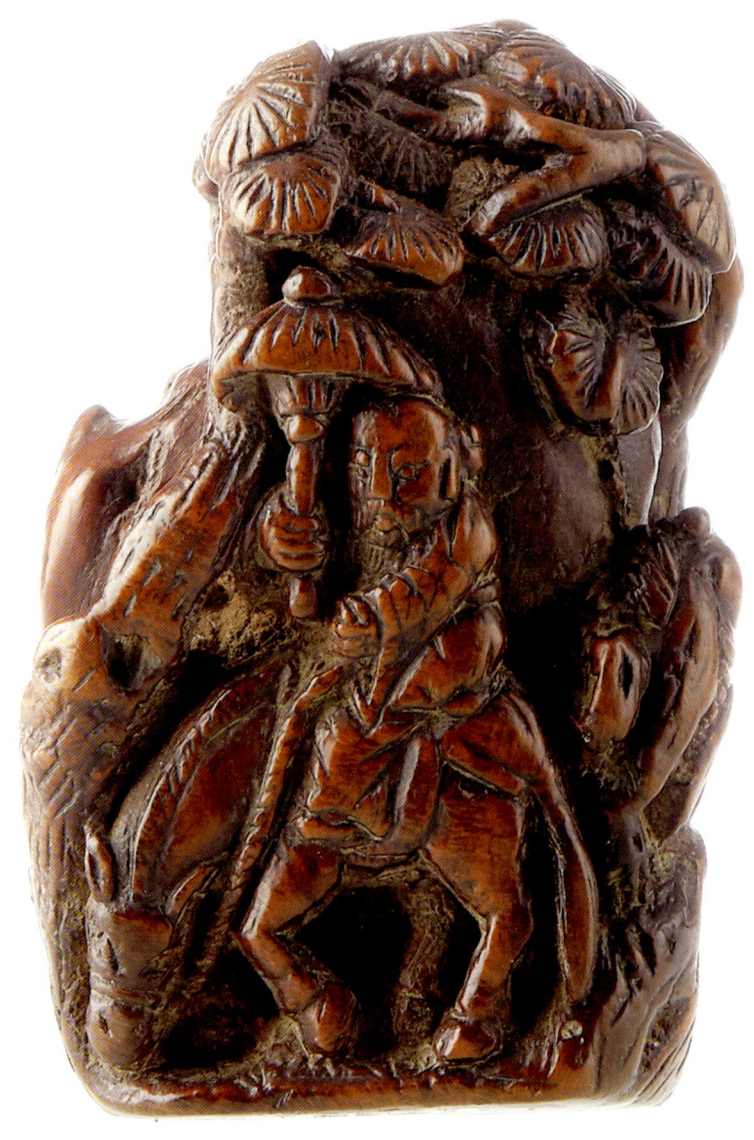

Fig. 3.2: Toggle in the shape of Lu You on a donkey, China, c.1700–1940. Wood, 45 x 30 x 23 mm. Gift of Alastair Morrison, 1992. Powerhouse Collection. Object 92/533.

Entering the picture

Some figurative toggles were carved as a scene (or even *mise-en-scène*) that provides a backdrop or narrative context to a figure. Being situated in a narrative context, these miniaturised figures evoke a more expansive vision. Jonathan Hay relates this effect to the experience of *ruhua* (入画), 'entering the picture': when the viewer beholds and contemplates an object modelled from narrative, it triggers multiple associations and an imagination of 'unbounded pictorial space'.[4] On many occasions in Chinese culture, this ruhua experience of metaphoric or narrative exploration could be aroused by a subtle combination of pictorial and literary cues.

A rich example of the toggle as a vehicle for such narrative and aesthetic journeying is the Lu You toggle (fig. 3.2), which depicts the Southern Song poet Lu You (陆游, 1125–1210) riding a donkey and holding an umbrella as he travels below a canopy of jagged pine trees and rocks. A large cicada is carved on a pine tree to the figure's right. This toggle directly references the famous poem *Jianmendao zhong yuweiyu* (剑门道中遇微雨), 'Encounter Light Rain Crossing the Sword Gate Path', written by Lu You in 1172, when he was reappointed to Sichuan as a senior officer for military affairs. The poem reads,

> 'With my clothes covered in dust mixing wine stains, I have encountered many dispiriting occasions along this long journey.
> Has my life only confirmed me as a poet? I enter the Sword Gate Path on a donkey as it drizzles.'[5]

Lu expressed his disappointment regarding his post not long after he fought briefly at the front line of the war between the Han-led Song Empire (960–1279) and the Jurchen-led Jin Empire (1115–1234). When he wrote this poem at the age of forty-seven, Lu felt dejected that he could not fulfil his ambition to fight off the Jurchen invasion; he felt underappreciated by the court and lamented the thought of spending his life as a poet.

Historically, many literati—members of the elite scholar-bureaucrat class—felt disappointed by affairs of the imperial court, and expressed such feelings through their poems and paintings, often set in idyllic 'mountains and waters'. Indeed, so prevalent is such a setting in literati art that *shanshui* (山水—*shan*, 'mountain', *shui*, 'water') has become a general term for all ink painting of landscapes in the literati style. The representation of a scholar on a donkey, travelling across a rocky mountain path lined with pine trees, is a familiar motif in both literature and art. It has become a symbol of the dream of literati who are unsuccessful or underappreciated politicians: to become a recluse living in or travelling through remote mountains after retiring from court. Such scenes could be found in one of the most representative snow landscape paintings from China: *Guanshan jixue tu* (关山积雪图), *Deep Snow in Mountain Passes* (fig. 3.1) by Ming dynasty (1368–1644) painter Wen Zhengming (文徵明, 1470–1559). In this handscroll, more than 4 metres long, Wen, one of the famed Four Scholars of Ming, depicted a remote, snowy path on Mount Guan. One can see many figures crossing the snow mountain on donkeys.[6]

A quiet and unfettered world, far from the upheavals of official service, was the archetypal subject of literati longing in imperial China. The gnarled trees and cold solitude also hinted of exile or at least a kind of rejection. The simplicity of travelling in solitude vividly represents the complex desire of many scholars. Despite its more rustic or *quotidienne* finish, the Lu You toggle knowingly references this motif of elite poetry and ink painting, signalling a pictorial and literary space for its beholder and his circle. As Hay states, 'The juxtaposition of presentational and representational ideas in a single artefact generates metaphoric space from the relation between the two.[7] The toggle, a particularly small and discrete example of such a 'single artefact', is a physical presentation; at the same time it embodies the 'representational idea' the disappointments or compromises of urban politics and a yearning for peace, or at least solitude, in remote nature. Carrying the toggle might be a reminder of this individual, counter position, expressed through metaphoric, literary narrative, asserting the self amid the upheavals of the court and noisy urban life.

Animated adornment

The idea of metaphoric space is taken further in the 'Journey to the West' toggle (fig. 3.5). This toggle was carved to show a scene from the historical novel *Xiyouji* (西游记) *Journey to the West*, one of the most enduringly popular Chinese classics, attributed to Ming dynasty writer Wu Cheng'en (吴承恩, c.1500–82). It features the monk Tang Sanzang (唐三藏), a character based on Xuanzang 玄奘, the famous monk from the Tang dynasty (618–906) on his horse, leading three supernatural disciples— Sun Wukong (孙悟空, 'Monkey'), Zhu Bajie (猪八戒, 'Pigsy') and Sha Wujing (沙悟净, 'Sandy')—across mountains, temples and pagodas on their way to the lands of the West, in and around what is today northern India. *Journey to the West* was developed from Xuanzang's own work, *Datang xiyuji* (大唐西域记), *Great Tang Records on the Western Regions*, edited by his disciple *Bianji* (辩机) in 646, which narrates his nineteen-year journey to bring ancient Buddhist texts from India back to China.

Numerous versions of *Journey to the West* were produced during the Ming and Qing periods (1368–1911), yet the outline of the story remained similar, with the same key protagonists, who were illustrated as the story was reproduced. *Xiyouyuanzhi* (西游原旨), *The Original Gist of the Journey to the West*, written by Liu Yiming (刘一明, 1734–1821) around 1640, shows images of the enlightened monk Tang Sanzang with his white horse, determined to travel to the Sukhāvatī, Western Heaven (fig. 3.3).

The four lightly carved Chinese characters, *xi tian qu jing* (西天取经), at the base of the toggle, mean 'bringing scriptures from the Western Heaven' and would have been readily identified with the *Journey to the West* story and its protagonists. Holding the toggle, one could turn it to appreciate the four figures and recall familiar episodes about them (fig. 3.5). One might start with Zhu Bajie with his floppy pig ears, carrying his signature weapon— a Nine-Tooth Rake—while walking in front of the monk's horse, offering protection. Turning the toggle to the left, one sees Tang Sanzang, riding his white horse and crossing a temple in which a Buddhist god was enshrined. Sha Wujing carries luggage, following the horse. Turning the toggle further, one encounters the powerful yet rebellious disciple Sun Wukong, 'Sun the Wanderer', or the Monkey King, as he is often referred to in English. Sun Wukong, wearing a golden headband that allows the monk to control him when he misbehaves, seems to have just flown out of a pagoda; he looks over his shoulder, ever alert to hidden dangers. A gigantic spider-like demon extends its long, sharp legs, hovering on top of the toggle, looking down on its prey, the monk, below.

This motif specifically recalls the well-known episode of the spider demons and their *pangsidong* (盘丝洞), or 'Cave of the Silken Web', from *Journey to the West*. In this story, Tang Sanzang is captured by seven spider demons, disguised as beautiful maidens, who plot to eat the monk's flesh in

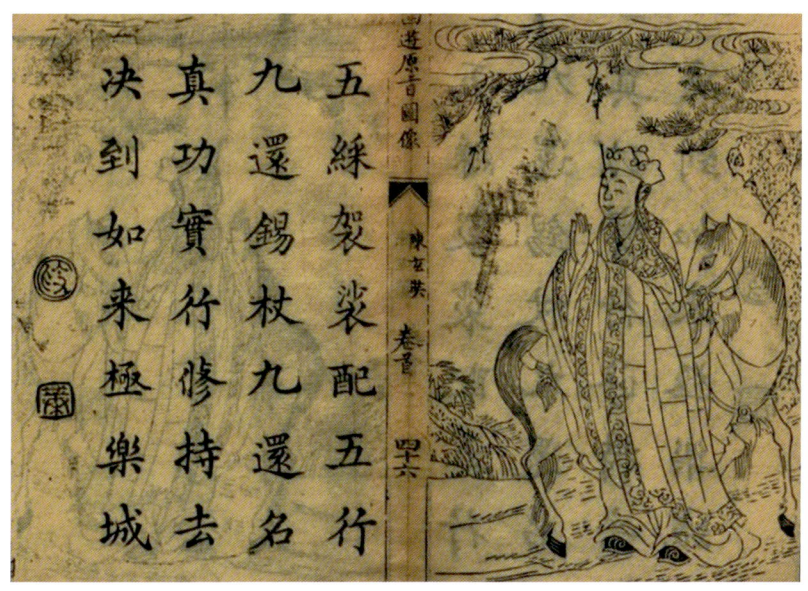

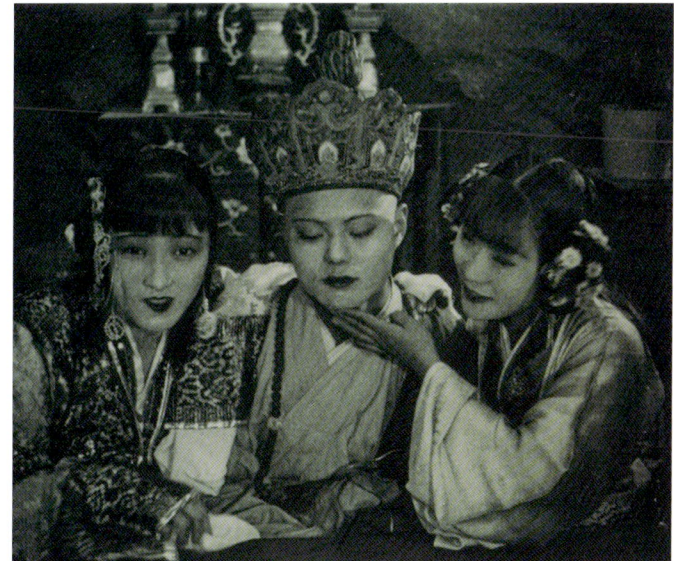

Fig. 3.3: Illustration and text on Xuan Zang's determination to the Western Heaven. Image from *The Original Gist of the Journey to the West*, written by Liu Yiming, printed by the Fellowship of Goodness, Changde Branch, Hunan (湖南常德同善分社), 1820. Collection of Gansu Provincial Library, 857.46/436.071.

Fig. 3.4: Still from *The Cave of the Silken Web*, directed by Dan Duyu, 1927. Shanghai Yingxi Company.

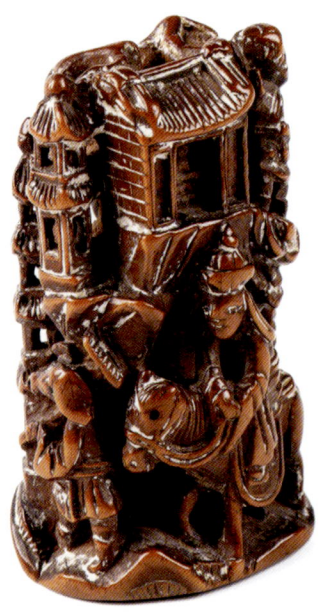
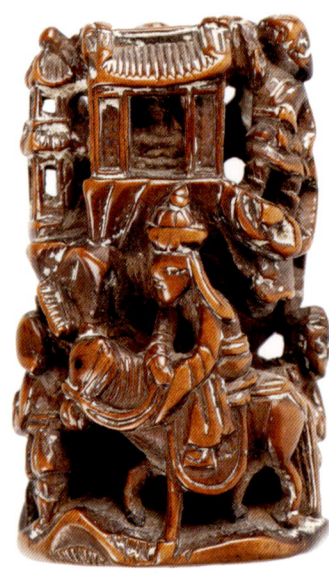
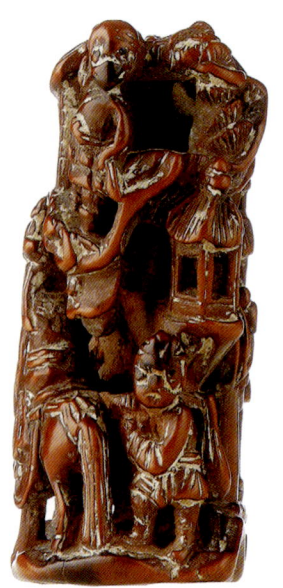
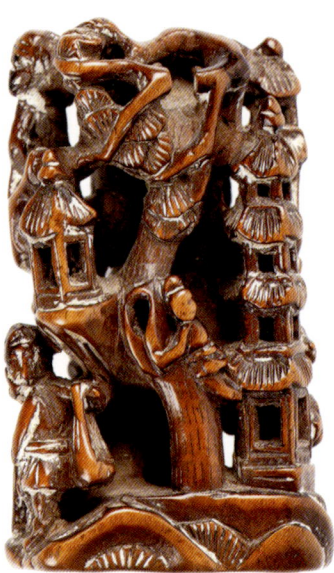

Fig. 3.5: Toggle depicting a scene from *Journey to the West*, China, c.1700–1940. Wood, 46 x 29 x 20 mm, Powerhouse Collection. Gift of Alastair Morrison, 1992. Object 92/584.

order to achieve immortality. The turning gesture one anticipates when contemplating this toggle enhances its affective dimension, which is not confined to fondling, rubbing and turning. It embodies a trajectory of story with one's bodily engagement, including the turning of hand, the tilting of head and the gazing of eyes anticipating the changing of figures.

Stewart has commented on the dramatic potential of miniature form, writing:

We see the essential theatricality of all miniatures. Our transcendent viewpoint makes us perceive the miniature as object and this has double effect. First, the object in its perfect stasis nevertheless suggests use, implementation, and contextualization. And second, the representative quality of the miniature makes that contextualization an allusive one; the miniature becomes a stage on which we project, by means of association or intertextuality, a deliberately framed series of actions.[8]

In a similar way, the 'Journey to the West' toggle's shape is exploited to present a temporal and narrative shift, featuring different key motifs of the 'Cave of the Silken Web' story, succinctly conjuring the drama of the novel across the toggle's limited surface. The series of actions conjured by this toggle might have been triggered by memories not only of the novel itself but also its adaptation in operas. During the Qing dynasty and into the early part of the Republican era (1912–49), different genres of Chinese opera featured many stories from *Journey to the West*, especially the 'Cave of the Silken Web', which was popular among both the imperial court and common people.[9]

While the exact date of production of this toggle remains unknown, it was collected in Beijing by Hedda and Alastair Morrison between 1940 and 1942.[10] By then, quite a few stories from *Journey to the West* had even been made into films.[11] Among these, 'The Cave of the Silken Web' was featured in various movies, including Dan Duyu's (但杜宇, 1897–1972) eponymous 1927 production (fig. 3.4), as well as sequels made in 1929 by the Shanghai Yingxi Company.[12] Testament to the broad and ongoing popular appeal of this episode from the novel, Dan's film was publicised in the most circulated newspaper in China, *Shen Bao*.[13] Moreover, as a result of the burgeoning print industry, photographs of the main protagonists were widely circulated in film advertisements, posters and production stills, while film reviews were featured in newspapers and popular illustrated pictorials.[14]

By holding, turning and appreciating the 'Journey to the West' toggle as a miniature stage, the owner may have projected a metaphoric space with series of actions informed by literature, illustration, opera and film on this popular story. As Edward S. Cooke, Jr., states, 'When handling the objects in use, users could literally feel these stories with their fingers. Just as stained-glass windows in churches provided a visual theology, moulded surfaces facilitated a felt folklore.'[15] The owner, through their interpretation of and personal attachment to the object at their waist and in their hands, gave meaning to the toggle as a miniaturised reflection of its time. The toggle is therefore an animated medium capable of connecting its owner to a cultural context that might exist between the past, present and future.

Amulets

Chanting and holding prayer beads (for example, *mala* beads in Hinduism and Buddhism, and rosary beads in Christianity) are wide-spread practices among many cultures that are often practised in private space. Like the prayer beads, miniature religious statuettes are intimate and portable compared to large-scale statues, and often are worshipped in private spaces such as the home or worn as personal amulets. They represent the gods and immortals who listen to prayers and protect worshipers. Such personal amulets might take the form of toggles carved in the shape of Buddhist and Daoist gods as well as immortals. Worn around the waist, these toggles channelled prayers to the gods and were intended to bring good fortune, health, longevity and fulfilment to their owners.

Miniature religious figures can be found in the Powerhouse Collection. One toggle, possibly representing Shou Xing (寿星), god of longevity, features the figure of a bald, bearded man with his eyes closed (fig. 3.6), making a bow. Dressed in a traditional long robe, Shou Xing leans on a rock with a pine tree at his back. The pine tree, a type of evergreen that lives for more than 1000 years, is a typical Chinese symbol of longevity. One can see that this Shou Xing toggle was well loved, as it appears that frequent fondling has smoothed the hard wooden edges, producing a lustre cultivated by the owner's hand. As Margaret Duda writes,

> Hold an old wooden toggle in your hand. Close your eyes. Let your fingers roam slowly over the ridges and valleys. Feel the surface made smooth by centuries of fondling. Soon you will come to understand why earlier generations believed that a toggle embodied transcendent truths and talismanic powers.[16]

The talismanic power and tactile magic are triggered by the owner's mix of cultural and sensory elements. Religious figures were often carved in colossal forms of a few metres high, expanded, physically to magnify and glorify the spiritual authority of the god. Such monumental religious sculptures have been installed in temples, churches and shrines as conduits for the worship of believers. Miniaturised figures, however, connect the visual and the haptic, perception and touch, to conjure a metaphoric presence that extends well beyond the physical dimensions of the toggle. To borrow the words of the English poet and painter William Blake, it is to 'see the world in a grain of sand' and 'hold infinity in the palm of your hand'.[17]

Personal miniatures

Stewart called miniatures an 'object of person', and the choice of what toggle to wear was probably a personal matter.[18] This intimate dimension to the connection between a toggle and its owner might be found in the miniature wooden abacus toggle (fig. 3.7) with moveable beads made of bone. The outer wooden frame was carved with auspicious patterns, including a motif of double copper coins with round outer shapes and squared central holes, symbolising good fortune. In addition to these traditional motifs, this toggle was carved with Chinese characters indicating an exact date on two sides of the frame: 'the fifteenth day of the third month, the twelfth year of Tongzhi Reign'. According to the lunar calendar used in imperial China the twelfth year of the Tongzhi reign was 1873, while the fifteenth day of the third moon of that year would correspond to 11 April on the Gregorian calendar.[19] Interestingly, the bottom of this miniature abacus also features a hidden sliding lid or panel, allowing the toggle to double as a tiny box, concealed behind the delicately carved abacus.

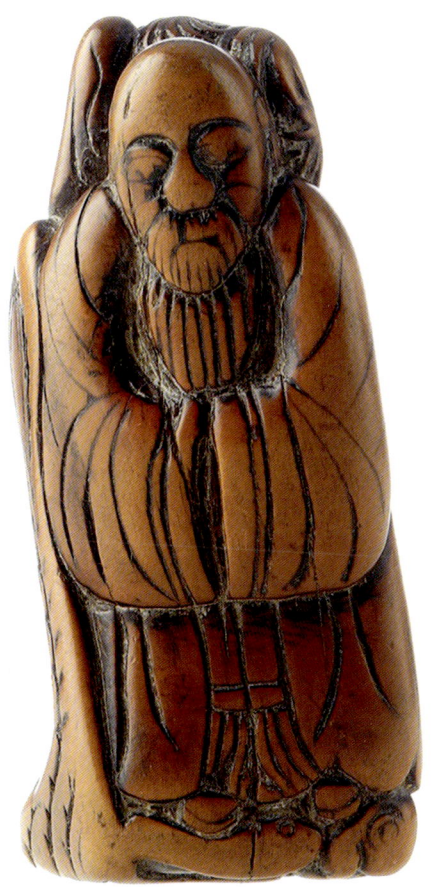
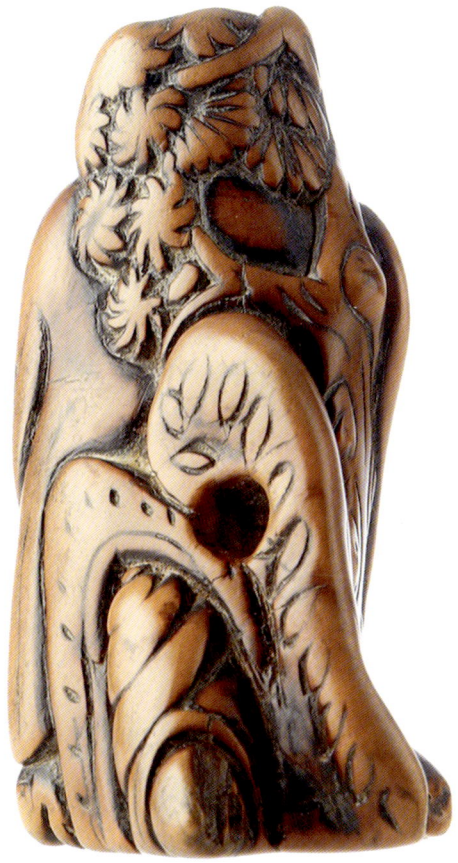

Fig. 3.6: Front and back views;
toggle in the Shape of Shou
Xing, China, c.1700–1940.
Wood, 62 x 30 x 47 mm.
Gift of Alastair Morrison, 1992.
Powerhouse Collection.
Object 92/531.

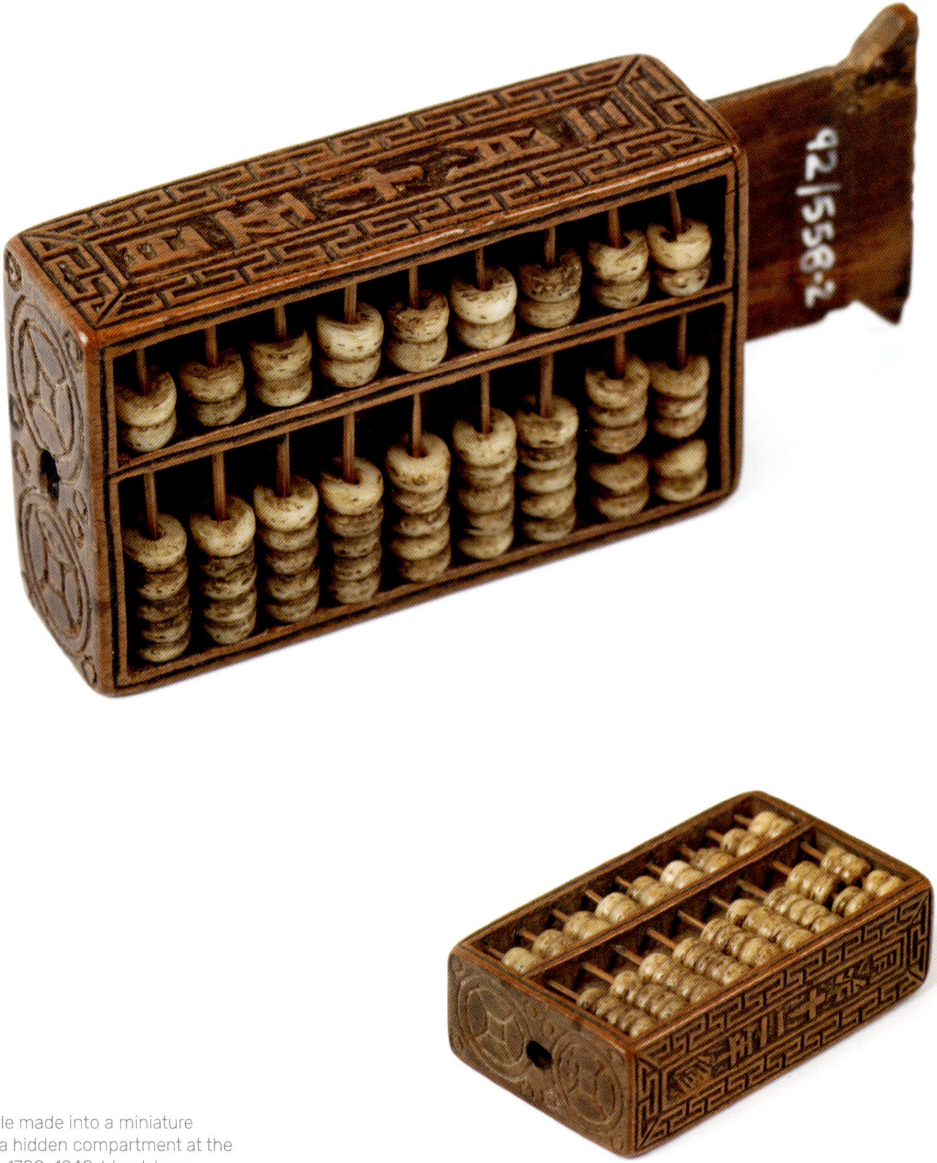

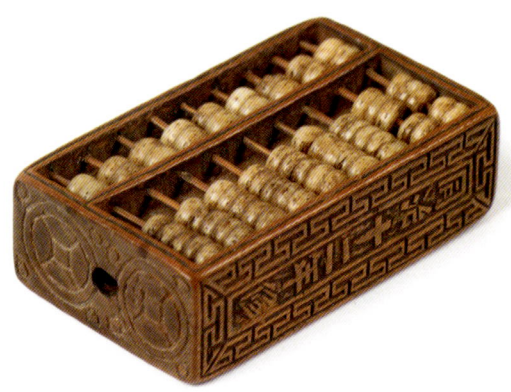

Fig. 3.7: Toggle made into a miniature abacus, with a hidden compartment at the back, China, c.1700–1940. Wood, bone, 11 x 38 x 22 mm. Gift of Alastair Morrison, 1992. Powerhouse Collection. Object 92/558.

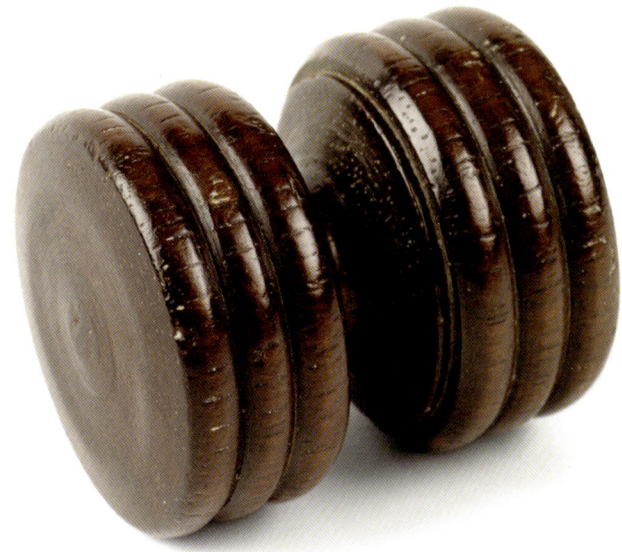

Fig. 3.8: Toggle in the shape of a Chinese diabolo, China, c.1700–1940. Wood, 35 x 30 (diam) mm. Gift of Alastair Morrison, 1992. Powerhouse Collection. Object 92/549.

It is tempting to presume that the owner of this abacus toggle might have been a merchant or from a wealthy merchant family, where the use of a real abacus for everyday business would have been familiar and significant. They might have hidden a personal or business seal in the disguised compartment. However, the excellent condition of the wooden frame, showing very minimal wear, indicates that this toggle was not often handled or used. The exact date carved on the abacus—the only such example in the Powerhouse Collection—might mark a special personal occasion—a birthday, for example. This toggle could have been one of the objects for the *zhuazhou* (抓周) celebration.

Zhuazhou literally means 'catch' (*zhua*) of the 'first year' (*zhou*), a traditional custom celebrating a baby's first birthday. On this occasion, parents would place a variety of objects typically a book, writing brush, copper coins, scissors, an abacus and other precious objects made of jade, gold or silver in front of the child, who would be dressed in new clothes and surrounded by family members. When the child would 'catch' (select) an item, this was considered a sign of their future career, their personality or particular talent. A brush or book would indicate a career in the bureaucracy, a pair of scissors a talent for a craft, while an abacus or copper coins a future in commerce.[20]

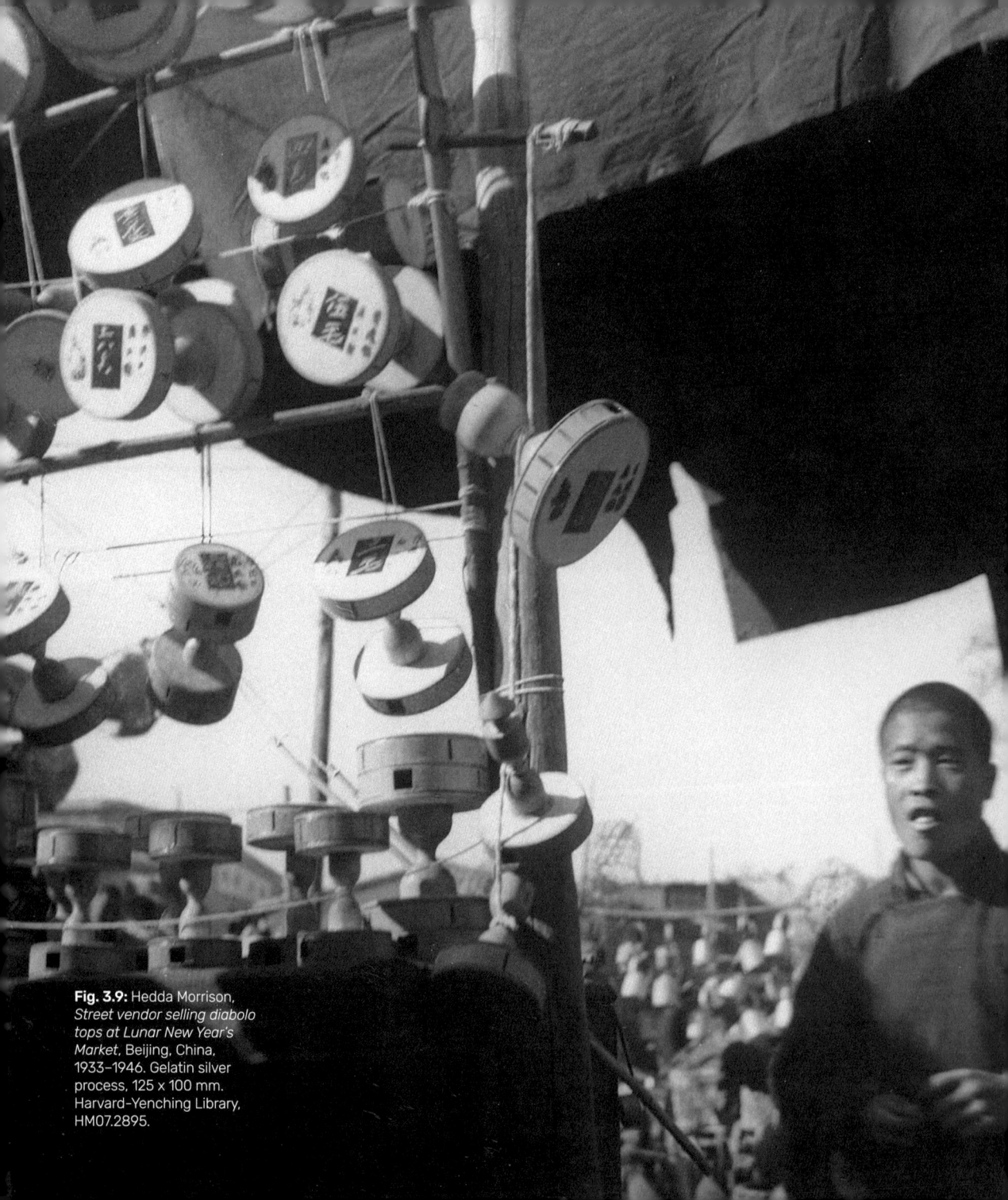

Fig. 3.9: Hedda Morrison, *Street vendor selling diabolo tops at Lunar New Year's Market*, Beijing, China, 1933–1946. Gelatin silver process, 125 x 100 mm. Harvard-Yenching Library, HM07.2895.

This small sculpture might have been later repurposed as a toggle because a baby picked it at the *zhuazhou* ceremony, or perhaps it was made by parents who wished to ensure a successful commercial career for their child.

While it is impossible to identify precisely why this miniature abacus toggle was made and who might have owned it, this unique object reveals how toggles could also create spaces of deeply personal significance. Its fine condition suggests it may have been tucked away, only taken out for special occasions or treasured in private. This sense of personal significance, the air of mystery and even secrecy associated with such complex miniature objects, is what British Museum curator John Mack alluded to when he wrote:

> the most important, symbolically motivated or powerful may be the least in scale; that the miniature occupies a contained space; that it may be controlled, possessed; but yet that it has at its heart an inherent mystery, which may be a matter of aesthetics or … of hidden verities.'[21]

While toggles could and did display the tastes of their owners, at the same time, their discreet sizes made it possible for owners to keep aspects of their desires or memories private.

Playthings

Just as the abacus might have related to a childhood ritual, there are instances where toggles were miniature replicas of everyday children's playthings, symbolising joy and new life. These replica toys, historically popular around Beijing, where most of the toggles in the Powerhouse Collection were collected, provide an important insight into the street life of China's imperial capital even at the time of their collection in the early twentieth century.

A toggle (fig. 3.8) made of dark-brown polished wood replicates a Chinese diabolo, a traditional toy played with by children in the street. Known as *kongzhu* (空竹), 'hollow bamboo' or *kongzhong* (空钟), 'hollow bell', Chinese diabolos consist of two dumbbell-like hollow discs made of bamboo or wood, connected by a rod that functions as an axle. To play, one must keep the diabolo spinning on a string, the ends of which are connected to sticks held in both hands. Agitating the sticks on either side of the diabolo spins and balances it, while also producing a loud, reverberating sound. Such a game may have first been recorded in the late Ming dynasty book *Dijing jingwulue* (帝京景物略), *Resume of Sights and Goods of the Imperial Capital* (first published in 1635) by Liu Tong (刘侗, c. 1593–1636) and Yu Yizheng (于奕正, 1597–1636). In this book, the Chinese diabolo only had a single disc and was spun on the ground. During the Qing dynasty, this toy developed into its characteristic double-disc form and method of play, recorded in *Yanjing zaji* (燕京杂记), *Yanjing Miscellaneous* (published date unknown, circa late nineteenth or early twentieth century).[22]

Throughout the nineteenth and early twentieth centuries in Beijing, the Chinese diabolo was played during springtime, as the weather started warming and the capital's street life became more vibrant. Markets selling a variety of children's toys, among other things, were set up around temples, especially the May market near the City God Temple around Xuanwu Gate.[23] Hedda Morrison captured a glimpse of one market vendor selling diabolos at Chinese New Year in the 1930s or 1940s (fig. 3.9).

Another popular street game during the Ming and Qing dynasty in Beijing was *zhi beishi* (掷贝石), literally meaning to 'throw' (*zhi*), knucklebones (*beishi*). As recorded in *Rixia jiuwenkao* (日下旧闻考), *Hearsay of Old Matters Under the Sun*, a Beijing gazetteer published in the Qianlong era (1735–96), this game was played by children during mid-autumn, around the tenth month of the year on the lunar calendar, when many sheep ankle bones were available because lamb was a popular food of the season.[24] A variety of knucklebone games have, of course, been shared by numerous cultures around the world for centuries. The Nicholson Collection at the Chau Chak Wing Museum includes a set of three knucklebones possibly used by children as games from Tell el Duweir (Lachish), Tel Lakhish, Israel (fig. 3.11) and a single knucklebone from Arpachiyah, Tell Arpachiyah, Iraq, dated to the Halaf-Ubaid period (6500–4000 BCE).[25]

The Powerhouse Collection includes a finely carved rock crystal toggle in the form of a large knucklebone (fig. 3.12). In China, knucklebone games were widely played historically in and around the north, and knucklebones have been common in the nomadic cultures of the region, where lamb is a staple food. Such games were known as *gachuha* in Manchu and *shagai* in Mongolian. In Mongolian culture, knucklebones have been used as toys, gifts and toggles. Beijing, the imperial capital, had a sizable community of resident Mongolians during the Qing dynasty.[26] One can imagine that even later, when Hedda and Alistair Morrison were in Beijing, they may still have seen knucklebones used as children's toys in the street. One can see a pair of knucklebones used as toggles for a small bag purchased in Mongolia in the 1990s, with strings threaded through a drilled hole in the bone (fig. 3.10). Knucklebones are still used as humble decorative objects today.

Chinese toggles miniaturise symbolic content into a small object, carried or hidden in a personal space. They are limited by their contained physicality, yet they prompt reflection, imagination and connection. Through this small selection from the Powerhouse Collection, we see how a toggle could conjure a cultural realm, how it could be an amulet or memento channelling personal desire and memory, how it could represent a figure from history or folklore, connecting reality and fantasy, and how it could be a miniature plaything that symbolised simple, everyday pleasures. The discreet scale of toggles implies an 'exaggeration of content'[27] that expands in response to the holder and beholder. They are objects of the time, contextualising and connecting the stories, cultures and histories of the 'metaphoric space'[28] the owner inhabited and actively fashioned.

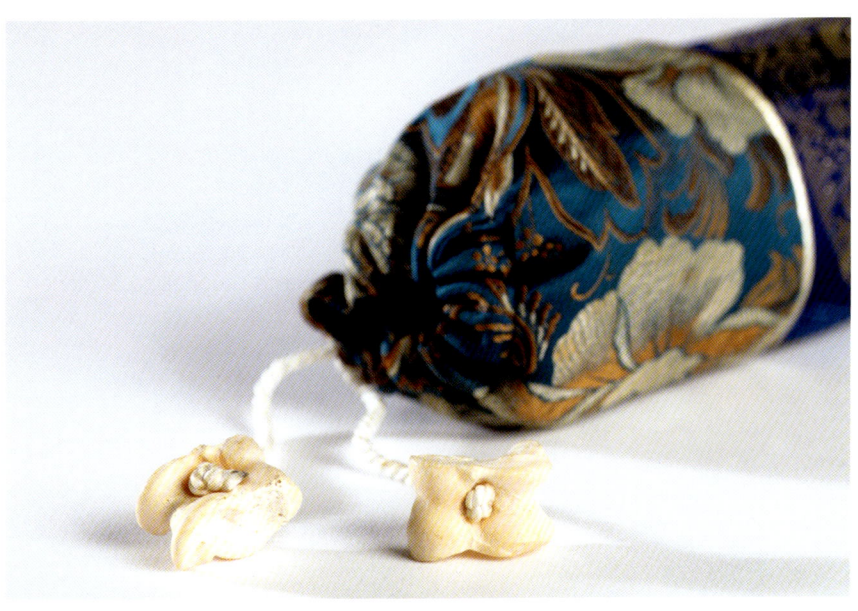

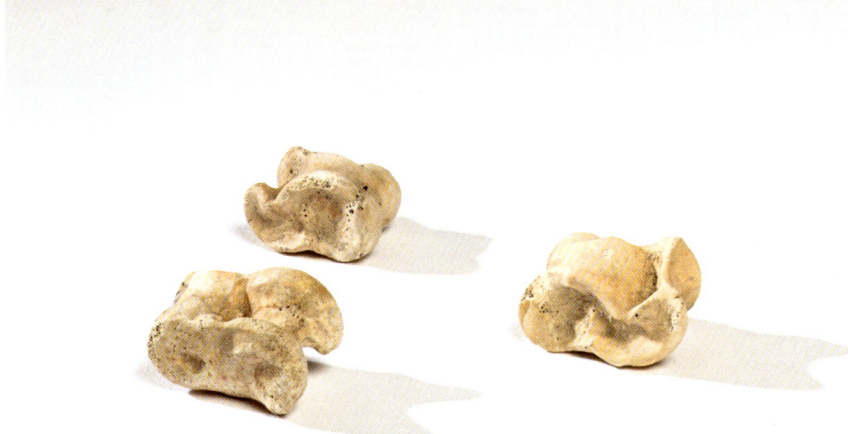

Fig. 3.10: Bag with a pair of knucklebone toggles, Mongolia, 1999. Knucklebones, textile, 35 x 25 mm (each). Courtesy of Dr Olivier Krischer. Image: Chau Chak Wing Museum;

Fig. 3.11: Toy knucklesbones, Tell el Duweir (Lachish), Tel Lakhish, Israel, date unknown. Bone, 35 x 25 mm (each). Nicholson collection, Chau Chak Wing Museum, donated by the Wellcome-Marston Trustees, 1952. Object NM52.193.1-3. Image: Chau Chak Wing Museum.

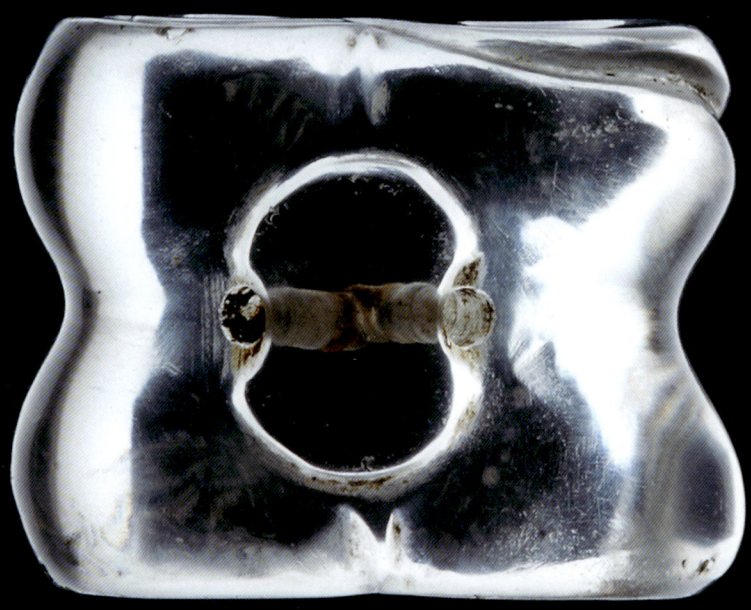

Fig. 3.12: Toggle in the form of a knucklebone, China, c.1700–1940. Rock crystal, 20 x 30 x 24 mm, Powerhouse Collection, Gift of Alastair Morrison, 1992. Object 92/695.

1. Wu Hung 巫鸿, '"明器" 的理论和实践――战国时期礼仪美术中的观念化倾向' ['Theory and Practice of Burial Objects: Tendency of Conceptualizing Etiquette Art in the Warring States Period'], 文物 [*Cultural Relics*], no. 6, 2006, p. 73. See also Yu Haiguang 于海广, '山东龙山文化的大型墓葬分析' ['Analysis of Large-scale Tombs of Shandong Longshan Culture'], 考古 [*Archaeology*], no. 1, 2000. pp. 61–7.

2. See Chen Shuxia's chapter 4 for a discussion of 'pleasurable things'.

3. Susan Stewart, 'The Miniature', in *On Longing: Narratives of the Miniature, the Gigantic, the Souvenir, the Collection*, Duke University Press, Durham and London, 1993, pp. 37–68.

4. Jonathan Hay, 'The Surfacescape's Resources', in *Sensuous Surfaces: The Decorative Object in Early Modern China*, University of Hawaii Press, Honolulu, 2010, pp. 171–3.

5. Translated by the author. The whole poem in Chinese is 《剑门道中遇微雨》：衣上征尘杂酒痕, 此身合是诗人未? 细雨骑驴入剑门。

6. See Andong Lu, 'Deciphering the Reclusive Landscape: A Study of Wen Zheng-Ming's 1533 Album of the Garden of the Unsuccessful Politician', *Studies in the History of Gardens and Designed Landscapes*, vol. 31, no. 1, 2011, pp. 40–59.

7. Hay, 'Decorative Objects', p. 82.

8. Stewart, 'The Miniature' p. 54.

9. See Fang Wenxi 方问溪, '清廷平秘内升署本: 盘丝洞' ['Qing Imperial Court Drama *Pingmi Neisheng*: The Cave of Silken Web'], 戏剧月刊 [*The Theatre Monthly*], no. 12, 1932, pp. 178–94. See also Zhao Yulong 赵毓龙, Feng Wei 冯伟, '舞台蝶变: 清宫大戏《昇平宝筏》对《西游记》案头叙事的因与革' ['Butterfly Metamorphosis on Stage: The Inheritance and Reform of Qing Imperial Drama the Precious Raft of Peaceful Times from Closet Drama Journey to the West'], 艺术广角 [*Art Panorama*], no. 5, 2019, pp. 34–41.

10. Some of the toggles in the Powerhouse Collection were collected by Alastair Morrison when he worked in Shanghai and Chongqing during the Pacific War (1941–45). See Alastair Morrison, *The Bird Fancier: A Journey to Peking*, Pandanus Books, Canberra, 2001.

11. Cheng Jihua 程季华, Li Shaobai 李少白, Xing Zuwen 邢祖文, 中国电影发展史 [*A History of the Development of Chinese Cinema*], China Film Publishing House 中国电影出版社, Beijing, 1998, pp. 86–9.

12. 'The Cave of the Silken Web', *The Chinese Mirror: A Journal of Chinese Film History*, https://web.archive.org/web/20131007031150/http://www.chinesemirror.com/index/2011/09/cave-of-the-silken-web-1927.html, (viewed August 2022).

13. See Shaoyi Sun, 'Fantasy, Vampirism and Genre/Gender Wars on the Chinese Screen of the Roaring 1920s', in Lin Feng and James Aston (eds), *Renegotiating Film Genres in East Asian Cinemas and Beyond*, Palgrave Macmillan, Cham, 2020, p. 100.

14. Wei Chenjie 魏晨捷, '透视《盘丝洞》：中国20年代电影与传统印刷媒介的互动' ['The Cave of the Silken Web in Perspectives: The Interaction Between Chinese Cinema and Traditional Print Media in the 1920s'], 当代电影 [*Contemporary Cinema*], no. 2, 2015, pp. 73–6. For more details on visual and textural archival materials related to the film *The Cave of the Silken Web*, see also Xue Ning 薛宁, '《盘丝洞》文图史料概况' ['The Historical Articles and Pictures of *Spiders*'], 当代电影 [*Contemporary Cinema*], no. 2, 2019, pp. 73–5.

15. Edward S. Cooke Jr., 'Touch', in *Global Objects: Toward a Connected Art History*, Princeton University Press, Princeton and Oxford, 2022, p. 245.

16. Margaret Duda, *Traditional Chinese Toggles: Counterweights and Charms*, Editions Didier Millet, Singapore, 2011, p. 23.

17. William Blake, 'Auguries of Innocence', c.1803. requoted from John Mack, 'Visualising Small Worlds', in *The Art of Small Things*, Harvard University Press, Cambridge, 2007, p. 77.

18. Stewart, 'The Miniature' pp. 37–68.

19. The Gregorian calendar was officially used in China when the Republic of China was established in 1912.

20. See Hu Pu-an 胡朴安, 中华全国风俗志 [*Gazettes of Chinese Customs*], Tai Tat Press 大达图书供应社, Shanghai, 1936. Requoted from Li Songling 李松龄 and Qu Chunhai 屈春海, '话说抓周习俗' ['On the Customs of Zhuazhou'], 文史知识 [*Chinese Literature and History*], no. 10, 1991, pp. 51–5.

21. Mack, 'Epilogue', p. 208.

22. Sun Xiaoning 孙小宁, '明、清两代北京的民间儿童游戏' [Children's Folk Games During Ming and Qing Period], 体育文史 [*Literature and History of Physical Education*] no. 1, 1990, p. 21.

23. ibid.

24. ibid.

25. Lesley Beaumont, Nicola Harrington and Candace Richards, 'Play', in *Children in Antiquity: Greece and Egypt*, Sydney University Museums, Sydney, 2015, p. 8, 14.

26. See Nicola Di Cosmo and Dalizhabu Bao, 'Introduction: A Brief Survey of Manchu-Mongol Relations Before the Qing Conquest', in *Manchu-Mongol Relations on the Eve of the Qing Conquest: A Documentary History*, Brill, Leiden, 2003, pp. 1–14. Also see Yang Shengmin 杨圣敏, '多民族在北京地区交往交流交融的历史缩影' ['A Historical Epitome of Multi-ethnic Exchanges in Beijing'], 中国教育新闻网 [*Education News of China*], http://www.jyb.cn/rmtzcg/xwy/wzxw/202201/t20220119_676656.html (viewed October 2022). Originally published in 中国民族教育 [*Ethnic Education of China*], no. 1, 2022. pp. 61–3.

27. Mack, 'Epilogue', p. 208.

28. Hay, 'Decorative Objects', p. 82.

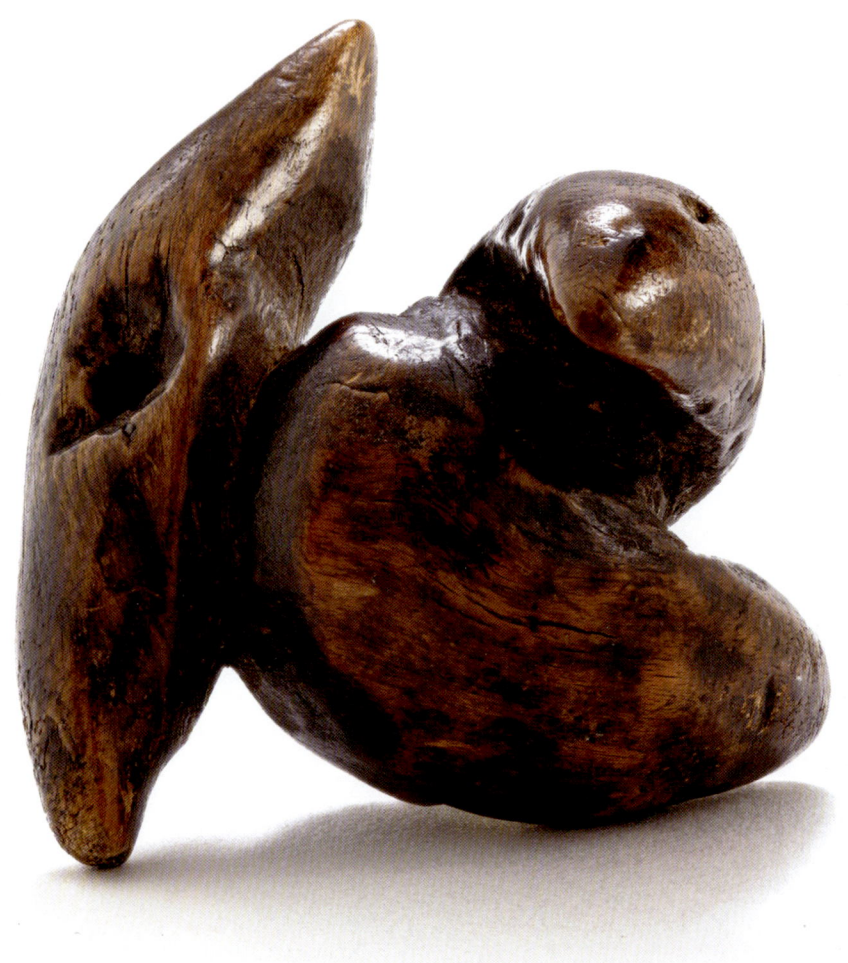

Fig. 4.1: Toggle in an abstract form, China, nineteenth to twentieth century. Wood, 35 x 40 x 40 mm. University Art Collection, Chau Chak Wing Museum. Gift of Todd Barlin, 2023. Object UA2023.5. Image: Chau Chak Wing Museum.

4. Chinese toggles at play: *bawan* and the cultivating hand

Chen Shuxia

Much of the research on historical Chinese art and aesthetics to date has been dominated by approaches that focus on visuality, particularly through forms of painting and calligraphy. For this reason, art historian Jonathan Hay has criticised the lack of critical attention in contemporary Western art-historical literature given to decorative objects and focuses on a more affective aesthetics related to pleasure.[1] Such attention to the significant role of decorative objects in everyday life was highlighted in *Xianqing ouji* (闲情偶寄, 1671), *Sketches of Idle Pleasure* by the famous Ming and Qing playwright and novelist Li Yu (李渔, 1610–80), who called them *wanhao zhiwu* (玩好之物), or 'pleasurable things'. As one of the most influential representatives on creative thinking during the Ming and Qing periods, Li's emphasis on the feelings and needs of ordinary people, as well as connections between pleasure, cultivation and objects,[2] provides a productive framework for understanding the art and material culture of the time.

The pleasant sensory experience of fondling a small, scrupulously carved object has been an important part of aesthetic appreciation and leisure in China. By using the term *bawan* (把玩), literally meaning 'to hold' or 'handle' (*ba*) and 'to play with' (*wan*), the Chinese term emphasises an active and intentional touching of the object, to explore its tactile form, its surfaces and textures. Drawing on examples of toggles from the Powerhouse Collection and Chau Chak Wing Museum's Art Collection, this chapter explores a mediated cultivation of aesthetic pleasure and reciprocity between people, objects and materiality,[3] emphasising the significant role of the user's hand and forms of touch in this often-overlooked facet of aesthetic experience and connoisseurship.

The cultivating hand

The skin is the body's largest organ, literally sensing our world. Through touch, the hand and fingers obtain information on the properties of objects, such as size, shape, texture, temperature, hardness and weight. Compared to the eyes, the skin assumes an arguably more important role in building a sense of reality regarding the external world within which we are defined. Modern psychology also refers to 'the intelligent hand', emphasising the significant function of the hand in a person's exploratory and cognitive development, language and culture.[6]

Yet this significant sense of touch is rarely considered within the realm of aesthetics or art history. The superiority of visuality in conventional art history, and the distanced gaze from the modes of display and infrastructures (plinths, walls, galleries) originated in Europe and spread to the non-Western world through colonialism around the late eighteenth century.[7] This hierarchy and aesthetic imperialism in the Western canon is criticised by Edward S. Cooke, Jr.: 'The European misunderstanding of art began valuing the cerebral over the manual, the head over the body, the visual over the haptic and other senses, and the aesthetically autonomous over the socially functional.'[8]

Chinese toggles, as everyday functional decorative objects, would not make the list of so-called fine arts classified by a European convention that centres around general rather than personal contemplation, which tactile appreciation entails. This personal contemplation can be demonstrated by feedback from post-graduate students in the course 'Exhibiting and Collecting Asian Art' at The University of Sydney, following an Object-Based Learning session at the Chau Chak Wing Museum. Students were guided by the author and co-curator of the exhibition *Chinese Toggles: Culture in Miniature* in the China Gallery. Following the curator's tour, students handled two Chinese toggles from the Art Collection of the Chau Chak Wing Museum in a study room. These students were very aware of the different presentations of toggles: the exhibition positioned the toggles in display cases as 'exceptional examples of [purely] aesthetic crafts', and the handling session facilitated better appreciation of toggles as 'intimate and familiar adornments and tools'.[9] The everyday nature of an unadorned toggle in an abstract form (fig. 4.1) invited tactile engagement, like a fidget cube, inspiring students to feel it 'along its surfaces and squeeze tightly into the curves of its form.'[10] Through this private activity of handling, students gradually felt more familiar with its physicality, and that helped them to create personal connections

to the toggle, its previous owners and its history.[11] A similarly intimate encounter has been shared by the acclaimed British ceramicist and writer Edmund de Waal; when he fondled a wooden Japanese *netsuke* (根付) (arguably a descendant of the Chinese toggle) in his pocket, it evoked a flood of personal memories of his family.[12]

During the Object-Based Learning session, long-term tactile engagement with particular kinds of small objects is strongly linked to kinds of aesthetic 'cultivation'. In Chinese, the verb *yang* (养) commonly means to 'nurture', 'raise' or 'care for', and is used to refer to growing flowers, keeping a pet or forging relationships. Importantly, such practices take time and ongoing effort. Many kinds of aesthetic leisure and the pleasure derived from them relate to the 'cultivation' of objects. For example, the lustrous patina on old clay teapots, which is highly valued by collectors, is formed by 'cultivating' the pot through the way it is used over time. With long-term *bawan* or 'playful handling', the sweat and oils of the hand, considered 'nutrients', moisten and smooth certain objects, depending on their materials. Often called *shouze* (手泽), 'hand lustre', this colour and luminance are important indicators historically for the beauty and value of the object among Chinese collections.

Australian collector Todd Barlin, who has acquired around sixty Chinese toggles, echoes the significance of patina created by long-term handling:

> I understand that these toggles had a long life of their own in rural areas of China, where they were lovingly worn, and with a deep belief in their good fortune, they were handled and admired and given a deep warm patina over long use and handling, and that they were possibly owned by more than one generation of a family.[13]

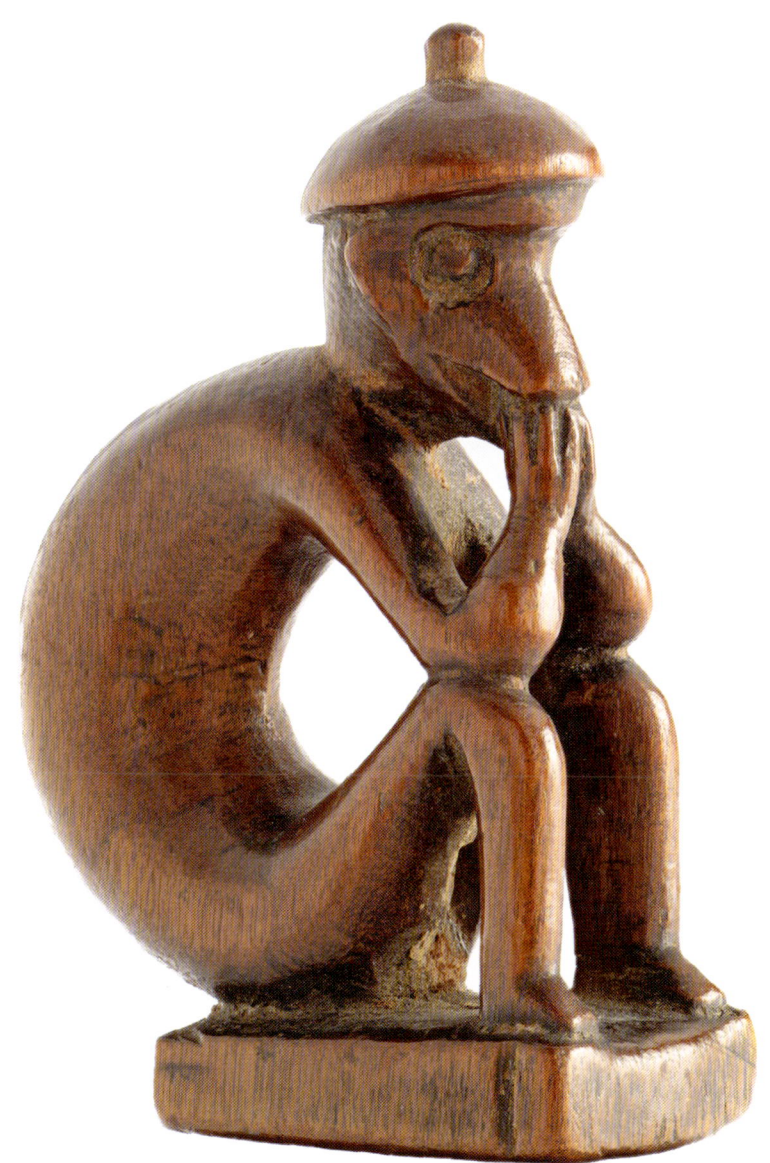

Fig. 4.2: Toggle in the shape of a curve-backed monkey, nineteenth century. Wood, 60 x 44 mm, Todd Barlin Collection of Asian Art. Image: Chau Chak Wing Museum.

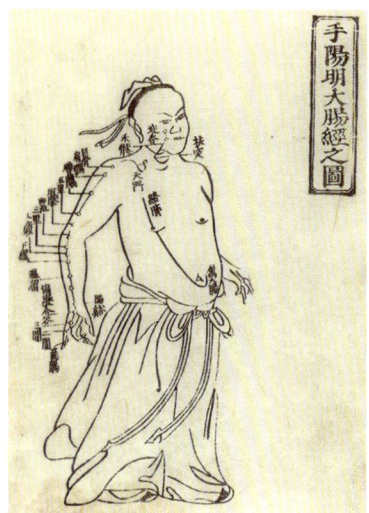

Fig. 4.3: 'The large intestine meridian of the hand shown by Yangming's acupoints (手阳明大肠经之图)' illustrated in Hua Shou (滑寿, c.1304–1386), *Expression of the Fourteen Meridians* (十四经发挥), 1341. Collection of National Library of Medicine, United States. 8105422.

This warm patina, or hand lustre, can be found in one of Barlin's favourite toggles in the shape of a curve-backed monkey (fig. 4.2). The lustre and the smooth texture of the monkey's back demonstrates much handling. Touch plays an important role in aesthetics, reflecting the connection between time and texture[14] that results from consistent 'nurturing' by its owner.

However, it is also possible to say that while one is 'nurturing' the object, the object in turn cultivates the owner or collector. Objects are not just passive signifiers; they are also active participants.[15] Barlin shares his passion for the monkey toggle:

> The monkey with the highly curved back, which I never saw another so elegant in form, could easily be compared to the best Henry Moore or Brancusi sculpture, something of great beauty, refined and elegant … I do pick them up and look at them, but one of the best things in collecting is sharing the beauty with others.[16]

The monkey toggle connects Barlin with sculptural form in the modern world and, more importantly, evokes joy by being handled and shared with friends.

In traditional Chinese medicine, the hand and fingers are important parts of the meridian system, featuring acupuncture points for treating disorders of the body and mind (fig. 4.3). Handling small objects with the fingers or in the palm of the hand is a good way to stimulate these acupuncture points, as an everyday practice of health cultivation. The relationship between tactile appreciation and cultivation has been special for the Chinese. Although toggles functioned as counterweights, the choice of materials, such as stone, ivory and wood, and the specially carved round, flat or broad shapes, avoiding sharp edges, catered to a delight in their caress.[17] Most toggles in the Powerhouse Collection were probably handled in this way, as they often show clear signs of smoothness and wear, despite being made of very diverse materials. Each material has its particular cultural significance for self-cultivation and tactile pleasure. As Hedda and Alastair Morrison commented, 'Essentially, these are small objects, often rounded and a pleasure to handle—fine toggles ought to be fondled—and capable of being strung.'[18]

Walnut toggles

Among the toggles in the Powerhouse Collection, some are made from natural, organic objects, including seashells, roots and nuts such as walnut. Walnut, known as *hetao* (核桃) in Chinese, symbolises harmony, as *he* is a homophone for harmony, *hexie* (和谐), and peace, *heping* (和平). In addition to such auspicious associations, walnuts were fondled as 'pleasurable things' in the imperial court for centuries, particularly during the Ming and Qing periods.[19] Termed *wenwan hetao* (文玩核桃), 'literati walnut', or *roushou hetao* (揉手核桃), 'rubbing walnut', the chosen walnut is not simply an ordinary nut. Literati walnuts and walnut carvings were for fondling and were appreciated by many elites,

including emperors such as the Qing dynasty Qianlong Emperor (乾隆帝, 1711–99).[20] An old Beijing saying recorded in the *Beijingzhi* (北京志, 2007), *Beijing Chronicle*, indicates the walnut's significant social status: 'The three treasures of the Beile masters are thumb rings, walnuts and caged birds.'[21] *Beile* (贝勒), meaning 'lord' or 'prince' in Manchu, generally refers to the aristocratic class in Chinese.

In the collection of the Palace Museum in Beijing, there are more than ten pairs of walnuts that belonged to the Qing court. It is believed that these walnuts were produced in the mid-to-late Qing period. Each pair was housed in a brocade or rosewood box with beautiful auspicious decorations. One pair in a brocade box might

Fig. 4.4: Toggle in the shape of a walnut, China, c.1700-1940. Ivory, silk, 30 mm (diam.) x 20 mm, Powerhouse Collection. Gift of Alastair Morrison, 1992. Object 92/640.

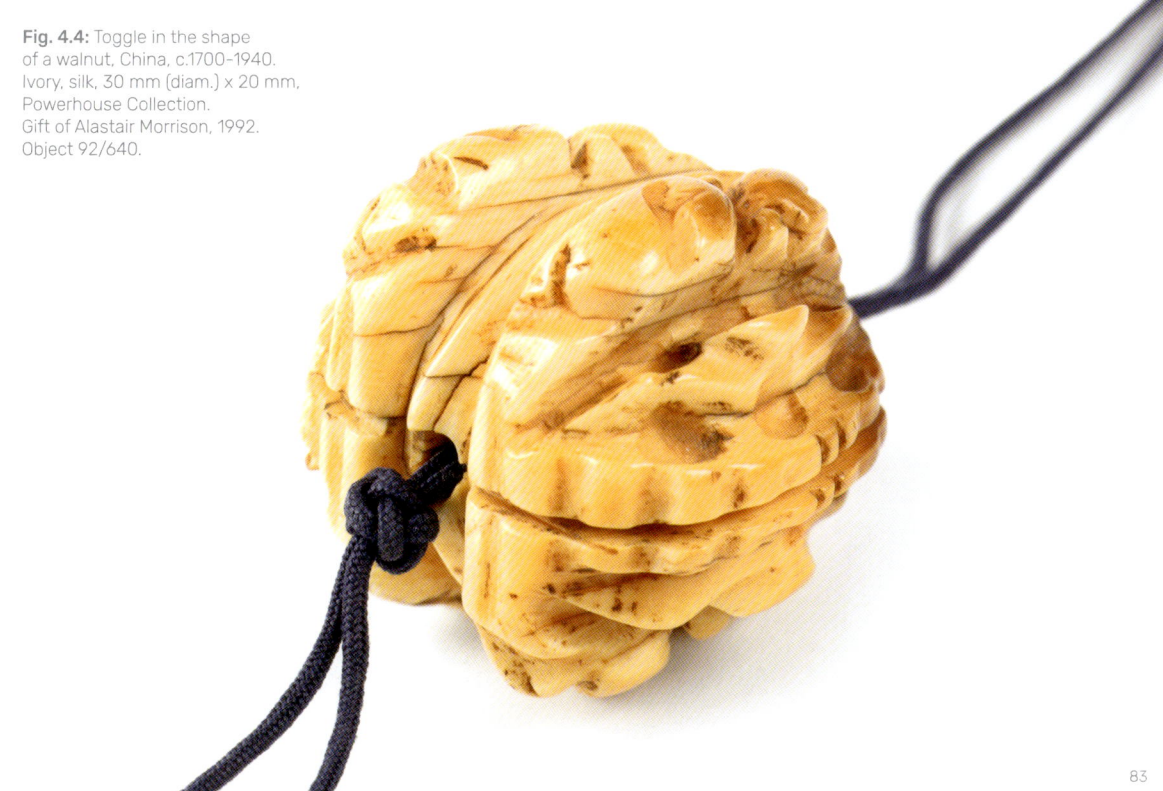

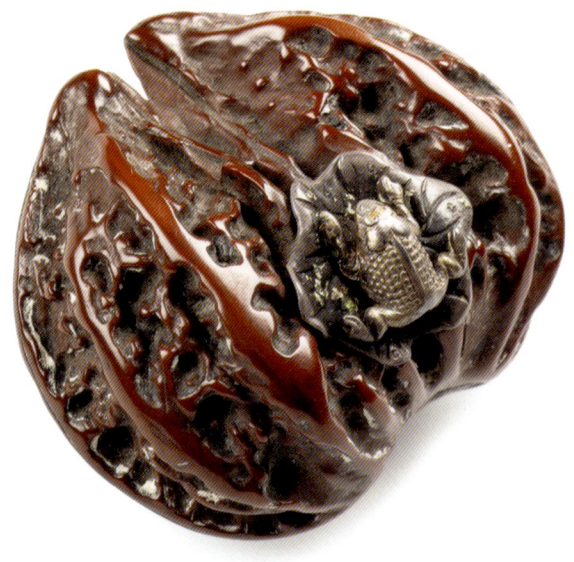

Fig. 4.5: Toggle made from a walnut decorated with a frog on a lotus leaf, China, c.1700–1940. Lacquered walnut, metal, silver alloy, 40 x 43 x 33 mm, Powerhouse Collection. Gift of Alastair Morrison, 1992. Object 92/480.

Opposite:
Fig. 4.6: Burlwood tobacco case with walnut toggle with *luohan* relief carvings, China, nineteenth century. Wood, walnut, 45 x 20 x 75 mm. University Art Collection, Chau Chak Wing Museum. Gift of Todd Barlin, 2023. Object UA2023.4. Image: Chau Chak Wing Museum.

have belonged to a member of the royal family named Dan Beile (丹贝勒), as his name was written on a note attached to the lid. As one of the three treasures of Qing aristocrats, walnuts became associated with a high social rank. Once walnuts were imbued with such high social status and auspicious meaning, they became popular for both urban elites and common people. According to scholar I-YI Hsieh, seeing them in people's hands would have been part of 'an ordinary urban scene' in Beijing.[23]

Fondling walnuts was not just a gesture of social status; it was believed that the swirling and rubbing of a pair of walnuts could improve one's health. One could rub, press, twist and pinch the hard and wrinkly walnut shell with fingers and palm, which could stimulate the veins and activate blood circulation.[24] In addition to health, fondling walnuts has also been seen

as a process of cultivating the walnut, turning it into a piece of art, for long-term handling builds up an agate-like red layer and a translucent lustre.[25] German Sinologist Ernest Cordes described a scene of an elderly man swirling a pair of walnuts in his palm in Beijing in the 1930s. The man told Cordes that it was important to play with the walnuts every day, reportedly saying: 'This renders the scent from our body onto the walnuts, in order to bathe them with it. They eventually will be filled with our lives, and as time goes by, they become a part of us.'[26] The accumulating time one spends rendering one's body scent to the walnut not only nurtures but also transforms it as a natural object that over time becomes part of the user and their life.

In one of only two English-language books dedicated to Chinese toggles (see Introduction, p. 14), Margaret Duda mentions a natural walnut

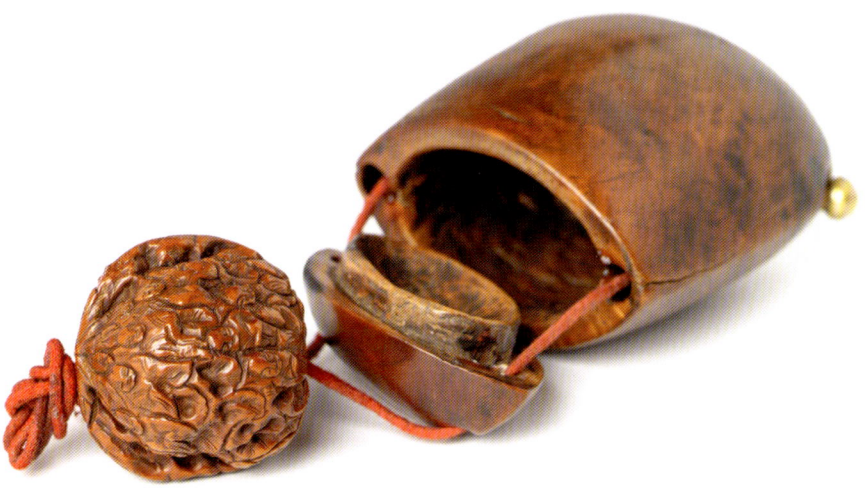

toggle tied to a tinder pouch, which was also attached to a pair of ivory toggles. Thinking this simple walnut toggle was incongruous with the full ensemble of the eating kit and tinder pouch it accompanied, presumably owned by a prosperous person, Duda suggested it might be a replacement for a lost ivory carving.[27] This seems plausible, and invites comparisons between the two materials. On the other hand, the reverse transformation is also possible: in the Powerhouse Collection we find an ivory toggle carved in the shape of a walnut (fig. 4.4).

As Schuyler Cammann has pointed out, the simplicity of using natural objects as toggles may not have attracted the interest of foreign collectors because they seek objects more representative of Chinese art.[28] Duda might have presumed that natural walnut was too unadorned to be of significant interest to

a Chinese person, yet this somewhat rustic simplicity is exactly what has attracted many Chinese people to them, especially the literati, who highly appreciate the aesthetic of *zhuo* (拙)—simplicity and clumsiness as a beguiling form of sophistication.[29] As the Qing Buddhist calligrapher and landscape painter Shi Tao (石涛, 1642–1707) wrote, 'Chaos is opened up when I put brush to paper to achieve clumsiness by discarding cleverness.'[30] Despite their ordinary appearance, toggles fashioned from natural objects were 'characteristic of the Old Chinese folk tradition' and relatively common.[31] Considering this, it may be that the walnut toggle Duda discussed was not a replica but an original.

There is an excellent example of a walnut toggle in the Powerhouse Collection (fig. 4.5), that is adorned by a silver alloy frog or toad sitting on a lotus leaf and brilliantly demonstrates the auspicious meaning, social status and cultivating capacity of a simple walnut. The metal frog on a lotus leaf symbolises fortune, harmonious marriage and fertility. The frog, *wa* (蛙), is a homonym for 'baby', *wa* (娃) in Chinese, connoting the desire to have many children. The lotus leaf also symbolises a harmonious married life. The shell was deliberately lacquered to mimic the effect of being 'nurtured'. This toggle was strung through the tough shell and attached to personal belongings such as a tobacco case. With the smooth and glossy outer layer of both the walnut and the silver frog, we can imagine that the owner caressed this toggle frequently, 'channelling' themselves into the toggle. American archaeologist Ruth Van Dyke describes this as a 'circular process by which everything we create also creates us.'[32]

Another demonstration of the preference for organic seed as a material for decorative art is the nineteenth-century example of a walnut toggle from the Chau Chak Wing Museum's collection that is attached to a burlwood tobacco case (fig. 4.6). The shell of the walnut was smoothed and carved into many small, abstract *luohan* (罗汉), or arhat relief carvings. With the protection of many luohan and a smooth and round shape, this walnut toggle invites caresses from its owner. As with the elderly man in 1930s Beijing, the owner has nurtured this walnut and it in turn has become part of its owner. Being attached to each other, the owner and the toggle are equally affective in their mutual cultivation and intimate engagement through the hand.

Jade toggles

Such inter-relation and mutual cultivation can also be found in jade toggles. These are among the finest stone toggles in the Powerhouse Collection. Toggles made of precious materials like jade were probably used by wealthier merchants and cultural elites during the Qing and early Republican periods.

Jade has been a significant substance in Chinese culture for millennia. Jade vessels have been described by art historian Wu Hung as 'the highest ceremonial tool, a symbol of royal power and a medium for communicating with heaven and spirits' in ancient China.[33] Jade often symbolises the virtues of a cultured gentleman, his benevolence, righteousness and piety. Such virtues of jade come from jade's material nature: translucent yet relatively hard. In Chinese culture, a virtuous person is often described as being as warm and smooth as jade, a saying that can be traced back to *Shijing* (诗经), the *Book of Songs*—the earliest anthology of poetry, collected between the early Western Zhou dynasty and the mid-Spring and Autumn period (between the eleventh and seventh centuries BCE).[34] The properties of jade have been described as both 'warm' and 'cool', depending on the source, but either way they make apparent that jade is best perceived not visually but through touch: the hand feels the texture and temperature of jade, its mellowness and mild warmth or coolness arousing peace and harmony. As Hedda Morrison wrote in her 1985 book, *A Photographer in Old Peking*,

> Jade was of special importance in old China. For the Chinese it was the most valued of precious stones and imbued with many magical and curative properties … Jade was used for many ceremonial and religious purposes. Not only was it appreciated for its beauty but also for the cool, almost sensuous feeling it conveyed when handled and for the sonorous notes emitted by jade chimes.[35]

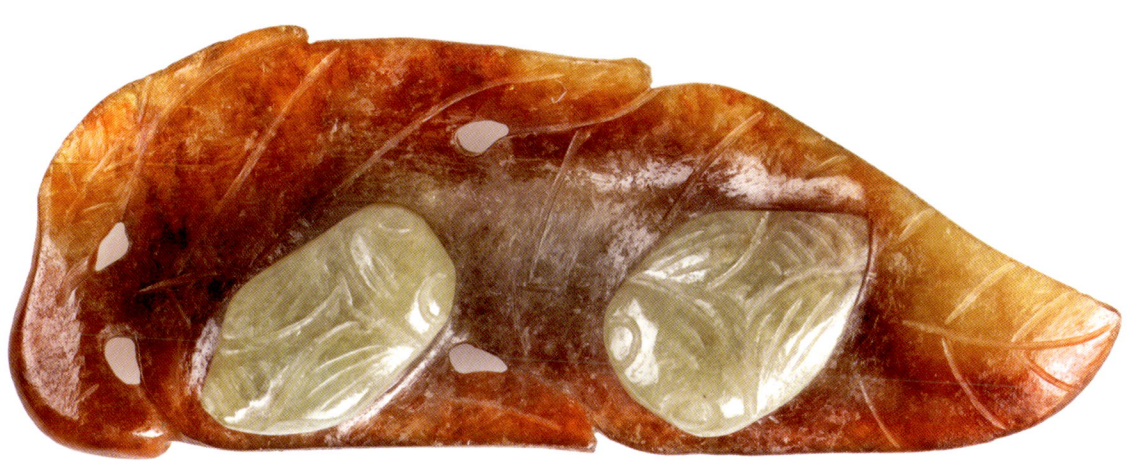

Fig. 4.7: Toggle in the shape of two cicadas
on a leaf, China, c.1700–1940. Jade,
11 x 75 x 28 mm, Powerhouse Collection.
Gift of Alastair Morrison, 1992. Object 92/472.

Jade has been regarded not only as a sartorial accessory, for dress or personal adornment, but also as a potent protective charm. Hence, the spiritual connection between jade and the individuality of its user has been widely discussed in both ancient and contemporary China.[36] Methods of cultivating jade, called *panyu* (盘玉), were also written in various classics on jade, especially during Qing dynasty.[37] *Pan* here means 'winding around' or 'revolving', referring to the finger movement involved in rotating the object in one's hand, not unlike the movement between the fingers and palm when rubbing a pair of walnuts. Late Qing and early Republican-era collector Liu Datong (刘大同, 1866–1952) offered one of the most detailed methods of *panyu* in his book *Guyubian* (古玉辨, 1940), *Archaic Jade Identification*.[38] He emphasised the importance of using human *qi* (气) to cultivate the jade by wearing it around the waist, especially the method of *yipan* (意盘) or 'mindful cultivation'. Liu wrote,

> Many people don't understand the method of *yipan*: you have to hold it in the hand, to play with it and to treasure it. From time to time, you need to caress it and imagine the virtue of jade. This would change my temperament, cultivate my nature and purify my life without selfish desire. Such utmost sincerity would affect bronze and stone.[39]

The fondling cultivates the jade, to make it smooth with lustre. In return, contemplating the virtues of jade cultivates and protects the user.

Jade's hard-yet-smooth texture has also made it a symbol of longevity and immortality. Jade was used as an offering to heaven in ancient rituals and for funeral objects. During the Han dynasty (206 BCE–220 CE), a jade cicada might be placed in the mouth of the deceased to protect the corpse and help the spirit become immortal. Indeed, cicadas are a significant motif in Chinese jade culture, with a long history. The jade cicada first appeared in the late Neolithic Age: those of the Hongshan culture (4700–2900 BCE), Dawenkou culture (4000–2300 BCE) and Liangzhu culture (3300–2300 BCE) were the earliest.[40] In Chinese culture, the cicada has been a symbol of longevity, nobility, purity and rebirth or deathless spirit, due to its long life and its ability to shed its exoskeleton. While the funeral practice of placing a jade cicada in the deceased's mouth fell out of popularity after the Eastern Han dynasty (25–220), the cicada motif has remained significant in decorative objects and paintings through to the present. Jade cicadas regained their popularity after the Ming dynasty, with the location of more abundant sources of jade and the technical development of jade-carving skills.[41] (Jade-carving techniques and processes are discussed in detail in chapter 5.)

The Powerhouse Collection features a jade toggle with the motif of a cicada sitting on twin pomegranates (plate 31, p. 194). Pomegranates have many seeds, and one word for seed *zi* (籽), is also a homonym of 'sons' in Chinese. Pairing seeds with a cicada, this jade toggle indicates boosted fertility and undying spirit, and would have been worn and fondled to express the hope for many male heirs to carry on the family line.

Another jade toggle was carved in the shape of a leaf on which sit two pale green cicadas (fig. 4.7). Here, the motif of cicadas on a red-coloured leaf refers to the Chinese idiom *jinzhi yuye* (金枝玉叶), 'golden branches and jade leaves', which describes the decendants of an imperial family or a noble person. In colloquial Chinese, cicadas are

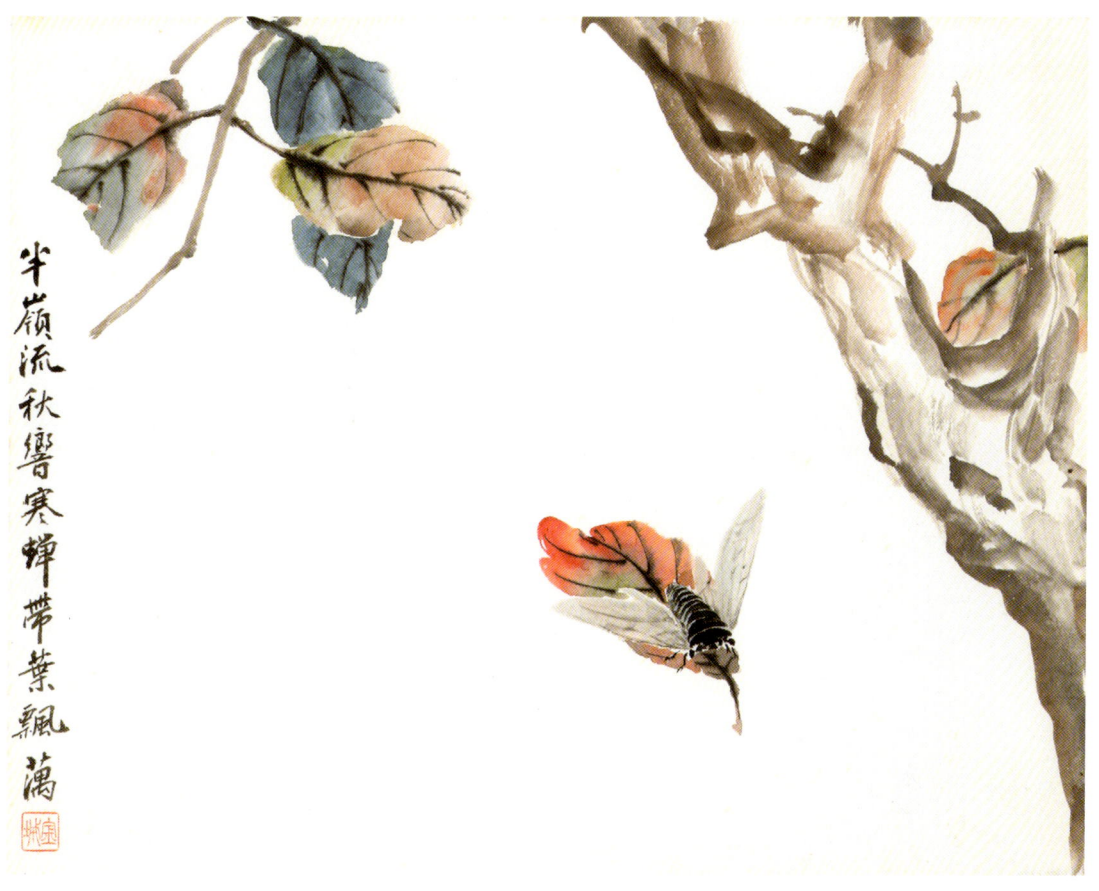

半嶺流秋響寒蟬帶葉飄滿

Fig. 4.8: Jin Cheng, *Cicada Floating on a Falling Leaf*, China, early twentieth century. Coloured ink on paper, 22.5 x 33 cm, University Art Collection, Chau Chak Wing Museum. Object UA1990.370.
Image: Chau Chak Wing Museum.

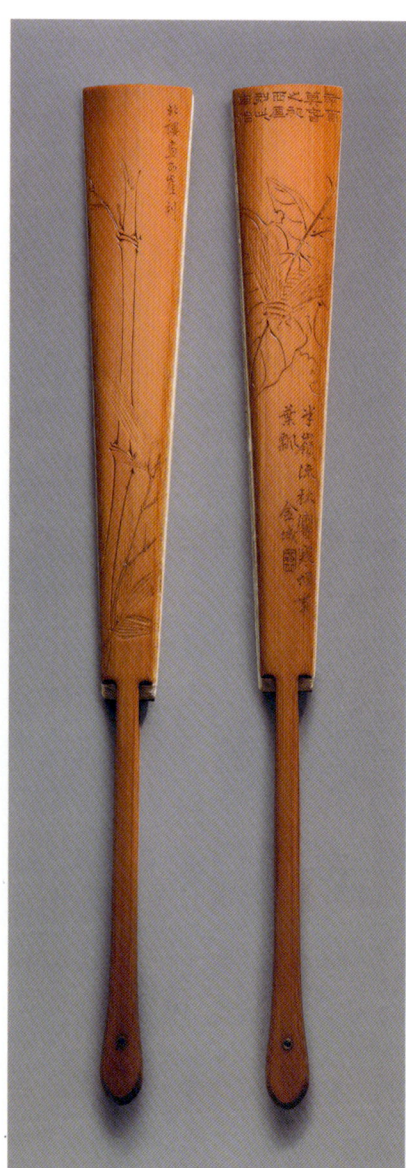

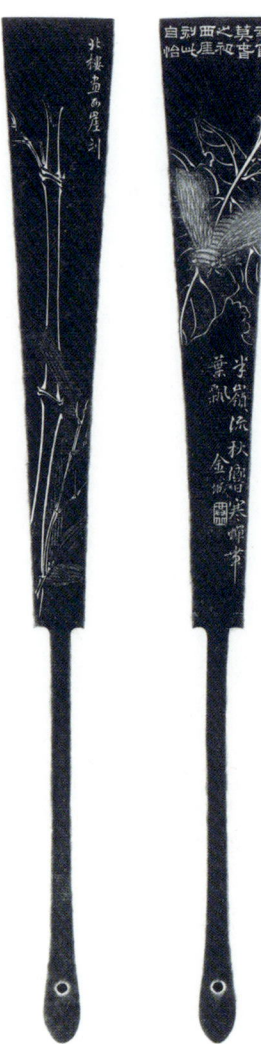

Fig. 4.9: Left: Painted by Jin Cheng, carved by Jin Xiya. Fan ribs with motifs of wind, bamboo, cicada and leaf, China, 1921. Right: Ink on bamboo, paper, 31.6 x 3.5 x 2.6 cm. Rubbings of the fan ribs. Image from auction catalogue of Beijing Poly International 2018 Spring Auctions, *Jiansong Ge Collection: A Soft Breeze in a Mindscape: Engraved Art Objects in the Chinese Scholar's Studio*, 2018, unpaginated. Private collection.

also known as *zhiliao* (知了), which is a homophone of tree branches, *zhi* (枝). Such auspicious wordplays are common sources of aesthetic meaning in Chinese art. This toggle reflects on such traditions and was skillfully carved to capitalise on the different colours of this single piece of jade.

Many Chinese cultural motifs are transmitted or translated across different mediums and genres. As noted above, the cicada motif was turned into funeral objects. It was also the subject of many classical poems and ink paintings. A *Cicada Floating on a Falling Leaf* (fig. 4.8) by Jin Cheng (金城, 1878–1926)—a businessman and influential ink painter who was one of the leaders of the Beijing art circle in the early twentieth-century depicts a cicada, wings outstretched, on a falling red leaf, floating at the centre-right of the painting. A few autumn leaves on a branch occupy the top left and right side of the painting. The inscription on the left reads *banling liuqiuxiang, hanchan daiyepiao ou* (半岭流秋响, 寒蝉带叶飘 漚), meaning 'the sound of autumn fills the mid valley; a cicada floats through the air on a falling leaf. Painted in the Hut of Lotus Root.'[42]

The pictorial motif of one or more cicadas on a leaf has been a popular subject for many painters in both pre-modern and modern China. The same motif of a cicada on a leaf, bearing the same inscription, can be found carved on the rib of a fan (fig. 4.9) made in 1921 by Jin Cheng's younger brother, Jin Xiya (金西崖, 1890–1979), a famous bamboo-carver.[43] Jin Cheng was credited as the painter and Jin Xiya was the carver. Rubbed with ink, the intaglio carving depicts a cicada on a maple leaf, wings open, facing down to the left.

A similar motif can also be found on an embroidered bag (fig. 4.10) acquired by Hedda Morrison in Beijing in the 1930s or 1940s, the same time she was collecting the jade toggles with cicada carvings. Even in the black-and-white photograph, one can discern the delicate needlework and many colours, differentiated by multiple shades of grey on the wings and body of the cicada. An endless mystic knot is attached to the insect, symbolising the never-ending cycle of life.

The motif of the cicada could clearly be depicted across different mediums. It could be written in poetry, drawn in a painting, carved into sculpture and embroidered as a bag. This transmedial quality of Chinese plastic representation was emphasised by Hay when he questioned the conventional division between the pictorial and the sculptural in Western art:

> The primacy of the pictorial in decorative depiction also allowed artisians to explore with ease the additional, intermediary possibilities between two-dimensional picturing and plastic depiction in the round, making extensive use of relief carving and moulding. The incorporation of figurative representation into decorative surface thus constituted a continuum of technical possibilities from two-dimensional to fully three-dimensional.[44]

The relief carving of pale-green cicadas on an autumn leaf in the Powerhouse Collection is a three-dimensional adaptation of a pictorial design that had been depicted in ink painting, bamboo-carving and embroidery in early modern China. Reproduced in jade, with a solid volume the form encourages a more intimate connection with the object by the collector or owner. The tactility of the toggle strengthens a sense of identification with a rich palimpsest of cultural significance that may express something of the owner's desires.

As the discussion here argues, Chinese toggles not only represent a largely lost

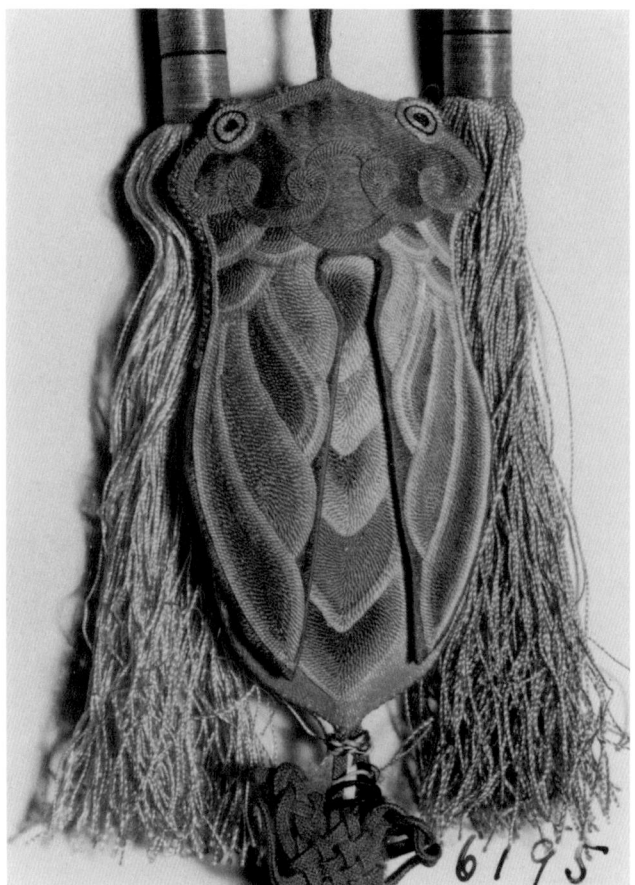

Fig. 4.10: Hedda Morrison, *Insect-shaped Embroidered Bag with Tassels and Endless Mystic Knot*, Beijing, China, 1933–46. Gelatin silver process, Harvard-Yenching Library, HM08.6195.

sartorial tradition but also, as 'pleasurable things', they bring to our attention the tradition of *bawan* and sensory experience as an important and often overlooked aspect of Chinese aesthetics. This chapter celebrates the important role of the user as cultivator, continuing to 'make' the objects and add aesthetic value to them. These so-called decorative objects have long formed part of a complex aesthetics in which the materiality of an object and its user form a kind of reciprocal relationship premised on the slow, mindful practice of cultivation rather than a distant gaze. This tangible connection relied on an intimate handling and a sense of what we might now call 'relational' aesthetics, the evidence of which abounds in the patiently smoothed edges of this unique collection of Chinese toggles.

1. Jonathan Hay, 'The Surfacescape's Resources', in *Sensuous Surfaces: The Decorative Object in Early Modern China*', University of Hawaii Press, Honolulu, 2010.
2. Qi Shao, Xiaojing Wen and Paul E. White, 'Design Thinking Under the Qing Dynasty', in A *Brief History of Chinese Design Thought*, Shanghai Bookstore Publishing House and Springer, Shanghai and Singapore, 2022, p. 242.
3. Hanna B. Hölling, Francesca G. Brewer and Katharina Ammann, 'Material encounters', in Hanna B. Hölling, Francesca G. Brewer and Katharina Ammann (eds), *The Explicit Material*, Brill, Leiden, 2019, p. 5.
4. David Katz, *The World of Touch*, Lawrence Erlbaum Associates, New Jersey, 1989.
5. Susan J. Lederman and Roberta L. Klatzky, 'Hand movements: A window into haptic object recognition', *Cognitive Psychology*, vol. 19, no. 3, 1987, pp. 342–68.
6. Frank Wilson, *The Hand: How Its Use Shapes the Brain, Language, and Human Culture*, Pantheon Books, New York, 1998.
7. Shuchen Wang, 'Museum coloniality: displaying Asian art in the whitened context', *International Journal of Cultural Policy*, vol. 27, no. 6, 2021, pp. 724–5.
8. Edward S. Cooke Jr., 'Introduction', in *Global Objects: Toward a Connected Global History*, Princeton University Press, Princeton, 2022, p. 9.
9. Email correspondence between postgraduate student Benjamin Clay and the author, 31 May 2023.
10. Email correspondence between postgraduate student Danielle Brown and the author, 31 May 2023.
11. Email correspondence between postgraduate student Rose Hannan and the author, 1 June 2023.
12. Edmund de Waal, *The Hare with Amber Eyes: A Hidden Inheritance*, Picador, New York, 2010, pp. 10–13.
13. Email correspondence with the author on 14 March 2023.
14. Cooke Jr., 'Touch', p. 253.
15. Ruth M. Van Dyke, 'Materiality in Practice', in Ruth M. Van Dyke

(ed.), *Practising Materiality*, The University of Arizona Press, Tucson, 2015, p. 14.
16. Email correspondence with the author, 14 March 2023.
17. Schuyler Cammann, 'Chinese Toggles: Basic Types', in *Substance and Symbol in Chinese Toggles: Chinese Belt Toggles from the C. F. Bieber Collection*, University of Pennsylvania Press, Philadelphia, 1962, pp. 29–30.
18. Hedda and Alastair Morrison, 'Chinese Toggles: A Little Known Folk Art', *Arts of Asia*, vol. 16, no. 2, 1986, pp. 68–75.
19. Wu Wenlong 武文龙, '文玩核桃: 从产地到古玩圈' ['Play with Walnuts: from Product Place to Antique Circle'], 艺术市场 [*Art Market*], no. 23, 2012, p. 55.
20. According to Aisin-Gioro Puyi 爱新觉罗‧溥仪 in his autobiography 我的前半生 [*The First Half of My Life*] , (Qunzhong Chubanse, Beijing, 1964), he found a carved walnut in a rosewood curio box belonging to the Qinglong Emperor. See Mao Xianmin 毛宪民 and Zhang Baozhong 张保中, '清宫揉手核桃' ['The Rubbing Walnuts in Qing Court'], 紫禁城 [*Forbidden City*], no. 1, 1995, p. 46.
21. Compilation Committee of Beijing Local Chronicles 北京市地方志编撰委员会 (ed.), 北京志 [*Beijing Chronicle*], Beijing Publishing House 北京出版社, Beijing, 2007.
22. Mao and Zhang, 'The Rubbing Walnuts in Qing Court', p. 27, 46.
23. I-Yi Hsieh, 'On Touching: Connoisseurship of Literati Walnuts in Beijing', in Peter Stewart and Christina M. Anderson (eds), *Connoisseurship*, Oxford University Press, Oxford, 2023, p. 216.
24. Wu, '文玩核桃: 从产地到古玩圈' ['Play with Walnuts: from Product Place to Antique Circle'], p. 56.
25. Gao Qing 高清 and Wang Baoqing 王保青, '浅论文玩核桃的文化品性' ['"On Literati Walnuts" Cultural Characters,'], 艺术品鉴 [*Appreciation*], no. 2, 2015, p. 313.
26. Requoted from I-Yi Hsieh, 'Nuts: Beijing folk art connoisseurship in the age of marketization', *Asian Anthropology*, vol. 15, no. 1, 2016, pp. 59–60. Original text by Ernest Cordes, '揉核桃的中国人' ['The

Chinese Man Who Rubs Walnuts'], Ling Shuang 凌霜 (transl.), 月报 [*Yue Bao*], vol. 1, no. 1, 1937, pp. 212–15.
27. Margaret Duda, 'Traditional Chinese Toggles', in *Traditional Chinese Toggles: Counterweights and Charms*, Editions Didier Millet, Singapore, 2011, pp. 18–19.
28. Cammann, 'Toggles from Natural Objects', pp. 39–40.
29. The idea of '*zhuo*' in Chinese art has been discussed widely from classical texts to contemporary writings on Chinese philosophy, aesthetics, literature and art. For more recent discussion on this concept in Chinese calligraphy and art see Qianshen Bai, *Fu Shan's World: The Transformation of Chinese Calligraphy in the Seventeenth Century*, Harvard University Press, Boston, 2003; Zhu Liangzhi 朱良志, '关于大巧若拙美学观的若干思考' ['Thoughts on the Aesthetics of the Great Artlessness as Clumsiness'], 北京大学学报哲学社会科学版 [*Journal of Peking University Philosophy and Social Sciences*], vol. 43, no. 3, 2006, pp. 33–41. See also David Adam Brubaker and Wang Chunchen, 'Philosophy of Chinese Ink Art', in *Jizi and His Art in Contemporary China*, Springer, New York, 2015, pp. 59–72.
30. Jianping Gao 高建平, 中国艺术的表现性动作: 从书法到绘画 [*The Expressive Act in Chinese Art: from Calligraphy to Painting*] , Zhang Bing 张冰 (transl.), Anhui Educational Publishing House 安徽教育出版社, Anhui, 2012, p. 354.
31. ibid.
32. Van Dyke, 'Materiality in Practice', p. 8.
33. Wu Hung 巫鸿, '"材质"与中国艺术的起源' ['"Material Quality" and the Origin of Chinese Art'], in Wu Hung 巫鸿 (ed.), 艺术与物性 [*Art and Materiality*], Shanghai Fine Arts Publishing House 上海书画出版社, Shanghai, 2023, p. 23.
34. In *Book of Songs: The Airs of the States* (诗经‧国风), mainly folk songs of a love theme, it reads 言念君子, 温其如玉 (when I miss my husband, I think of his warmth like a jade).
35. Hedda Morrison, *A Photographer in Old Peking*, Oxford University Press, Hong

Kong, 1985, pp. 165–6.
36. See Wu, '"材质"与中国艺术的起源' ['"Material Quality" and the Origin of Chinese Art'], p. 28.
37. Chen Xing 陈性 (ed.), 玉纪 [*The Discipline of Jade*], first published in 1839; Wu Dacheng 吴大澂, 古玉图考 [*Illustrations on Archaic Jade*], Chung Hwa Book Company 中华书局, Taipei, 1991 (first published in 1889); Chen Yuanxin 陈原心, 玉纪 [*The Discipline of Jade*], first published during Qing Dynasty; Liu Datong 刘大同, 古玉辨 [*Archaic Jade Identification*], Shanghai, People's Fine Art Publishing House 上海人民美术出版社, Shanghai 2018 (first published in 1940).
38. Liu, *Archaic Jade Identification*, 1940.
39. In Chinese: 意盘之法, 人多不解一必须持在手内, 把玩之、珍爱之, 时时摩挲、意想玉之美德, 足以化我之气质, 养我之性情, 使我一生纯正而无私欲之蒙昧。Requoted from Lin Feng 林峰, '试说盘玉' ['On Panyu'], 紫禁城 [*Forbidden City*], no 1, 2001, p. 37.
40. Zheng Jianming 郑建明 and He Yuanqing 何元庆, '中国古代的玉蝉' ['Ancient Jade Cicada in China'], 汉江考古 [*Hanjiang Archaeology*], no. 1, 2006, p. 44. Also see Zhu Naicheng 朱乃诚, '汉代玉蝉研究' ['Research on Han Dynasty Jade Cicadas'], 文博学刊 [*Journal of Archaeology and Museology*], no. 1, 2019, pp. 4–16.
41. Zhu, '汉代玉蝉研究' ['Research on Han Dynasty Jade Cicadas'], pp. 15–16.
42. The character 溝 is an alternative writing for 藕, lotus root, which is the name of Jin Cheng's studio, 藕庐, the Hut of Lotus Root. In an earlier Qing Dynasty album leaf of twelve paintings *Landscape, Figures, Flowers and Birds, Grass and Insects* (1749), Qing painter Hua Yan 华岩 (1682–1756) also depicted one green cicada with both wings opened, floating on a falling leaf. The inscription on the left is the same as Jin Cheng's. See Christie's Hong Kong, *Chinese Arts Auction Records*, 26 November 2007, Live auction 2386, Lot 932.
43. Wang Shixiang 王世襄 (ed.), 竹刻 [*Bamboo Carving*], People's Fine Art Publishing House 人民美术出版社, Beijing, 1991, p. 42.
44. Hay, 'The Surfacescape's Resources' p. 171.

Part III
Materiality

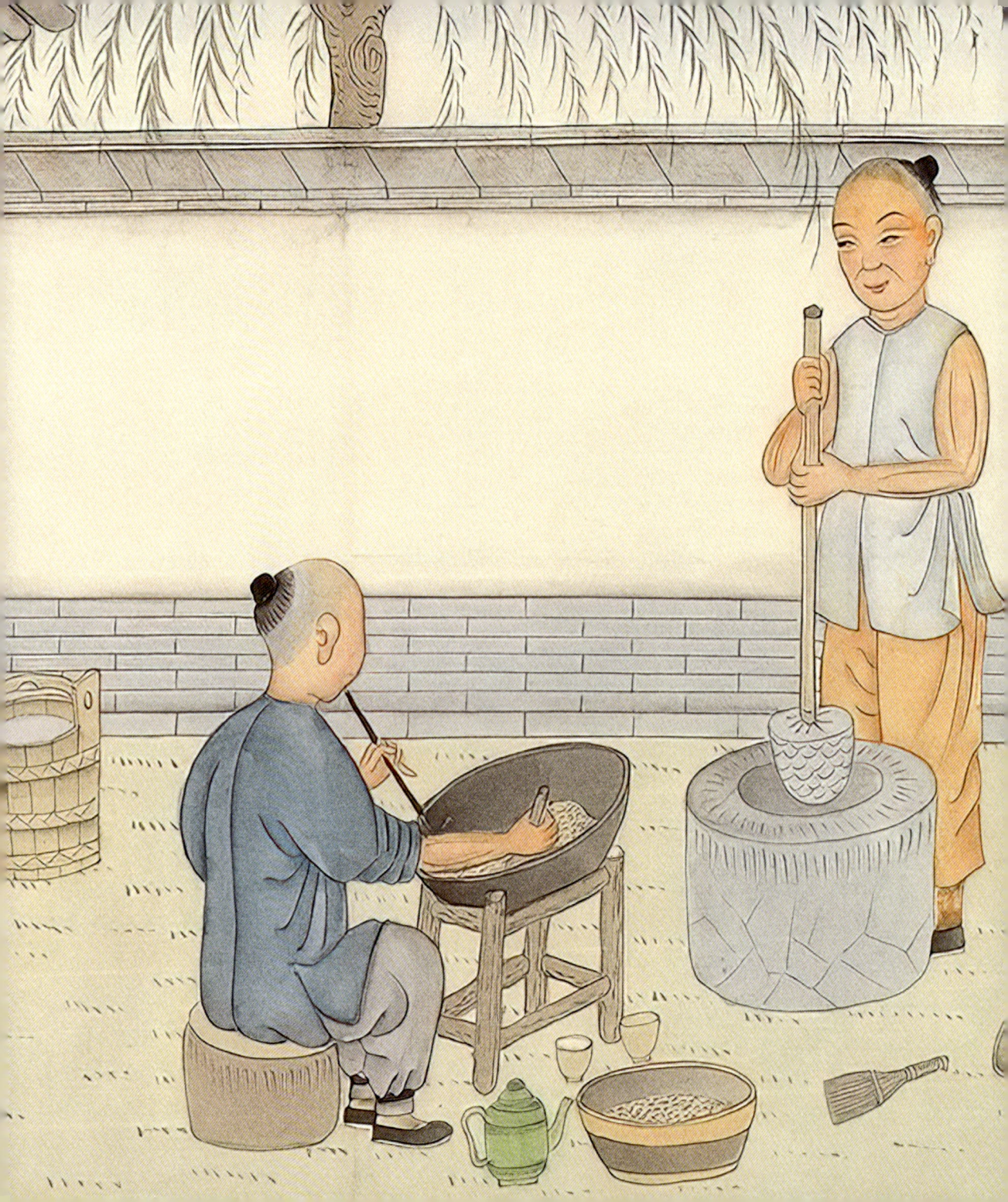

5. Jade toggles and carving in the Qing dynasty

Gu Fang and Chen Shuxia

As discussed in chapter 4, jade is significant in China, both culturally and materially.[1] The art of jade carving in China boasts a history of some 8000 years. A classical Chinese text states, *yubuzhuo, buchengqi* (玉不琢，不成器), 'without carving, jade cannot become a vessel'. This means that without sculpting, jade cannot be transformed into an object of appreciation. The craft was made an official profession by the Song dynasty (960–1279) imperial court, where a special institution called the Jade School was established. Jade carving reached the pinnacle of its technological sophistication in the Qing dynasty (1644–1911)[2], which was one of five significant developmental periods for jade carving in imperial China.[3]

There are twenty-five jade toggles in the Powerhouse Collection, most of which are believed to have been used by a more affluent class than toggles made of more humble materials such as wood, used by common people. Most jade toggles in the Powerhouse Collection are highly likely to have been produced during the Qing dynasty and the early part of the Republican era (1912–1949). English literature in jade-carving techniques and process during the Qing dynasty is very limited.[4] The earliest publication is the 1906 two-volume catalogue *The Bishop Collection: Investigations and*

Studies in Jade, with a small print run of only 100 copies that were mostly gifted to heads of states in Europe and Asia, including the Qing dynasty Guangxu Emperor (光绪帝, 1871–1908).[5] The catalogue includes translations of two major Chinese texts on jade: Qing collector Tang Rongzuo's (唐荣祚) *Yushuo* (玉说), *A Discourse on Jade* and Qing dynasty painter Li Chengyuan (李澄渊), *Yuzuotu* (玉作图), *Illustrations of Manufacture of Jade*. Both Tang Rongzuo and Li Chengyuan were originally invited to write about and illustrate jade objects by British physician and amateur orientalist Stephen Wootton Bushell (1844–1908),[6] who was the principal author of the *Bishop Collection* catalogue.

Given the limited access to this significant but rare book on jade in English, this chapter is drawn mostly from illustrations from Li Chengyuan's *Illustrations of Manufacture of Jade*—arguably the most detailed book introducing the ancient jade-carving process.[7] This chapter provides a comprehensive yet detailed discussion of jade-carving processes and techniques during the Qing dynasty. It helps readers to understand how the many jade toggles in the Powerhouse Collection were produced, and how such mature carving techniques made a significant impact on the styles and aesthetics of jade toggles.

While research on the makers of Chinese toggles is absent from current literature (both Chinese and English), this chapter is intended as a reference to the production of jade products in China's early modern and modern eras.

The use of jade in the Qing dynasty was ubiquitous, being found among emperors and their consorts, dignitaries and noblemen, as well as among commoners.[8] Jades range from imperial seals signifying the emperors' authority, ritual vessels for worshipping gods and ancestors, writing tools such as paperweights or brush pots for literati and home decoration such as vases and practical utensils used every day, to costume ornamentation like buttons and women's jewellery, including hairpins and pendants.[9] Jade toggles in the Powerhouse Collection represent important Chinese material heritage, comprising ornaments with auspicious motifs of flora, fauna, human figures and landscapes typical of jade products.[10]

Jade-carving in the Qing dynasty can be broadly divided into three procedures: design, carving, and mounting. This chapter will focus on the design and carving procedures of twelve jade toggles in the Powerhouse Collection, which together offer a detailed view of the production process of one type of Chinese toggle.

Jade selection and design

The Eastern Han (25–220) Chinese dictionary *Shuowen jiezi* (说文解字), *The Origins of Chinese Characters* states, *Yu, shizhi meizhe* (玉，石之美者), 'Jade is a stone of beauty'. Jade has been regarded as a beautiful stone throughout China's long history. The jade-carving industry judged each type of raw jade by two criteria: selection and grade.

Selection refers to judging whether an item was jade or not; that is, whether it could be used as raw material for carving. In Chinese culture and the jade-carving industry, jade included a broad range of stones.[11] There were at least twenty types of stones used in the Qing dynasty as jade, including the 'four famous jades': Hetian jade (和田玉), Xiuyan jade (岫岩玉), Dushan jade (独山玉) and Lantian jade (蓝田玉); in addition, there were quartzite jade, crystal, lapis lazuli, turquoise and coral.[12] While the types of jade were numerous, its material features had been established across many centuries, and therefore 'selection' was easy for those in the sector to judge. Factors included the variety of jade and the minimum standards for an application, as well as the type, form, use, and commercial potential of the resulting product or products.

Grade, also known as quality, refered to a hierarchy of material across various forms of jade. The quality of jade was primarily evaluated by observation of its external features. The key to choosing jade, the first step in jade carving, was the ability to recognise grade. The raw material is precious, and each piece of jade has a scope of application, so as a general rule, different products were designed according to the distinctive characteristics of each piece.

Excavated from deep within the earth through mines, jade had a complex quality, so it was necessary to grasp the internal and external characteristics of the raw material. A process of examining the stone to ascertain its condition allowed features such as the texture and colour of the jade to be ascertained. Once these had been clearly understood, prospective forms could be considered, and so the design phase could begin. Attention to the combined beauty of material and style was a prime requisite for designing a jade object in the Qing dynasty and the wholeness of the stone was of vital

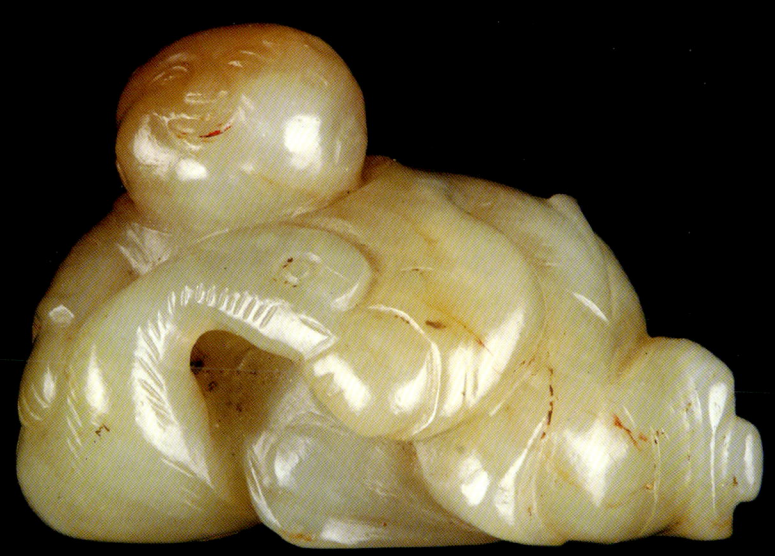

Fig. 5.1: Toggle depicting a boy embracing a goose, China, c.1700–1940. Jade, 22 x 37 x 25 mm, Powerhouse Collection. Gift of Alastair Morrison, 1992. Object 92/514.

importance. If there were any visible blemishes or cracks on the surface of an object, it was deemed to be deficient, no matter how perfect the form may have been. Imperfections must be completely removed, or if complete removal was unfeasible, steps had to be taken to hide them, or make them less conspicuous. This was called *wazangzheliu* (挖脏遮绺), 'removing blemishes and hiding cracks', in the Qing jade-carving industry. In order to set off the beauty of jade, motifs had to be suitable for the characteristics of the stone, for each jade had its own distinctive attributes. Some had a smooth and delicate texture, some were a riot of colour, some were transparent, others were glossy. Expressing the beauty of the special features of a piece of jade was of great importance.

The design for carving had to be executed with the available tools. In addition, the jade should not be damaged due to its specific properties. Some types of jade are brittle, so to prevent damage they should not be minutely carved, whereas other types of jade are tough and suitable for fine craftmanship. Designs were expected to bring out the characteristics of jade and the beauty of the craft; only an appropriate combination of the two could give birth to an outstanding object.

Designers were the backbone of jade production and required a diverse range of knowledge and skills. Material selection, design and craft were the fundamental skills that a jade designer needed to master. Taking the jade toggle carved with 'attributes of a scholar' motifs as an example (plate 24, p. 186), one can understand the skill and knowledge of this designer from its material selection, market and taste. This toggle was made from a rectangular block of semi-translucent pale yellow-green serpentine jade and depicts a relief carving of the *siyi* (四艺), 'four arts' of a Chinese scholar: *qin* (琴), a Chinese plucked zither,

qi (棋), a Go chess board and two jars for Go pieces, *shu* (书), a thread-bound book and *hua* (画), two scrolls of paintings. These symbolic objects are connected by the stem of a vine, expressing the ambitions of the owner: to embody the four arts and be a talented, cultured person. One might mistake this yellow serpentine jade as the precious beeswax-yellow tremolite jade, which was considered the best of Qing dynasty jades due to its rarity.[13] The maker of this toggle would have been aware of the market value of yellow tremolite jade and the auspicious meaning of yellow as the imperial colour. However, their client might have been an aspiring scholar who could not afford the yellow tremolite jade (mostly white in colour) yet was longing for a career in the imperial court; in that case, the cheaper, softer and lighter serpentine jade with similar beeswax-yellow colour would be the perfect choice. The designer of the 'Attributes of a Scholar' toggle skilfully combined the selection of jade and the motifs of the design, resulting in a piece of art tailored for the client's class and taste.

With these skills, craftspeople could design and carve jade independently, realising their own creative potential and providing the foundation for guiding others. In jade production, carvers should have themselves been designers, but because of the deeply entrenched production process and the limitations on technical knowledge, it was impossible for everyone to have a comprehensive set of skills. Few jade carvers possessed design skills, and designers with excellent carving skills were even fewer.

When the design was complete, the motifs were outlined in ink on the surface of the jade so that the carvers could produce a finished product. A layer of wax was often applied over the ink to prevent it from being removed by water and sand in the carving process. Influenced by Ming period (1368–1644) jade design conventions, the artistic motifs of Qing dynasty jades embody auspiciousness, based on the principle of *youtu bi youyi, youyi bi jixiang* (有图必有意，有意必吉祥), 'images expressing meaning, meaning bringing auspiciousness'[14] and through combinations of figures, animals, plants, artifacts, landscapes and antique patterns.[15] The popularity of auspicious motifs in jade design reflected a growing middle class and their taste during the Qing period.[16] Jade toggles held by Powerhouse Museum manifest this approach during the eighteenth to early twentieth centuries.

The toggle in the shape of silkworms and mulberry (plate 25, p. 187) was made of semi-translucent white jadeite with one area of pale amber-coloured patination. Two silkworms were carved around the mulberry leaves, with small indentations to indicate the eaten holes. A cocoon is on the underside. Sericulture has thousands of years of history in China, and the celebrated product of silk has been an important export that has generated great wealth for the Chinese. Hence, the silkworm is an important symbol of industry and wealth.

The toggle depicting a boy embracing a goose (fig. 5.1) refers to the famous story of Wang Xizhi (王羲之, 303–61), one of the greatest calligraphers in Chinese history, and his obsession with a goose. It is believed that he observed the movement of the goose's feet as it swam in order to improve his calligraphic wrist technique.[17] The motif of a boy embracing a goose symbolises the refinements of a scholar, and parents' wishes for their sons to become scholars like Wang Xizhi.

During Ming and Qing periods, *bon mots* homophone became a popular feature of art and craft practices.[18] One can find such attributes across many toggles in the Powerhouse Collection. For example, a toggle in the shape of paired persimmons (fig. 2.11) indicates the meaning of wishes fulfilled, *shishi ruyi* (事事如意). Persimmon, *shi* (柿), in Mandarin Chinese, shares the same pronunciation as the word for things or affairs, *shi* (事). The red colour of ripe persimmons also symbolises a flourishing career and life.

Other popular designs also include the twelve signs of the Chinese zodiac. A toggle in the shape of a pig (plate 58, p. 221) realistically depicts both a zodiac sign and one of the most common domestic animals. The pig, with its simple temperament and value as livestock, symbolises a content and affluent life in Chinese culture.

Jade carving and finishing

The jade-carving industry had already matured by the Ming dynasty. A jade workshop at the time would have been commercially processing materials, as indicated in the Ming dynasty encyclopedia *Tiangong kaiwu* (天工开物, 1637), *The Exploitation of the Works of Nature*, written by the scientist Song Yingxing (宋应星, 1587–1666).[19] With the rapid development of jade manufacture during the Qing dynasty, the jade-carving industry specialised in different carving processes, and there were collaborations between differently focused workshops.[20] Jade manufacture was carried out in handicraft workshops, and the process was divided into four procedures: *kaiyu* (开玉), 'cutting the jade'; *zhuozhi waixing* (琢制外形), 'carving the raw jade into the desired shape'; *zhuankong taotang* (钻孔掏膛), 'drilling the hole and hollowing the interior'; and *shanghua paoguang* (上花抛光), 'carving patterns and polishing'.

The first step was to cut the jade, specifically to pare off loose stone on the surface of the raw jade with such tools as a framesaw or a string saw. When sawing, one covered the jade

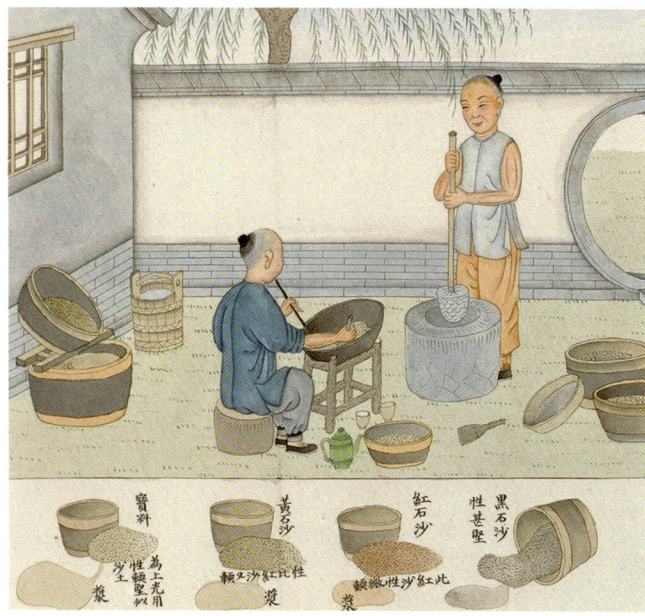

Fig. 5.2: Pounding and grinding stone sand (捣沙、研浆). Li Chengyuan, *Illustrations of the Manufacture of Jade*, 1891. Album of twelve leaves, ink and colour on silk.

in a mix of water and finely crushed sand (known as jade-grinding sand) to reduce the heat from friction but increase the amount of friction. The jade-grinding sand, collected from riversides, was initially placed in a mortar and pounded repeatedly with a pestle (fig. 5.2); then water was added for settling and filtering, and finally it was sieved, separated according to particle size, and categorised as coarse, medium, fine or powder, for application in the various steps of jade-cutting. The powdered sand, resembling flour, was called *baoliao* (宝料), 'treasure material' and was specifically used for the final polishing of jade. The *tiaoju* (条锯), framesaw, also known as *datiao faju* (大条法锯), large-framed straight saw, was a straight steel saw. The string saw, also called *gongziju* (弓子锯), a bow saw, comprised bow-shaped bamboo and a bowstring made of multiple strings of twisted wire. When cutting jade, two sawyers pulled the saw back and forth, one of

whom (or else a hanging kettle) added mortar comprising a mixture of water and coarse sand onto the contact point of the saw and the jade (figs 5.3 and 5.a). The hardness of jade is generally over 6 on the Mohs scale, higher than that of saw blades, so it was not the saw alone, but rather the mortar inserted by the movement of the saw, that slowly ground away the piece of raw jade.

The second step was to carve raw jade into the shape of the desired object on a lathe. The lathe used for processing raw jade was a jade-grinding workstation, also known as *mucheng* (木橙), 'wooden bench' (fig. 5.4). It was formed by a wooden frame and comprised a bench surface, a bench groove, a pot stand, a support frame, a seat and treadles. There were two wooden plates on the front and the back of the bench surface to support a shaft made of either wood or iron, the diameter of which is about 50–60 mm. The end of the shaft was

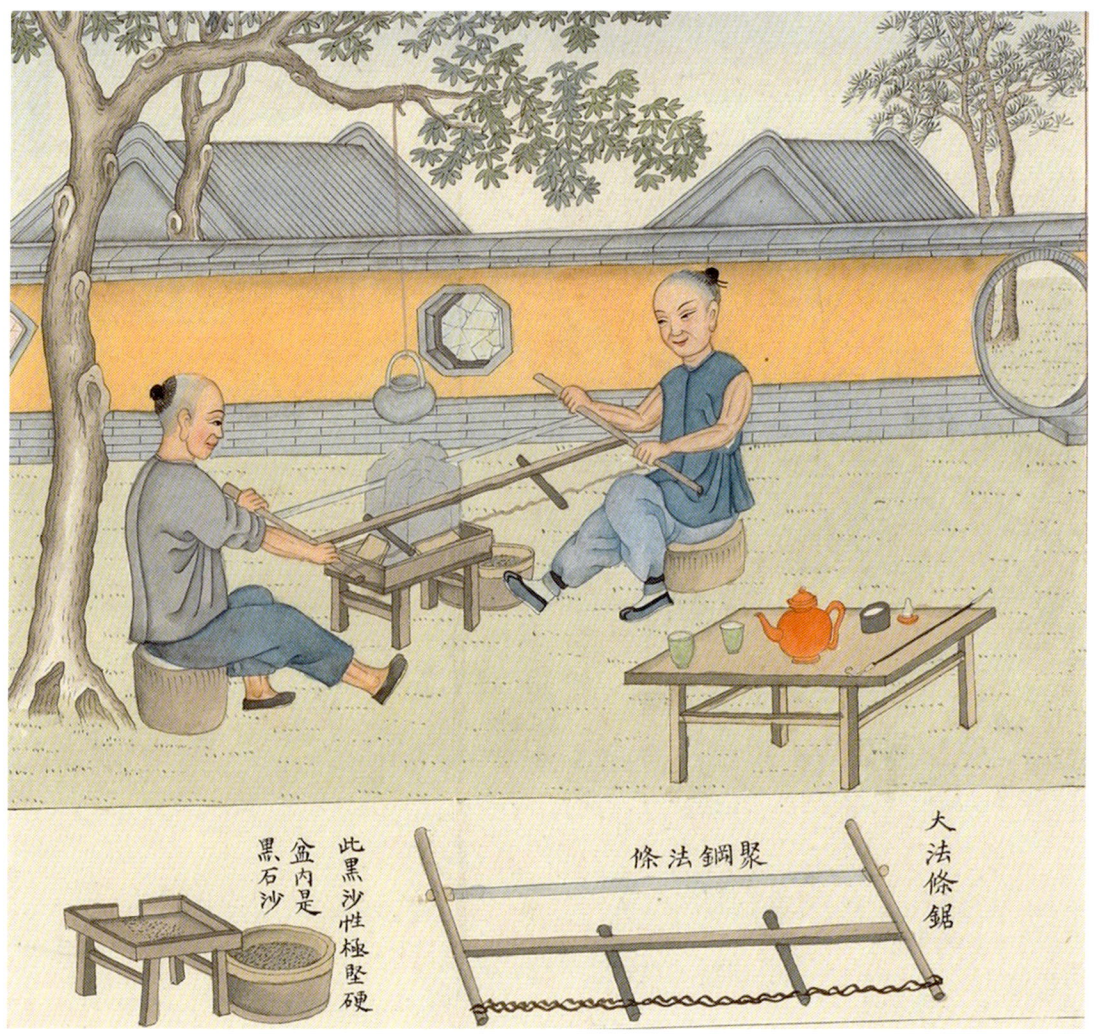

大法條鋸　條法鋼聚　此黑沙性極堅硬　盆內是黑石沙

Fig. 5.3: Sawing open crude jade with the help of stone sand (开玉). Li Chengyuan, *Illustrations of the Manufacture of Jade*, 1891. Album of twelve leaves, ink and colour on silk.

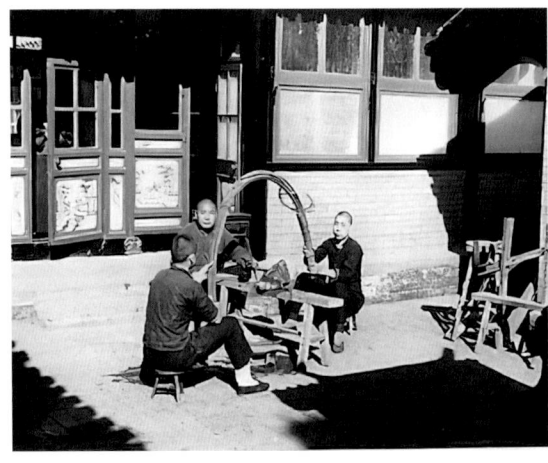

Fig. 5.a: S. Howard Hansford, photograph of jade-carvers, in S. Howard Hansford, *Jade, Essence of Hills and Streams: The Von Oertzen Collection of Chinese and Indian Jades* (Cape Town and London, 1969).

attached to a jade-carving tool made of iron, and the middle was wrapped with a rope and connected to the treadles. The diameter of the iron tool was about 20mm. The end of the shaft was attached to the jade-carving tool, and a string or leather strap hanging in the middle of the shaft was connected to the treadles. These were made of bamboo, with one end lying on the footrest of the seat. A craftsman sat on the seat, and his feet worked the treadles to make the string or leather strap move up and down, causing the shaft to turn back and forth. The craftsman's left hand gripped a piece of raw jade, supporting it and keeping it vertical, and aligning it with a spinning disc-shaped tool (the grinding wheel). His right hand clenched a ball of wet mortar made of medium sand, constantly touching the disc of the grinding wheel, with his right palm held against the raw jade in his left hand. With some mortar between the surface of the cut and the disc of the wheel, the turning wheel correctly and precisely carved the raw jade through friction along the inked lines.

If a piece of raw jade was too heavy and inconvenient to hold in the hand, a steelyard could be employed to hold it for carving. The bench groove was in the shape of a dustpan, to store the grinding sand and jade objects. An iron pot was placed on the pot stand in front of the bench groove, in order to catch used water and sand. The jade grinding workstation was fitted with a cutting grinder (a thin circular steel plate), an impact grinder (a circular steel ring), and a polishing grinder (a heavy circular steel plate). The cutting grinder was used to cut the raw jade into semi-finished products of square blocks or square strips (fig. 5.5), then the impact grinder was applied to grind away the unnecessary edges and corners (fig. 5.6), and finally the polishing grinder was employed to polish the surface of the object (fig. 5.7). In this way, the general shape of a jade object was completed.[22]

The third step in the manufacturing process was to drill a hole and hollow out the inside of the carved jade object to form an empty vessel such as a vase, incense burner or snuff bottle. Drilling and hollowing were critical processes in jade manufacture. Drilling skills in the Qing dynasty were advanced, but tools were basic: there were only solid and hollow drills. The solid

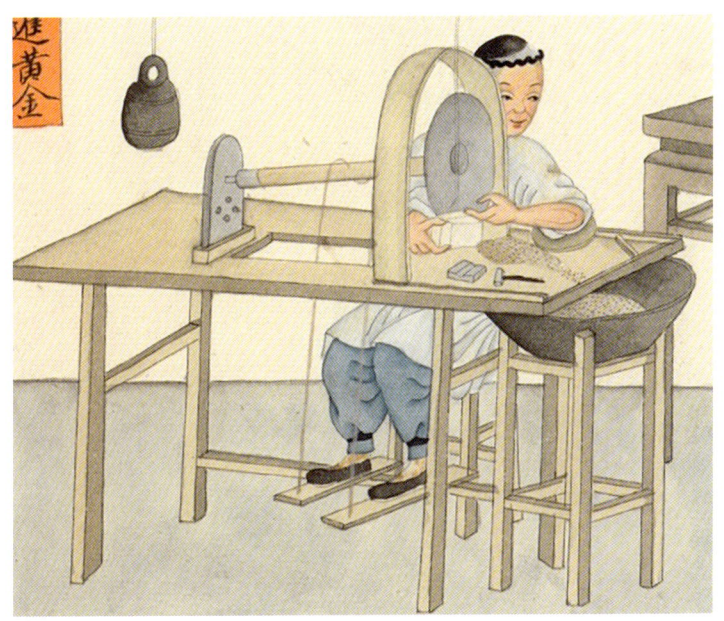

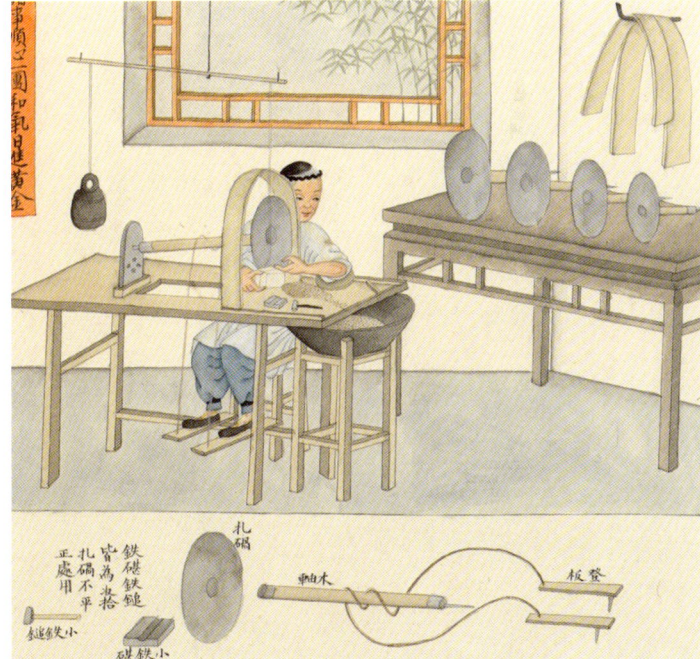

Top to bottom:

Fig. 5.4: The machine used to slice jade into oblong slabs (磨玉机), Li Chengyuan, *Illustrations of the Manufacture of Jade*, 1891. Album of twelve leaves, ink and colour on silk;

Fig. 5.5: Slicing the jade into square or oblong slabs (扎碢), Li Chengyuan, *Illustrations of the Manufacture of Jade*, 1891. Album of twelve leaves, ink and colour on silk.

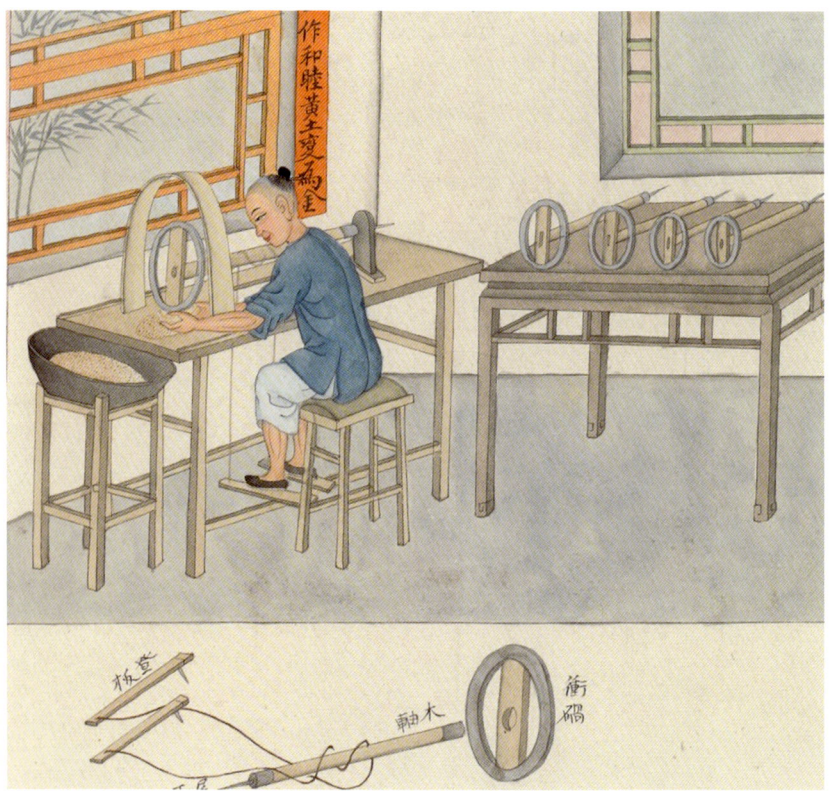

Fig. 5.6: Removing the sharp
edges and corners from the
jade (冲碢), Li Chengyuan,
*Illustrations of the Manufacture
of Jade*, 1891. Album of twelve
leaves, ink and colour on silk.

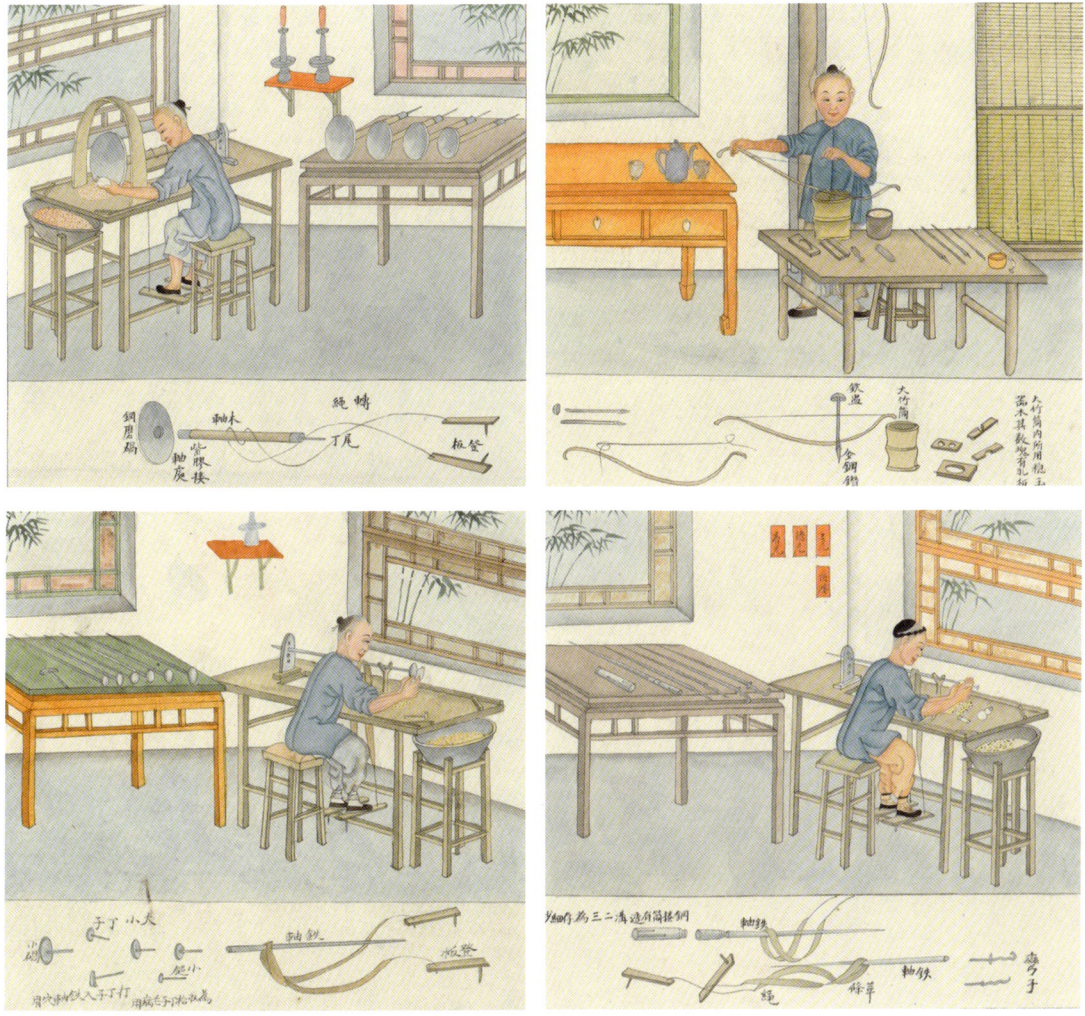

Clockwise from top:

Fig. 5.7: Grinding the jade until the surface is smooth (磨碢), Li Chengyuan, *Illustrations of the Manufacture of Jade*, 1891. Album of twelve leaves, ink and colour on silk; **Fig. 5.8:** Piercing holes on small objects such as snuff bottles (打眼), Li Chengyuan, *Illustrations of the Manufacture of Jade*, 1891. Album of twelve leaves, ink and colour on silk; **Fig. 5.9:** Hollowing the interior (掏膛), Li Chengyuan, *Illustrations of the Manufacture of Jade*, 1891. Album of twelve leaves, ink and colour on silk; **Fig. 5.10:** Carving ornamental designs on jade (上花), Li Chengyuan, *Illustrations of the Manufacture of Jade*, 1891. Album of twelve leaves, ink and colour on silk.

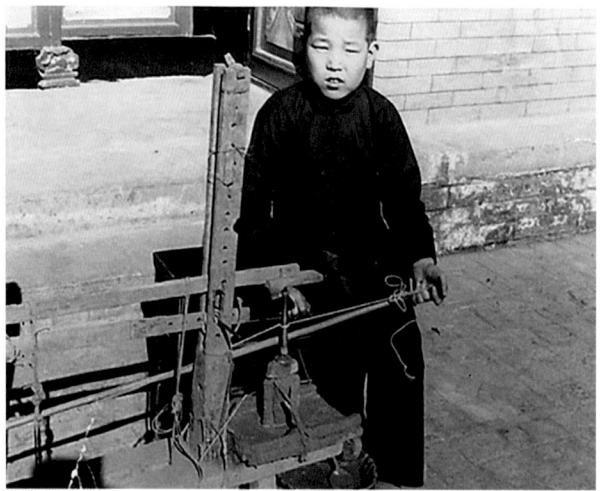

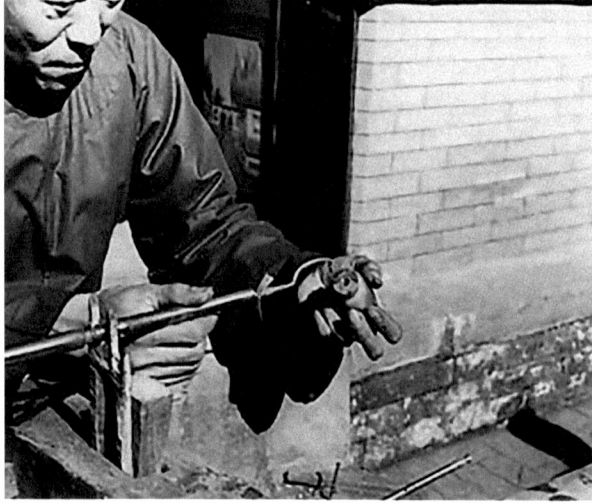

Fig. 5.b & c: S. Howard Hansford, photographs showing jade-carving, in S. Howard Hansford, *Jade, Essence of Hills And Streams: The Von Oertzen Collection of Chinese and Indian Jades* (Cape Town and London, 1969).

drill was relatively long and slender, resembling a nail, and was used for boring small holes. The hollow drill was a steel tube for drilling the inside of the jade object. A slit left on the side of the steel tube allowed the entry and exit of mortar.

There were two drilling methods: vertical and horizontal. Vertical drilling involved boring a hole by hand by pulling a drilling rod; it was suitable for larger containers such as vases and incense burners. For vertical drilling, a container in the shape of a wooden bucket was used, inside of which sat a supporting frame holding the jade object, and the drilling rod pulled by a bowstring (figs 5.8 and 5.b). In this procedure, the hollow drill attached at the bottom of the drilling rod entered the inside of the jade object and produced a cylinder of jade. The craftsmen would then strike the cylinder gently with a hammer to break the jade off for removal. Horizontal drilling involved attaching a drill to the end of the shaft on the jade-grinding workstation; it was suitable for making smaller containers such as pipes and snuff bottles, and for hollowing out vessels with small openings and large insides, including vases (figs 5.9 and 5.c). The tools for hollowing were a set of steel shafts with bent hooks of various sizes. The hooks entered through the opening, turning and grinding with the help of fine sand mortar; this gradually hollowed out the inside and eventually produced an object with a small opening and a large hollow. The walls of snuff bottles of the Qing dynasty can be as thin as a piece of paper and even float on water, being aptly named 'water floaters' (水上漂), a testament to advanced hollowing skills.

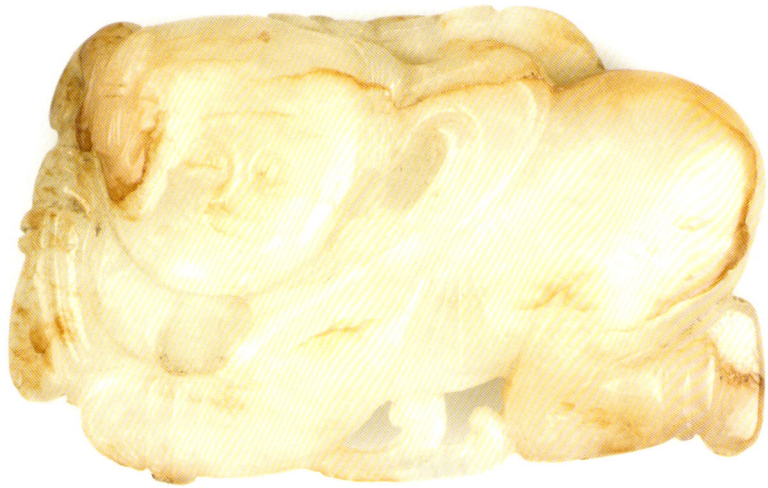

Fig. 5.11: Toggle depicting Liu Hai kneeing forward and holding a bundle of strings with cloud swirls and coins, China, c.1700–1940. Jade, 5 x 62 x 37 mm. Powerhouse Collection, Gift of Alastair Morrison, 1992. Object 92/500.

The fourth step focused on the surface of the jade by carving various relief patterns, also known as *shanghua* (上花), or 'adding patterns', followed by polishing. First, nail-shaped tools were used on the surface, the turning of the round nail cap etching shallow lines on the exterior of the object (fig. 5.10). Apart from the etched lines, techniques of relief-carving and openwork were often applied to bring out more vivid patterns. Relief carving was divided into relief on flat surfaces and relief on three-dimensional surfaces (also known as rounded relief carving). After unwanted parts had been removed to highlight the patterns, an outline was sketched on the patterned section to finely carve a layered design. Removing unwanted material further brought to life images such as figures, flowers and birds, grass and insects, garment patterns, landscapes, trees, pavilions and terraces. The two toggles in the shape of Liu Hai in the Powerhouse Collection are great examples of flat relief carving (fig. 5.11) and rounded relief carving (fig. 5.12).

Carving openwork patterns like the Liu Hai toggle (fig. 5.12) initially required drilling (fig. 5.13); then into the resulting hole was inserted a wire with two ends fixed to bow-shaped bamboo to form a bow saw (also known as an engraving bow). Cutting was then done according to the lines drawn on the surface of the object (fig. 5.14). Patterns emerge as in papercutting; this was called *toudiao* (透雕) or *loudiao* (镂雕), meaning fretwork. Such jade-carving techniques were employed as early as the Warring States Period (c.475–221 BCE) but only gained popularity after the Yuan dynasty (1271–1368).[23]

Jade objects boasting features such as carved lines, relief and openwork engraving required ample labour and materials, and so must have been considered exquisite pieces of art. A good example is the toggle in the shape of a *lingzhi* mushroom with clouds (fig. 5.15). The fretwork on the clouds provides multiple holes for attachment.

The jade carving technique of *qiaose qiaodiao* (俏色巧雕), 'natural texture in fine engraving',

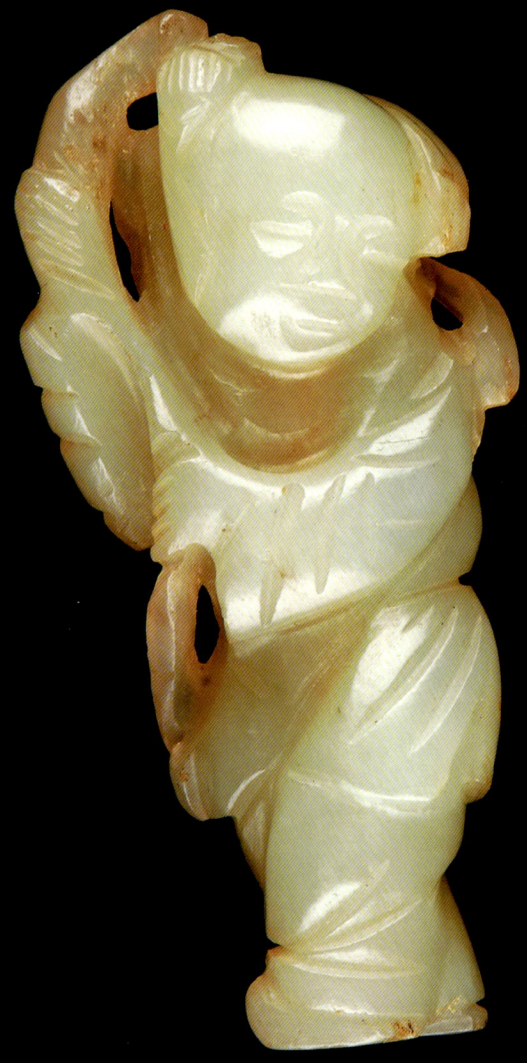

Fig. 5.12: Toggle depicting Liu Hai standing and carrying a branch of leaves, China, c.1700–1940. Jade, 10 x 55 x 25 mm, Powerhouse Collection. Gift of Alastair Morrison, 1992. Object 92/508.

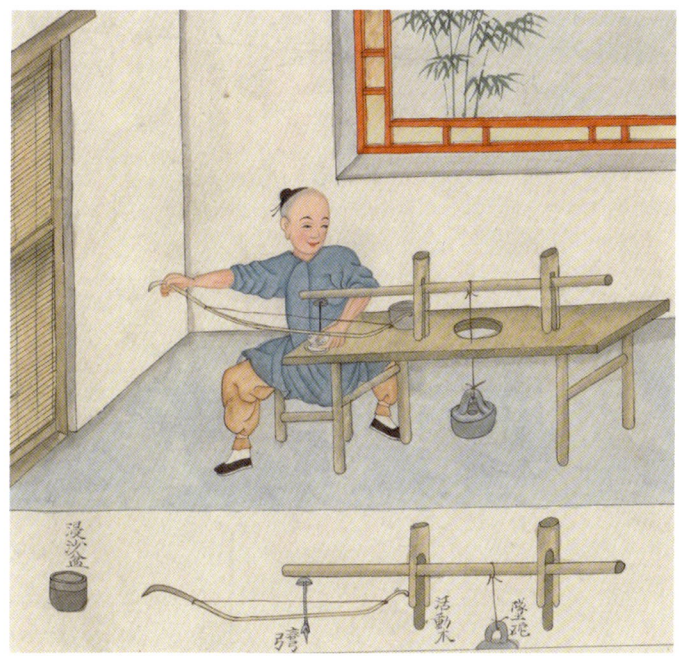

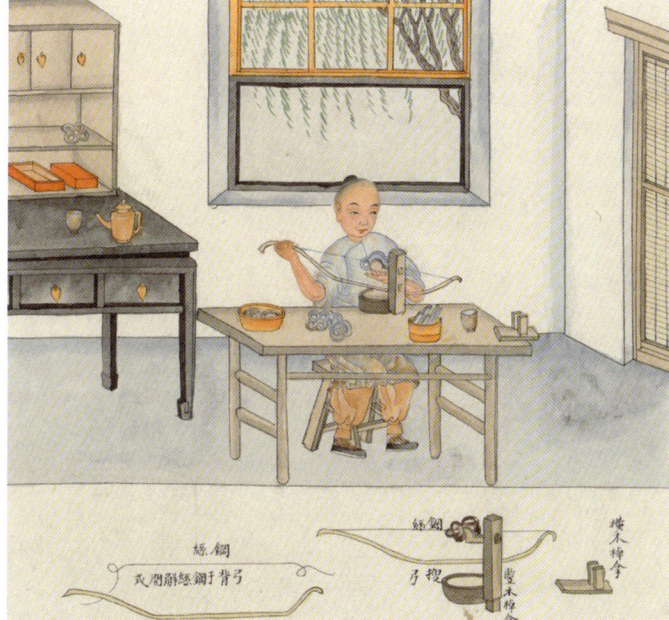

Fig. 5.13: Piercing holes on jade with diamond borer (打钻), Li Chengyuan, *Illustrations of the Manufacture of Jade*, 1891. Album of twelve leaves, ink and colour on silk.

Fig. 5.14: Carving openwork with wire on bow (透花), Li Chengyuan, *Illustrations of the Manufacture of Jade*, 1891. Album of twelve leaves, ink and colour on silk.

can be traced back to the Song dynasty.[24] The technique was also commonly used during the Qing dynasty, utilising the colour, surface hue and texture of raw jade. By blending the elements of the stone into the design, a perfect harmony between the material and artistic interpretation could be achieved, enhancing the ornamental and aesthetic quality of the jade object.[25] Such carving techniques can be found in a few jade toggles in the Powerhouse Collection, such as that depicting a boy riding on a dragonfish and holding a lotus stem (plate 47, p. 210). It is beautifully carved to utilise the natural white and dark-grey jade, symbolising one's children's success.

The final concern in this fourth manufacturing step was to meticulously buff or polish the surface of carved jade. Polishing was the process of buffing the surface to refine it to a mirror-like finish. This process enabled the surface to reflect the light as evenly as possible, achieving a state of brightness and smoothness that brings out the inner warmth and subtlety of jade. Polishing was generally carried out with a wooden disc called a 'wooden wheel', (fig. 5.16), or with a disc covered in ox hide, called a 'hide wheel', (fig. 5.17), which is supplemented with a powder-like 'treasure material'. Hedda Morrison lived in Beijing for thirteen years, giving her dual interests of toggle collecting and photography many opportunities to merge, such as when she captured a jade polisher at work (fig. 5.18). Reflecting on this period in her 1985 book *A Photographer in Old Peking*, she noted 'In the 1930s, the carving of jade was mainly for jewellery and ornaments, many of which were exported. Some of the finest jewellery, especially green jades, were reworked pieces derived from heirlooms of impoverished gentry.'[26] While we cannot identify what kind of jade product this man is polishing, it is clear that he is working on a wooden wheel, with a cup and dish also sitting on the machine bench.

In addition to wood, polishing implements could be made of natural shellac, gourds, bristles, cloth and fine stones. After jade was buffed by the wheel, its surface was washed free of dirt and stains before being waxed, oiled and wiped. These were important steps after buffing, as they served to remove minute flaws and smooth out subtle areas of unevenness. When applied to the surface, both wax and oil added vibrancy to an object, making it appear moist, as well as filling in tiny indentations to enhance the reflection of light. Waxing involved dropping melted wax onto the jade surface after it was baked hot and removing the wax after cooling to ensure no residual wax was visible. Oiling involved immersing jade objects in heated oil and wiping them when hot to ensure the oil was evenly distributed. Bamboo or wooden sticks were used for removing the wax, while a soft cotton cloth, preferably with oil absorption properties, was used for wiping the oil. Wax and oil also protected the jade surface from dirt. With their surfaces gleaming and protective layers in place, the jade objects were ready to be placed into the hands of their new owners.

Mounting

The goal of mounting, for jades of the Qing dynasty, was to enhance and protect the objects. Court jades usually had bases and boxes. Some were packaged as sets, with glass cases on the bases and silk ribbons, silk tassels and silver and gold inlays. We will not elaborate further on Qing dynasty jade mounting in this chapter as such practices were a rare outlier when compared to the wider function of toggles as sartorial decorations typically attached as counterweights to other accessories, such as small pouches or cases. There are no mountings for the jade toggles in the Powerhouse Collection. However, there are metal mountings on some other toggles, with ring hooks for a connecting string

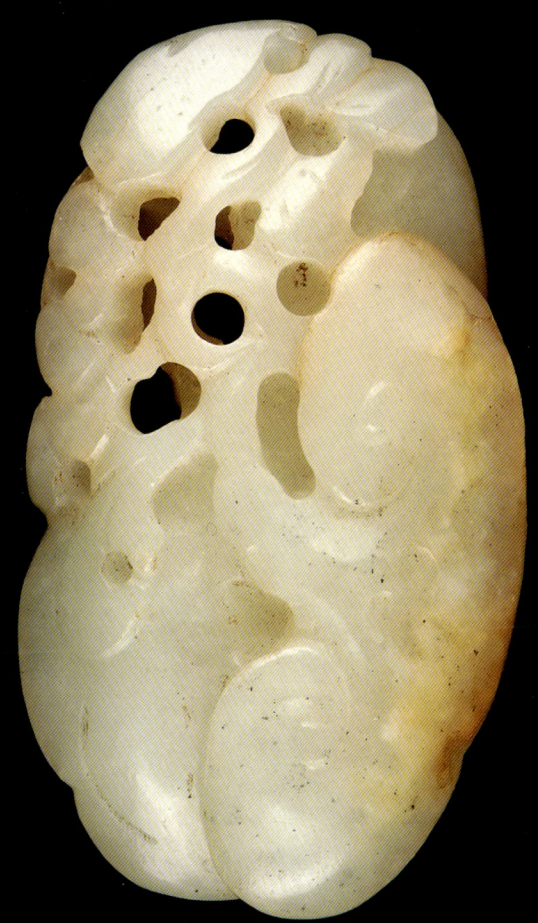

Fig. 5.15: Toggle in the shape of
a *lingzhi* mushroom with clouds,
China, c.1700–1940. Jade,
12 x 50 x 30 mm, Powerhouse
Collection. Gift of Alastair Morrison,
1992. Object 92/507.

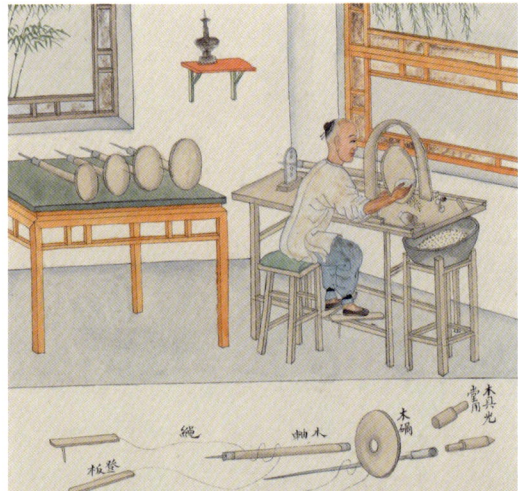

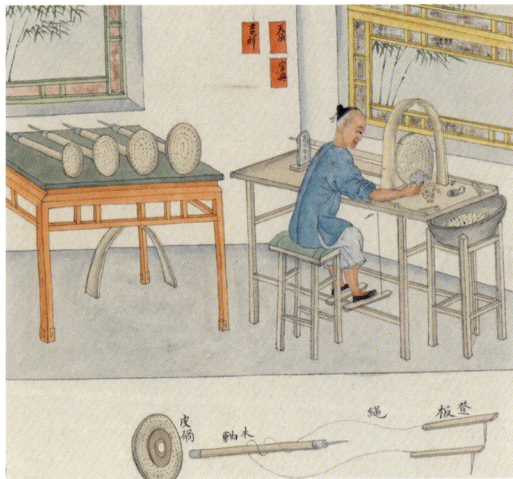

Fig. 5.16: Polishing with wooden wheel (木碢), Li Chengyuan, *Illustrations of the Manufacture of Jade*, 1891. Album of twelve leaves, ink and colour on silk;

Fig. 5.17: Brightening with leather wheel (皮碢), Li Chengyuan, *Illustrations of the Manufacture of Jade*, 1891. Album of twelve leaves, ink and colour on silk.

to go through (plate 68, p. 230). There might have been jades mounted in precious metals like silver and gold that were used as toggles, given that jade pendants have been used over millennia as decorative accessories, but no examples have come to light as part of this study or appear within the collection.

Aspects of Qing-era quality

The finest jade objects in the Qing dynasty appeared mainly during the reign of the Qianlong Emperor (1735–96). The developed economy, advanced technology and Qianlong's fascination with jade (the government was in charge of the mining and use of jade materials, prohibiting private mining) all contributed to the unprecedented prosperity of the jade-carving industry.[27] The centre of jade carving under the Qing dynasty was Suzhou, Jiangsu province, where the quality of the work produced was characterised by five aspects.

The first aspect of Qing-era quality that was acknowledged was the careful selection of raw materials. As outlined above in 'Jade selection and design', simply by observing uncut raw material, craftspeople could consistently judge the quality of the jade and could often choose the best pieces to work with. A Qing-era toggle in the shape of water caltrop from the Powerhouse Collection (plate 61, p. 224), for example, is made from a high-quality, semi-translucent white tremolite jade that suggests a careful selection process.[28]

The second stand-out aspect of Qing-era jade was its meticulous attention to the surface. Regardless of size, many Qing-era objects appear smooth and cleanly polished, fully displaying the attributes of their inherent beauty, with the touch of their lustrous curves giving rise to a feeling of fineness, as tender as a baby's skin, like another toggle in the shape of a lingzhi fungus (plate 59, p. 222).

The third aspect is exquisite and creative forms. Whether carved three-dimensionally or on a flat surface, Qing-era designs are considered graceful and unique. The lines and patterns, fluent and flowing, combine the solid with the delicate without a trace of hesitation or heavy-handedness. Among the many works featured here, fault can rarely be found.

Superb carving is the fourth aspect of Qing-era quality, and another that ties closely to the processes outlined in this chapter. Lightweight objects with thin walls are particularly difficult to carve, testifying to proficiency and advanced skills. Such artwork is evenly carved and has a distinctly transparent look; together with undulating patterns, this gives rise to a three-dimensional feel.

Finally careful attention to detail was valued in Qing-era objects as it offered a sense of seeing the breadth of the world through the miniature. Small jade pieces of the time, Chinese toggles in particular, are finely carved and gracefully crafted, having a rich three-dimensional effect. Managing to be miniature, detailed and three-dimensional all at once required ingenious utilisation of the kinds of carving techniques outlined in this chapter. These can be seen in the toggle in the shape of two pomegranates (plate 31, p. 194).[29]

The sage Confucius stated, 'Gentlemen liken virtue to jade', meaning that the moral character of an upright gentleman is as fine and firm as jade, which, when turned into objects that can demonstrate the five aspects of Qing-era quality and more, also represent

the status and rank of its wearer. Over thousands of years, jade craftspeople have used their hands and common tools to carve ordinary pieces of jade into exquisite objects, demonstrating the beauty of its uncorrupted form and imbuing it with rich cultural significance. Jade craft of the Qing dynasty was the pinnacle of the Chinese art of jade carving, with complicated processes, clear divisions of labour, careful attention to materials and striving for perfection. The perfect union of jade and human culture is also demonstrated in the diverse Chinese jade toggles in the Powerhouse Collection.

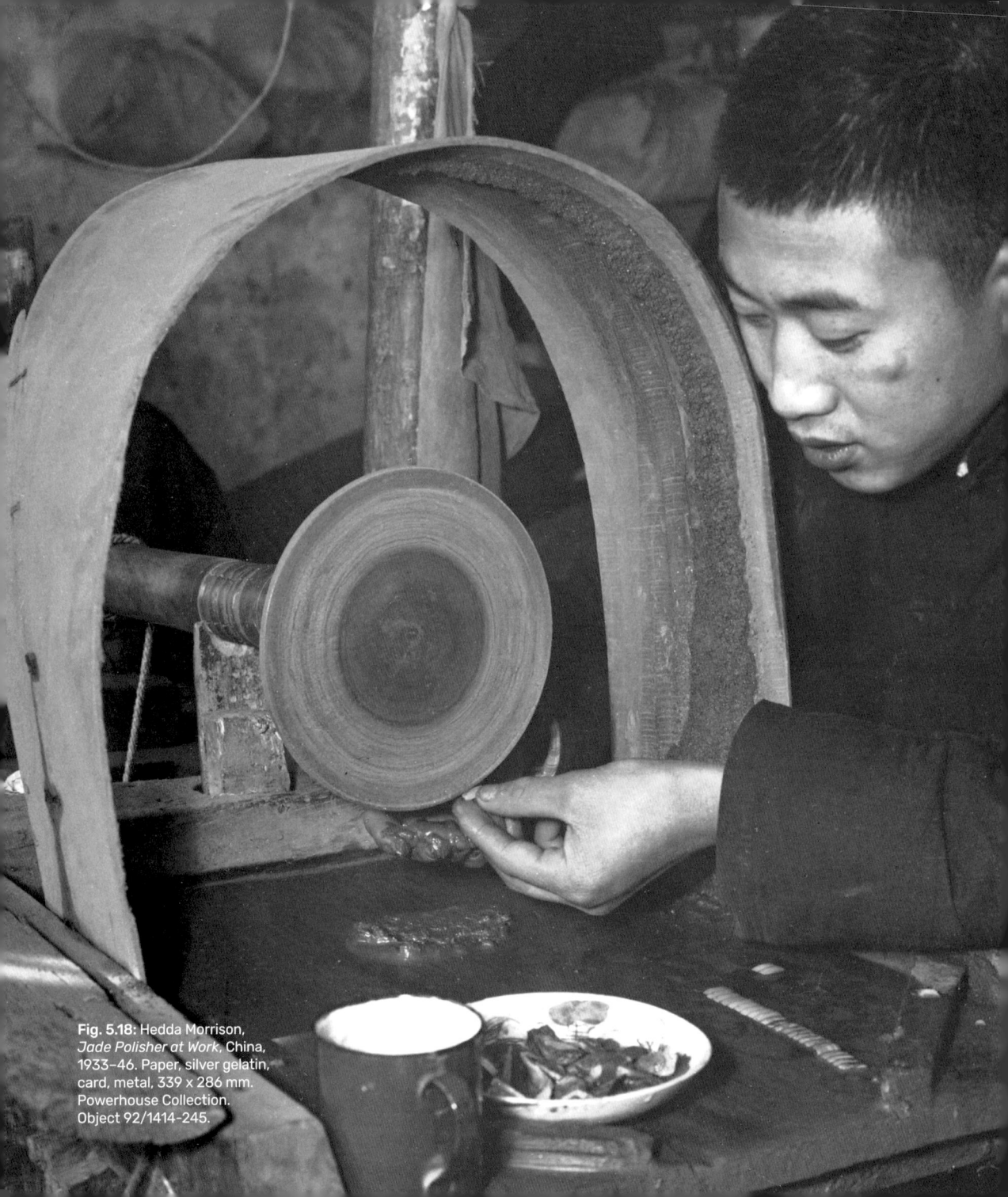

Fig. 5.18: Hedda Morrison, *Jade Polisher at Work*, China, 1933–46. Paper, silver gelatin, card, metal, 339 x 286 mm. Powerhouse Collection. Object 92/1414-245.

1. For discussion on the cultural significance of jade in China, please see previous chapter by Chen Shuxia.

2. Luo Xingbo, 'Sculpture', in Hua Jueming, Li Jinsong, and Wang Lianhai (eds), *Chinese Handicrafts*, Daxiang Publishing House and Springer, Zhengzhou and Singapore, 2022, p. 677.

3. These five periods are: the late Neolithic Age (c.3500–2070 BCE), the late Shang Dynasty (1600–1046 BCE), the Zhanguo period (475–221 BCE), the Han Dynasty (206 BCE–220 CE), and the Qing Dynasty (1644–1911). See Mingying Wang and Guanghai Shi, 'The Evolution of Chinese Jade carving Craftmanship', *Gems & Gemology*, Vol. 56, No. 1, 2020, p. 30.

4. One important English publication is S. Howard Hansford, *Chinese Jade Carving*, Lund Humphries, London and Bradford, 1950.

5. Catalogue entry of The Bishop Collection. The Metropolitan Museum of Art, New York, *The Bishop Collection: Investigations and Studies in Jade*, The Bishop Collection, accession no. 139.3 N48F, https://www.metmuseum.org/art/collection/search/680379 (viewed July 2023).

6. Heber R. Bishop, Stephen Wootton Bushell, Tadamasa Hayashi, George Frederick Kunz and Robert Lilley, *The Bishop Collection: Investigations and Studies in Jade*, De Vinne Press, New York, 1906. Known copies are in the collections of the Jade Ware Department of National Palace Museum, the Libraries of the Metropolitan Museum of Art, New York, and Tokyo National Museum.

7. Xu Lin 徐琳, '切磋琢磨—中国史前至汉代的治玉工艺' ['Cutting, Grinding, Carving and Polishing: Early Jade Craftmanship from Prehistory to the Han Dynasty'], 养德堂珍藏中国古玉器二 [*Chinese Archaic Jades From The Yangdetang Collection*

PART II], Christie's, Hong Kong, 2018, pp. 9–10.

8. Zhang Ruixiang 张睿祥, Yang Xiaoping 杨筱平 and Ou Xiuhua 欧秀花, '从神坛走向民间：中国古代玉器的发展历程' ['From the Altar to the Common People: The Development of Ancient Chinese Jade Artifacts'], 文物鉴定与鉴赏 [*Identification and Appreciation to Cultural Relics*], no. 11, 2018, p. 86.

9. He Song 何松, '中国清代玉器的主要成就·艺术特征·文化内涵' ['Major achievement, art characteristics and cultural connotation of the jade carvings of Qing Dynasty of China'], 超硬材料工程 [*Superhard Material Engineering*], vol. 18, no. 1, 2006, pp. 56–57.

10. Zhang Zhang 张章, '清代玉器的纹饰特点与风格研究' ['On the characteristics and styles of jade products in the Qing Dynasty'], 艺术品鉴 [*Appreciation*], no. 23, 2018, pp. 11–12.

11. Wang Yuchang 王裕昌, '中国玉文化之管见———兼谈中国的制玉材质' ['Views on Chinese Jade Culture and Jade Materials'], 丝绸之路 [*Silk Road*], no. 8, 2012, p. 61.

12. For more details about different types of jade rocks, please see chapter six.

13. Wang, '中国玉文化之管见———兼谈中国的制玉材质' ['Views on Chinese Jade Culture and Jade Materials'], p. 63.

14. Wang Yamin 王亚民, '玉器、玉文化及民间藏玉' ['Jade ware, jade culture and private jade collections'], 紫禁城 [*Forbidden City*], no. 5, 2010, p. 13.

15. Wang, '中国玉文化之管见———兼谈中国的制玉材质' ['Views on Chinese Jade Culture and Jade Materials'], p. 61.

16. He, '中国清代玉器的主要成就·艺术特征·文化内涵' ['Major achievement, art characteristics and cultural connotation of the jade carvings of Qing Dynasty of China'], p. 58.

17. Please see Qing dynasty

calligrapher and historian of calligraphy Bao Shichen's 包世臣 (1775–1855), 艺舟双楫 [*Two Oars for the Boat of Art*], 1844.

18. Jiang Yonghu 江用虎, 安徽怀宁文物管理所藏明清时期民间佩玉 ['Collection of Everyday Jade Toggles from Ming–Qing Period in Anhui Huaining Cultural Relics Management Office'], 收藏界 [*Collection World*], no. 12, 2009, p. 38.

19. In *The Exploitation of the Works of Nature*, Song noted, 'The craftsman would determine the price of the jade [provided by the client], then carve it [玉工辨璞高下定价，而后琢之].'

20. Zhang Yufu 张玉甫, '明代琢玉大师陆子冈与苏琢史略考' ['Ming Dynasty Jade carving master Lu Zigang and Suzhou Jade carving history'], 中国民族博览 [*Chinese National Expo*], no. 2, 2020, p. 87.

21. This section is based on one publication and one major documentary on jade carving procedures. Zhao Yongkui 赵永魁 and Gu Fang 古方, '制玉工艺' ['The art and craft of jade-carving'], in Gu Fang 古方 (ed.), 中国古玉器图典 [*The Pictorial Handbook of Ancient Chinese Jades*], The Cultural Relics Publishing House 文物出版社, Beijing, 2007, pp. 27–41; 琢玉工艺 [*The Art and Craft of Jade Carving*], film, Beijing Jade Factory 北京玉器厂, The Institute of Archaeology, Chinese Academy of Social Sciences 中国社会科学院考古研究所, Beijing, 1976. Six techniques of carving, including drilling, wheel-cutting, sawing, flexible string sawing, riffling and point or blade abrasion are recognised in recent searches on Chinese nephrite jade. See Margaret Sax, Nigel D. Meeks, Carol Michaelson, and Andrew P. Middleton, 'The identification of carving techniques on Chinese jade', *Journal of Archaeological Science* no. 31, 2004, pp. 1413–28.

22. For details on the significance of using grinding workstations in jade production in Chinese history,

please see Yang Boda 杨伯达, '关于琢玉工具的再探讨' ['Revisiting jade carving tools'], 南阳师范学院学报 [*Journal of Nanyang Normal University (Social Sciences)*], no. 2, 2007. pp. 72–6.

23. Wu Mo 吴沫, '中国汉代玉器的工艺进步和艺术创新——以安徽出土的汉代玉器为例' ['Technological progress and artistic innovation of Chinese Han Dynasty jade wares: sampling the Han Dynasty jade wares unearthed in Anhui'], 宝石和宝石学杂志 [*Journal of Gems and Gemmology*], vol. 23, no. 3, 2021, pp. 56–7.

24. Japanese art historian on Chinese art Ōmura Seigai (1868–1927) mentioned this jade carving technique in his book 中国美术史 [*Chinese Art History*], Chen Binsu 陈彬苏 (transl.), Commercial Press 商务印书馆, Shanghai, 1930.

25. Wang Mingying 王铭颖 and Shi Guanghai 施光海, '从宝玉石学角度浅析玉雕俏色艺术' ['A Brief Analysis of the "Qiaose" Jade from the Perspective of Gemmology'], 美术学 [*Fine Art Research*], no. 3, 2020, p. 77.

26. Hedda Morrison, *A Photographer in Old Peking*, Oxford University Press, Hong Kong, 1985, p. 165–6.

27. Luo Xingbo, 'Sculpture', in Hua Jueming, Li Jinsong and Wang Lianhai (eds), *Chinese Handicrafts*, Springer and Elephant Press, Singapore and Zhengzhou, 2022, p. 668.

28. Wang, '中国玉文化之管见———兼谈中国的制玉材质' ['Views on Chinese Jade Culture and Jade Materials'], p. 63.

29. Gu Fang 古方, '明清时期的苏州玉雕' ['Jade carving in Suzhou during Ming–Qing period'], 收藏家 [*Collectors*], no. 10, 2021, pp. 239–42.

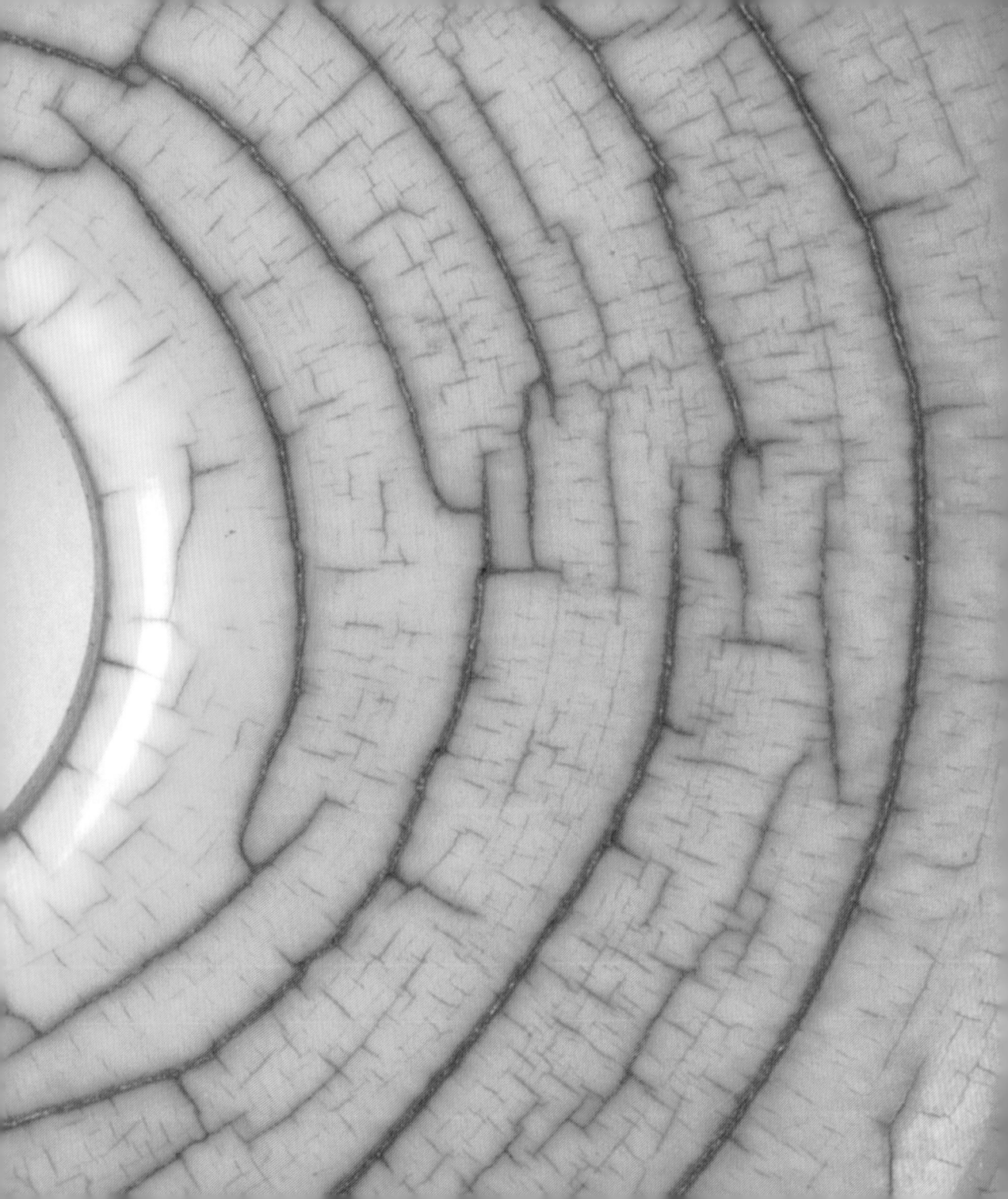

6. Material matters: the scientific analysis of Chinese toggles

Elizabeth A. Carter, Lorraine Leung, Brad Swarbrick, Thérèse Harrison,
Chen Shuxia, Min-Jung Kim, Meredith Freeman, Paul Donnelly

This chapter presents analysis of the material composition of Chinese toggles using the most up-to-date methods. Increasingly nuanced identifications provide the opportunity to interpret and exhibit the collection to the public with greater accuracy. It has been noted in preceding chapters that Chinese toggles have been over-shadowed in profile and reputation by their better-known Japanese antecedents, *netsuke* (根付). Compared to netsuke, Chinese toggles are greatly under-represented in institutional and private collections, suffer from a lack of focused research, and are rarely exhibited in their own right. To redress this imbalance, we have collaborated to produce the first materials analysis of Chinese toggles.[1]

The insights that follow are the result of a range of complementary analytical methods intended to provide objective insights into the materiality of a set of historical objects. With greater clarity and increased knowledge of the materials employed we have been able to confirm or qualify more subjective earlier attributions made by collectors, conservators and curators. For this first ever comprehensive scientific study on the materiality of Chinese toggles we will focus on the most complex of toggle materials—the broader categories of jade and ivory. The use of X-ray fluorescence (XRF) and the vibrational spectroscopic techniques of near-infrared (NIR) and Raman spectroscopy, together with renewed close visual analysis, have provided a toolbox of methods for reaching more accurate and objective identification. This scientific work forms part of a broader project that seeks to reposition and reimagine the history of toggles in Asia, conducted alongside in-depth collection research and an exhibition on one of the two largest toggle collections in the world—that of Powerhouse Museum, collected by Hedda and Alastair Morrison.

Apart from a number of small museums, where they are categorised merely as 'pendants' or 'carvings' of jade or ivory, toggles are not often found in the collections of cultural institutions, and particularly not those with the resources for serious examination. As such, this research forms not only part of a debut of the Morrisons' collection, but also an introduction to toggles as objects. Except for a short article by the Morrisons in 1986,[2] and a symposium paper by Min-Jung Kim in 2008,[3] the existence of the collection has not been communicated to broader international audiences.

Using the information available to them when they were collecting in the mid-twentieth century, the Morrisons categorised the types of toggle materials relatively well, and most of the current museum documentation is based on the donors' original attributions. The collection has been catalogued according to the many material types represented, including wood, ivory, jade, agate, stone, jet, crystal, glass, seed, metal, amber, shell and so on. However, having been purchased from antique dealers in Beijing in the 1930s and 1940s, the toggles' dates of production are unknown. Some of the materials, including ivory and jade, are inconsistently identified: some are categorised in general and others in more specific terms. For example, the categories of animal materials include 'ivory', 'antler' and 'horn', with some specifically noted as elephant tusks, mammoth tusks, and sperm whale teeth; the minerals categorised as 'jade' include jadeite, nephrite, and other materials. Curatorial research on these objects, their materials, and categorisations has led to questions that the current analysis can better answer.

Chinese artisans imported mammoth ivory from Siberia for their carvings for hundreds of years, and so it was of interest to know whether some toggles were made from mammoth tusks. It was known that Indian elephants' tusks had been used for more than a thousand years, and African tusks were used since the eleventh century, beginning with the Song dynasty (960–1279). Could mammoth ivory be identified among the toggles?[4]

To properly understand the materiality, cultural context and production methods of toggles, XRF and other methods were incorporated within a multi-disciplinary approach. By combining expertise across disciplines, this project presents a unique opportunity that fuses curatorial and conservation knowledge with cutting-edge scientific research to better understand the processes and production methods behind cultural objects and the materials they are made from.

Scientific analysis is pivotal to improving our understanding of the materials and the practices that contribute to cultural heritage. Furthermore, it provides the foundational information required to optimise the techniques used in research, conservation, preservation and restoration. The rare nature of objects in cultural collections demands analysis techniques that do not cause damage or irreversible change—that is, non-destructive techniques. It is also important that the methods employed allow for rapid data collection to handle the large scale of material that requires analysis.

Initial identification of ivory, horn, bone, and jade

Conservators routinely assess the condition of objects and are trained in identifying the materials and methods of production. An initial macroscopic examination of the morphology of those Chinese toggles nominated as ivory and bone was carried out by museum conservators. Horn and bone were included in the analysis, as there can be misattribution of these materials as ivory, a more prestigious material that makers could try to emulate with these more available, cheaper options.

Criteria for the identification of ivory and assignment to a particular species included the presence of Schreger lines visible in the cross-sectioned material and then by quantifying the angle formed by the intersection of the Schreger lines to ascertain whether the cementum enamel junction is visible. Schreger lines that formed an angle of <100 degrees are categorised as mammoth, while Schreger lines that formed an angle of >100 degrees are categorised as elephant (fig. 6.1A).[5] Criteria for the identification of horn or bone included the

A. Elephant

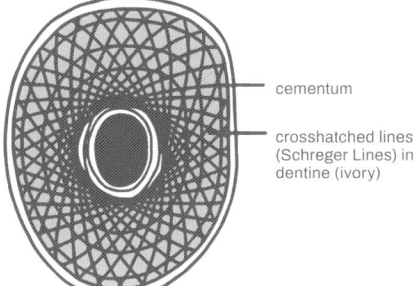

cementum

crosshatched lines
(Schreger Lines) in
dentine (ivory)

B. Walrus

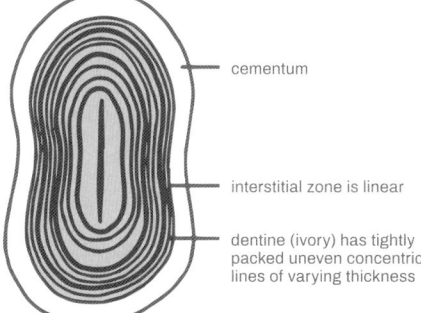

concentric rings in cementum

primary dentine (ivory)

transition ring

a secondary dentine wuith
marbled or "oatmeal"
apperaence

C. Warthog

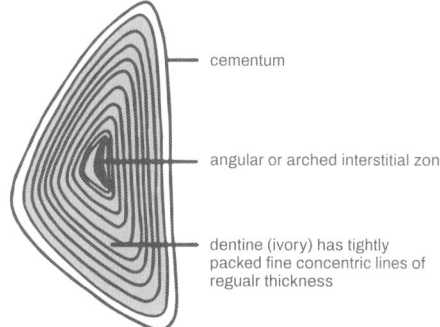

cementum

interstitial zone is linear

dentine (ivory) has tightly
packed uneven concentric
lines of varying thickness

D. Hippopotamus

cementum

angular or arched interstitial zone

dentine (ivory) has tightly
packed fine concentric lines of
regualr thickness

E. Sperm and killer whales

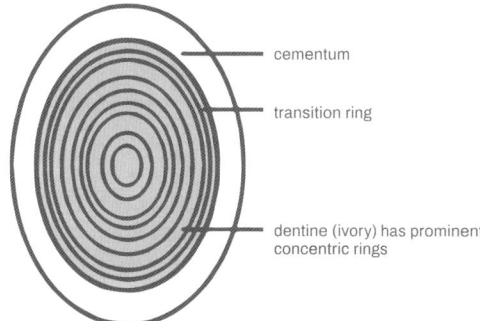

cementum

transition ring

dentine (ivory) has prominent
concentric rings

Fig. 6.1: Schematic diagrams of
different types of ivory illustrating
the key features, including
Schreger lines, that are used to
distinguish between species.
Copyright N. Sotoudeh (Mucca Design).

presence of a textured central area porous in nature, exhibiting blood vessels or nerve pits, and a visible dentine layer.

Twenty-nine toggles were assessed by four conservators. Twenty-eight toggles had been noted as ivory in the Museum's accessioning description and one as horn. After macroscopic examination, however, one toggle could not be confirmed as ivory, and two toggles that were accessioned as ivory were identified as either bone or horn. Of the remaining twenty-five toggles identified as ivory, three had contested species attribution; on morphology alone, and without microscopic analysis at higher magnification to reveal the Schreger lines, conservators could not agree if they were elephant or mammoth.

There are well-documented limitations to macroscopic examination of morphology in small, carved ivory objects, including inability to detect with the naked eye a clear cementum-dentine junction, which is used to orient the sample to confirm the outer Schreger lines. Other limitations can relate to possible disruption and distortion of the Schreger lines. These type of changes in ivory morphology can result from the carving and working of the object, overworking the surface to obtain a glossy finish, painted and decorative finishes applied to the object, or from physical damage resulting in the loss of material.

Scientific identification

Scientific analysis allows for objective identification to confirm or correct the suspected materiality of an object that has been classified based on a visual assessment. To investigate the elemental compositions and chemical compositions of ivory and jade in this project, a combination of X-ray fluorescence (XRF) and the vibrational spectroscopic techniques of near-infrared (NIR) and Raman spectroscopy were employed.

Elements within any material are arranged in a specific configuration unique to that material and are held together by chemical bonds. In some instances, using only one technique can provide material identification, but, typically multiple techniques are used for improved specificity and selectivity. XRF spectroscopy is used to identify the elements present within a sample—for instance iron (Fe), silicon (Si), or calcium (Ca)—and vibrational spectroscopy is used to understand the chemical environments of molecules. A deeper understanding of the chemical structure of the samples can be achieved through these two forms of data analysis working alongside each other, leading to better classification of the toggles.

XRF spectroscopy is widely used for the analysis of cultural heritage objects and historical materials, often employed as an initial tool for gaining an elemental understanding of material composition. When a sample is irradiated with high-energy X-rays, the sample will emit fluorescent X-rays of a specific energy level that is characteristic for each element. Advancements in portability, affordability, sensitivity and detection limits have given rise to the widespread use of hand-held units in conservation labs, and in the field for the assessment of samples in remote locations.

Vibrational spectroscopy (comprised of infrared and Raman spectroscopy) measures the energy required by chemical bonds within a sample to vibrate when exposed to infrared (IR) or, in the case of Raman spectroscopy, NIR, visible or ultraviolet (UV) radiation. These interactions produce a spectrum, which then provides information about the chemical composition and molecular

A

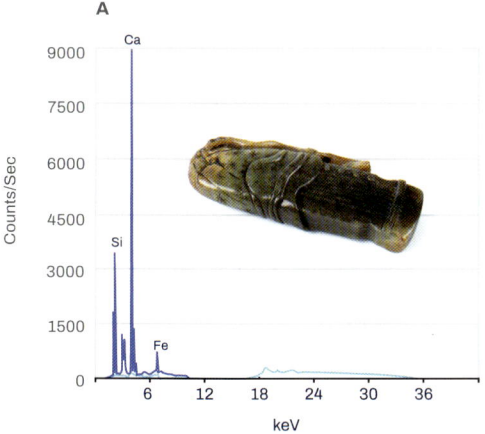

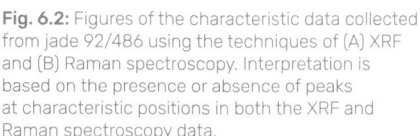

B

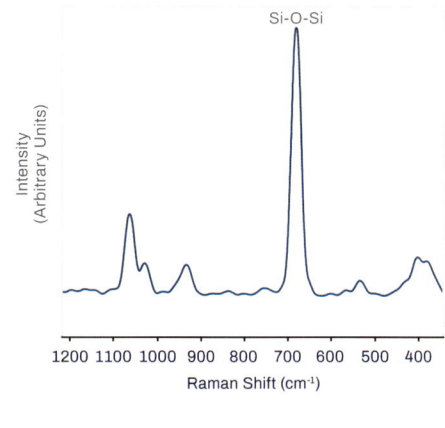

Fig. 6.2: Figures of the characteristic data collected from jade 92/486 using the techniques of (A) XRF and (B) Raman spectroscopy. Interpretation is based on the presence or absence of peaks at characteristic positions in both the XRF and Raman spectroscopy data.

structure of the sample. These techniques are widely used because they are non-destructive (and in some instances non-contact), require little to no sample preparation, and allow for in-situ analysis.

There is a range of instrumentation that allows for analysis from the microscopic level through to the macroscopic.

Figure 6.2 provides an example of data collected from a jade toggle (92/486) using XRF and Raman spectroscopy. The XRF spectrum (fig. 6.2A) is used to identify the various elements present within the sample, which are observed as narrow emission lines with characteristic energy for the elements silicon (Si), calcium (Ca), and iron (Fe). However, not all elements can be measured with this technique, in particular lighter elements such as carbon, hydrogen and oxygen. The corresponding Raman spectrum (figure 6.2B) was collected from the same object. The most intense peak is due to the chemical bonds that

exist between the silicon and oxygen atoms within the sample. This identifies the presence of oxygen, which is otherwise not able to be detected by XRF spectroscopy. By comparing the data across these two techniques, it is possible to identify the material, in this instance actinolite, which will be discussed in greater detail below.

Scientific analysis of ivory

For thousands of years, ivory has been used as a medium for artistic expression. Though ivory is known to be a rare material, it is also a generic term describing the teeth and tusks of marine and terrestrial mammals, such as the elephant, mammoth, sperm whale, hippopotamus, narwhal and walrus; wart hog and pig tusks also come under this classification.

Chemically, ivory contains both an organic and inorganic component. The organic component consists of collagen, which provides elasticity and tensile strength, making ivory particularly valuable as a carving medium.[6] The inorganic host matrix is carbonated hydroxyapatite ($Ca_{10}(PO_4)_6(CO_3)H_2O$), which provides ivory with its rigidity and compressional strength.

The vibrational technique of NIR spectroscopy has been traditionally used in the pharmaceutical and agricultural industries. NIR spectral data is rich in information from molecules that contain CH (carbon-hydrogen), NH (nitrogen-hydrogen) or OH (oxygen-hydrogen) groups.

Recent research has illustrated the potential of handheld NIR spectroscopy to distinguish between rhinoceros horn and ivory samples,[7] and to discriminate between ivory from African, wild Asian and domesticated Asian elephants.[8] Data analysis can be complicated due to broad overlapping bands (fig. 6.3A), which often require the use of multivariate statistical methods (also known as chemometrics) to enable information to be extracted from the spectra and presented visually as groupings of related material, converting data into knowledge.

Methodology

Samples

Eighty-eight objects were provided for analysis, which were originally categorised as elephant (twenty-three), mammoth or elephant (eighteen), ivory (thirty-three), unknown (eight), bone (one), tooth (three), antler horn (two).

NIR spectroscopy

All objects were investigated using a handheld spectrometer (MicroNIR OnSite, Viavi Solutions Inc., California, USA). The system consists of a linear variable filter, an indium gallium arsenide (InGaAs) array detector, and two vacuum-sealed tungsten lamps as radiation source. This spectrometer acquires data over the spectral range of 908–1676 nm (11013–5966 cm^{-1}), related to second and third overtones of the C-H, O-H and N-H bands, and is optimal for diffuse reflectance sampling. Experimental parameters used were based on the Power et al. 2018 study.[9] Spectra were collected by measuring each toggle at five random positions on each side for a total of 10 spectra per object. Data were collected in diffuse reflectance mode, with an integration time of 12.7 ms and the co-addition of 100 scans.

Data analysis

Spectra were imported into VEKTOR DIREKTOR (Ver 1.1 KAX Group, Australia). VEKTOR DIREKTOR is a chemometrics software platform that allows the investigation of complex spectroscopic data using exploratory, multivariate regression and multivariate classification methods. The main method of analysis used was principal component analysis (PCA) on processed spectra.

Results and discussion

An example of the data collected from the handheld NIR system is presented in figure 6.3A. Characteristic spectral features are attributed to proteins (C–H from collagen, N–H from protein residues), and water (O–H) that interacts with proteins. Although the broad spectral features are difficult to interpret, there is a wealth of data that can be mined using multivariate statistical analysis (MVA or chemometrics). MVA is used to investigate the variability of the data and its source (exploratory data analysis), to allow model(s) to be developed to predict, for instance, the identity of any toggles analysed in the future (multivariate classification). In this study, principal component analysis (PCA) was the technique used to explore the NIR data collected from the toggles. PCA is used to find the hidden structure within large, complex data sets revealing important groupings, and allowing for visualisation of data trends.[10]

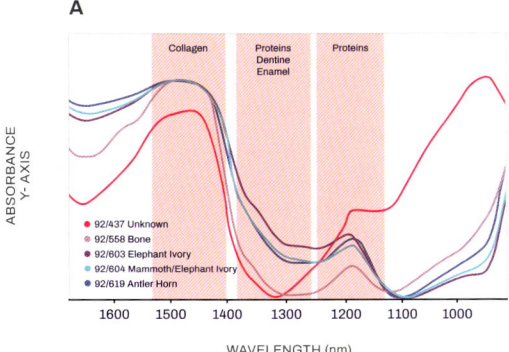

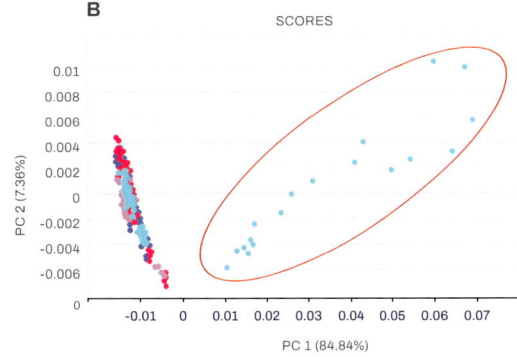

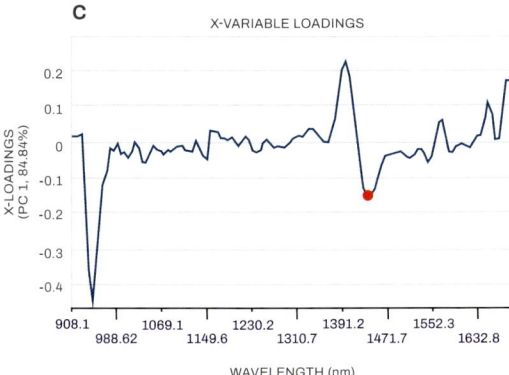

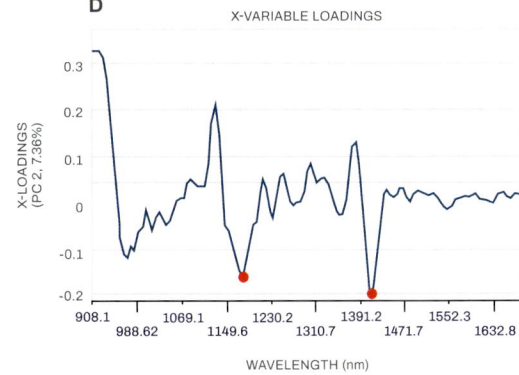

Fig. 6.3: (A) Characteristic near infrared (NIR) data collected from representative toggle groups illustrating the broad spectral features and similar profile obtained from a subset of the toggles. Principal component analysis (PCA) of NIR data illustrating the influence of pigment. (B) PC1 vs PC2 scores plot showing two clusters of data, the red circle surrounds data collected from the highly pigmented objects. (C) and (D) Loadings plots for PC1 and PC2, respectively, with red dots highlighting the CH functionality which separate objects 92/437 and 92/477. The loadings between 900–950 nm confirm that these objects have more pigment than the other toggles.

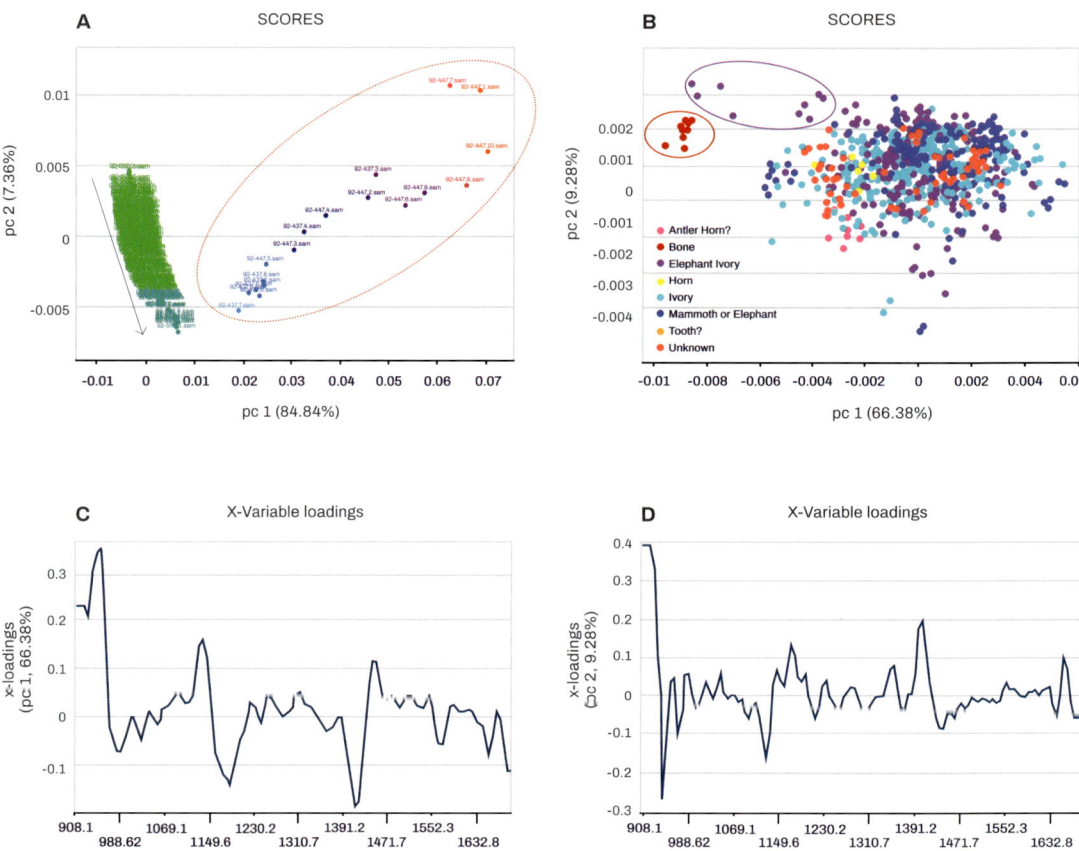

Fig. 6.4: (A) PCA scores plot, as seen in Fig. 6.3(B) plotted to investigate the intensity of the variable at 945 nm. Objects 92/437 and 92/447 show a little overlap, however, object 92/447 may be more intensely coloured than 92/437. A potential colour trend is observed in the negative PC2 direction, likely associated with reduced amounts of pigmentation. (B) Recalculated PCA scores plot with data from objects 92/437 and 92/447 removed. The objects classed as bone (red circle) are separated from the ivory objects and due to the small sample size, this is an indicative observation. Data collected from object 92/608 (purple circle) clusters between the bone and ivory toggles, and potentially is representative of an object made from bone. (C) and (D) are the loadings plots for PC1 and PC2, respectively. The PC1 loadings of this model are the same as the PC2 loadings of the previous model (Fig. 6.3C) indicating that the PC1 loadings of the first model were attributable to the highly pigmented objects.

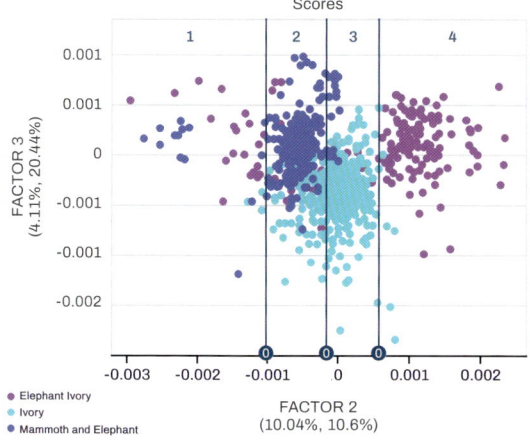

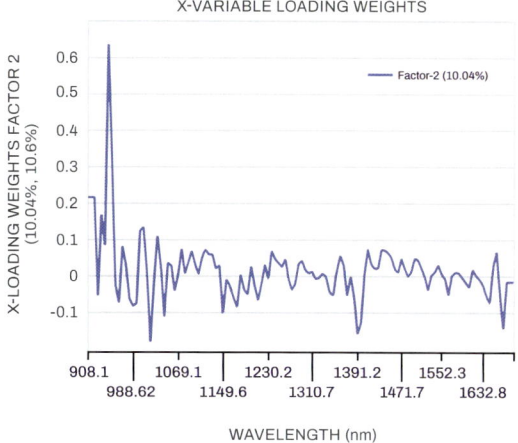

Fig. 6.5: (A) Factor 2 vs. Factor 3 scores plot shows a much clearer separation of the objects into distinct groups and reveals the potential misclassification of some elephant ivory toggles as mammoth. (B) Variable loadings plot.

Figures 6.3B–D present a series of plots from the initial PCA of the data collected from all eighty-eight samples. Figure 6.3B is a scores plot, a map of the sample relationships, illustrating that most of the data is similar and clusters together, with a second dispersed group separated along both axes, PC1 and PC2. These axes are the principal components (PCs) that describe the variability in terms of trends or, in some cases, the differences as unique clusters in a data set. The plots in figures 6.3C and 6.3D, called loadings plots, are used to identify what variable(s) are being used to describe the observed trends or clusters. Preliminary analysis revealed a pair of toggles, objects 92/437 and 92/447, as outliers, which was attributed to the pigments applied to them (red-circled data in figure 6.3B). The loadings plots of PCs 1 and 2 in figures 6.3C and D, respectively, describe

~92% of the total data variability and confirm the influence of the pigments on these objects, as seen in the 950–900 nm region, which is typically associated with the onset of colour, due to proximity to the visible region of the electromagnetic spectrum. In figure 6.4A, the data has been grouped and colour-coded, based on the intensity of the absorbance band at 945 nm. This data suggests that object 92/447 is more intensely coloured than 92/437. In addition, there appears to be a potential trend in the data, circled in the red dotted line, suggesting varying colour levels, possibly related to the heterogeneity of the sample being assessed by NIR.

One of these pigmented ivory toggles, 92/447, is a basic button-shaped disc. It has a central, mottled dark-green band, flanked by a lighter olive-green colour. From its appearance, one would not identify this material as ivory.

Attribution	Scientific	Curatorial / Conservation		
Object Number and description	**Zone**	**Morrison's catalogue (c. 1946)**	**Powerhouse catalogue (post 1992)**	**Australian Museum (2022)***
92/608 Dress accessory, toggle, ivory, monkey holding baby, China, c. 1700-1940	1, 2	Elephant	Mammoth	Mammoth
92/612 Dress accessory, toggle, basket vase of flowers, ivory, China, c. 1700-1940	1, 2	Elephant	Elephant	Elephant
92/617 Dress accessory, toggle, Plant of Immortality, ivory, China, c. 1700-1940	1	Elephant	Elephant	Elephant
92/622 Dress accessory, toggle, in the shape of a slice of lotus root, ivory, China, 1700-1940	1, 2	Elephant	Elephant	Elephant
92/603 Dress accessory, toggle, lantern, ivory / metal, China, c. 1700-1940	2	Elephant	Mammoth	Mammoth
92/606 Dress accessory, toggle, ball, ivory / metal, China, c. 1700-1940	2	Elephant	Mammoth	Mammoth
92/613 Dress accessory, toggle, butterfly, ivory, China, c. 1700-1940	2	Elephant	Elephant	Elephant
92/677 Dress accessory, toggle, spreader, ivory, China, c. 1700-1940	2, 3	Elephant	Elephant	–
92/676 Dress accessory, toggle, ivory / metal, China, c. 1700-1940	3	Elephant	Elephant	Elephant
92/683 Dress accessory, toggle, in the shape of an egg, ivory, China, c. 1700-1940	3	Elephant	Mammoth	Mammoth
92/625 Dress accessory, toggle, Buddha's hand citron, lotus, ivory, China, c. 1700-1940	4	Elephant	Mammoth	Mammoth
92/632 Dress accessory, toggle, fig, ivory, China, c. 1700-1940	4	Elephant	Elephant	Elephant
92/640 Dress accessory, toggle, walnut, ivory, China, c. 1700-1940	4	Elephant	Elephant	Elephant
92/643 Dress accessory, toggle, lotus, ivory, China, c. 1700-1940	4	Elephant	Mammoth	Mammoth
92/644 Dress accessory, toggle, lotus pod, ivory, China, c. 1700-1940	4	Elephant	Elephant	Elephant
92/654 Dress accessory, toggle, mythical lion, ivory, China, c. 1700-1940	4	Elephant	Elephant	Mammoth
92/658 Dress accessory, toggle, lion, ivory, China, c. 1700-1940	4	Elephant	Elephant	Mammoth
92/659 Dress accessory, toggle, lion, ivory, China, c. 1700-1940	4	Elephant	Elephant	Elephant
92/661 Dress accessory, toggle, in the shape of old man holding sceptre, ivory, China, c. 1700-1940	4	Elephant	Elephant	Elephant
92/663 Dress accessory, toggle, in the shape of a reclining scholar with a long beard, ivory, China, 1700-1940	4	Elephant	Elephant	Elephant
92/667 Dress accessory, toggle, pine tree, ivory, China, c. 1700-1940	4	Elephant	Elephant	Elephant
92/672 Dress accessory, toggle, prunus flower, ivory, China, c. 1700-1940	4	Elephant	Elephant	Elephant
92/683 Dress accessory, toggle, in the shape of an egg, ivory, China, c. 1700-1940	3	Elephant	Mammoth	Mammoth
92/684 Dress accessory, toggle, in the shape of an egg, ivory / textile, China, c. 1700-1940	?	Mammoth or Elephant	Mammoth	Elephant
92/686 Dress accessory, toggle, temple slit drum, ivory, China, c. 1700-1940	4	Elephant	Mammoth	Mammoth
Dyed Toggles				
92/447 Dress accessory, toggle, button-shaped disc, probably ivory or bone, China, c. 1700-1940	–	Unknown	Walrus tusk	Walrus
92/437 Dress accessory, toggle, tusk point, ivory, China, c. 1700-1940	–	Unknown	Antler	Antler

*At the invitation of the Powerhouse in 2022, conservators from the Australian Museum were invited to macroscopically inspect the toggles for comparison with the original attributions.

Table 1: Summary of curatorial re-evaluation of ivory toggles based on factorial analysis of NIR spectra. Tentative identification based on statistical analysis of NIR data in four zones: Zone 1 - Inconclusive, Zone 2 - Mammoth, Zone 3 - Ivory (non-descript), Zone 4 - Elephant Ivory

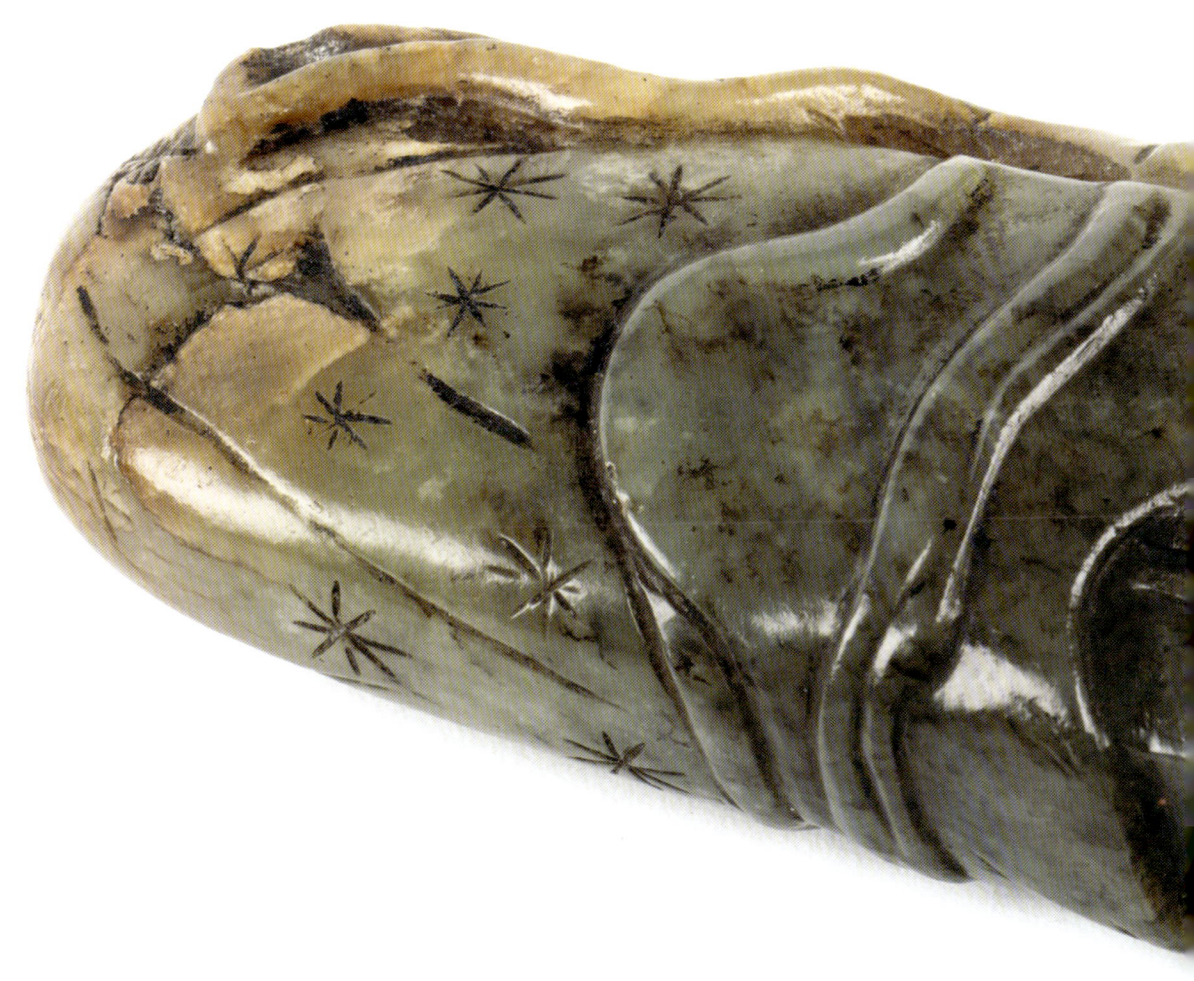

With this deliberate colouring and highly polished surface, the maker might have been trying to mimic the texture and appearance of jade, which was culturally considered more precious than ivory.

The data was re-analysed after removing the strongly influencing data collected from the pigmented 92/447 and 92/437 (fig. 6.4B). This revealed that the object originally categorised as bone (data circled in red) was now more distinctly grouped away from the ivory objects. The data from object 92/608 (circled in purple) is also observed to cluster closely next to bone, suggesting that this object is bone, not elephant ivory. This is an indicative observation at this stage, and any future study would require an increased number of bone objects to build a more robust statistical model.

A general assessment was undertaken to determine the identification of the unknown toggle material (data not shown). Examination of two objects (92/675 and 92/682) of unidentified material was assessed against antler horn, other horn and bone. This suggested that the two objects possibly identify as antler horn; neither object was classified as bone. Further analysis was undertaken using the multivariate classification method known as partial least squares discriminant analysis (PLS-DA). Figure 6.5 shows a much clearer separation of toggles broadly categorised as ivory into four distinct groups and reveals the potential for misclassification of some elephant ivory sample objects as mammoth. The PLS-DA algorithm considers previous classification assessments, using trained assessors to classify the data, and can be used in conjunction with NIR spectroscopy to determine whether subjective analyses can be objectively verified.

The tentative identification of groups in the four zones are (1) mammoth (2) mammoth (3) ivory (non-descript) and (4) elephant ivory. Based on this information, a total of twenty-seven objects, overlapping in the zones, were identified for curatorial re-evaluation (table 1). Close examination of the information in table 1 reveals that seven of the objects originally believed to be elephant ivory were re-attributed to mammoth ivory. In several instances, the visual assessment by the curators differed (for example, objects 92/654 and 92/658), highlighting the benefits of non-subjective techniques to support the visual assessment of these material types.

Conclusion of ivory analysis

NIR spectroscopy is a rapid and inexpensive technique that offers an attractive option for satisfying all the non-invasive criteria that are required by a collecting institution for sample analysis. In this study eighty-eight toggles were analysed by collecting data from ten areas per sample within approximately six hours, and the data was then analysed with a range of multivariate statistical analyses. This allows for rapid screening of the objects and can confirm the initial attribution of objects by the curators, potentially highlighting objects that may have been misclassified and thus require further examination, both visually and spectroscopically. Twenty-seven objects were identified as requiring re-evaluation. In several instances, the visual assessment by the conservators differed from the original curators' identification, highlighting the need for a non-subjective technique to support the visual assessment of these material types.

Compositional analysis of jade

Jade (*yu*) is a broad term that can include many types of rocks and minerals.[11] Rocks are made from the solid crystals of one or more minerals, while minerals are composed of elements. Broadly, amphibole, serpentine, turquoise and agate were considered the four main types of jade rocks in imperial China (see chapter 5, p. 98).[12] In the broader Chinese context, the range of rocks and minerals considered to be jade is vast, ranging from anorthite, zoisite and malachite to variscite, amblygonite, pyrophyllite and beyond.[13] Amphibole was the most significant of the four jades most prized in China.[14] For the purposes of the investigation of the toggles from the Powerhouse Collection, jade has been categorised into three main groups: amphibole jade, serpentine jade and other jades.

Jade has been used as a culturally significant material around the world, in areas such as Taiwan, New Zealand and Mesoamerica.[15] *Pounamu* in New Zealand, also known as greenstone, is generally considered nephrite but can encompass semi-nephrite, bowenite and serpentinite.[16] The earliest examples of worked jade in China can be traced back to the early Neolithic site of Xiaonanshan in Heilongjiang Province.[17] The prominence and significance of jade in the mid to late Neolithic period in China is highlighted by the term *yuqi shidai* (玉器时代), 'Jade Age'.[18] Jade was first used in ancient rituals as offerings to heaven and a medium through which to communicate with the gods.[19] During the Zhou Dynasty (1046–256 BCE), grouped jade pendants were worn as belt accessories by aristocrats and cultural elites, as symbols of social status and virtue.[20] Only kings of the Zhou wore grouped pendants made of amphibole or serpentine jade, demonstrating

the greater prestige associated with these jade types. Other aristocrats wore a mixture of jades and other stones, such as agate, turquoise and crystal.[21]

Amphibole jade

Amphibole jade is also commonly known as nephrite. Nephrite can be a mixture of tremolite-ferro-actinolite group minerals with a felted microcrystalline habit.[22] Nephrite jade consists of sodium, magnesium, iron, silicon, oxygen and hydrogen ('ideal' formula: $Ca_2(Mg,Fe)_5Si_8O_{22}(OH)_2$). Semi-nephrite, a tremolite-ferro-actinolite series rock without the felted crystal texture, can also be considered an amphibole jade.[23]

Serpentine jade

Serpentine jade generally refers to jadeite, a pyroxene mineral rock with a non-fibrous texture.[24] Jadeite is composed of sodium (Na), aluminium (Al), silicon (Si) and oxygen (O) ('ideal' formula: $NaAl(Si_2O_6)$). Serpentine can also encompass serpentine minerals such as antigorite ('ideal formula: $Mg_6(Si_4O_{10})(OH)_8$), lizardite and chrysotile.

Other jades

For this case study 'other jades' will include rocks and minerals that do not fall under the amphibole or serpentine umbrellas.

Data analysis

Toggles 92/454, 92/472 and 92/486 were selected for compositional analysis as a preliminary investigation into the jade toggle collection held by Powerhouse. Raman and X-ray spectroscopy are well established analytical techniques used for the identification of jade. All data was collected at Powerhouse in Sydney, using portable and handheld instruments, allowing for the rapid, non-destructive and in-situ analysis of the toggles.

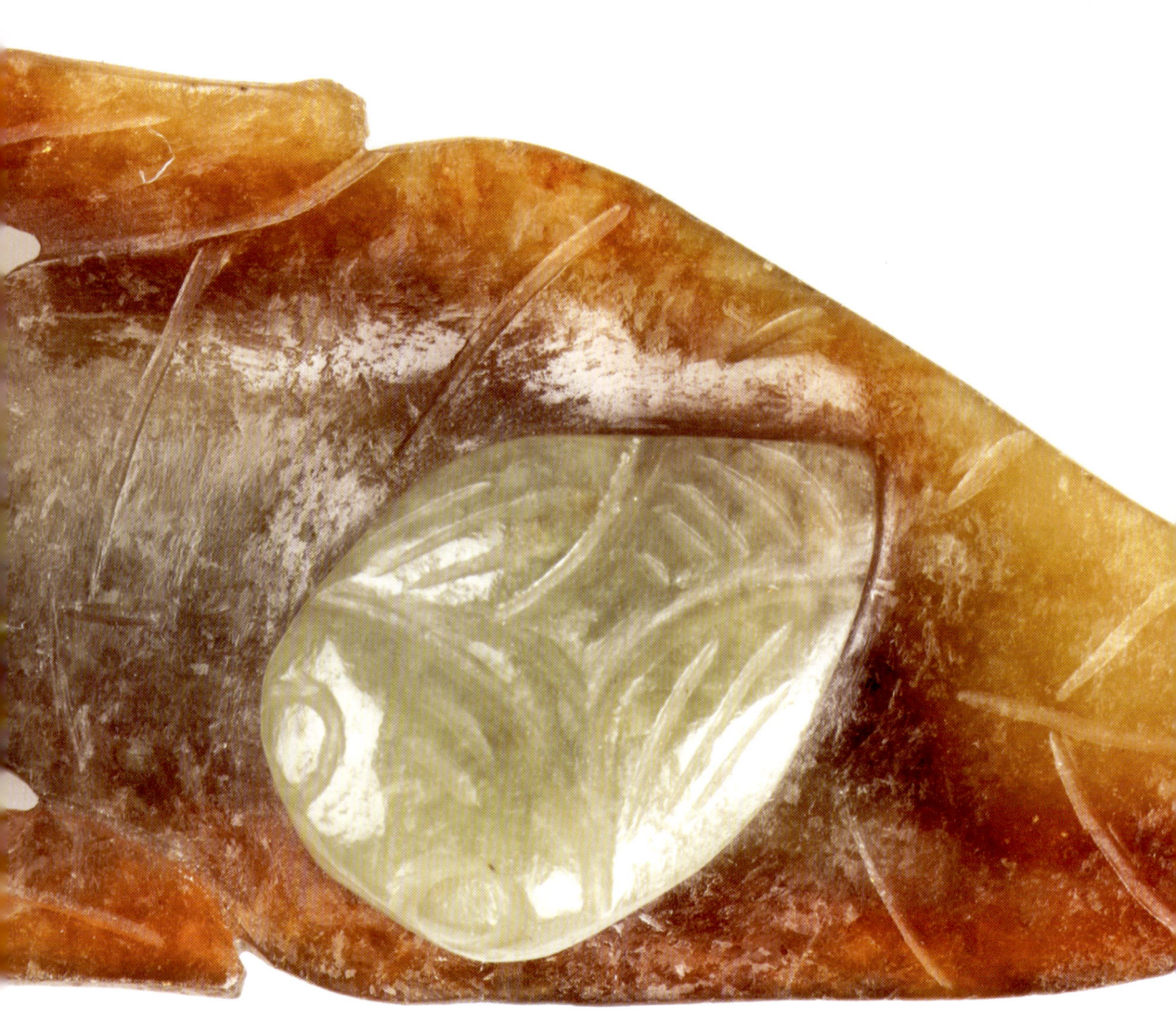

The jade toggle carved in the shape of a *qin* wrapped in textile (92/486, plate 63, p. 226) reminds us of one of the 'four arts' of Chinese scholars: mastery of the *qin*, a stringed instrument like a zither. Such motifs of the Chinese zither could also be found in the 'Attributes of a Scholar' jade toggle (92/454, plate 24, p. 186). As discussed in chapter 5, the choice of jade for this toggle was deliberate, representing the cultured nature of a gentleman. According to B*ook of Rites: Jade Algae*, one of the core classics in the Confucius canon describing ceremonial rites of the Zhou dynasty, edited during the Warring States period (c. 475–221 BCE) and early Han dynasty (206 BCE–220 CE), 'the ancient gentleman must wear jade any time, and the jade does not leave his body without special reason.'

Methodology

Samples

A total of thirty-four objects were identified by Raman spectroscopy as amphibole (twenty-one), serpentine (four), other materials (four), inconclusive (five). This section focuses on toggles 92/454, 92/472 and 92/486.

Raman spectroscopy

Raman spectra were collected using a Bruker Raman BRAVO handheld spectrometer (Bruker, Ettlingen, Germany) with sample excitation achieved using a Duo LASER™. The latter instrument uses patented Sequentially Shifted Excitation (SSE™) technology to mitigate fluorescence issues often encountered with Raman analysis. The Duo LASER™ system uses two laser lines emitting at 785 and 852 nm, coupled to a CCD detector. Data was collected from 3200 to 300 cm^{-1}. The BRAVO handheld spectrometer has a fixed optical head, and

data was collected directly from the toggles. The flattest and smoothest surface of the object was selected, to ensure that the toggle was in direct contact with the sampling window and in focus. Spectra were acquired from multiple areas of each toggle in triplicate. The sample spot size was 2 mm. Data was collected and processed using OPUS™ software (Bruker, Ettlingen, Germany).

X-ray fluorescence

Elemental analysis was conducted using an Olympus Vanta Handheld XRF device (Olympus Corporation of Americas, Waltham, Massachusetts, USA). The XRF device was used with the preset Geochem2 method with a scan time of 40s (20s of 40kV energy beam, 71 µA and 20s of 10 kV energy beam, 83 µA). Spectra were collected from the smoothest and flattest area of the toggle, to ensure the sample was in maximum contact with the XRF window.

Results and discussion

Figures 6.6 to 6.8 show the data collected with Raman and XRF approaches from toggles 92/454, 92/472 and 92/486.

The use of Raman spectroscopy and portable X-ray fluorescence (XRF) assist in the chemical and elemental characterisation of sample 92/454 (fig. 6.6). The Raman spectrum of this sample (fig. 6.6a) and reference spectrum (fig. 6.6b) identifies the presence of antigorite ('ideal' formula: $Mg_6(Si_4O_{10})(OH)_8$) and can be categorised as a serpentine jade. Figure 6.6c presents the XRF data and confirms the presence of high levels of magnesium and low levels of silicon, calcium and iron impurities.

Figures 6.7a and b compare a Raman spectrum collected from toggle 92/472 and a reference spectrum of jadeite. The corresponding XRF data indicates high levels of silicon and aluminium (fig.6.7a, 'ideal' formula: $NaAl(Si_2O_6)$).

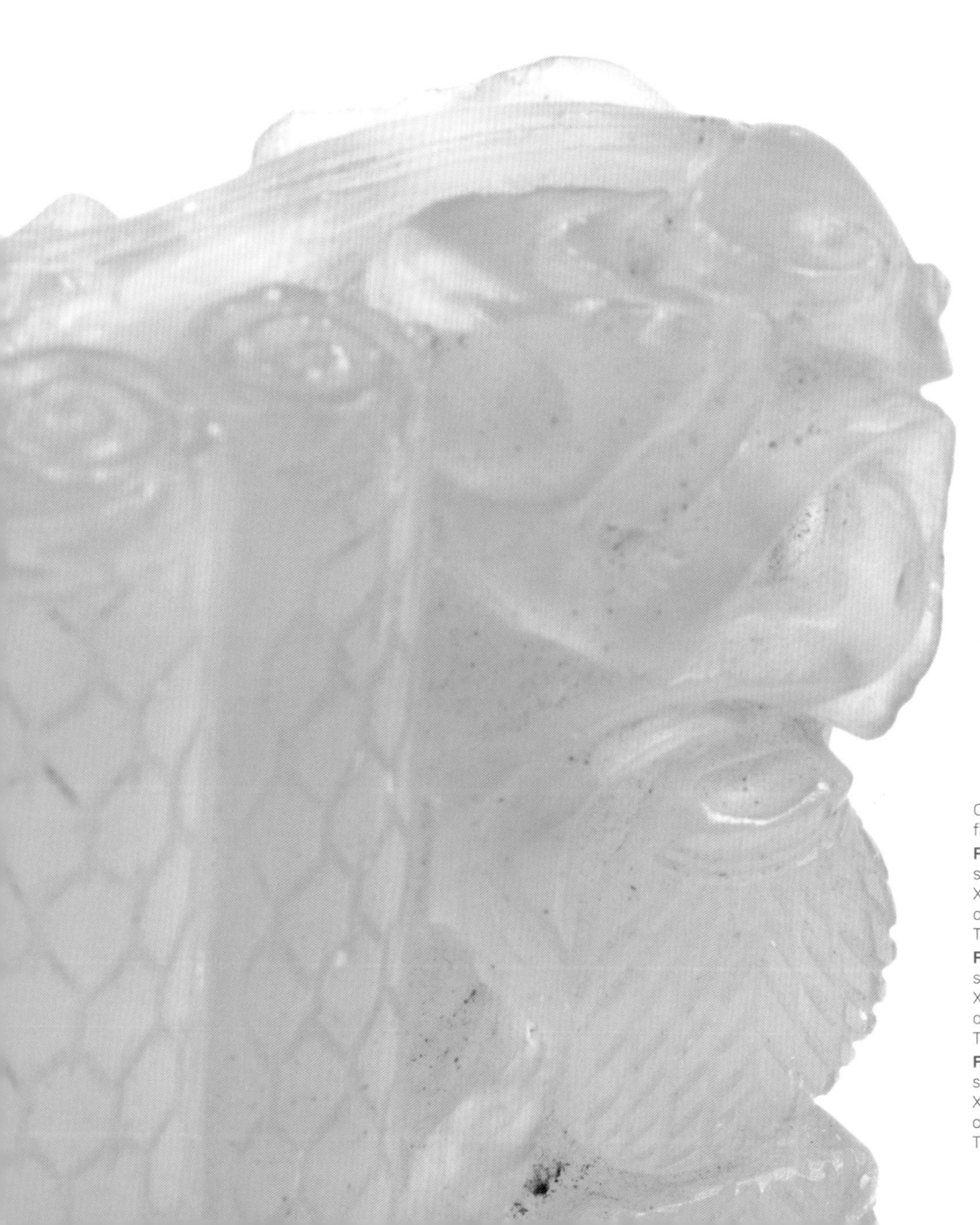

Opposite
from top:
Fig. 6.6: Raman
spectrum and
XRF data
collected from
Toggle 92/454.
Fig. 6.7: Raman
spectrum and
XRF data
collected from
Toggle 92/472.
Fig. 6.8: Raman
spectrum and
XRF data
collected from
Toggle 92/486.

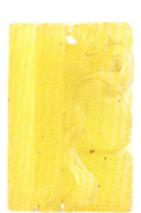

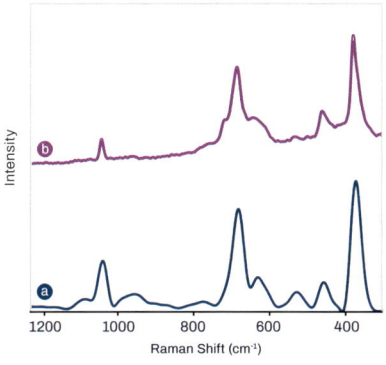

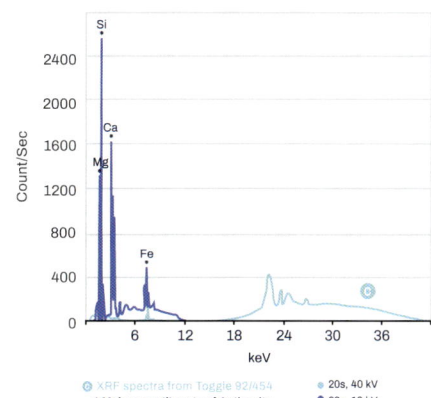

● a Raman spectrum from Toggle 92/454
● b Raman spectrum from Antigorite
(Lafuente B, Downs R T, Yang H, Stone N, 2015:R070228)

● c XRF spectra from Toggle 92/454   ● 20s, 40 kV
* Major constituents of Antigorite   ● 20s, 10 kV

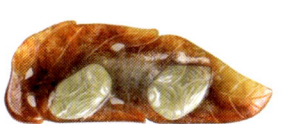

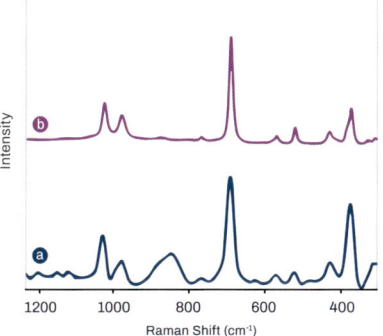

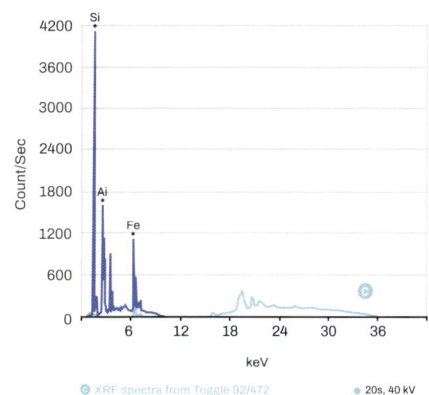

● a Raman spectrum from sample 92/472
● b Raman spectrum from Jadeite
(Laboratoire de Sciences de la Terre ENS-Lyon, 2022)

● c XRF spectra from Toggle 92/472   ● 20s, 40 kV
* Major constituents of Jadeite   ● 20s, 10 kV

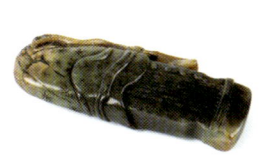

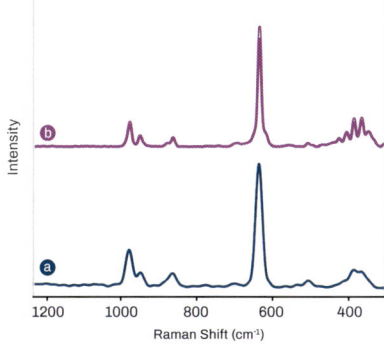

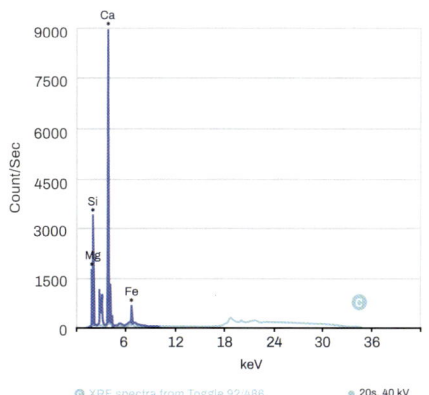

● a Raman spectrum from Toggle 92/486
● b Raman spectrum from Actinolite
(Lafuente B, Downs R T, Yang H, Stone N, 2015:X050001)

● c XRF spectra from Toggle 92/486   ● 20s, 40 kV
* Major constituents of Actinolite   ● 20s, 10 kV

Sodium (Na) is a light element (LE) and could not be measured, but the instrument calculated that the sample was comprised of 58.64% of LE. The Raman data identifies sample 92/472 as jadeite, a serpentine jade. This is further supported by the XRF data, which shows that no magnesium was detected in the toggle. Calcium, a common jadeite impurity, was detected in low concentrations.

The Raman spectrum of sample 92/486 (fig. 6.8a) is characteristic of actinolite, which is confirmed by the reference spectrum in figure 6.8b. The XRF data presented in figure 6.8a shows high amounts of Si, Mg, Ca and Fe, consistent with the 'ideal' formula of actinolite ($Ca_2(Mg,Fe^{2+})_5Si_8O_{22}(OH)_2$). The combined Raman and XRF data identify the presence of actinolite, suggesting that toggle 92/486 is a nephrite jade.

Using non-destructive analytical techniques, the chemical and elemental composition of toggles 92/454, 92/472 and 92/486 were characterised. Jade encompasses a wide range of materials, and the tested toggles fall underthe two major categories: amphibole jade and serpentine jade. The results of the XRF and Raman data reveals that the three jade toggles were composed of actinolite, jadeite and antigorite minerals.

Conclusion of jade analysis

XRF and Raman data provided complementary information to assist in the characterisation of toggles 92/454, 92/472 and 92/486. The in-situ analysis of the museum objects was rapid and non-invasive. The data obtained allows for the quick screening of artefacts that have been visually categorised as jade. The materials used to create these intricate jade toggles include actinolite, jadeite and antigorite. Characteristic Raman data allowed for discrimination between the different types of jade, with the XRF spectroscopic results providing supporting evidence.

Conclusion

Our understanding of the materiality of toggles has been enhanced by targeted scientific analysis conducted on toggles composed of ivory (elephant, mammoth, bone, antler/horn) and jade (amphibole, serpentine), using vibrational spectroscopic techniques of near infrared and Raman spectroscopy and X-ray fluorescence (XRF), respectively. Combined with visual and multivariate data analysis, this multi-disciplinary study demonstrates the value of questioning attributions to give greater clarity to a collection of this material complexity. Thanks to this analysis, the Powerhouse Collection is better understood and cultural objects can be presented to audiences with confidence.

1. The tested Chinese toggles in this study are identified with object numbers of Powerhouse Museum. For more details of these toggles, visit Powerhouse Museum website https://collection.powerhouse.com.au/ for a collection search using the object no.

2. Hedda and Alastair Morrison, 'Chinese Toggles: A Little Known Folk Art', *Arts of Asia*, vol. 16, no. 2, 1986, pp. 68–75.

3. The Powerhouse Collection was first presented at a symposium *Beijing-Xanadu: Past, Present and Future*, TAASA (The Asian Arts Society of Australia) 26 July 2008. A small exhibition titled Chinese Belt Toggles, which exhibited at the Powerhouse (4 July–27 September 2008). See 'Chinese belt toggles', *Australian Decorative & Fine Arts Societies*, vol. 17, no. 1, 2008.

4. Olga Krzyszkowska, *Classical Handbook 3: Ivory and Related Materials*, British Institute of Classical Studies, London, 1990, p. 22. On a world scale it has been estimated that during the nineteenth century alone, the trade in mammoth ivory reached enormous numbers. It is estimated that over the last 300 years the tusks of at least 45,000 mammoth have been sold. Referencing S. K. Eltringham, *Elephants*, Blandforde Press, Poole, 1982, p. 245.

5. Sarah Kelloway, Howell G.M. Edwards, Brad Swarbrick and Elizabeth A. Carter, 'Discrimination of Contraband Ivories Using Long Wavelength Portable *Raman* Instrumentation', in Peter Vandenabeele and Howell Edwards (eds), *Raman Spectroscopy in Archaeology and Art History*, 2018, pp. 123–40.

6. Howell G. M. Edwards and Dennis W. Farwell, 'Molecular and Biomolecular Spectroscopy', *Spectrochimica Acta Part A*, vol. 51, no. 12, 1995, pp. 2073–81; Howell G. M. Edwards, Dennis W. Farwell, T. Seddon and Jon K. F. Tait, 'Scrimshaw: Real or fake?

A Fourier-transform Raman diagnostic study', *Journal of Raman Spectroscopy*, vol. 26, no. 8–9, 1995, pp. 623–8. Michael D. Hargreaves, N. A. Macleod, Victoria L. Brewster, Tasmin Munshi, Howell G. M. Edwards and Pavel Matousek, 'Application of Portable Raman Spectroscopy and Benchtop Spatially Offset Raman Spectroscopy to Interrogate Concealed Biomaterials', *Journal of Raman Spectroscopy*, vol. 40, no. 12, 2009, pp. 1875–80.

7. A. C. Power, J Chapman, S. Chandra, J. J. Roberts, and D. Cozzolinio, 'Illuminating the Flesh of Bone Identification– an Application of Near Infrared Spectroscopy'. *Vibrational Spectroscopy*, vol. 98, 2018, pp. 64–8.

8. Apinya Chaitae, Ronnarit Rittiron, Iain J. Gordon, Helene Marsh, Jane Addison, Suttahatai Pochanagone and Nattakan Suttanon, 'Shining NIR light on ivory: A practical enforcement tool for elephant ivory identification', *Conservation Science and Practice*, vol. 3, no. 9, 2021, 486. doi 10.1111/csp2.486.

9. Power et al., 'Illuminating the flesh of bone identification'.

10. Brad Swarbrick, *Multivariate Data Analysis for Dummies*, Wiley, Chichester, 2012.

11. Rong Wang, 'Progress review of the scientific study of Chinese ancient jade', *Archaeometry*, vol. 53, no. 4, 2011, pp. 674–92.

12. Archaeological studies tend to classify amphibole, serpentine, turquoise and quartz types as the four main groups found in China. Rong Wang 王荣 and Wei-Shan Zhang, 'Application of Raman Spectroscopy in the Non-Destructive Analyses of Ancient Chinese Jades', *Journal of Raman Spectroscopy*, vol. 42, no. 6, 2011, pp. 1324–9.

13. Wang, 'Progress review of the scientific study of Chinese ancient jade'; Gu Yinghua 顾英华, ['历代玉器中闪石玉的材质分析' ['Material Analysis of

Amphibole Jade in Ancient Jade Artifacts'], 河南博物院刊 [*Henan Museum Journal*], no. 3, 2021, pp. 60–6.

14. Gu, '历代玉器中闪石玉的材质分析' ['Material Analysis of Amphibole Jade in Ancient Jade Artifacts'], p. 62.

15. Hsiao-Chun Hung, Yoshiyuki Iizuka, Peter Bellwood, Kim Dung Nguyen, Bérénice Bellina, Praon Silapanth, Eusebio Dizon, Rey Santiago, Ipoi Datan, and Jonathan M. Manton, 'Ancient Jades Map 3,000 Years of Prehistoric Exchange in Southeast Asia', *Proceedings of the National Academy of Sciences*, vol. 104, no. 50, 2007, 19745–50, doi: 10.1073/pnas.0707304104. Epub 2007 Nov 29. PMID: 18048347; PMCID: PMC2148369. Peter Coutts, 'Greenstone: the prehistoric exploitation of bowenite from Anita Bay, Milford Sound', *The Journal of the Polynesian Society*, vol. 80, no. 1, 1971, pp. 42–73; Winifred Creamer, 'Mesoamerica as a Concept: an Archaeological View from Central America', *Latin American Research Review*, vol. 22, no. 1, 1987, pp. 35–62.

16. Nicholas Matthew Cable, 'Greenstone Distribution Networks in Southern New Zealand', MA thesis. University of Otago, 2006.

17. Li Youqian 李有骞 and Yang Yongcai 杨永才, '黑龙江饶河县小南山遗址 2015 年 III 区发掘简报' ['Brief Report on the Excavation of Area III of the Xiaonanshan Site in Raohe County, Heilongjiang In 2015'], 考古 [*Kaogu*], no. 8, 2019, pp. 3–20.

18. Kwang-chih Chang, *The Archaeology of Ancient China*, Yale University Press, Connecticut, 1986; Elizabeth Childs-Johnson, 'Jade as Material and Epoch', in Sherman Lee (eds), *China: 5000 Years, Innovation and Transformation in the Arts*, Guggenheim Museum, New York, 1998, pp. 55–68; Elizabeth Childs-Johnson, 'The Jade Age Revisited,

ca. 3500–2000 BCE', in Elizabeth Childs-Johnson (ed), *The Oxford Handbook of Early China*, Oxford University Press, Oxford, 2020, pp. 101–17; Paola Demattè, 'The Chinese Jade Age: Between Antiquarianism and Archaeology', *Journal of Social Archaeology*, vol. 6, no. 2, 2006, pp. 202–26.

19. Shuyan Pei and Chuqiao Yu, 'Exploration on Jade Culture in West Liaohe River Basin in the Neolithic Age', *Advances in Social Science, Education and Humanities Research*, vol. 416, 2020, pp. 557–60.

20. Sun, Ji 孙机, '周代的组玉佩' ['On the Group Jade Body Ornament of Zhou Dynasty'], 文物 [*Cultural Relics*], no. 4, 1998, pp. 4–14; Ni Jianlin 倪建林, '战国时代的佩玉--中国古代玉器艺术鉴赏' ['Jade Pendants in the Warring States Period: Appreciating Chinese Ancient Jade'], 中国美术教育 [*Chinese Art Education*], no. 3, 2003, pp. 50–2.

21. Duo Limei 多丽梅, '佩玉将将: 组玉佩反映的古代礼仪等级制度' ['The Clanking of *Peiyu*: Grouped Jade Pendant and the Ancient Etiquette System'], 原道 [*Yuan Dao*], no. 2. 2015, p. 161.

22. George E. Harlow, Sorena S. Sorensen, Virginia B. Sisson, Guanghai Shi, 'The Geology of Jade Deposits', in Lee A. Groat (ed), *The Geology of Gem Deposits, Mineralogical Association of Canada Short-Course Series*, vol. 44, 2014, pp. 305–74.

23. Gina Barnes, 'Understanding Chinese Jade In A World Context', *Journal of the British Academy*, vol. 6, no. 1, 2018, pp. 1–63.

24. George E. Harlow and Sorena S. Sorensen, 'Jade (Nephrite And Jadeitite) and Serpentinite: Metasomatic Connections', *International Geology Review*, vol. 47, no. 2, 2005, pp. 113–46.

Part IV
Displaying culture in miniature

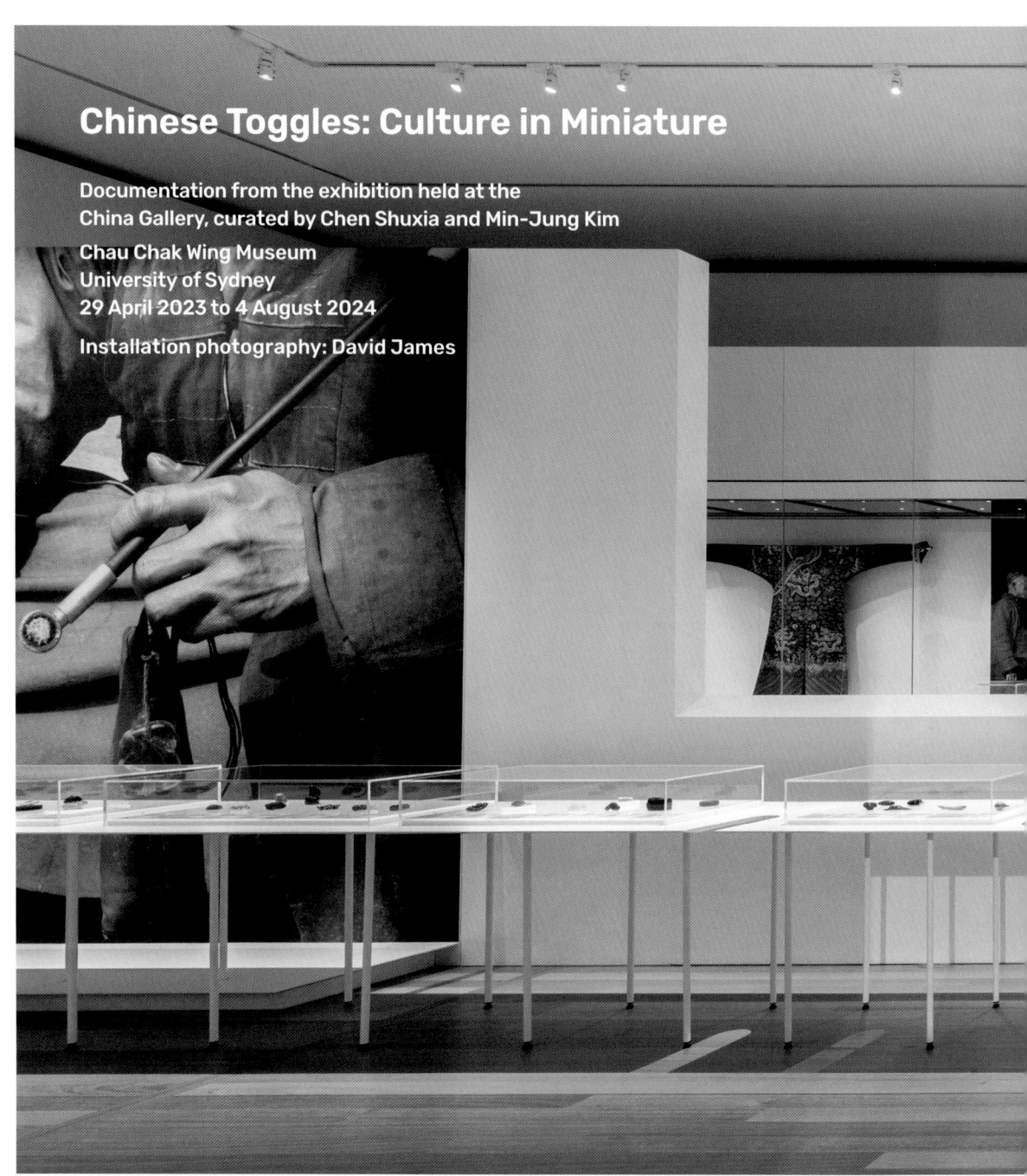

Chinese Toggles: Culture in Miniature

Documentation from the exhibition held at the
China Gallery, curated by Chen Shuxia and Min-Jung Kim

Chau Chak Wing Museum
University of Sydney
29 April 2023 to 4 August 2024

Installation photography: David James

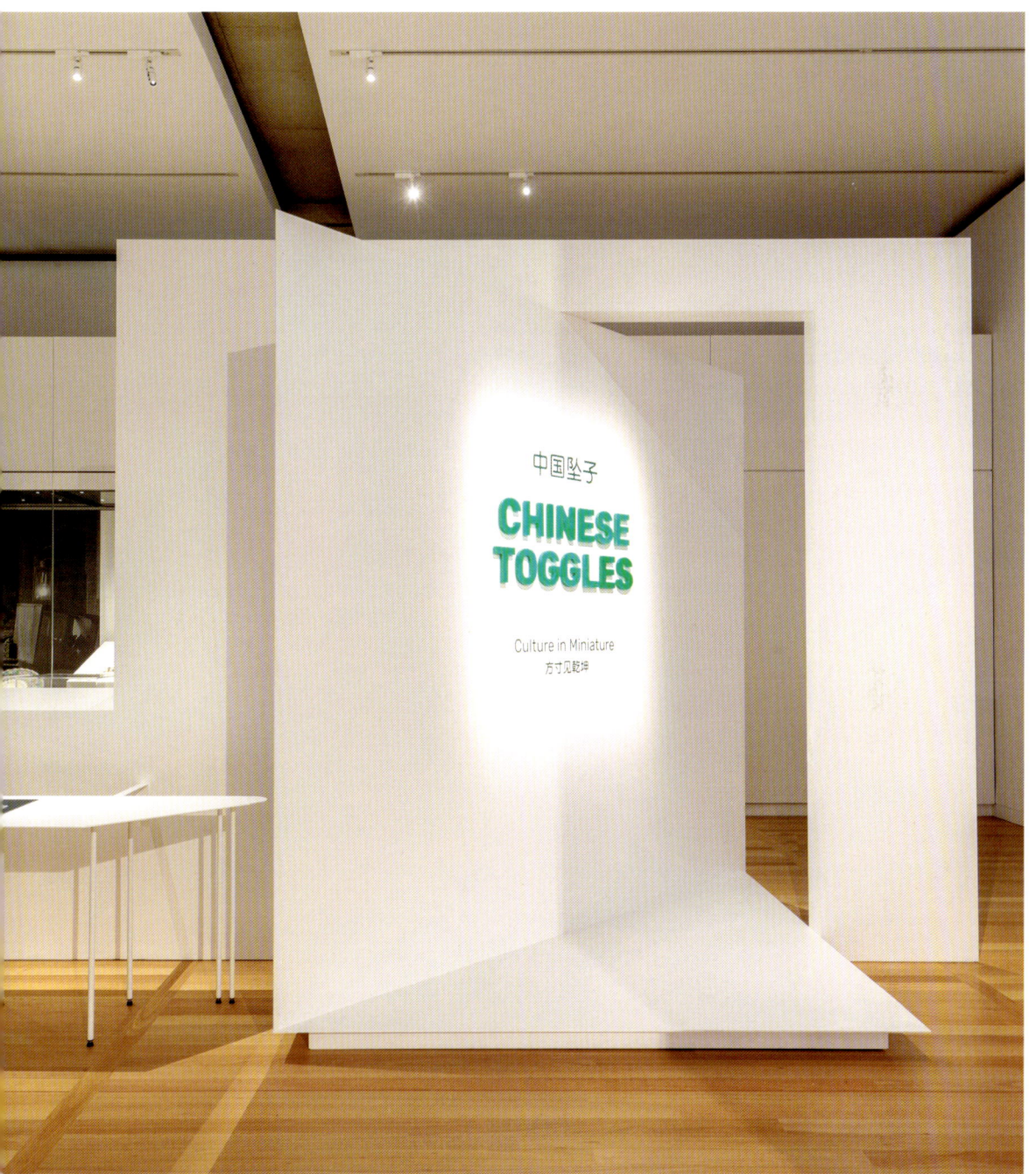

坠子与腰带文化
Toggles and belt-wearing culture

Traditional Chinese garments did not have the same pockets as those used in modern garments. In the Qing dynasty, an inner pocket was sometimes sewn on inside robes. Carrying pouches on a belt at the waist was common practice. Small pouches containing personal belongings such as money, spectacles, tobacco, and flint or knife sets were hung from the belt, tied by cords with toggles at the other end as counter-weights. Belt toggles are displayed here with pouches and robes, as well as images that demonstrate how they were typically worn.

传统中国服装没有现代服饰的口袋。清朝时期，内置口袋偶尔会缝入衣袍内。因此腰带上悬挂荷包 是常见的做法。人们会在腰带上挂着绳子束着的小荷包，里面装有诸如钱币、眼镜、烟草、打火石或套装刀具等个人物品，然后绳子另一端系着坠子来平衡重量。本单元不仅展示各种坠子，而且呈现荷包与长袍，以及描绘当时这些衣物饰品穿戴方式的图像。

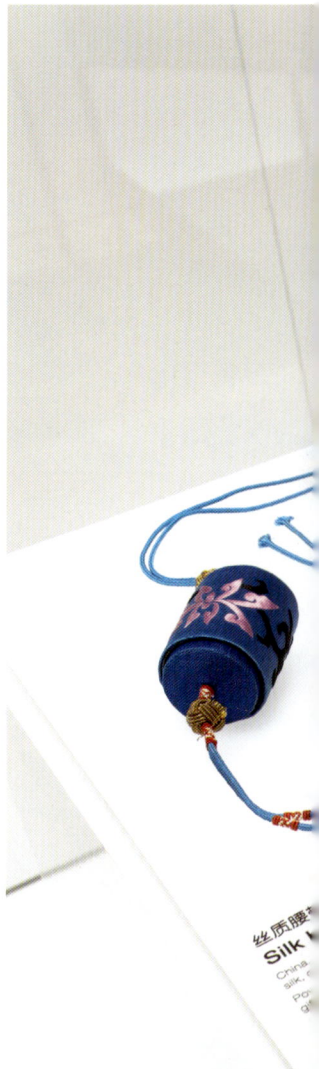

丝质腰
Silk
China,
silk,
Po-
g

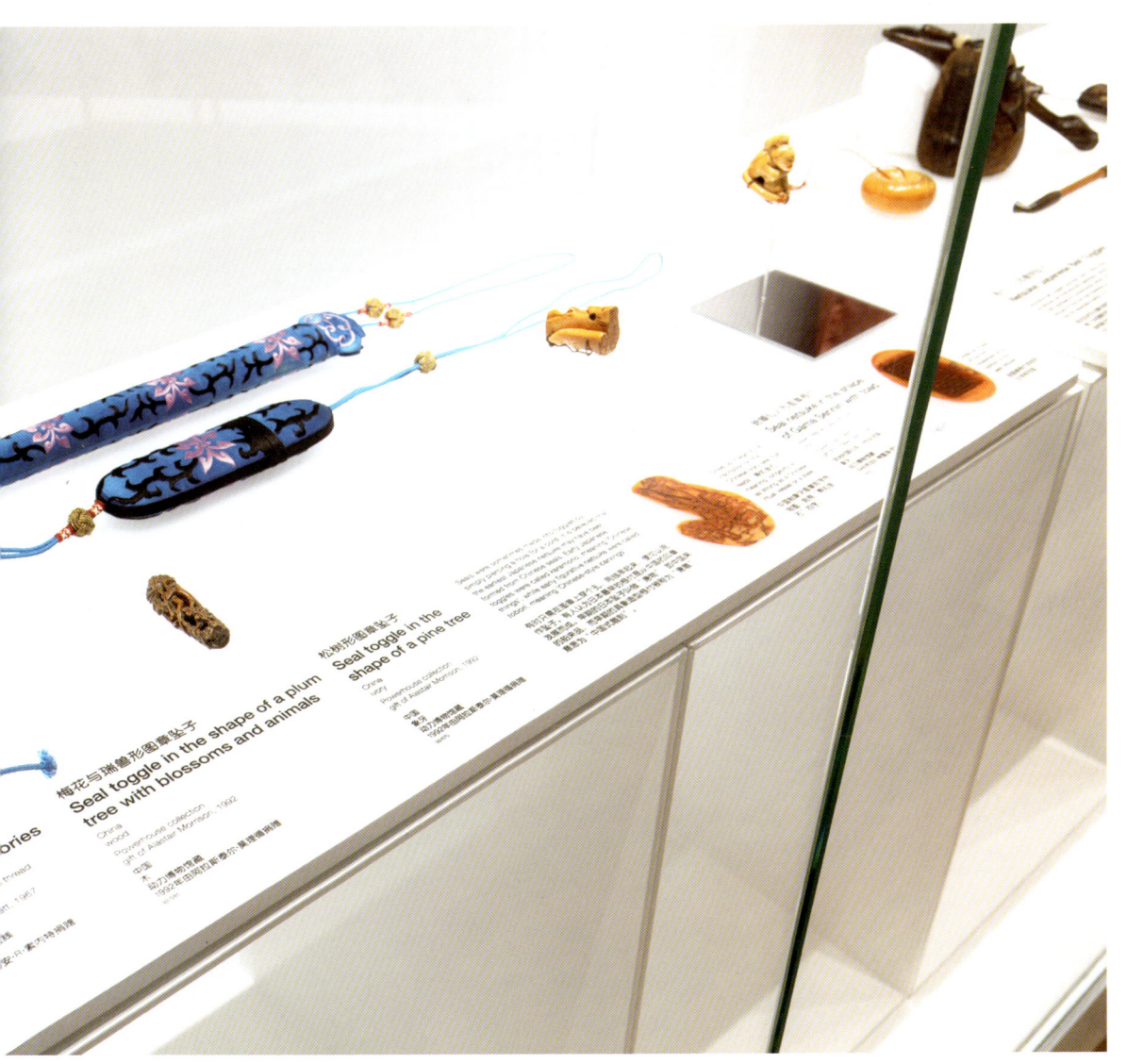

...ories

...thread

...ist, 1967

梅花与瑞兽形遮眉坠子
Seal toggle in the shape of a plum
tree with blossoms and animals
China
wood
Provenhouse collection
gift of Alastair Morrison, 1992
中国
运刀博物馆馆藏
1992年田阿拉斯泰尔·莫里森捐赠

松树形遮眉坠子
Seal toggle in the
shape of a pine tree
China
ivory
Provenhouse collection
gift of Alastair Morrison, 1992
中国
运刀博物馆馆藏
1992年田阿拉斯泰尔·莫里森捐赠

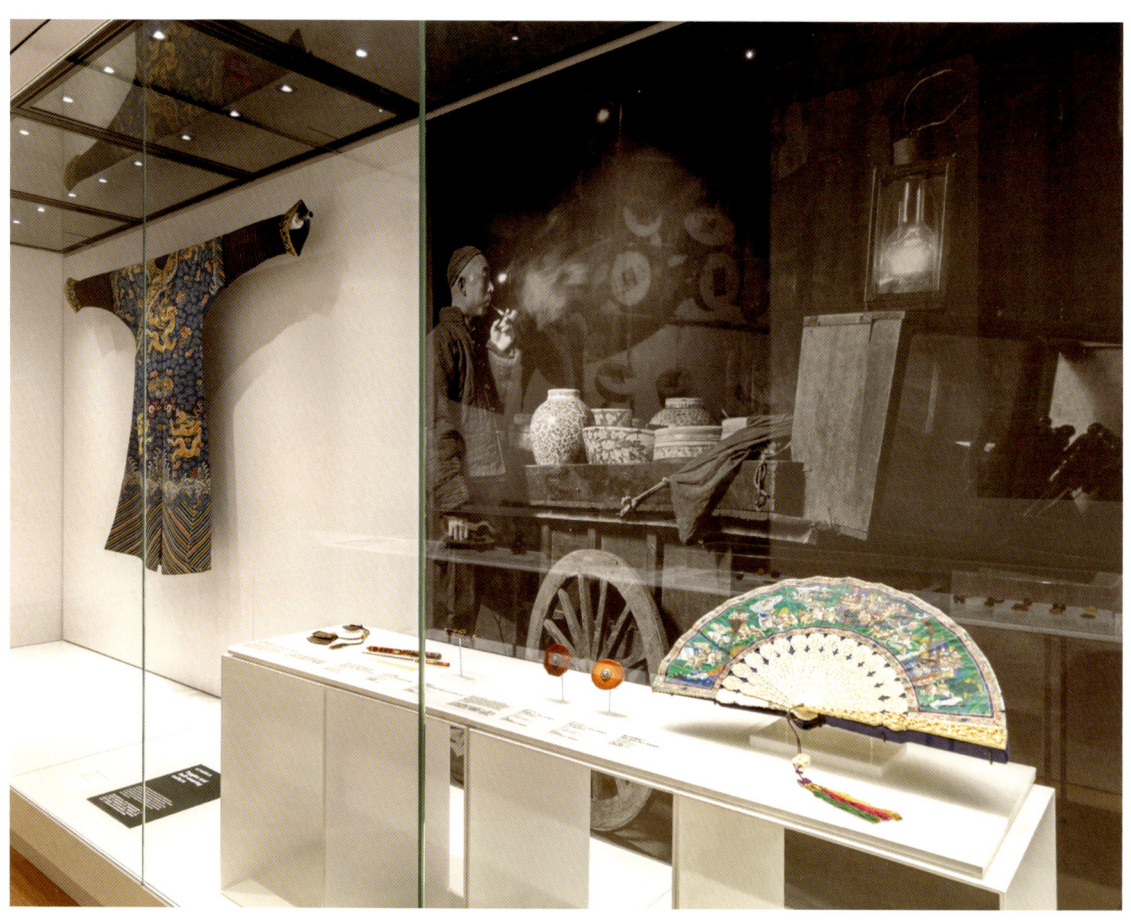

中国坠子的发展
Development of Chinese belt toggles

It is thought that the tradition of toggle-wearing probably arrived in China during the Yuan dynasty (1271–1368), a Mongol-led imperial dynasty. Toggles in the form of a miniature Mongolian knife set show the influence of that heritage by echoing the Mongol custom of carrying a knife set at the waist. The style of Chinese belt toggles was possibly influenced by Chinese fan toggle designs from the Song dynasty (960–1279). Belt toggles became more popular with the increased use of tobacco from the 1600s.

据传, 中国佩戴腰带坠饰的传统大抵滥觞于蒙古人统治的元朝 (1271年–1368年)。袖珍蒙古刀具形坠子效仿了蒙古人在腰间携带刀具的习俗, 并彰显了这一文化遗产的影响。中国腰带坠饰的风格可能自宋代 (960年–1279年) 以降借鉴于扇坠子设计。自17 世纪开始, 伴随着烟草消费的增长, 腰带坠饰更备受青睐。

根付：日本腰带坠子
Netsuke: Japanese belt toggles

Decorative belt toggles have been used in other Asian cultures. Japanese toggles, known as netsuke, are internationally celebrated, collected and studied. This delicate artform is still practised by contemporary artists. Netsuke were most often made from wood, lacquer or ivory but rare materials such as hornbill beaks were also used. It is possible that the Japanese tradition of netsuke has its origins in the Chinese tradition of *zhuizi*.

其他亚洲文化圈也使用装饰性的腰带坠子。日本坠子, 名为根付, 在国际上屡受赞誉, 被广为收藏和研究。当代艺术家仍对这一精致的艺术形式进行创作。根付多由木、漆或象牙制成, 但也时常使用如犀鸟喙等稀有材料。日本的根付传统的渊源和可能来自于中国的坠子传统。

收藏家：
海达和阿拉斯泰尔 · 莫理循伉俪
The collectors:
Hedda and Alastair Morrison

Hedda Morrison (1908–1991), nee Hammer, was a German photographer who moved to China in 1933 and, over more than a decade living in the country, produced a significant body of documentary images. In 1946, she married Alastair Morrison (1915–2009) who had been born in China to a New Zealander mother and Australian father—a prominent doctor-turned-journalist and later political advisor known as George 'Chinese' Morrison. The pair lived in Beijing, Hong Kong and Sarawak (Malaysia) before moving to Australia in 1967.

In 1940, they began collecting toggles they found in Beijing, and later in Shanghai, Chongqing and Singapore. Following Hedda's death, Alastair donated her photographic archive as well as the couple's impressive private collection of Asian art to the Powerhouse Museum. This included a collection of 279 Chinese belt toggles, one of the world's largest collections of the miniature wearable sculptures.

海达 · 莫理循（1908年–1991年），旧姓哈默，是一位德国摄影师，于1933年移居中国，并在中国生活了十多年，拍摄了大 量的纪实照片。1946年，她与阿拉斯泰尔 · 莫里森（1915年–2009年）结为伉俪。后者出生在中国，母亲是新西兰人，父亲是澳大利亚人。其父曾是一位医生，后转行为著名的记者与政治顾问，被称为乔治 · "中国的"莫理循。海达与阿拉斯泰尔夫妇曾在北京、香港和马来西亚的沙捞越生活，于1967年定居澳大利亚。

1940年，他们开始在北京、上海、重庆和新加坡等地收集坠子。海达去世后，阿拉斯泰尔将她的摄影档案与他们令人惊叹的亚洲艺术藏品捐赠给动力博物馆。其中有279件中国腰带坠子，为世界上最大的可穿戴袖珍品收藏之一。

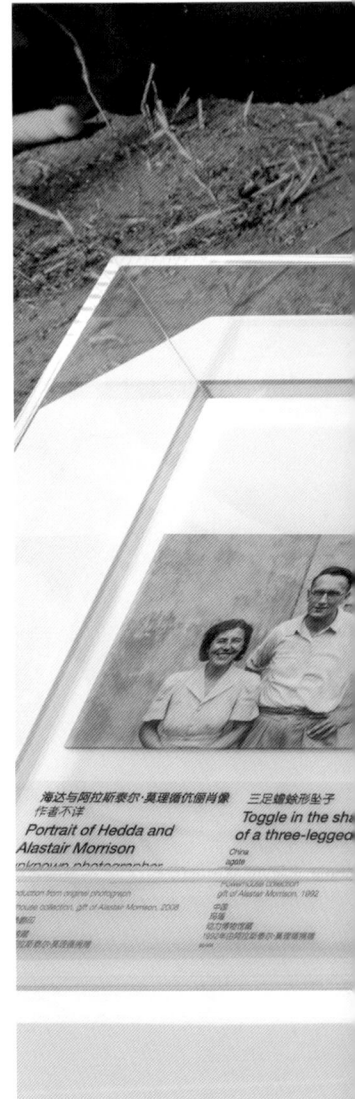

海达与阿拉斯泰尔 · 莫理循伉俪肖像
作者·不详
Portrait of Hedda and
Alastair Morrison
unknown photographer

三足蟾蜍形坠子
Toggle in the sh
of a three-legge
China
agate

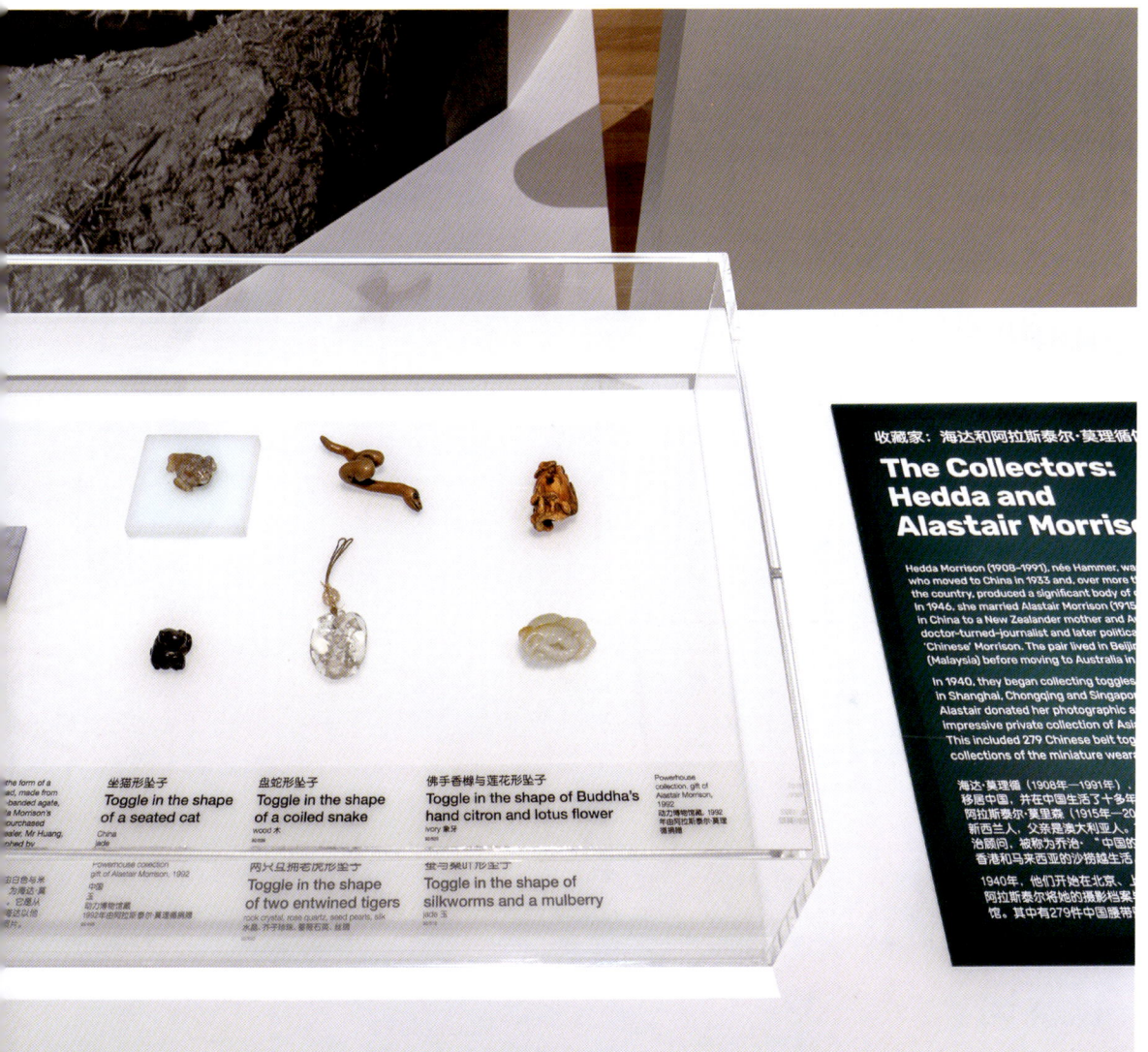

the form of a
...ed, made from
-banded agate,
...a Morrison's
...ourchased
...rer, Mr Huang,
...ched by

坐猫形坠子
**Toggle in the shape
of a seated cat**
China
jade

盘蛇形坠子
**Toggle in the shape
of a coiled snake**
wood 木

佛手香橼与莲花形坠子
**Toggle in the shape of Buddha's
hand citron and lotus flower**
ivory 象牙

Powerhouse
collection, gift of
Alastair Morrison,
1992
动力博物馆收藏，1992
年由阿拉斯泰尔·莫里
森捐赠

...白鲁与米
...为瑪达．真
...它是以
...海达以母

Powerhouse collection,
gift of Alastair Morrison, 1992
中国
玉
1992年由阿拉斯泰尔·莫里森捐赠

两只乌拥老虎形坠守
**Toggle in the shape
of two entwined tigers**
rock crystal, rose quartz, seed pearls, silk
水晶、齐牙珍珠、薔蓉石英、丝绸

蚕与桑叶形坠子
**Toggle in the shape of
silkworms and a mulberry**
jade 玉

收藏家：海达和阿拉斯泰尔·莫理循伉俪
The Collectors:
Hedda and
Alastair Morrison

Hedda Morrison (1908–1991), née Hammer, wa...
who moved to China in 1933 and, over more t...
the country, produced a significant body of ...
In 1946, she married Alastair Morrison (1915–...
in China to a New Zealander mother and A...
doctor-turned-journalist and later politica...
'Chinese' Morrison. The pair lived in Beijin...
(Malaysia) before moving to Australia in...

In 1940, they began collecting toggles...
in Shanghai, Chongqing and Singapore...
Alastair donated her photographic a...
impressive private collection of Asi...
This included 279 Chinese belt tog...
collections of the miniature wear...

海达·莫理循（1908—1991年），...
移居中国，并在中国生活了十多年...
阿拉斯泰尔·莫里森（1915—20...
新西兰人，父亲是澳大利亚人...
治顾问，被称为乔治·"中国...
香港和马来西亚的沙捞越生活...

1940年，他们开始在北京、上...
阿拉斯泰尔将她的摄影档案...
馆，其中有279件中国腰带...

寓意于物
Symbols and materials

Belt toggles had a practical use and a distinctive, often beautiful appearance, but perhaps more importantly they also expressed the wearer's wishes for good fortune, wealth, fertility or longevity. Toggles were typically carved into the shape of figures, plants, animals, or every-day objects and often reflected symbols drawn from Chinese history or mythology. Designs playing on homonyms—like-sounding words—were also popular and those made from or associated with materials believed to have magical or medicinal powers were highly prized. Most toggles were made of affordable wood. Ivory and jade toggles, used by a more affluent class, are popular among collectors. Other materials used include agate, brass, jet, seashells, amber, turquoise, bone, antler, and seeds.

腰带坠子具有实用价值和与众不同的美丽外观，但也许更为重要的是，坠子还寄托了佩戴者祈求好运、财富、生育或长寿的愿望。坠子通常被雕刻 成人物、动植物或日常用品的形状，并时常借鉴中国历史或神话中的符号。以同音字或谐音为主题 的设计也深受欢迎，而由被视为富有奇效或药用价值的材料制成的坠子则备受青睐。大多数腰带坠子是由普通木材制成。富裕人家使用的象牙和玉石坠子尤受收藏家垂青。其他材料包括玛瑙、黄铜 黑玉、贝壳、琥珀、绿松石、骨、鹿角与植物种子。

The lotus plant, including its flower, leaf, seed and root, is a significant symbol of purity, rebirth, fertility and strength in many Asian cultures influenced by Buddhism. These three toggles dynamically represent such symbolism, by exquisitely depicting the peaceful life of small creatures on the leaf, by replicating a slice of root with abstract patterns, and by ingeniously crafting the seed pod with movable seeds.

莲，无论是莲花、莲叶、莲子，还是莲藕，在众多深受佛教影响的亚洲文化中是纯洁、重生、多子多福和力量的重要象征。这三件坠子或以精巧的技艺描绘出栖居于莲叶上小生物的恬静生活，或用抽象的图案复制一块藕片，或巧妙地制作了带有可移动莲子的莲蓬，栩栩如生地体现了莲的象征意义。

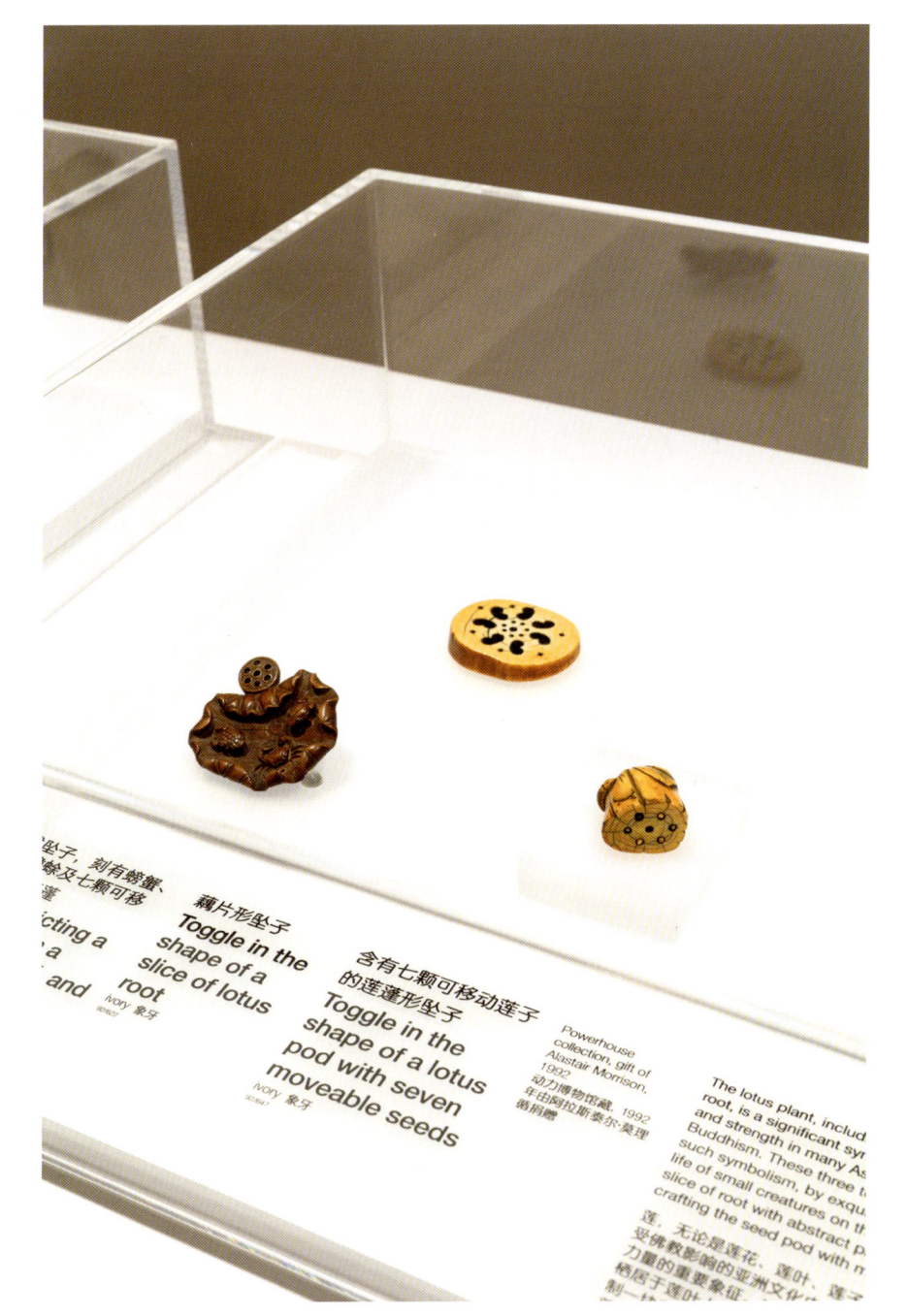

藕片形坠子
Toggle in the shape of a slice of lotus root
Ivory 象牙

坠子，刻有螃蟹、
蟋蟀及七颗可移

...cting a
...a
...and

含有七颗可移动莲子
的莲蓬形坠子
Toggle in the shape of a lotus pod with seven moveable seeds
Ivory 象牙

Powerhouse collection, gift of Alastair Morrison, 1992
动力博物馆藏，1992
年由阿拉斯泰尔·莫理
逊捐赠

The lotus plant, includ...
root, is a significant sy...
and strength in many As...
Buddhism. These three t...
such symbolism, by exqu...
life of small creatures on th...
slice of root with abstract p...
crafting the seed pod with m...

莲，无论是莲花、莲叶...
受佛教影响的亚洲文化...
力量的重要象征。藕片...
栩栩于莲叶的重要象征...
制一...

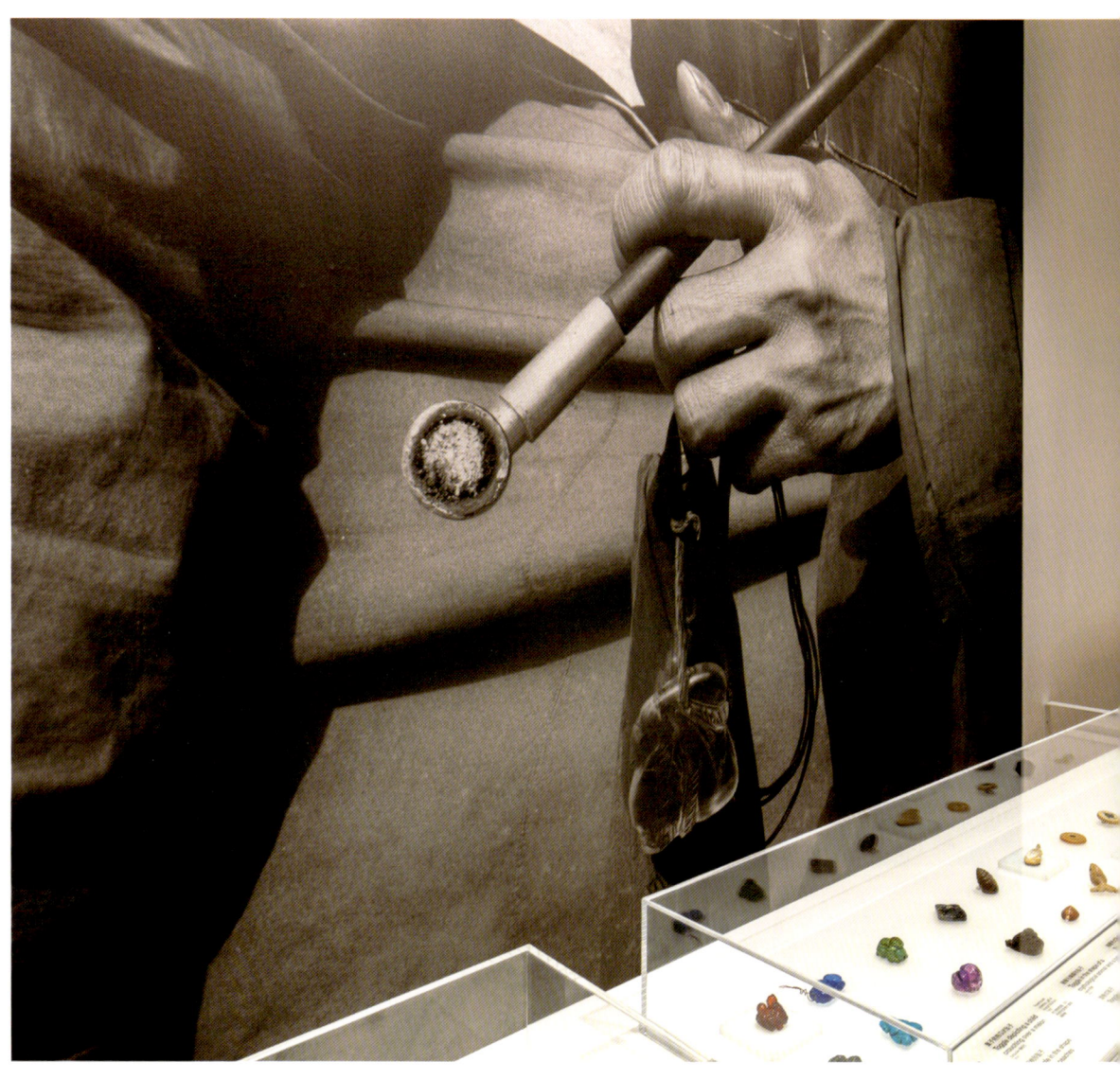

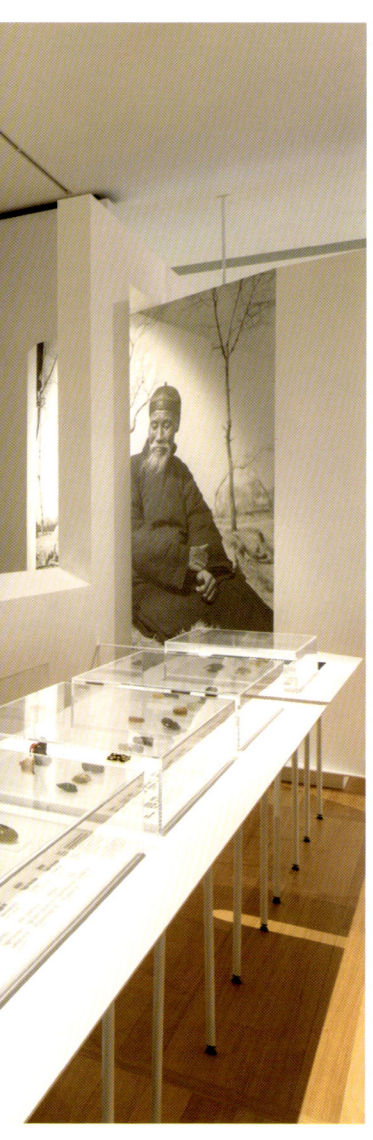

玉石
Stone/Jade

Techniques for carving stone, especially jade, were much developed during the Qing dynasty (1644–1911). During this period, it became more common for Chinese toggles to be made of various precious and semi-precious stones, distinguishing them from Japanese netsukes that were mostly made of wood and ivory. Gemstone toggles were worn by the more affluent classes due to the rarity of the stones and the relatively complex production process.

清代（1644年–1911年）的石雕技术，尤其是玉石雕刻技术的发展盛极一时。其时中国的坠子越来越普遍地采用各种宝石和半宝石制作，而与之不同的是，日本的根付大多仍由木头与象牙制成。由于宝石稀有，生产工艺相对复杂，宝石坠子多被富裕阶层所佩戴

象牙
Ivory

Carved elephant ivory has been unearthed in ruins in China dated to 1000 BC. In addition to being a material suited to detailed carving, ivory was also considered as medicine when ground into powder. Many of the toggles in the Powerhouse Collection are made of ivory, reflecting its popularity as a substance for decorative arts during late imperial China.

在中国的遗址中曾出土过公元前1000年的象牙雕刻。象牙不仅适合精雕细琢，而且待其磨成粉后，也是中药药材。动力博物馆藏的坠子多为象牙制成，反映了在晚期帝国时期的中国，象牙是流行的装饰艺术材料。

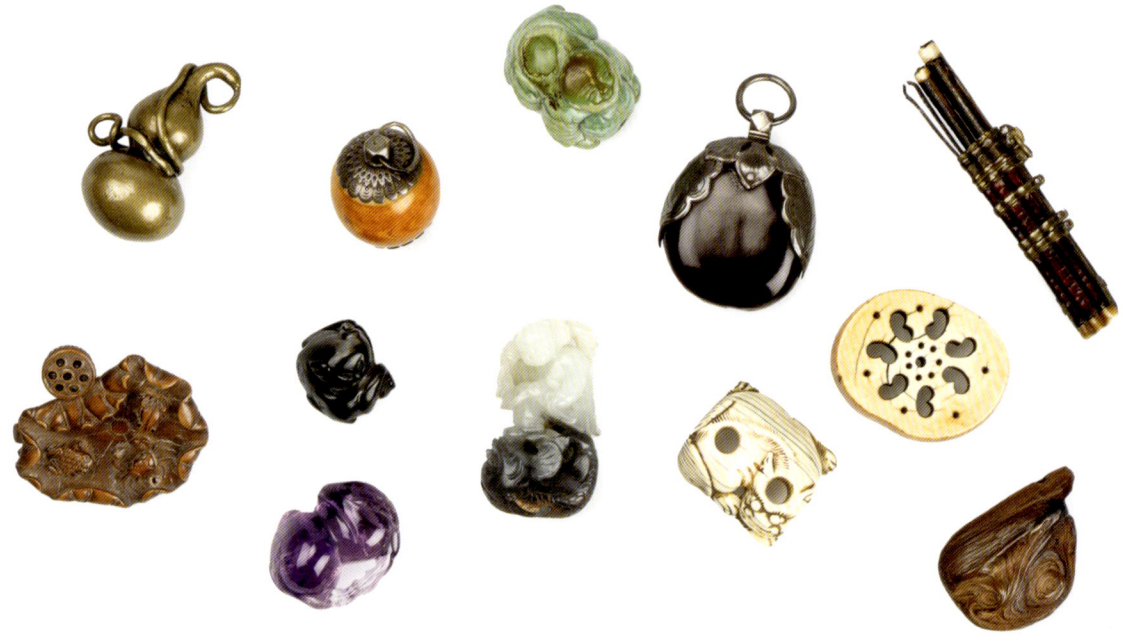

金属
Metal

Toggles made entirely of metal were rare
and generally only owned by wealthy people.
However, metal was often used to make
mounts, attachments or inlaid in toggles
made of other materials.

完全由金属制成的坠子甚是稀少，通常只有富
人才能拥有。但金属经常被用来制作首饰托、
附件或镶嵌于其他材料制成的坠子中。

木
Wood

Working-class people most commonly wore
toggles made of wood. Many wooden toggles
were probably carved by the wearers or
other amateur craftsmen. Yet the unadorned
simplicity of wood was also appreciated by
the scholar-gentry. Wood's durability and
suitability for carving made it the most versatile
material to produce more intricate patterns
and shapes for little toggles.

劳动阶层最常佩戴的是由木制的坠子。许多木制
坠子很可能是由佩戴者本人或其他业余工匠
雕刻而成。然而，这种返璞归真的特色也深受士大
夫阶层欣赏。木材的耐用性和适合雕刻的特性使
它成为最为通用的材料，可以雕镂更为精致图案
与形状的小坠子。

药用功能
Medicinal associations

Toggle makers often used decorative materials that were believed to have medicinal properties or auspicious connotations, such as antlers or gila beans. Symbols of longevity were believed by many to be as effective as medicinal potions.

坠子工匠使用诸如鹿角或樒藤子等通常被认为具有药用价值或吉祥寓意的材料作为装饰。在芸芸众生眼中，长寿的象征与药汤一样有效。

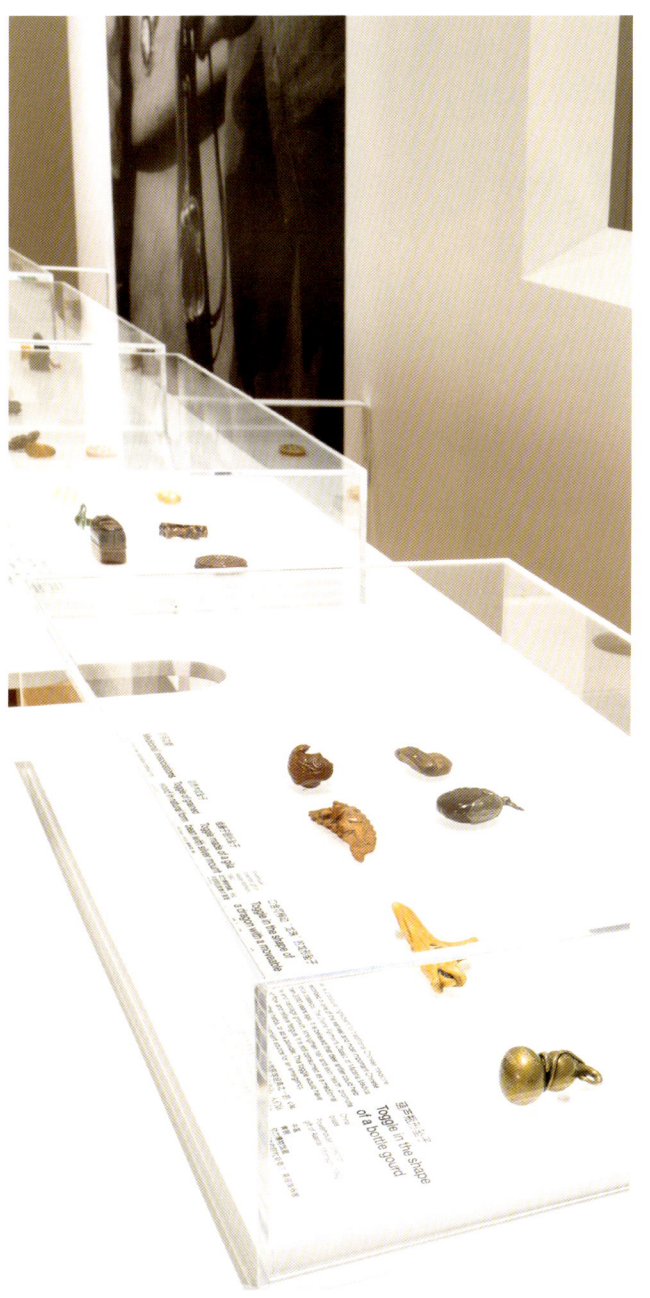

科学分析
Scientific analysis

The Chau Chak Wing Museum and the Powerhouse Museum partnered with Sydney Analytical, one of the University of Sydney's core research facilities that provides state-of-the-art instruments and technical expertise for sample characterisation, to study the materiality of many of the toggles on display. Portable and handheld instrumentation allowed for the rapid, non-destructive and in-situ analysis of the ivory and jade toggles. A combination of X-ray fluorescence, near infrared and Raman spectroscopy was used for scientific testing undertaken on selected ivory and jade toggles to establish their materiality. Scientific analysis allows for non-subjective identification to confirm the suspected materiality of an object which has been previously classified based on a visual assessment.

周泽荣博物馆和动力博物馆与悉尼大学的核心研究机构悉尼分析研究院合作，由后者提供最尖端的仪器和分析样品表征的技术专长，共同研究坠子的材质。便携式和手持式仪器可对象牙和玉石坠子实行快速、非破坏性的原位分析。采用X射线荧光、近红外和拉曼光谱相结合的方法，对甄选的象牙和玉石坠子进行科学测试，以判定其材质。科学分析可以客观鉴定原先基于视觉评估而分类的展品，明确其真实可证的材质。

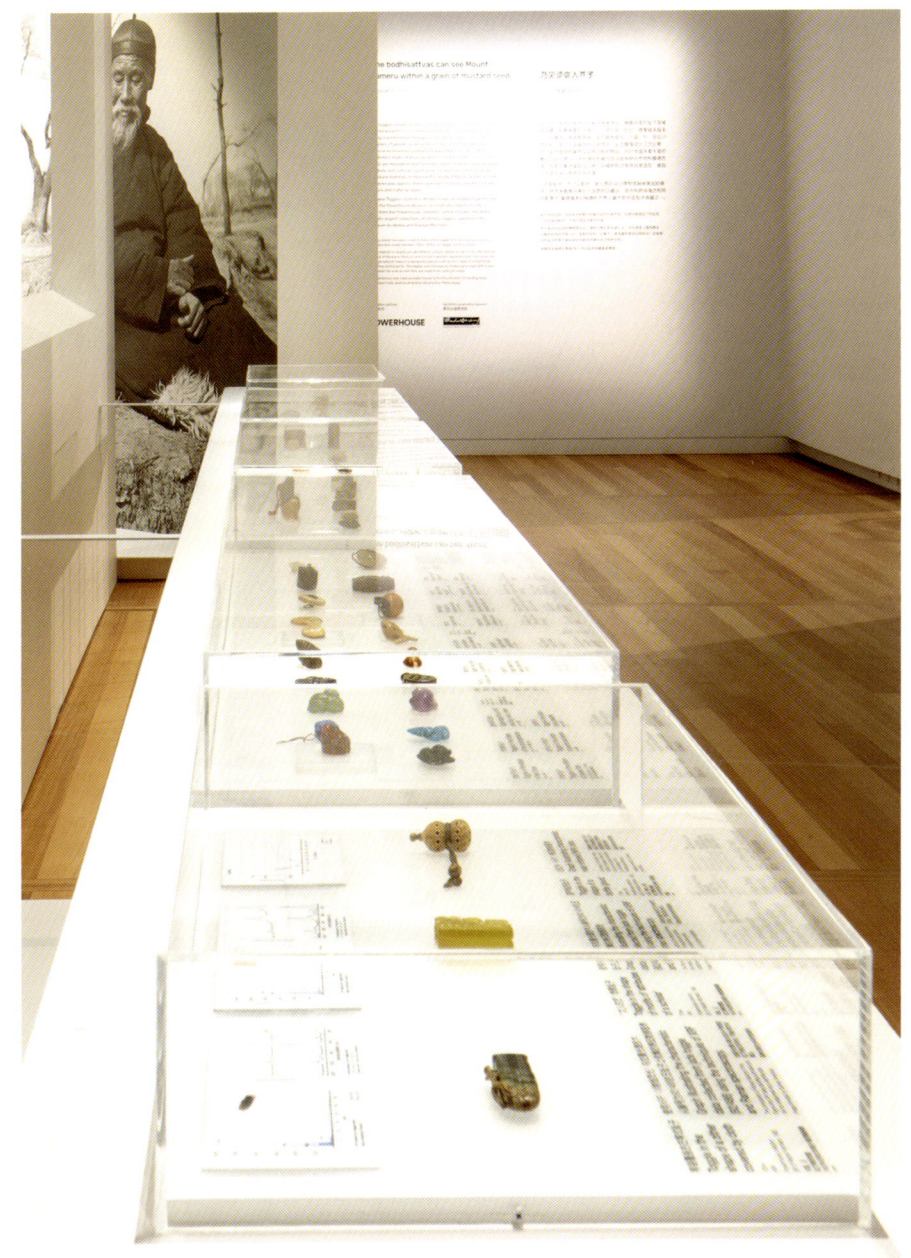

日常缩影
Everyday miniatures

Chinese belt toggles were sartorial accessories, tiny sculptures and everyday objects. Juxtaposing the toggles with some of the real-life objects they replicate, and artworks that share similar designs, helps us reflect on the pleasure of these miniature everyday artworks. Seeing these diverse objects in this context also highlights the custom of cross-medium representation in Chinese art and craft traditions.

中国的腰带坠子是时尚佩饰、精巧的小雕塑，亦是日常用品。将坠子置放在其所效仿的实物、以及具有类似设计图案的艺术品之间，有助于玩味这些日常的袖珍艺术品所带来的乐趣。这些不同种类的物品共聚一堂，彰显出中国艺术和工艺传统中跨媒介表现的传统。

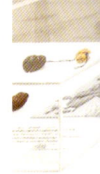

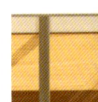

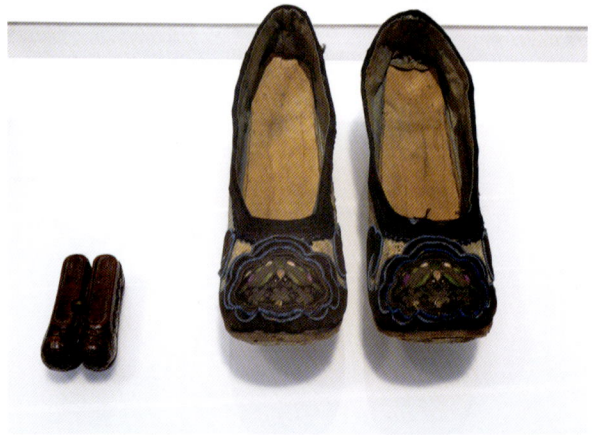

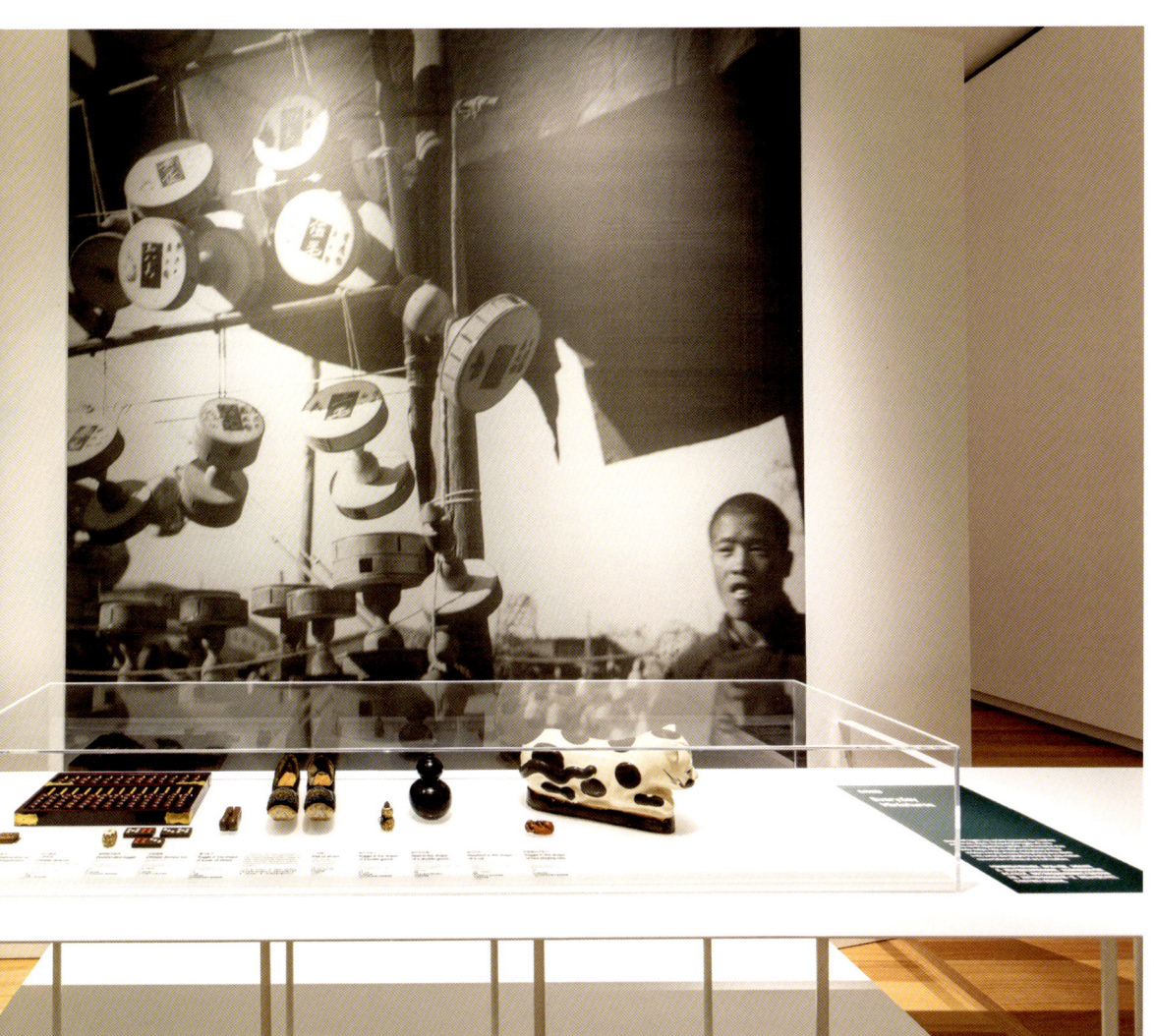

157

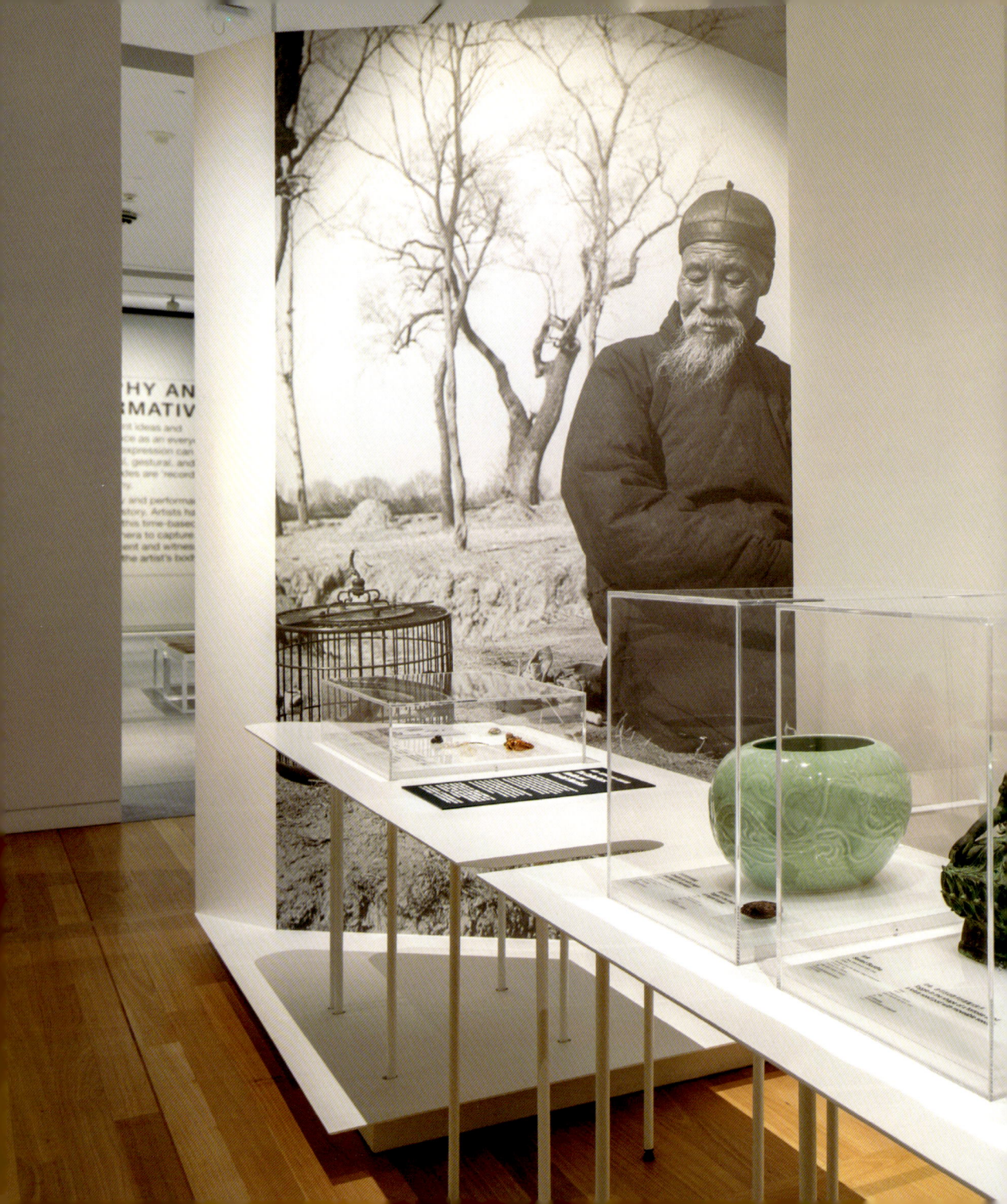

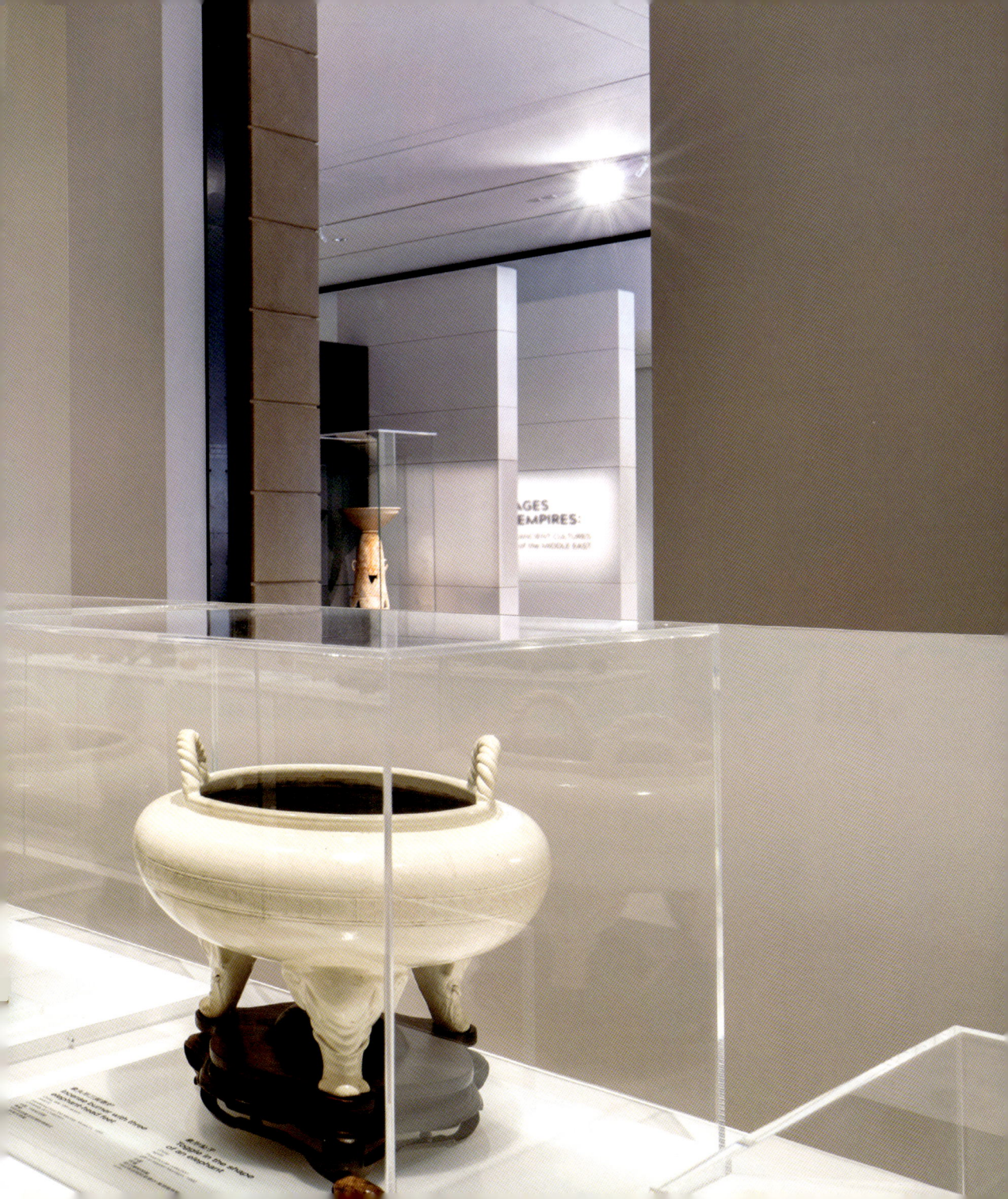

AGES
EMPIRES:
ANCIENT CULTURES
of the MIDDLE EAST

Image plates of exhibited toggles

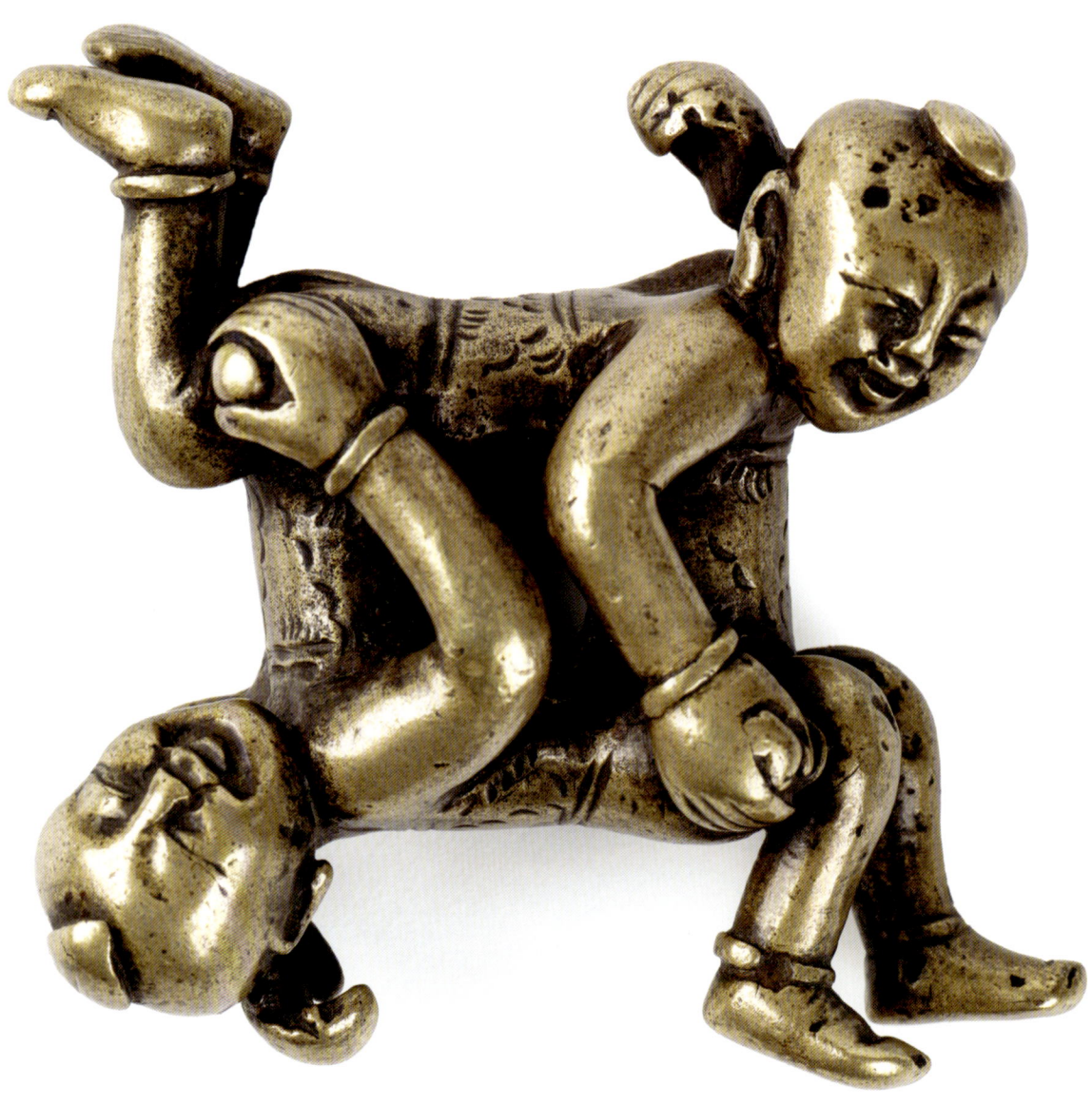

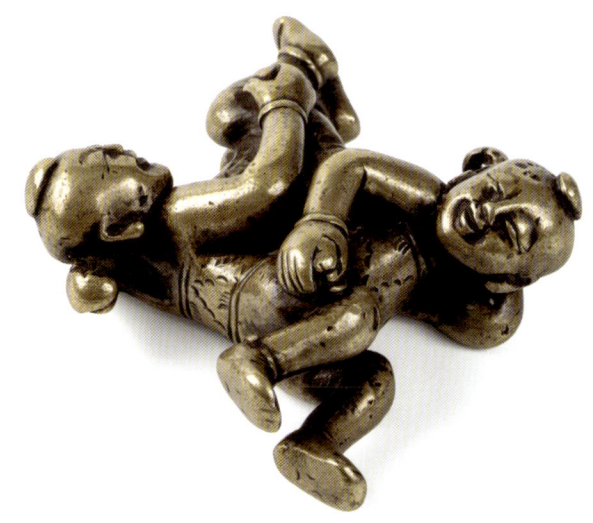

Plate 1

Toggle in the shape of 'Four Happy Boys'
"四喜子" 形坠子

China, c.1700–1940
Metal alloy
20 x 49 x 47 mm
Powerhouse Collection
Gift of Alastair Morrison, 1992

92/435

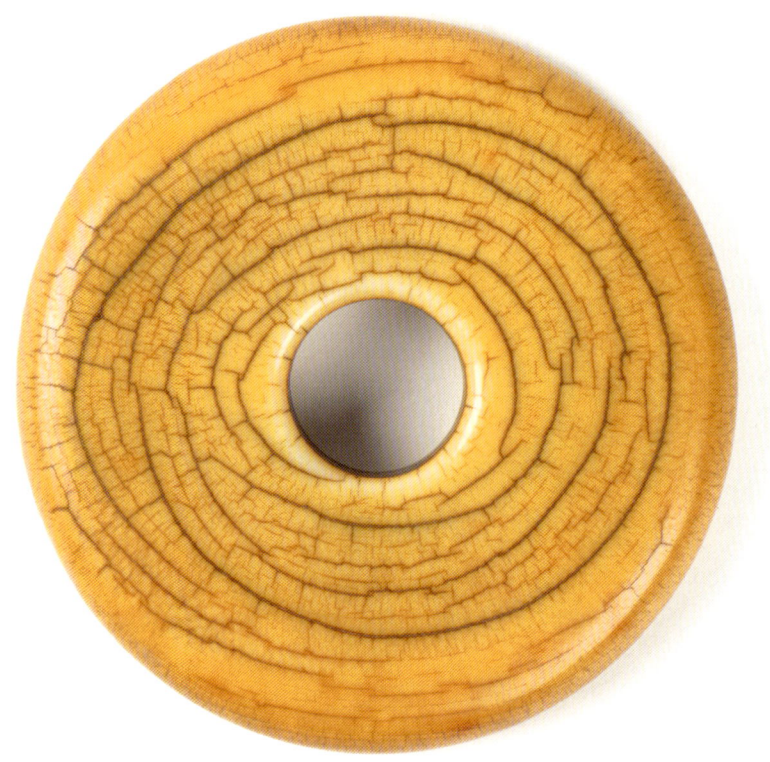

Plate 2

Toggle in the shape of a circular disc
圆盘式坠子

China, c.1700–1940
Ivory
49 (diam) x 7 mm
Powerhouse Collection
Gift of Alastair Morrison, 1992
92/618

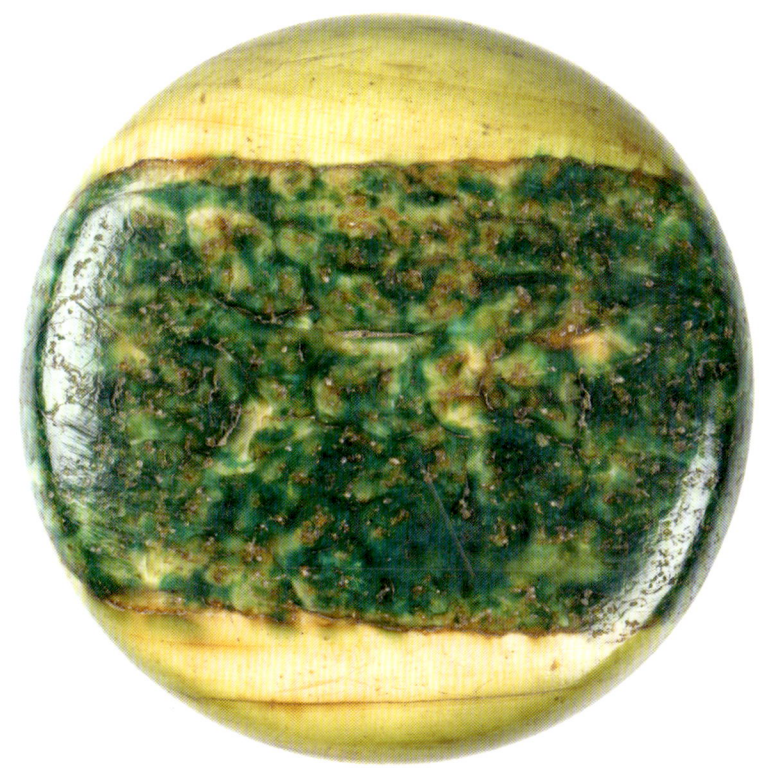

Plate 3
Button-shaped disc toggle
纽扣状圆盘坠子

China, c.1700–1940
Dyed antler
40 (diam) x 8 mm
Powerhouse Collection
Gift of Alastair Morrison, 1992
92/447

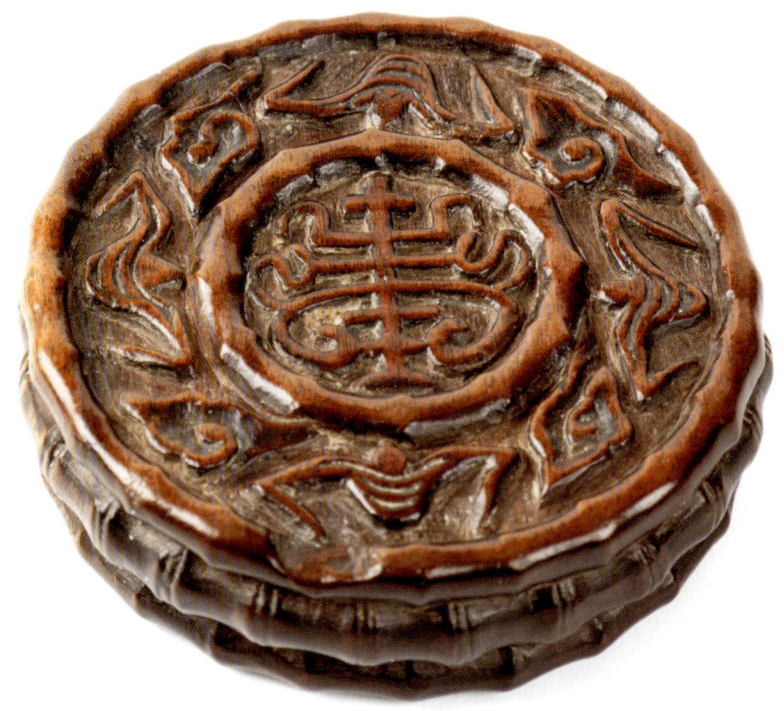

Plate 4

**Toggle in the shape of a disc depicting
the Chinese character *shou* (longevity)**
刻有"寿"字圆盘形坠子

China, c.1700–1940
Wood
55 (diam) x 15 mm
Powerhouse Collection
Gift of Alastair Morrison, 1992
92/552

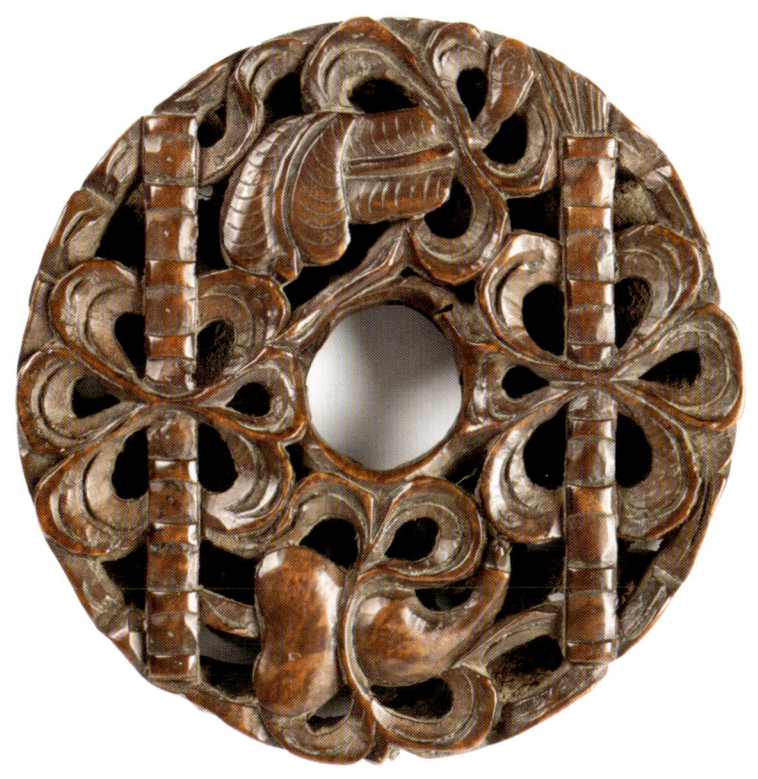

Plate 5

**Circular and hollowed toggle
with auspicious motifs**
祥纹镂空圆形坠子

China, c.1700–1940
Wood
14 x 62 mm
Powerhouse Collection
Gift of Alastair Morrison, 1992
92/551

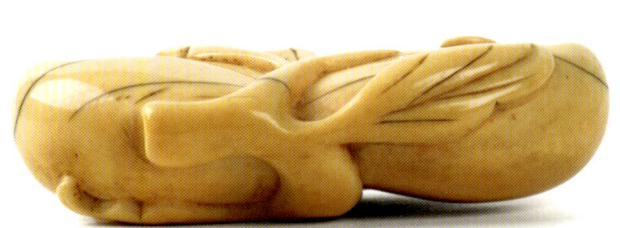

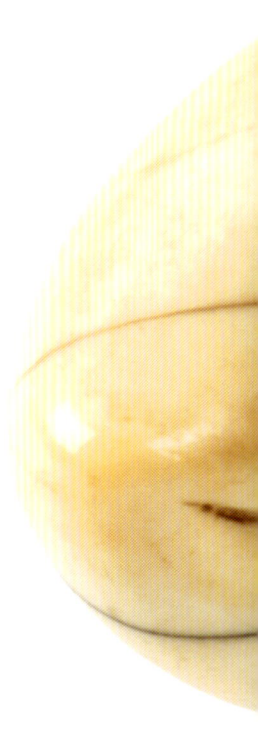

Plate 6

Toggle in the shape of two peaches
双桃形坠子

China, c.1700–1940
Ivory
30 x 50 x 13 mm
Powerhouse Collection
Gift of Alastair Morrison, 1992
92/637

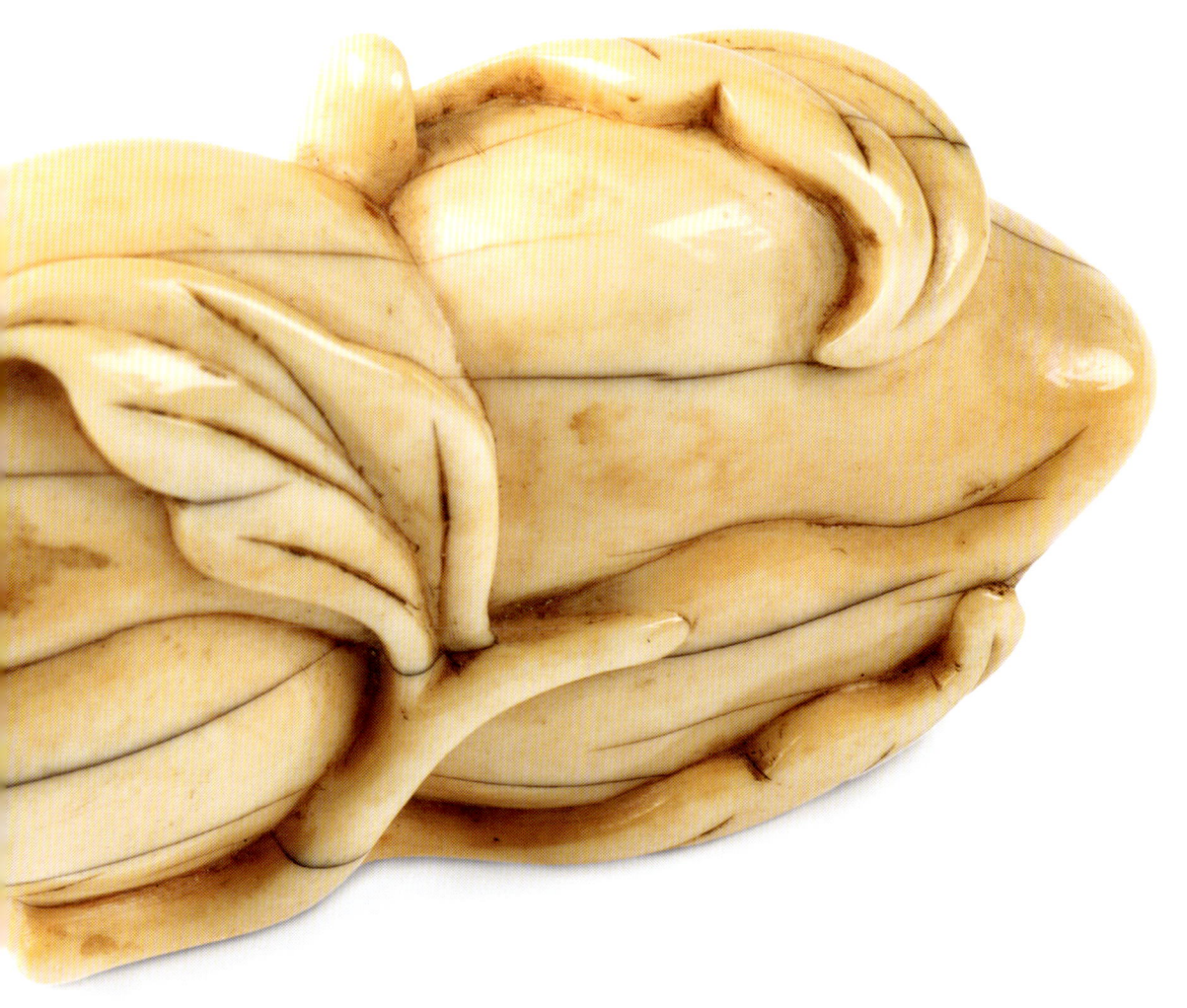

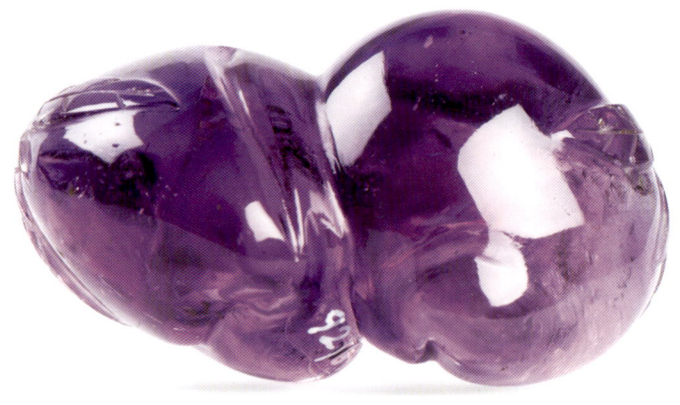

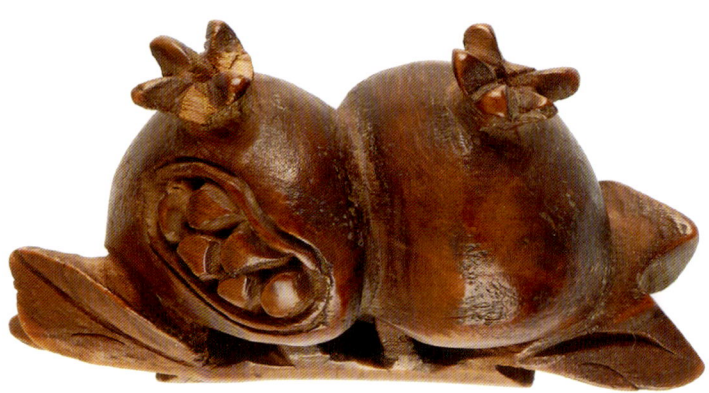

Plate 7

**Toggle in the shape
of two peaches**
双桃形坠子

China, c.1700–1940
Amethyst
33 x 43 x 23 mm
92/692

Plate 8

**Toggle in the shape
of two pomegranates**
双石榴式坠子

China, c.1700–1940
Wood
31 x 54 x 20 mm
92/591

Powerhouse Collection
Gift of Alastair Morrison, 1992

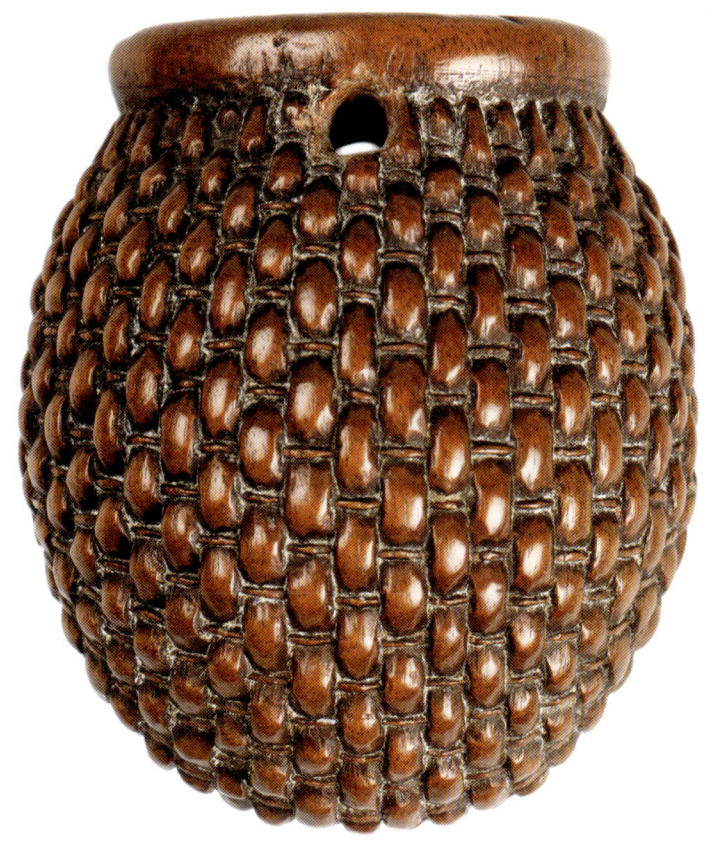

Plate 9
Toggle in the shape of a wicker bucket
柳条筐式坠子

China, c.1700–1940
Wood
35 x 24 x 29 mm
Powerhouse Collection
Gift of Alastair Morrison, 1992
92/569

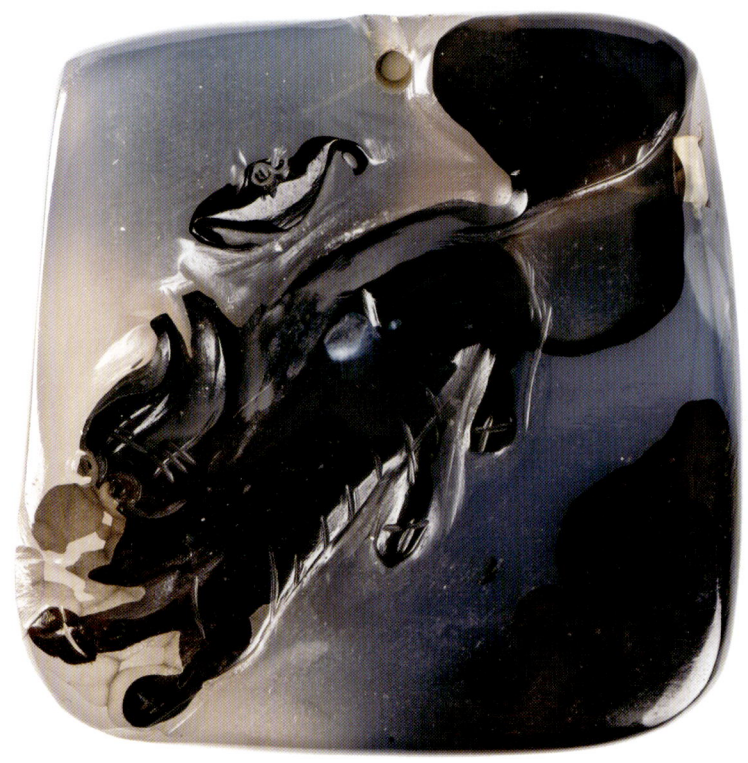

Plate 10
**Toggle in the shape of a mythological
animal and bat**
瑞兽与蝙蝠形坠子

China, c.1700–1940
Agate
9 x 41 x 30 mm
Powerhouse Collection
Gift of Alastair Morrison, 1992

92/452

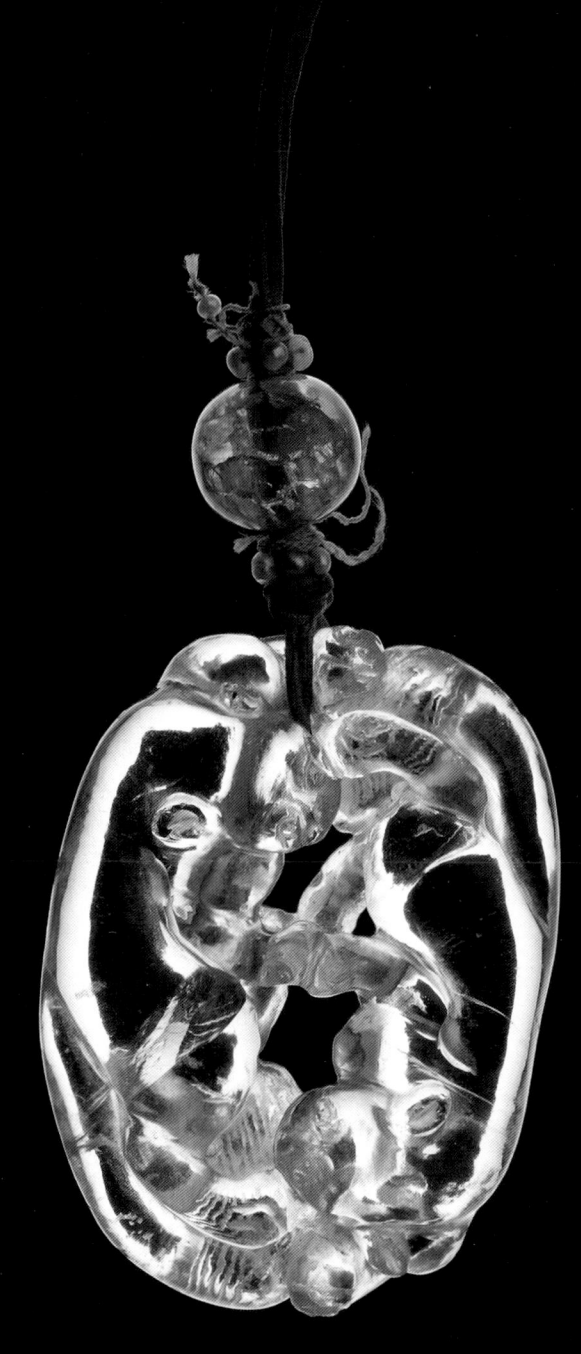

Plate 11

Toggle in the shape of two entwined tigers
两只互拥老虎形坠子

China, c.1700–1940
Rock crystal, rose quartz,
seed pearls, silk
119 x 36 x 15 mm
Powerhouse Collection
Gift of Alastair Morrison, 1992

92/693

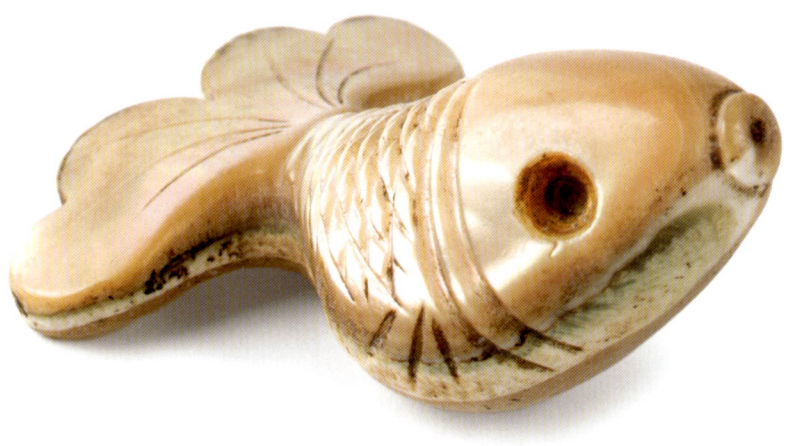

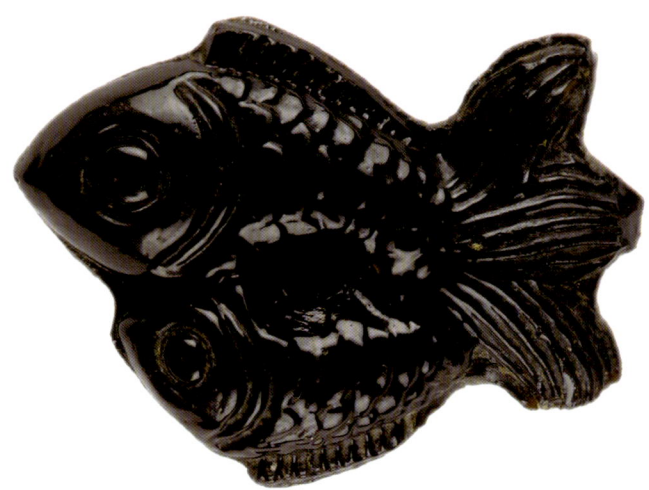

Plate 12

**Toggle in the shape of
a goldfish with a flat tail**
扁尾金鱼式坠子

China, c.1700–1940
Mother of pearl
54 x 42 x 22 mm
92/445

Plate 13

**Toggle in the shape
of paired fish**
双鱼形坠子

China, c.1700–1940
Jet, or possibly glass or obsidian
39 x 52 x 10 mm
92/493

Powerhouse Collection
Gift of Alastair Morrison, 1992

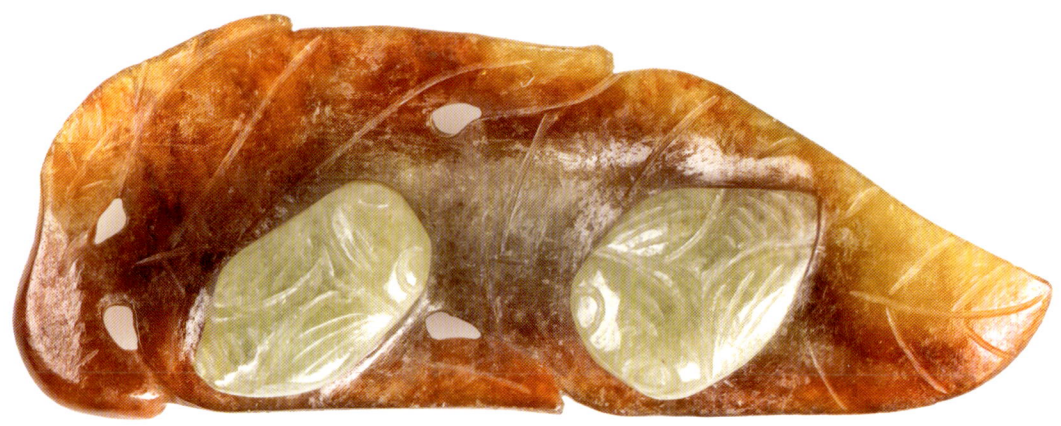

Plate 14

**Toggle in the shape of two
cicadas on a leaf**
双蝉栖叶形坠子

China, c.1700–1940
Jade
11 x 75 x 28 mm
Powerhouse Collection
Gift of Alastair Morrison, 1992
92/472

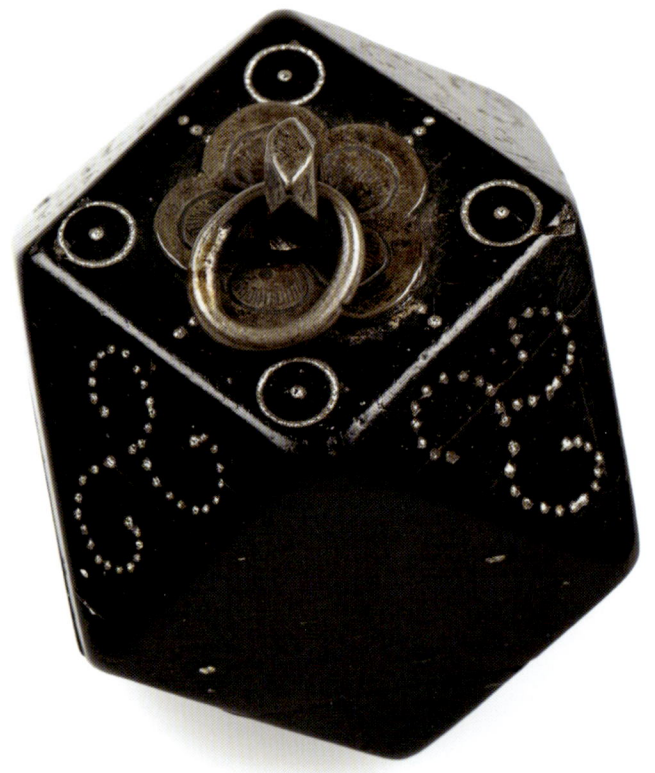

Plate 15

Toggle in the shape of a polygon
多边形坠子

China, c.1700–1940
Wood, inlaid with silver decoration
37 x 39 x 39 mm
Powerhouse Collection
Gift of Alastair Morrison, 1992
92/479

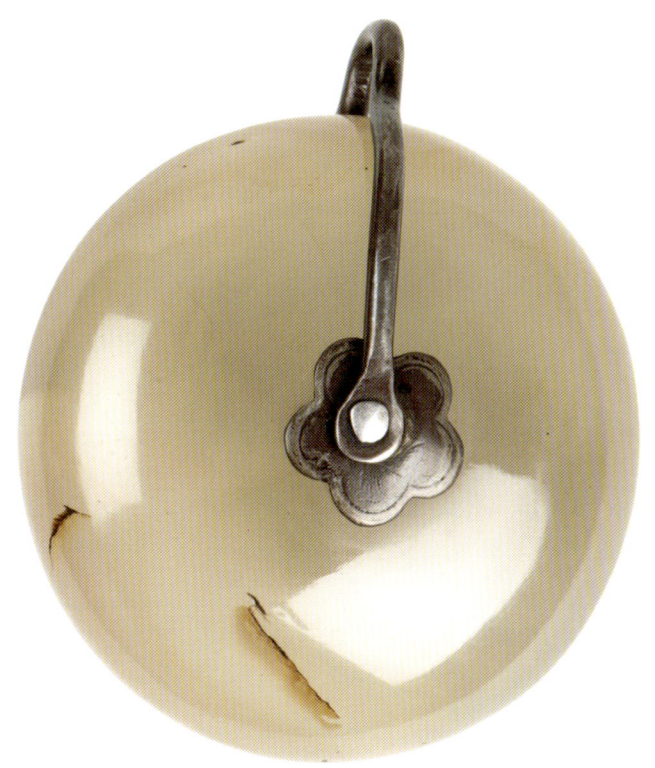

Plate 16
Disc-shaped toggle
圆盘状坠子

China, c.1700–1940
Agate, silver
29 x 57 x 49 mm
Powerhouse Collection
Gift of Alastair Morrison, 1992
92/473

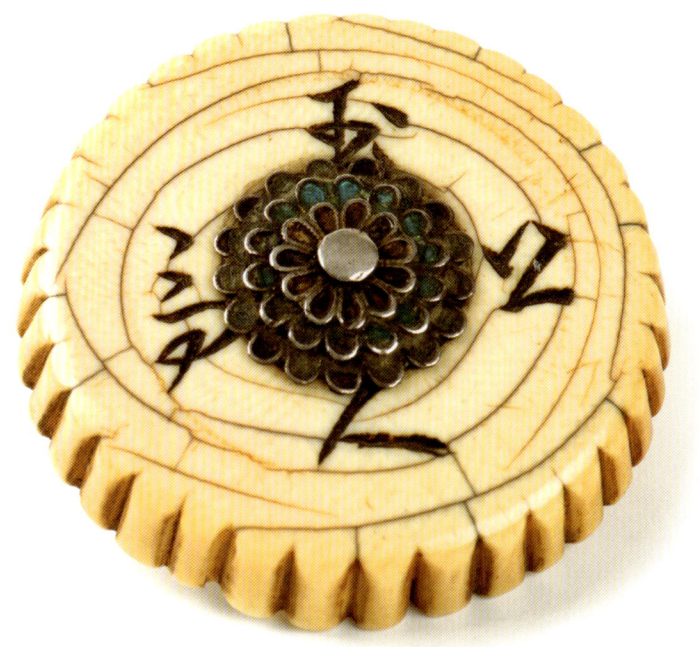

Plate 17
Disc toggle with cloisonné decoration
景泰蓝装饰圆盘坠子

China, c.1700–1940
Ivory, metal, enamel
40 (diam) x 7 mm
Powerhouse Collection
Gift of Alastair Morrison, 1992
92/604

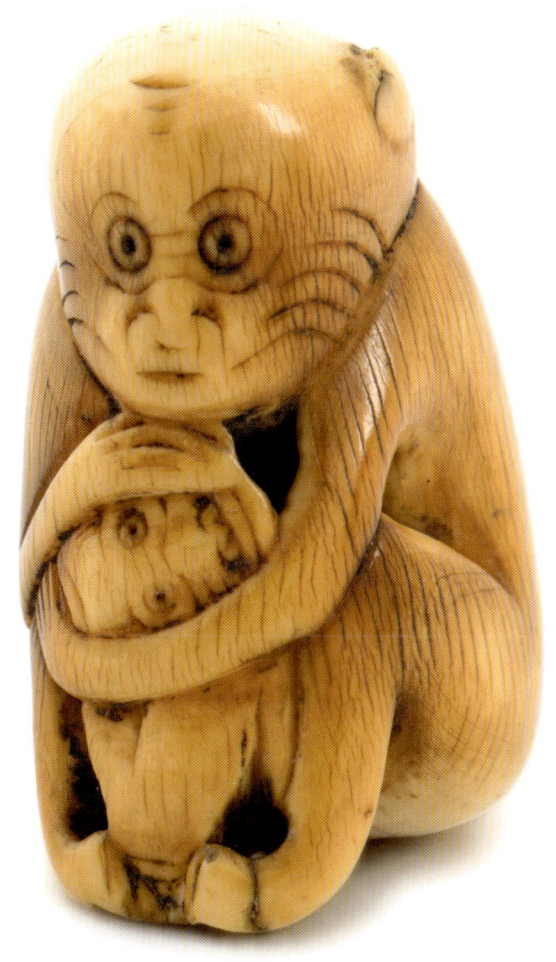

Plate 18

**Toggle in the shape of a monkey
holding baby**
猴抱嬰形坠子

China, c.1700–1940
Ivory
38 x 20 x 30 mm
Powerhouse Collection
Gift of Alastair Morrison, 1992
92/609

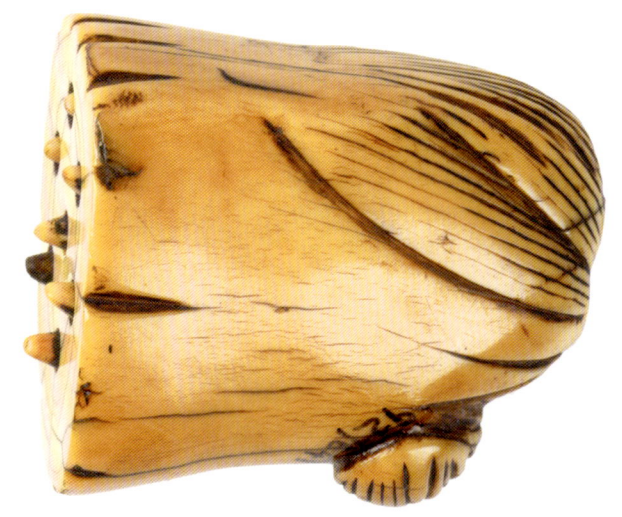

Plate 19

**Toggle in the shape of a lotus pod
with seven moveable seeds**
含有七颗可移动莲子的莲蓬形坠子

China, c.1700–1940
Ivory
35 x 27 x 18 mm
Powerhouse Collection
Gift of Alastair Morrison, 1992

92/647

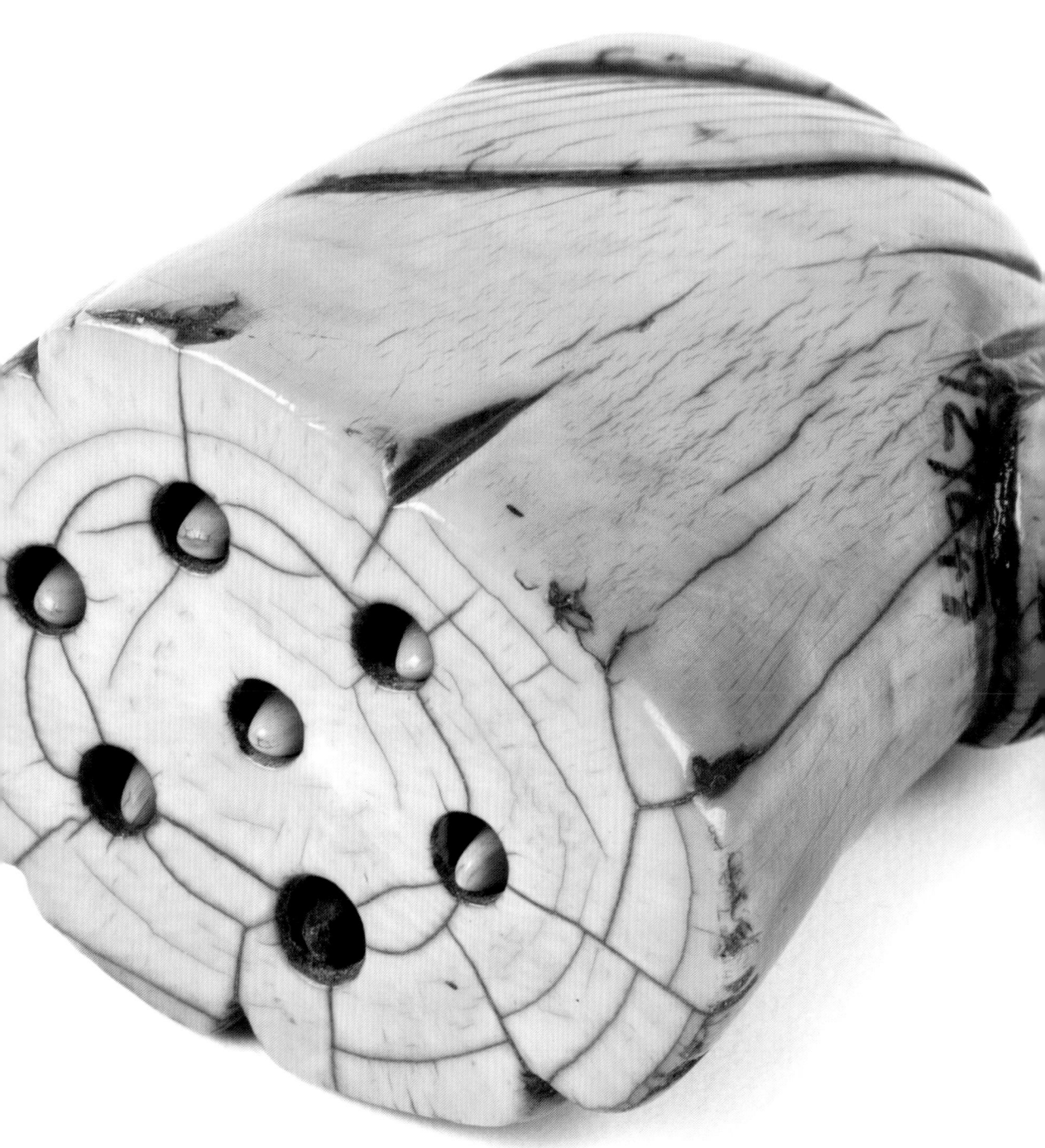

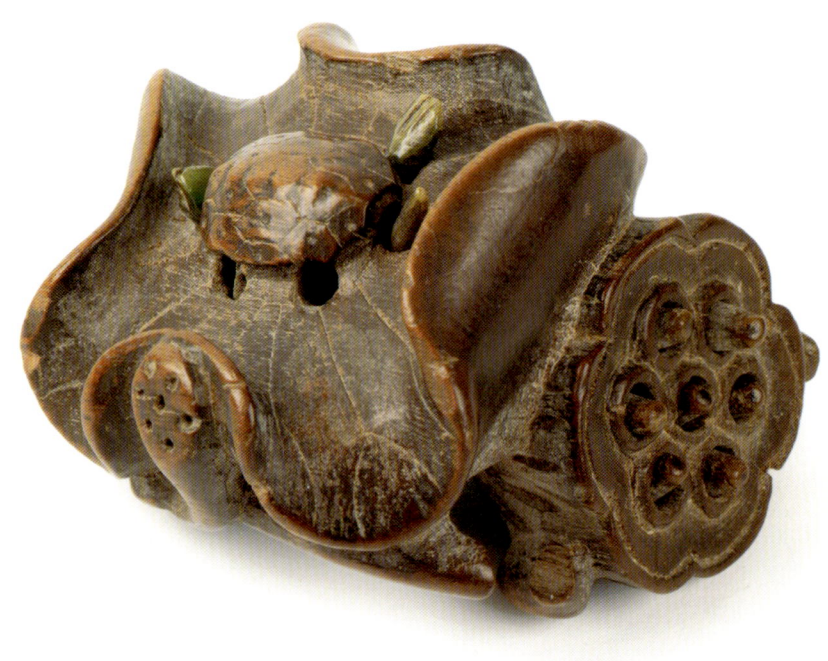

Plate 20

**Toggle in the shape of a tortoise and
lotus seed pod with moveable seeds**
乌龟、含可活动莲子的莲蓬式坠子

China, c.1700–1940
Wood
34 x 35 x 35 mm
Powerhouse Collection
Gift of Alastair Morrison, 1992
92/579

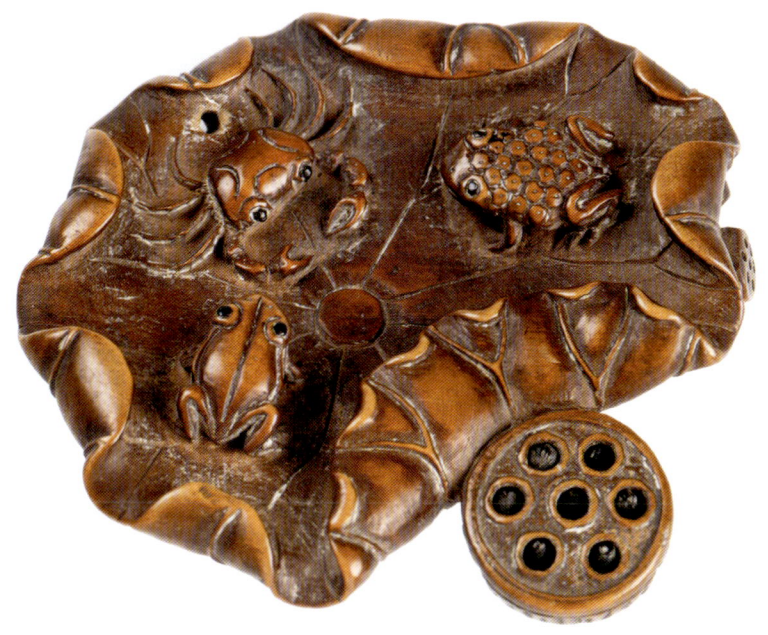

**Toggle depicting a lotus leaf with crab, frog,
toad, and a pod with seven moveable seeds**
莲叶式坠子，刻有螃蟹、青蛙、
蟾蜍及七颗可移动莲子的莲蓬

China, c.1700–1940
Wood
56 x 55 x 17 mm
Powerhouse Collection
Gift of Alastair Morrison, 1992
92/574

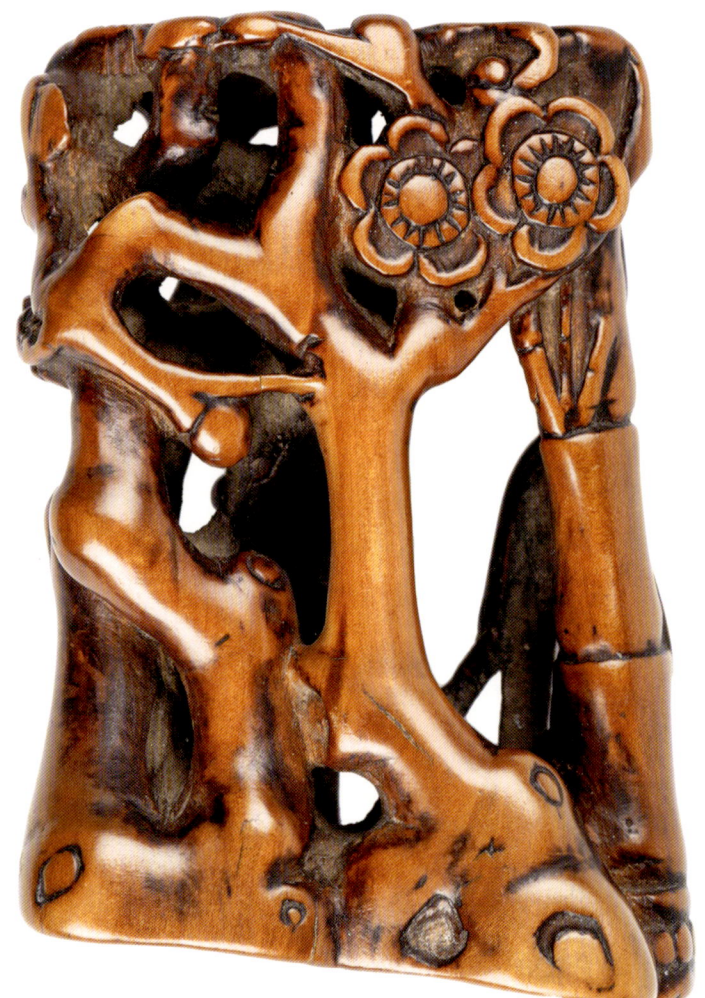

Plate 22

Toggle depicting bamboo, pine and prunus
"岁寒三友"竹、松、梅形坠子

China, c.1700–1940
Wood
50 x 44 x 19 mm
Powerhouse Collection
Gift of Alastair Morrison, 1992
92/588

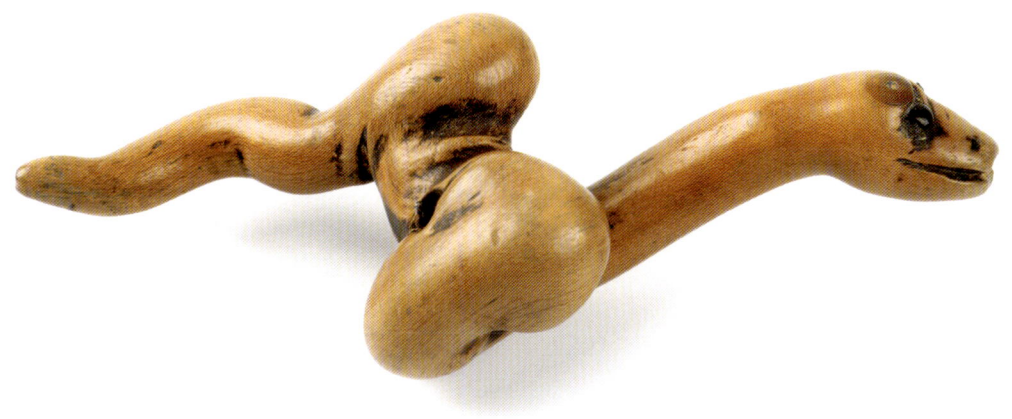

Plate 23

Toggle in the shape of a coiled snake
盘蛇形坠子

China, c.1700–1940
Wood
25 x 31 x 94 mm
Powerhouse Collection
Gift of Alastair Morrison, 1992

92/539

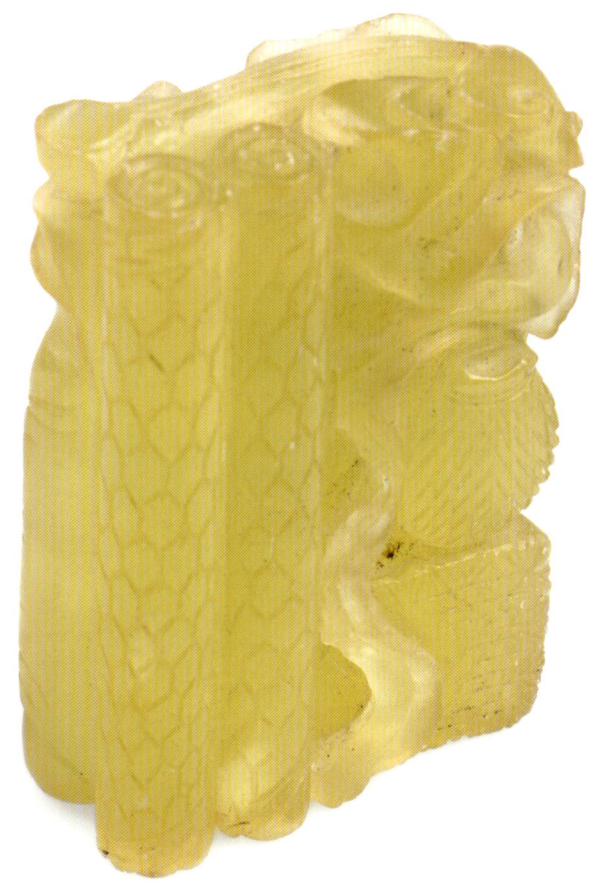

Plate 24

**Toggle in the shape of motifs
of 'attributes of a scholar'**
"文人四艺"饰图坠子

China, c.1700–1940
Jade
55 x 37 x 18 mm
Powerhouse Collection
Gift of Alastair Morrison, 1992
92/454

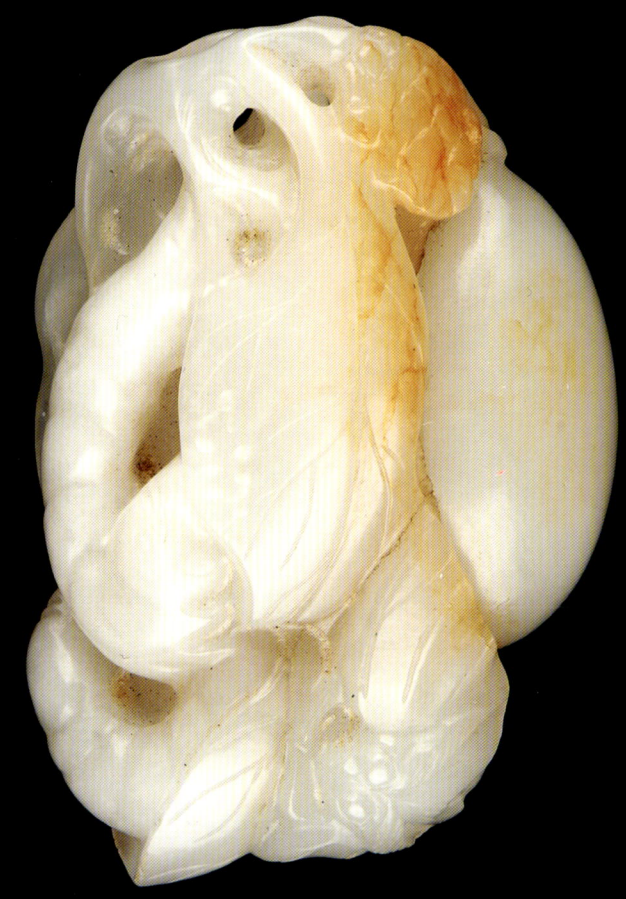

Plate 25

**Toggle in the shape of silkworms
and a mulberry**
蚕与桑叶形坠子

China, c.1700–1940
Jade
47 x 34 x 18 mm
Powerhouse Collection
Gift of Alastair Morrison, 1992
92/515

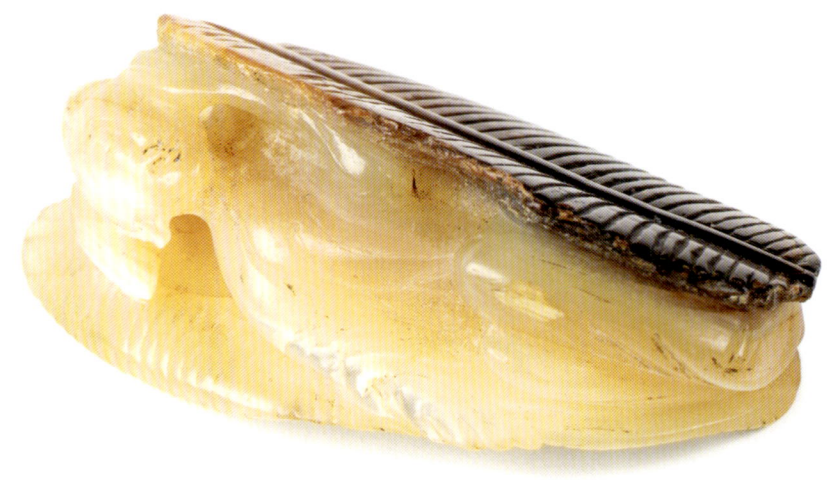

Plate 26
Toggle depicting a woman in banana leaves
香蕉叶伴妇人状坠子

China, c.1700–1940
Pearl shell
52 x 30 x 21 mm
Powerhouse Collection
Gift of Alastair Morrison, 1992
92/441

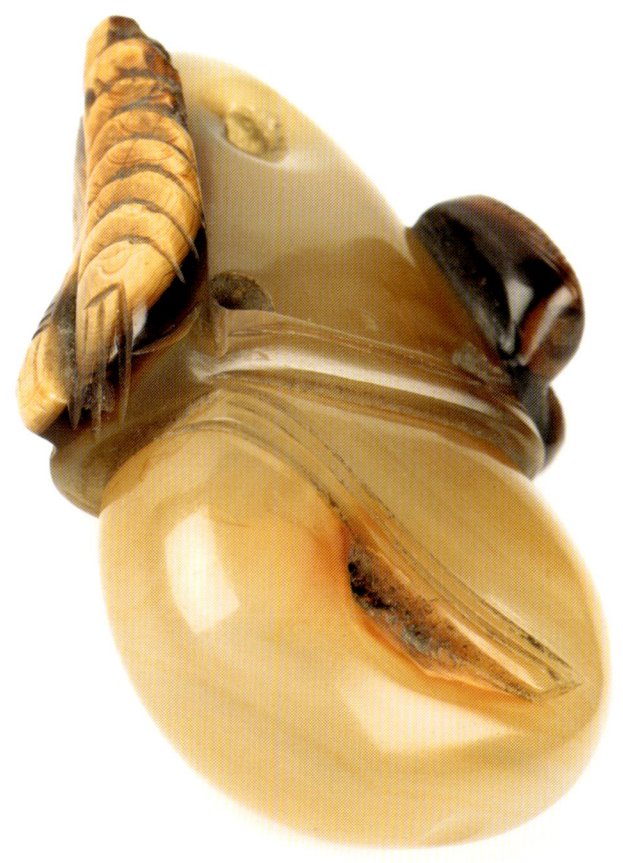

Plate 27

**Toggle in the shape of a gourd
and household implements**
葫芦与家庭用具式坠子

China, c.1700–1940
Honey-coloured agate
21 x 52 x 40 mm
Powerhouse Collection
Gift of Alastair Morrison, 1992

92/468

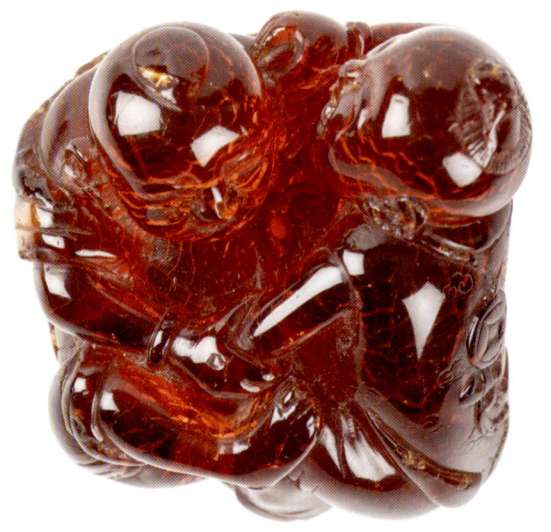

Plate 28

Toggle in the shape of two boys
双童子形坠子

China, c.1700–1940
Amber
29 x 30 x 25 mm
Powerhouse Collection
Gift of Alastair Morrison, 1992
92/707

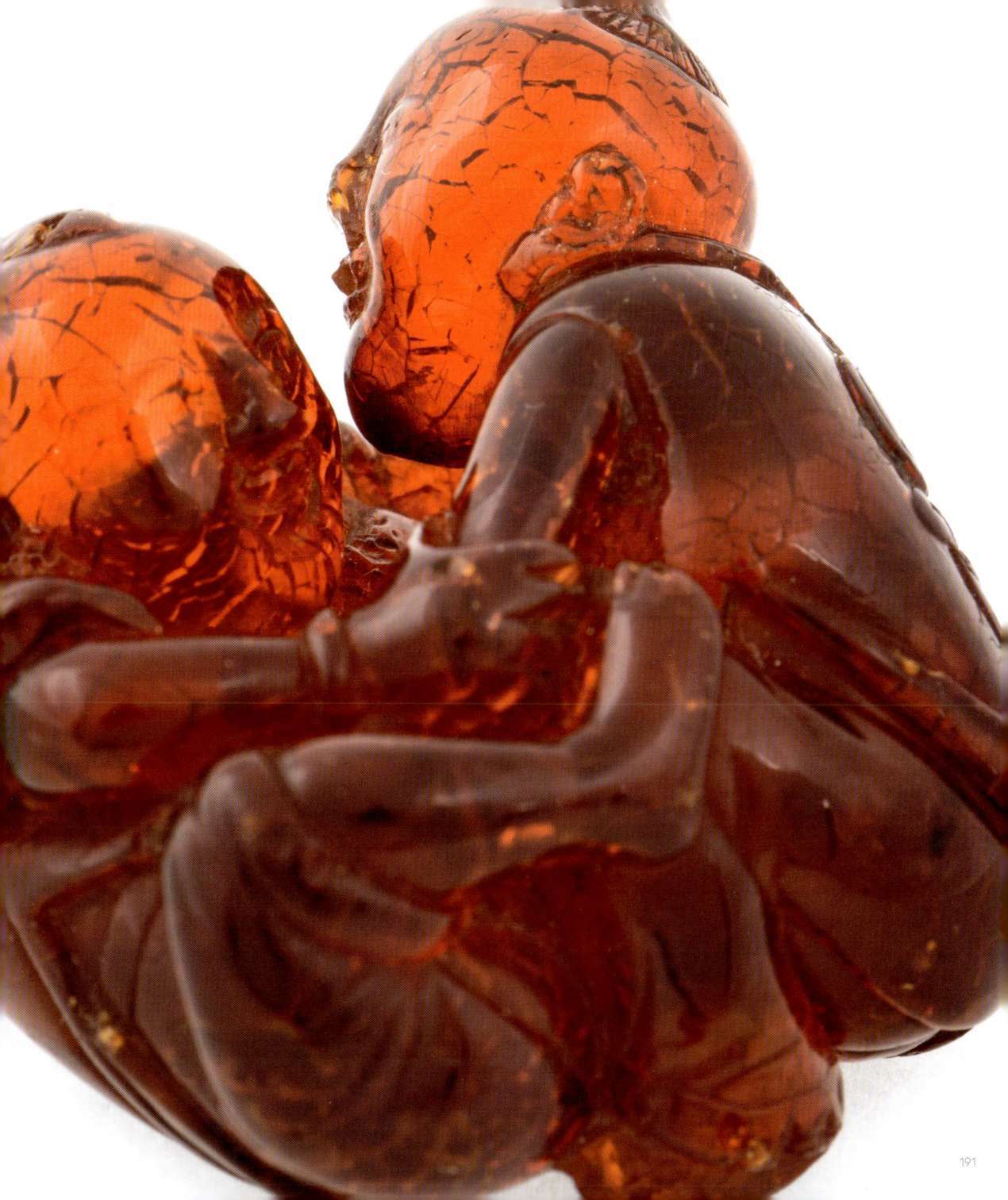

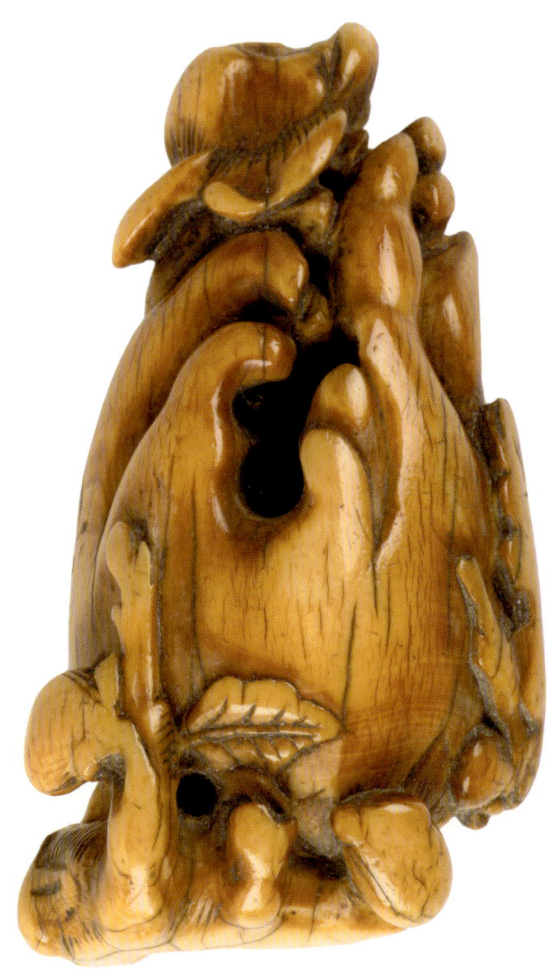

Plate 29

**Toggle in the shape of Buddha's
hand with a citron and lotus flower**
佛手、香橼与莲花形坠子

China, c.1700–1940
Ivory
32 x 60 x 20 mm
Powerhouse Collection
Gift of Alastair Morrison, 1992
92/625

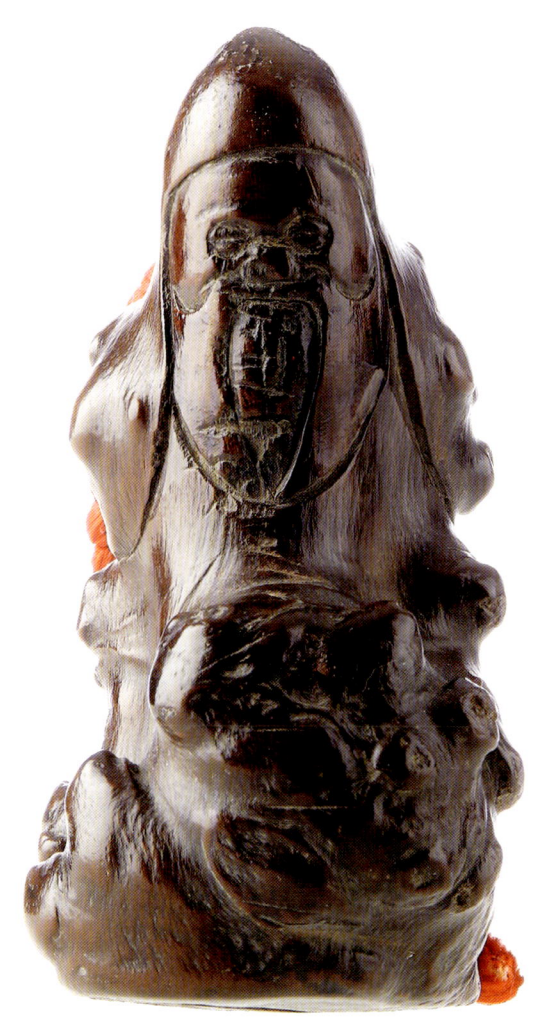

Plate 30

Toggle in the shape of Dongfang Shuo
东方朔形坠子

China, c.1700–1940
Wood, textile
69 x 42 x 35 mm
Powerhouse Collection
Gift of Alastair Morrison, 1992

92/532

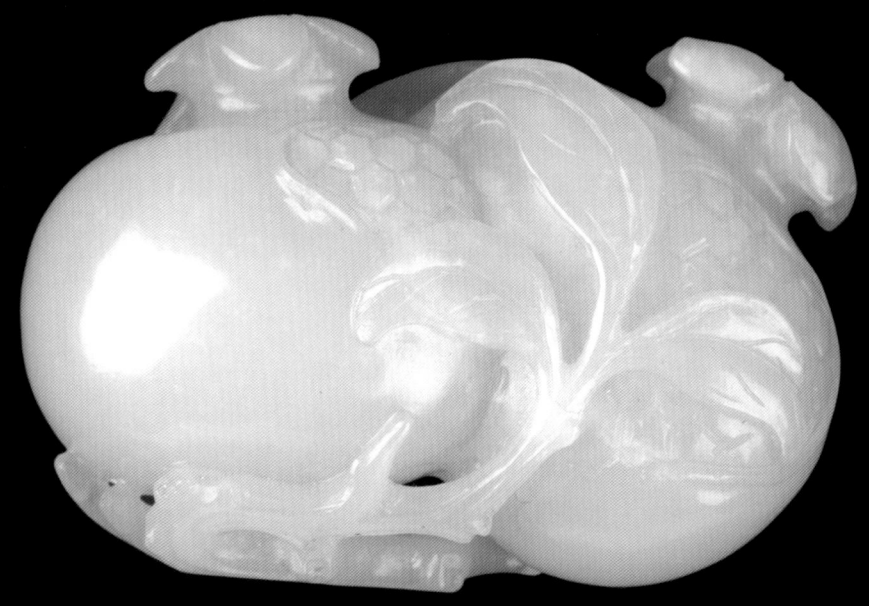

Plate 31

**Toggle in the shape of two pomegranates
and a cicada**
双石榴与蝉形坠子

China, c.1700–1940
Jade
35 x 52 x 23 mm
Powerhouse Collection
Gift of Alastair Morrison, 1992

92/511

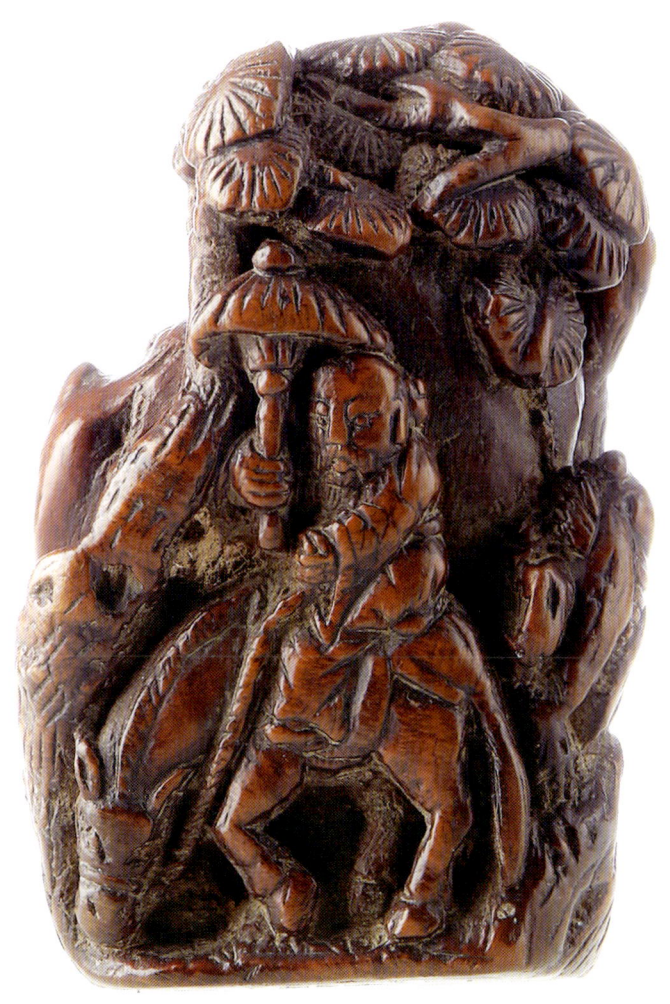

Plate 32

**Toggle in the shape
of Lu You on a donkey**
陆游骑驴形坠子

China, c.1700–1940
Wood
45 x 30 x 23 mm
Powerhouse Collection
Gift of Alastair Morrison, 1992

92/533

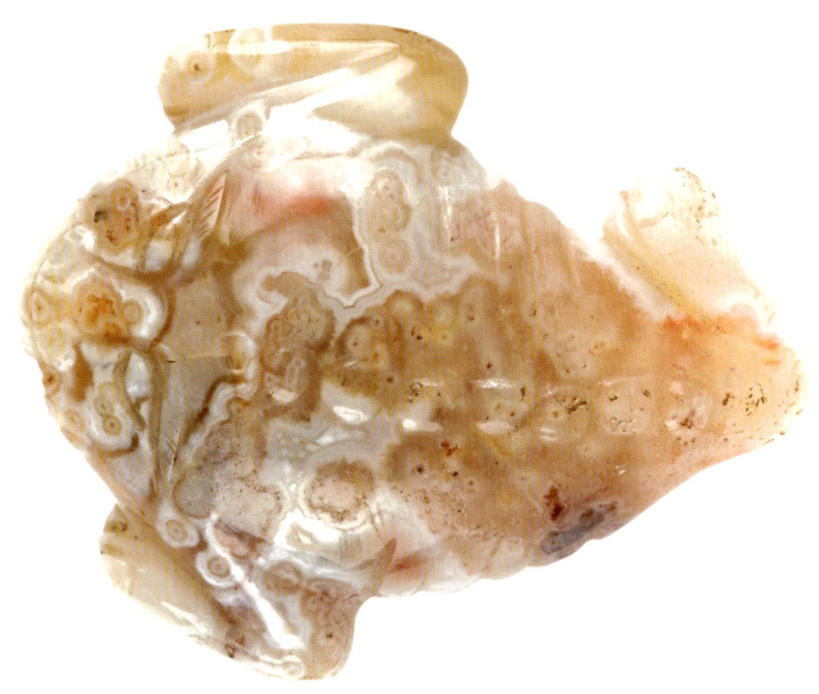

Plate 33

Toggle in the shape of a three-legged toad
三足蟾蜍形坠子

China, c.1700–1940
Agate
40 x 32 x 14 mm
Powerhouse Collection
Gift of Alastair Morrison, 1992

92/464

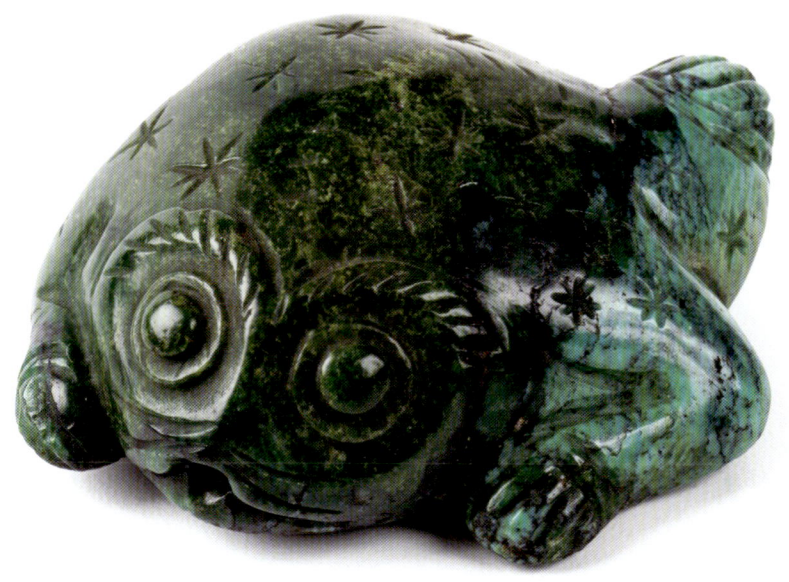

Plate 34

Toggle in the shape of a three-legged toad
三足蟾蜍形坠子

China, c.1700–1940
Turquoise
15 x 41 x 30 mm
Powerhouse Collection
Gift of Alastair Morrison, 1992

92/703

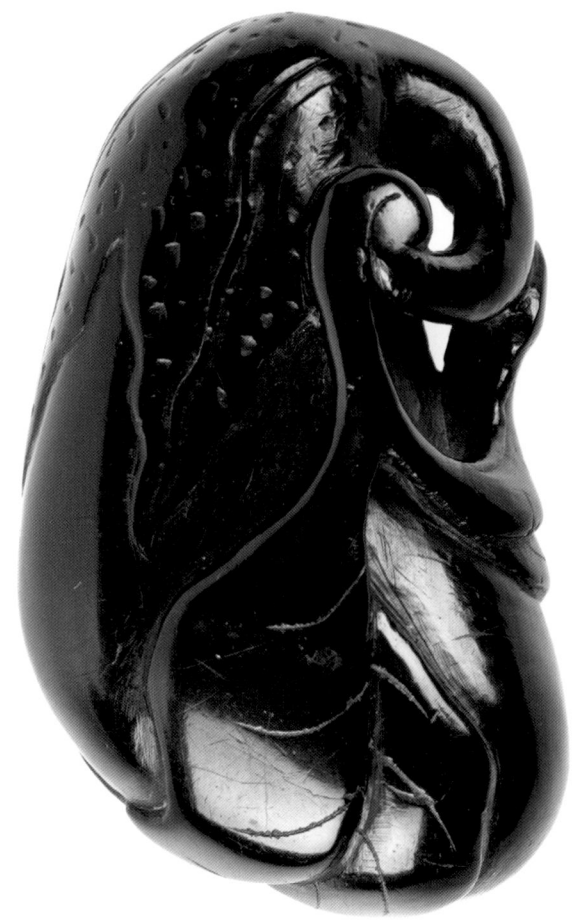

Plate 35

Toggle in the shape of an eggplant
茄子式坠子

China, c.1700–1940
Hardstone
51 x 36 x 21 mm
Powerhouse Collection
Gift of Alastair Morrison, 1992
92/497

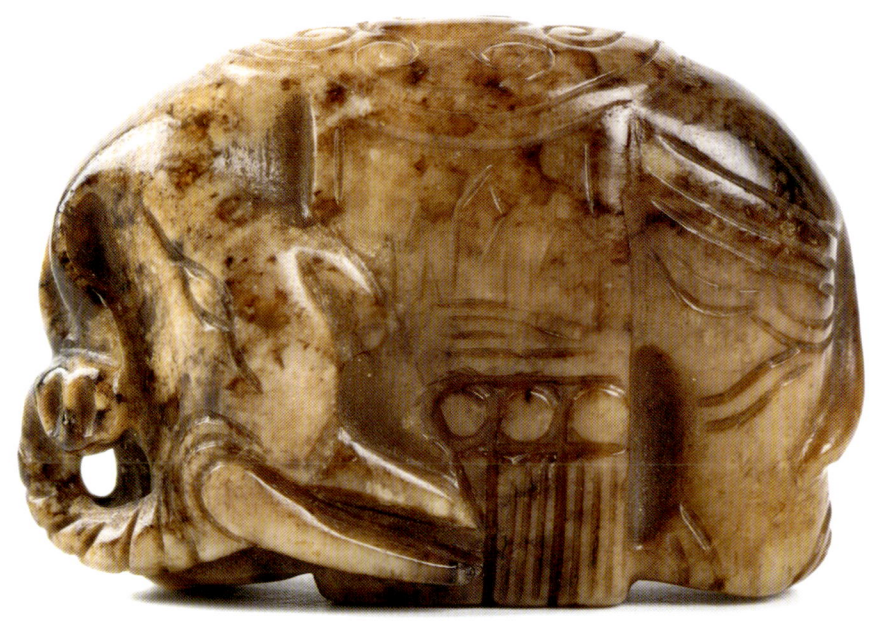

Plate 36

Toggle in the shape of an elephant
象形坠子

China, c.1700–1940
Agate
33 x 50 x 25 mm
Powerhouse Collection
Gift of Alastair Morrison, 1992
92/489

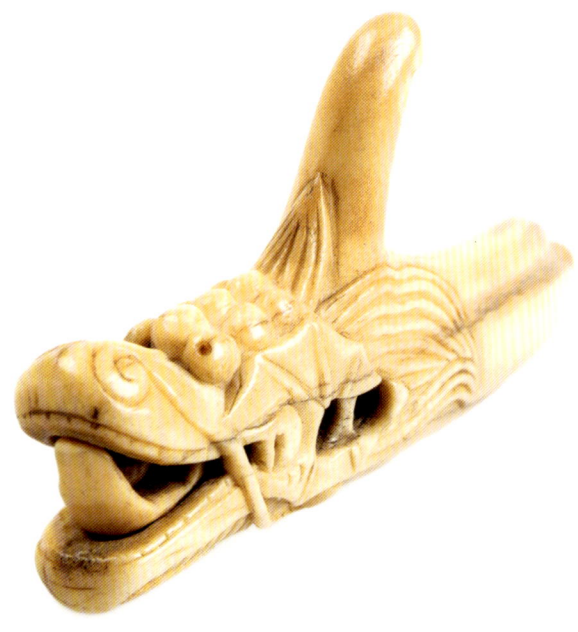
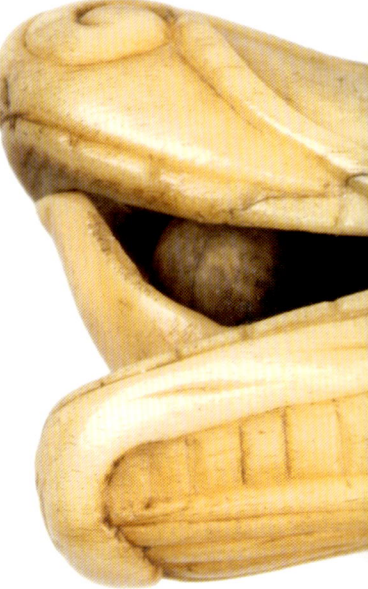

Plate 37

Toggle in the shape of a dragon with a moveable 'pearl' in its mouth
口含可移动"龙珠"的龙形坠子

China, c.1700–1940
Antler
29 x 44 x 20 mm
Powerhouse Collection
Gift of Alastair Morrison, 1992
92/673

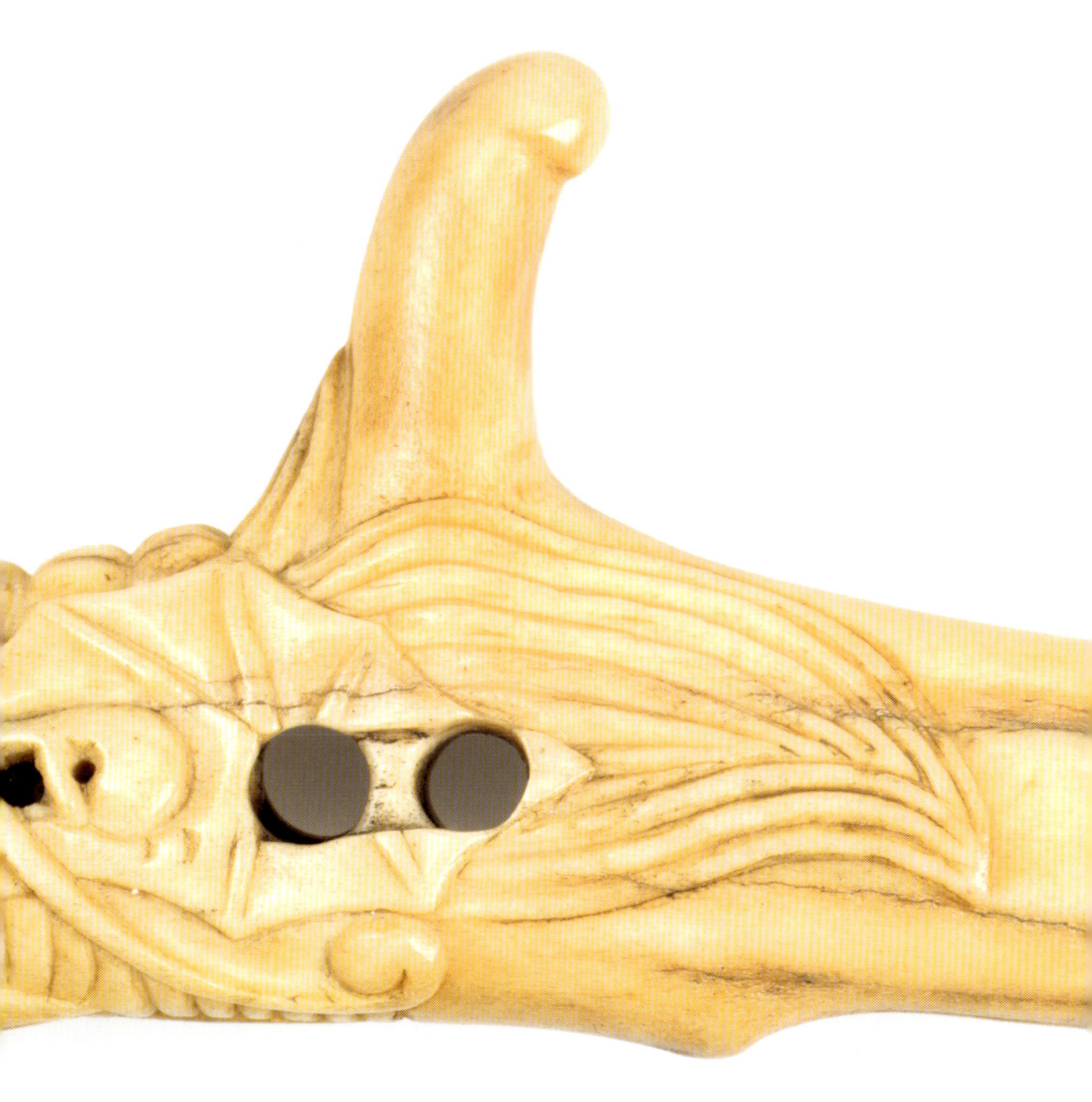

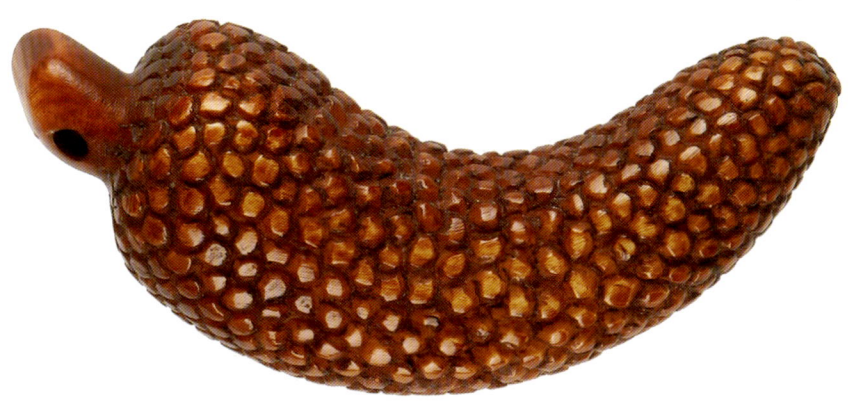

Plate 38
**Toggle in the shape
of a millet head**
黍穗式坠子

China, c.1700–1940
Ivory
56 x 15 x 19 mm

92/638

Plate 39
**Toggle in the shape
of a bean pod**
豆荚形坠子

China, c.1700–1940
Jade
63 x 35 x 13 mm

92/499

Powerhouse Collection
Gift of Alastair Morrison, 1992

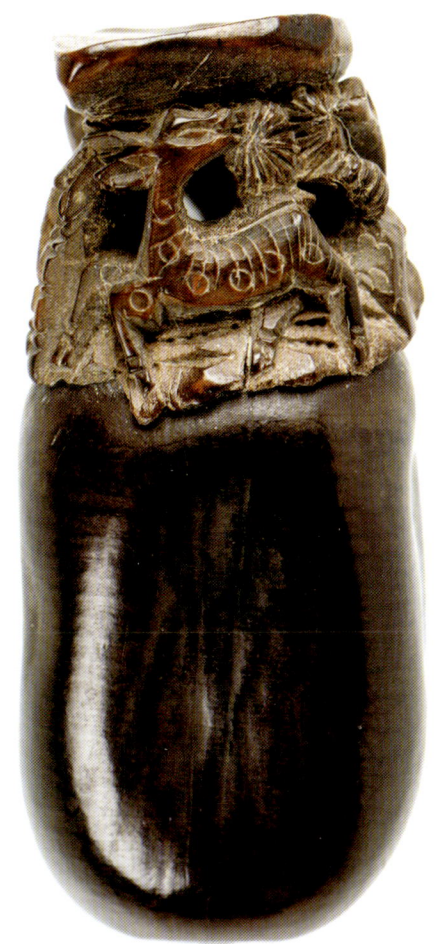

Plate 40

**Toggle made of a seed pod carved
with animal and foliage motifs**
种荚坠子，刻有动物与树叶饰图

China, c.1700–1940
Seed pod
35 x 11 x 12 mm
Powerhouse Collection
Gift of Alastair Morrison, 1992
92/529

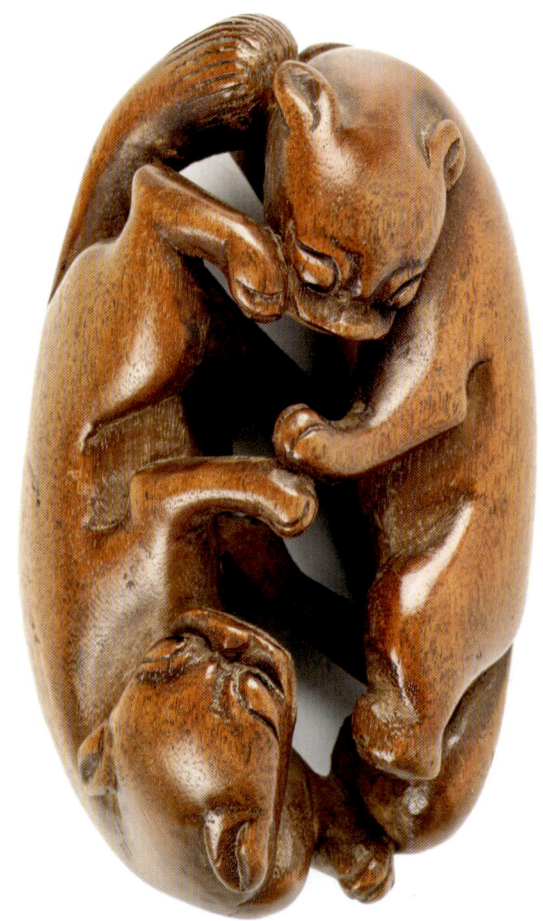

Plate 41

Toggle in the shape of two playing cats
双猫嬉戏式坠子

China, c.1700–1940
Wood
59 x 35 x 23 mm
Powerhouse Collection
Gift of Alastair Morrison, 1992
92/541

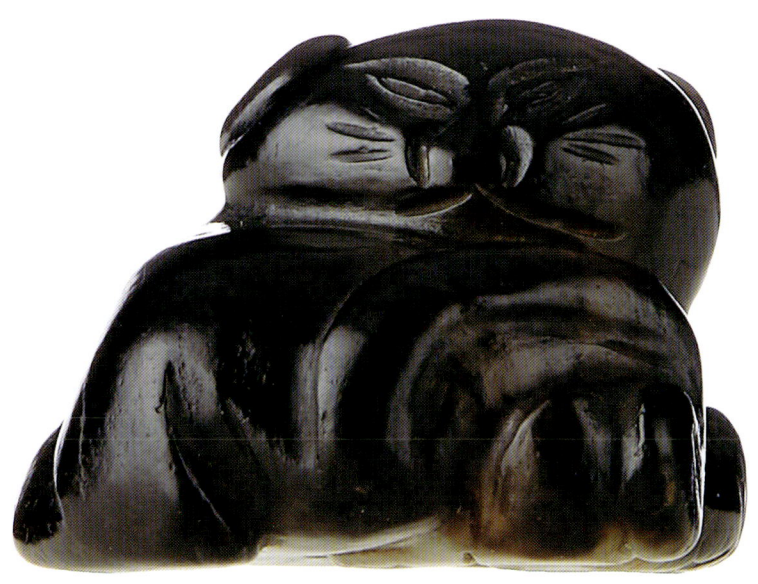

Plate 42

Toggle in the shape of a seated cat
坐猫形坠子

China, c.1700–1940
Jade
20 x 30 x 30 mm
Powerhouse Collection
Gift of Alastair Morrison, 1992

92/495

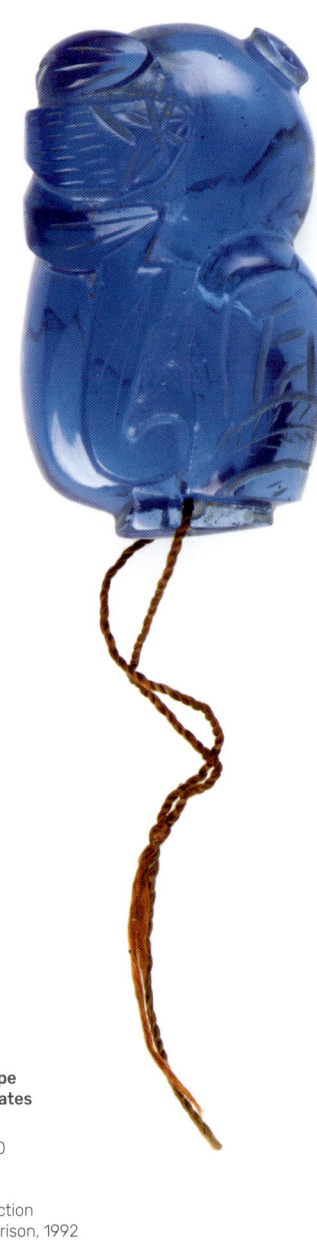
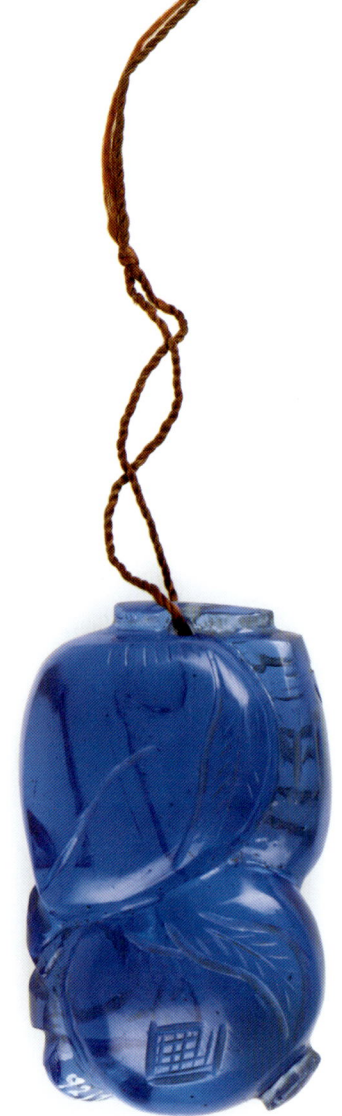

Plate 43

**Toggle in the shape
of two pomegranates**
双石榴形坠子

China, c.1700–1940
Glass, textile
44 x 27 x 15 mm
Powerhouse Collection
Gift of Alastair Morrison, 1992
92/701

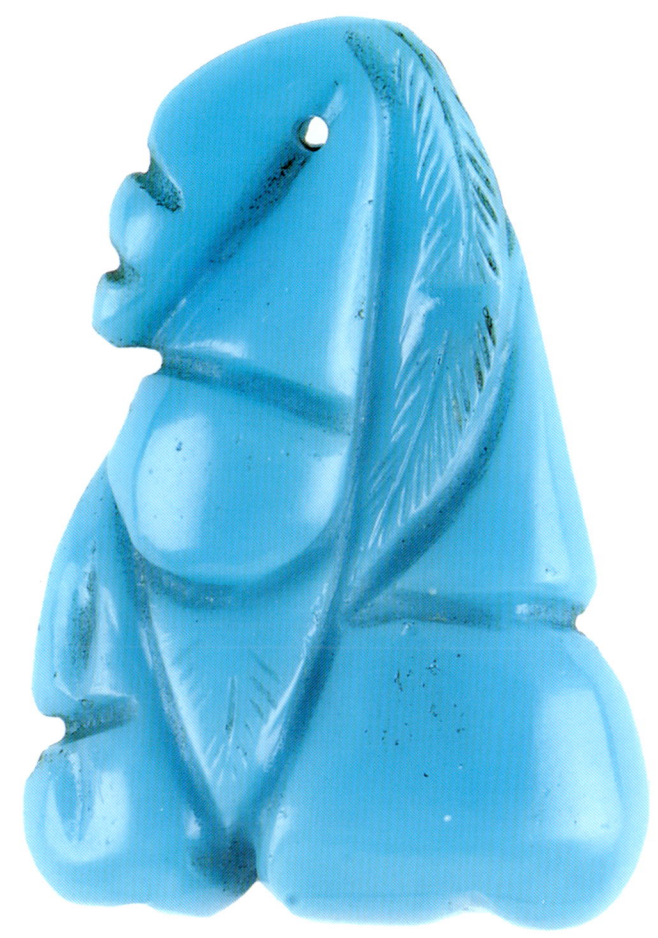

Plate 44

Toggle in the shape of gourds and leaves
葫芦与叶子形坠子

China, c.1700–1940
Glass
44 x 32 x 11 mm
Powerhouse Collection
Gift of Alastair Morrison, 1992

92/702

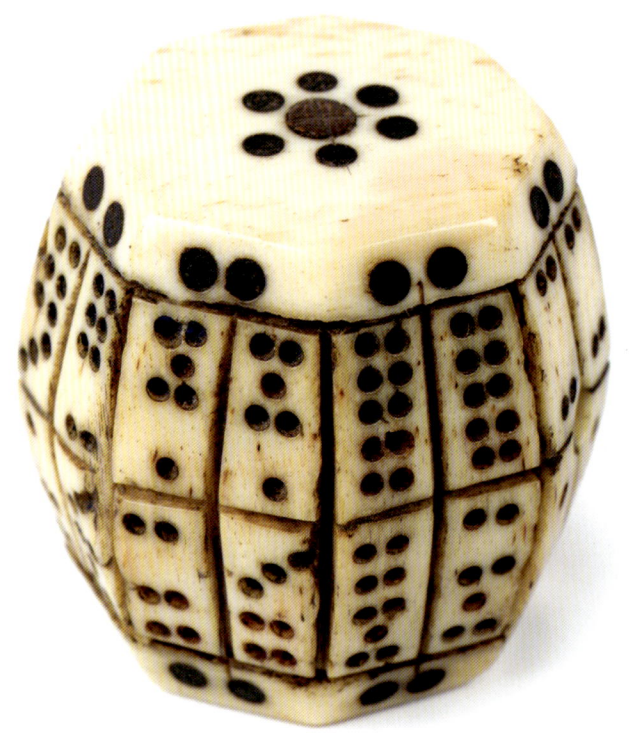

Plate 45

Domino dice toggle
骨牌骰子坠子

China, c.1700–1940
Bone
27 x 30 x 20 mm
Powerhouse Collection
Gift of Alastair Morrison, 1992

92/680

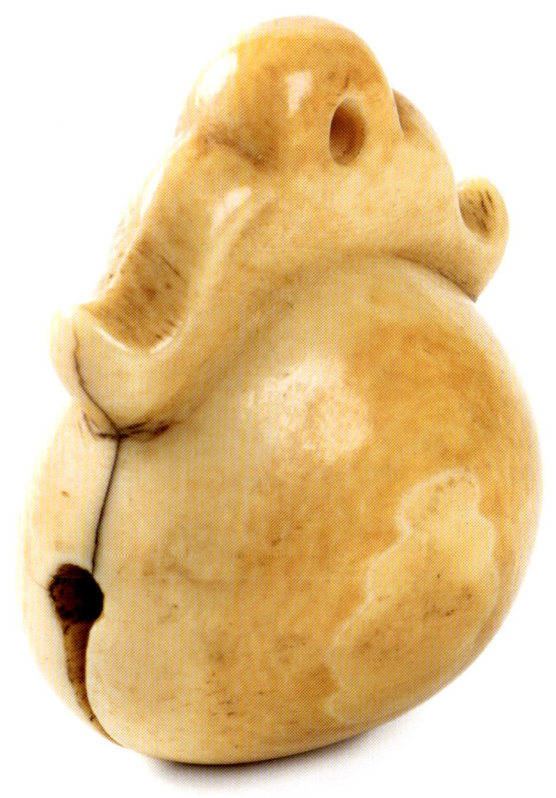

Plate 46

Toggle in the shape of a slit drum
木鱼式坠子

China, c.1700–1940
Ivory
40 x 35 x 23 mm
Powerhouse Collection
Gift of Alastair Morrison, 1992
92/685

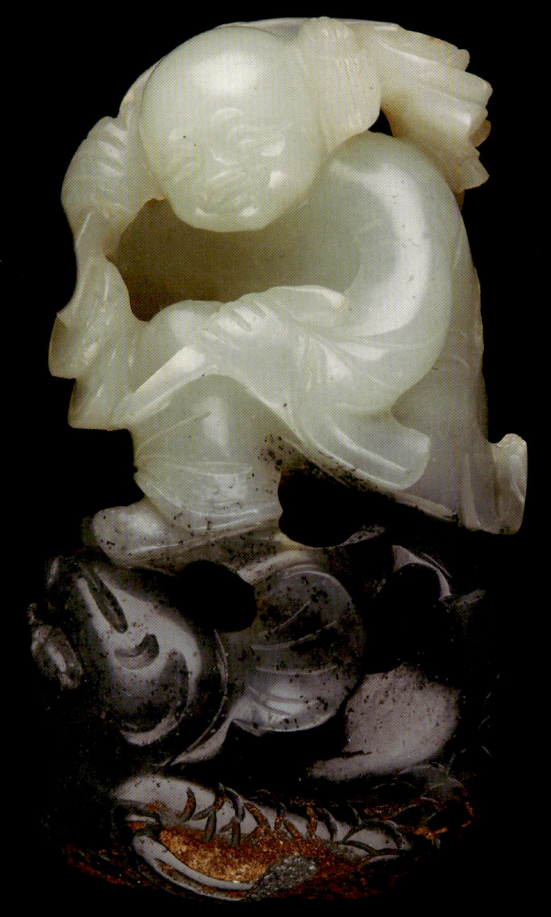

Plate 47

**Toggle in the shape of
a boy with a dragonfish**
童子骑龙鱼形坠子

China, c.1700–1940
Jade
57 x 33 x 19 mm
Powerhouse Collection
Gift of Alastair Morrison, 1992
92/498

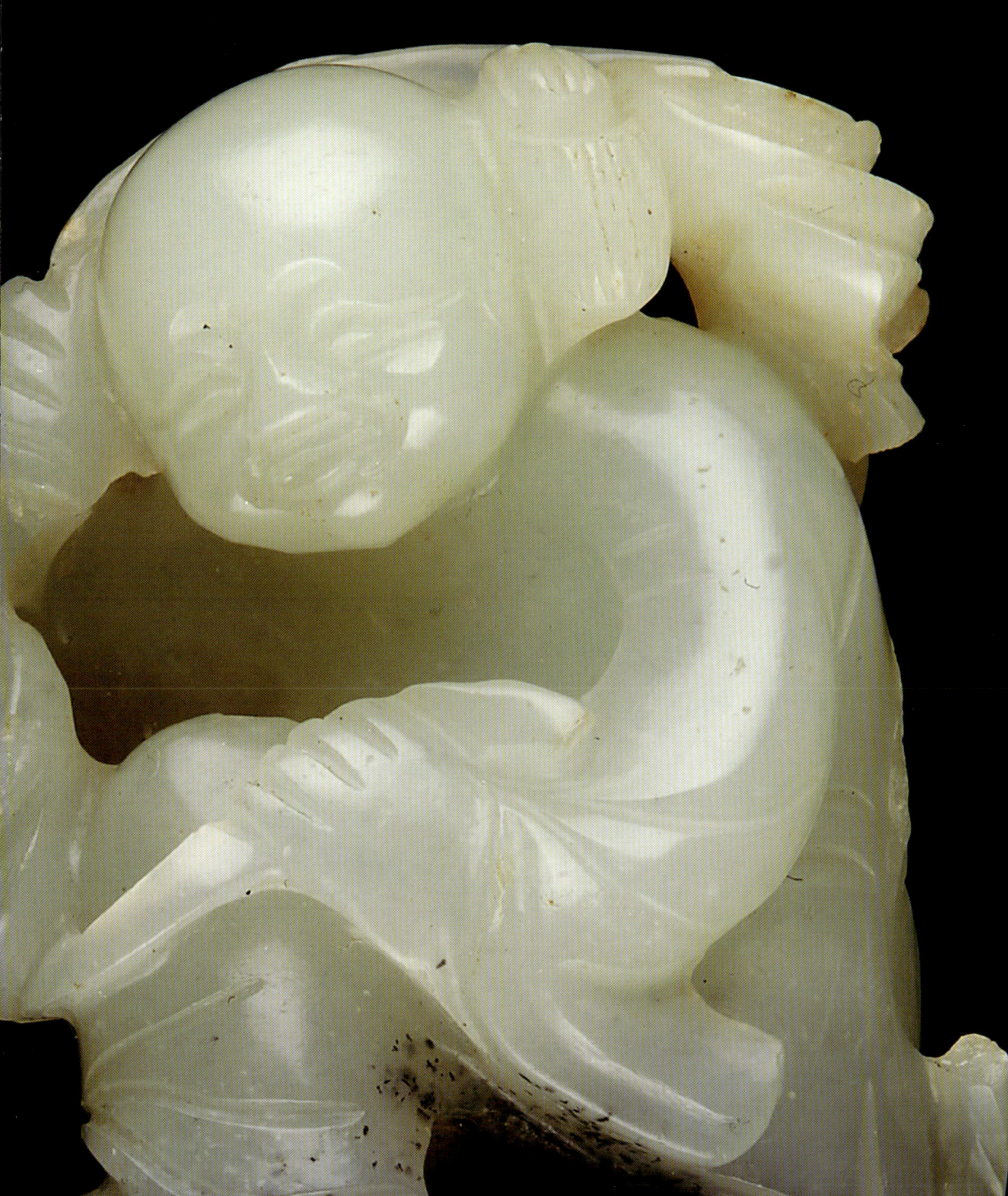

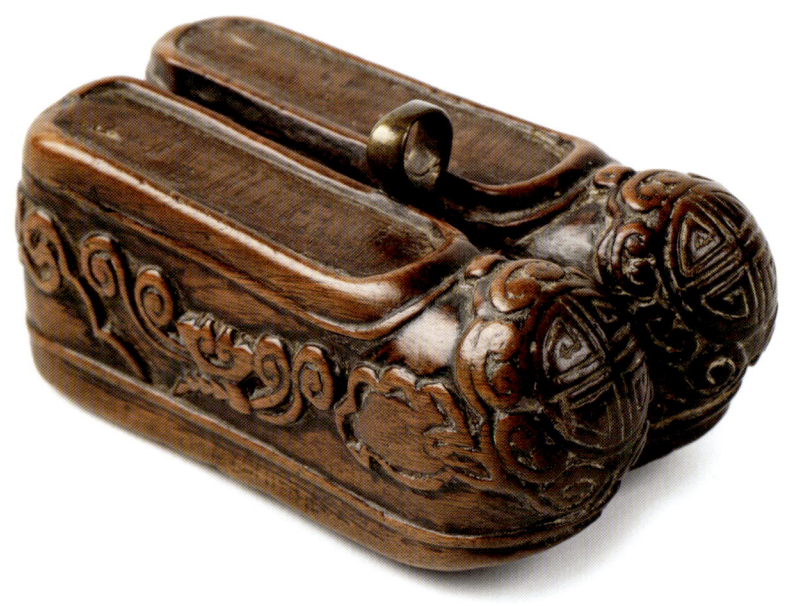

Plate 48

Toggle in the shape of a pair of shoes
履式坠子

China, c.1700–1940
Wood, metal
27 x 36 x 69 mm
Powerhouse Collection
Gift of Alastair Morrison, 1992

92/554

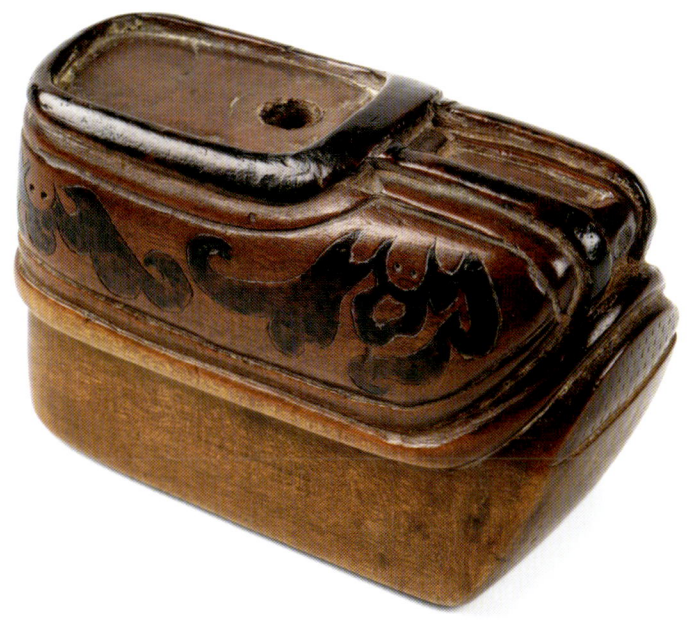

Plate 49

Toggle in the shape of a man's platform shoe
男士厚底靴式坠子

China, c.1700–1940
Wood
42 x 30 x 68 mm
Powerhouse Collection
Gift of Alastair Morrison, 1992
92/555

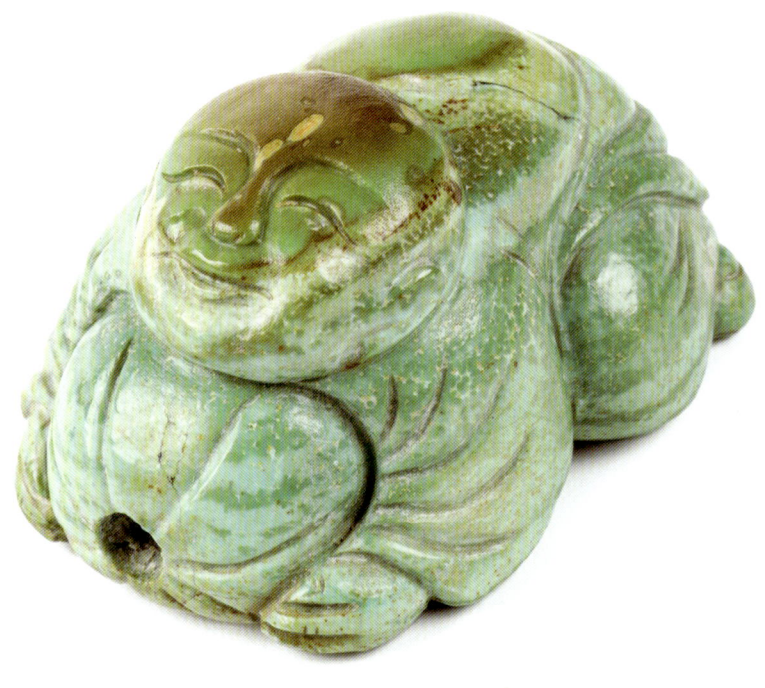

Plate 50

**Toggle depicting a child crouching
over a melon**
童子俯抱瓜状坠子

China, c.1700–1940
Turquoise
23 x 31 x 41 mm
Powerhouse Collection
Gift of Alastair Morrison, 1992

92/704

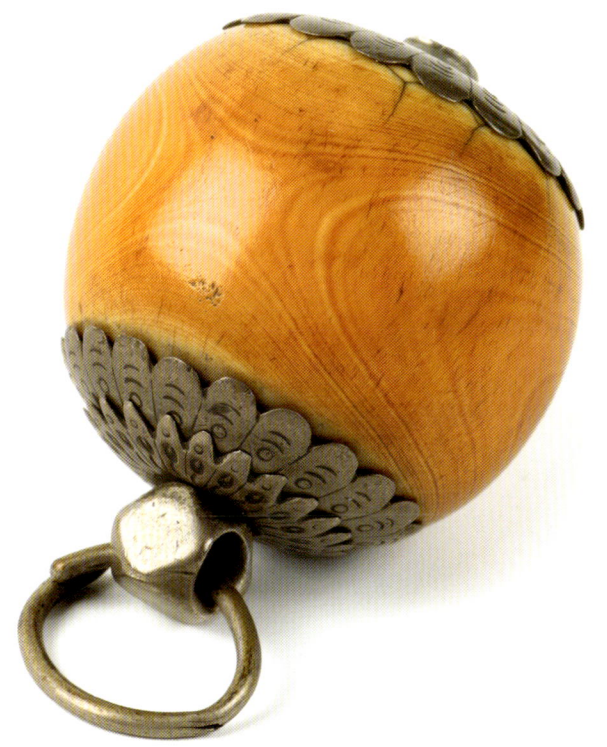

Plate 51
Toggle in the shape of a polished ivory ball
抛光象牙球形坠子

China, c.1700–1940
Ivory, metal
40 x 40 mm
Powerhouse Collection
Gift of Alastair Morrison, 1992
92/605

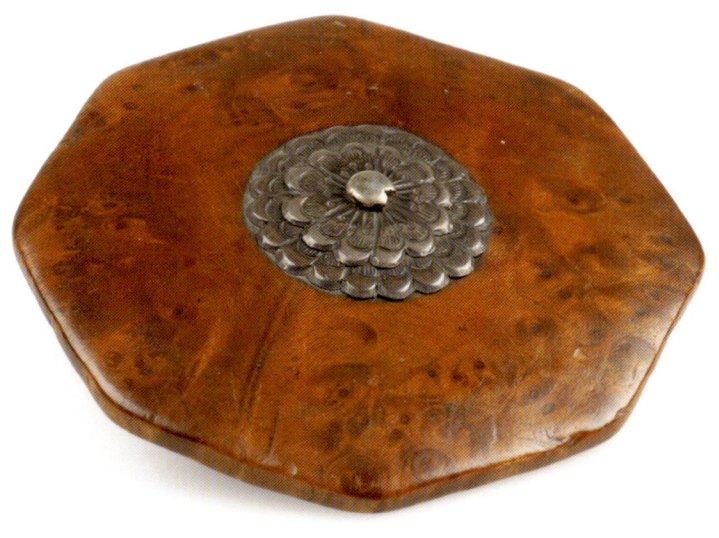

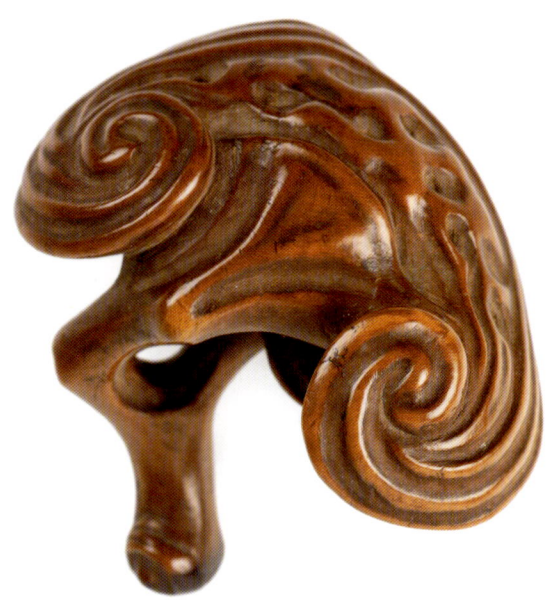

Plate 52

Toggle in the shape of a button
纽扣状坠子

China, c.1700–1940
Wood, silver
22 x 59 x 59 mm
92/475

Plate 53

**Toggle in the shape
of a *lingzhi* fungus**
灵芝式坠子

China, c.1700–1940
Wood
43 x 44 x 32 mm
92/522

Powerhouse Collection
Gift of Alastair Morrison, 1992

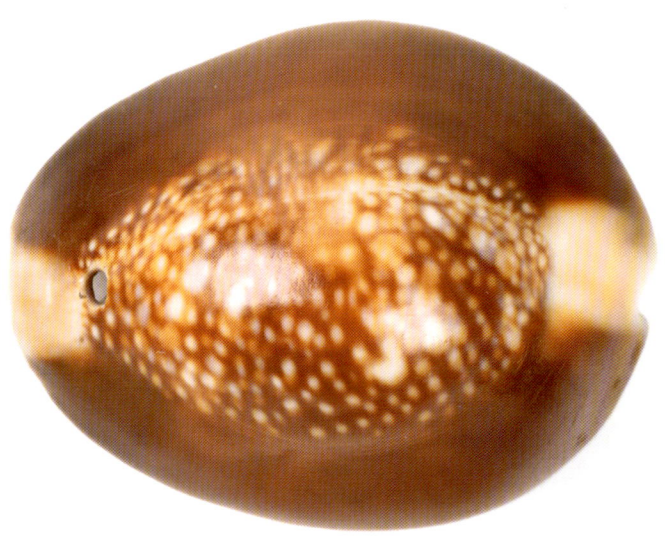

Plate 54

Toggle made from a natural cowry shell
玛瑙贝坠子

China, c.1700–1940
Cowry shell
15 x 33 x 25 mm
92/444

Plate 55

Toggle in the shape of a conch shell
海螺壳式坠子

China, c.1700–1940
Crystal
42 x 30 x 23 mm
92/457

Powerhouse Collection
Gift of Alastair Morrison, 1992

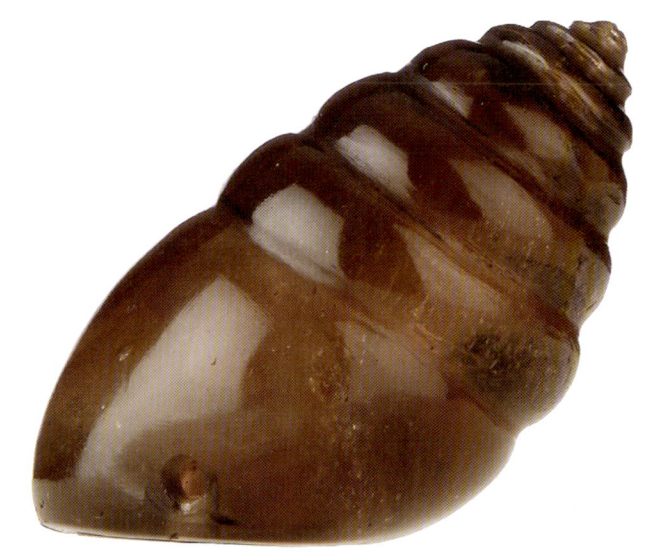

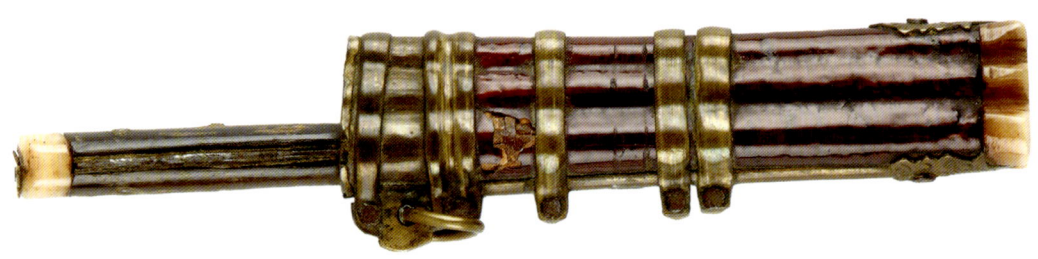

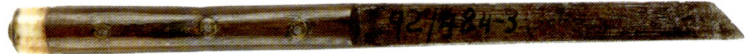

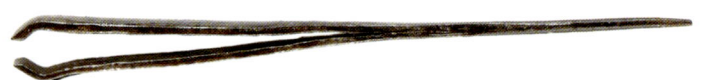

Plate 56
Toggle in the form of a knife set
刀具坠子

China, c.1700–1940
Wood, bone, metal
10 x 20 x 95 mm
Powerhouse Collection
Gift of Alastair Morrison, 1992

92/484

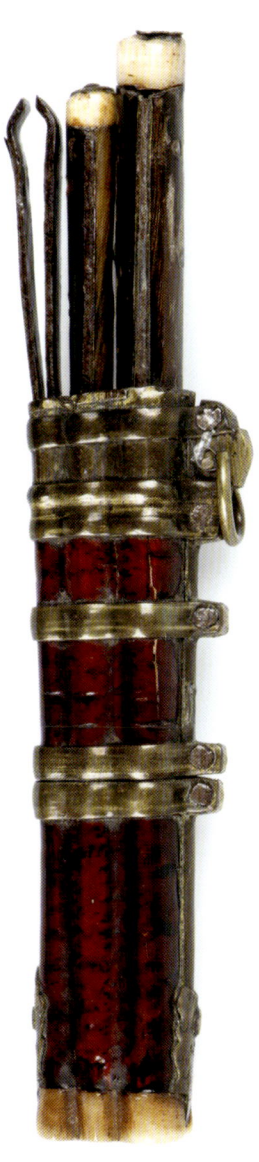

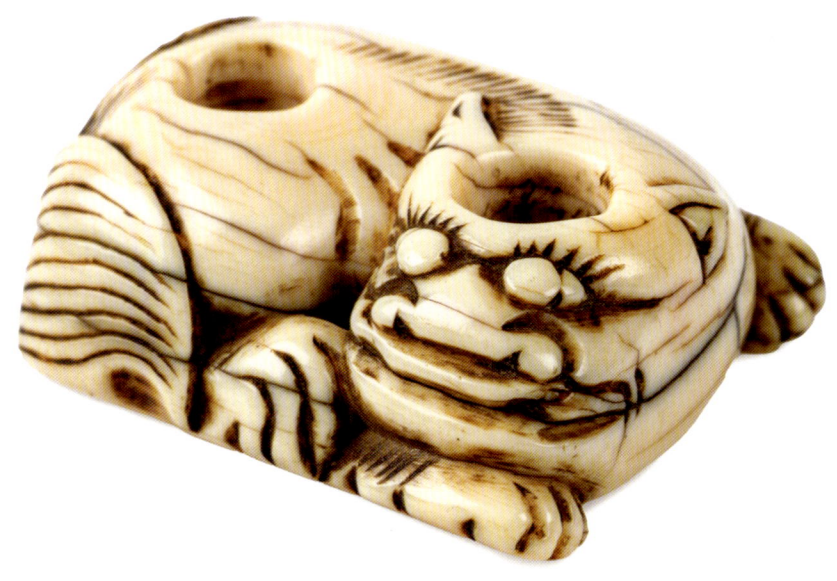

Plate 57
**Toggle in the shape of a lion-like
mythical animal**
狮样瑞兽形坠子

China, c.1700–1940
Ivory
35 x 37 x 18 mm
Powerhouse Collection
Gift of Alastair Morrison, 1992
92/653

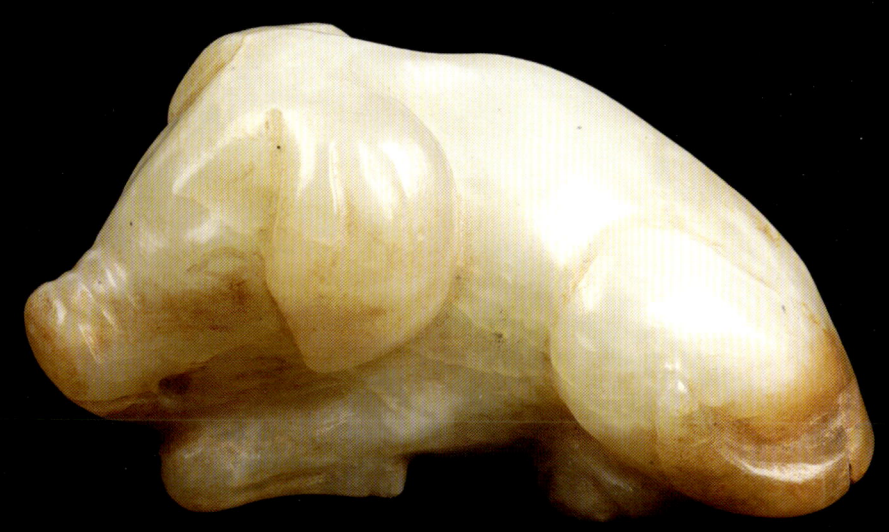

Plate 58

Toggle in the shape of a pig
豚式坠子

China, c.1700–1940
Jade
44 x 22 x 20 mm
Powerhouse Collection
Gift of Alastair Morrison, 1992
92/503

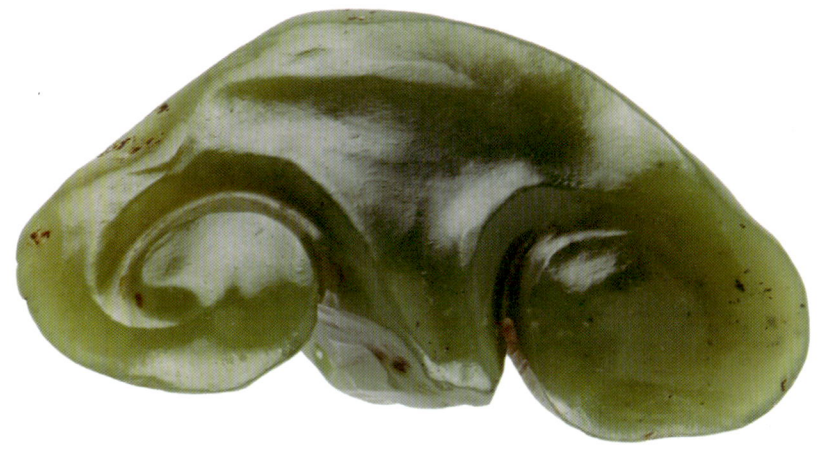

Plate 59

Toggle in the shape of a *lingzhi* fungus
灵芝式坠子

China, c.1700–1940
Jade
20 x 28 x 58 mm
Powerhouse Collection
Gift of Alastair Morrison, 1992

92/453

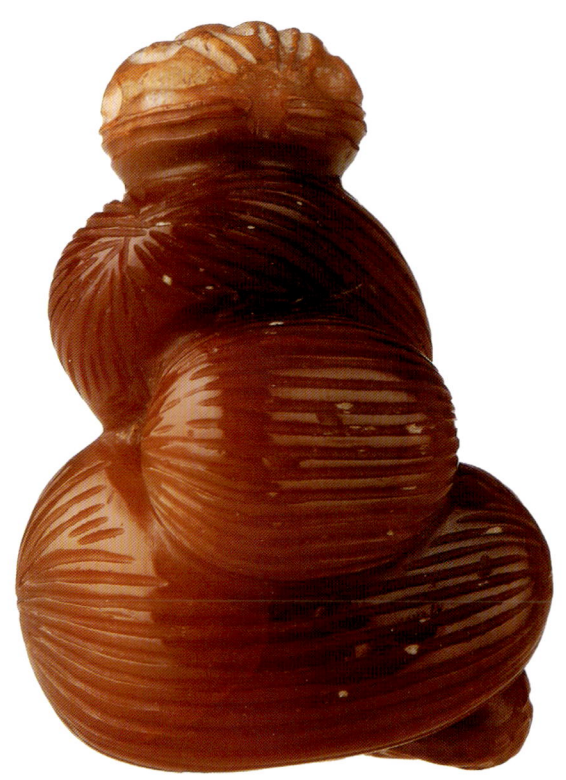

Plate 60

Toggle in the shape of jujubes and peanuts
红枣花生式坠子

China, c.1700–1940
Agate
28 x 45 x 32 mm
Powerhouse Collection
Gift of Alastair Morrison, 1992
92/469

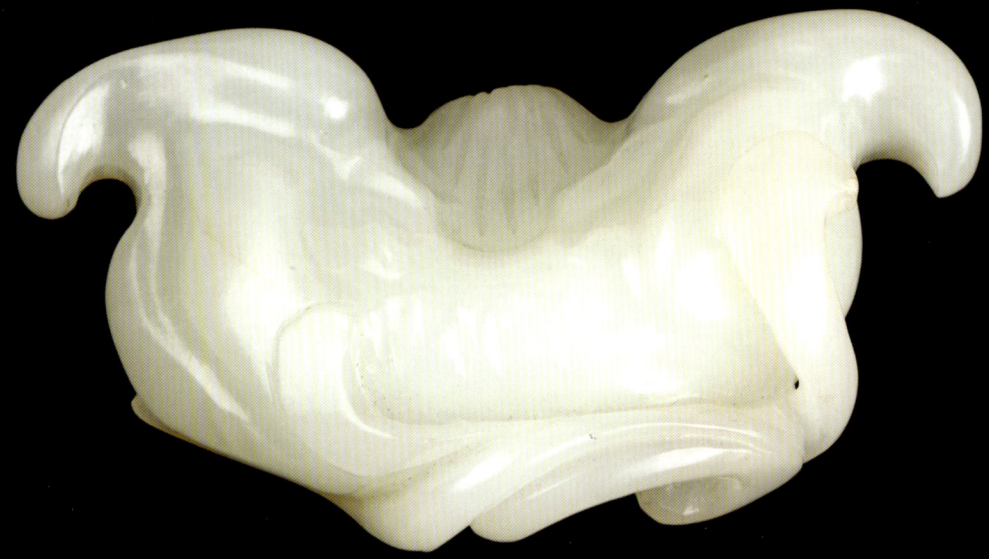

Plate 61
Toggle in the shape of a water caltrop
菱角式坠子

China, c.1700–1940
Jade
18 x 50 x 27 mm
Powerhouse Collection
Gift of Alastair Morrison, 1992
92/510

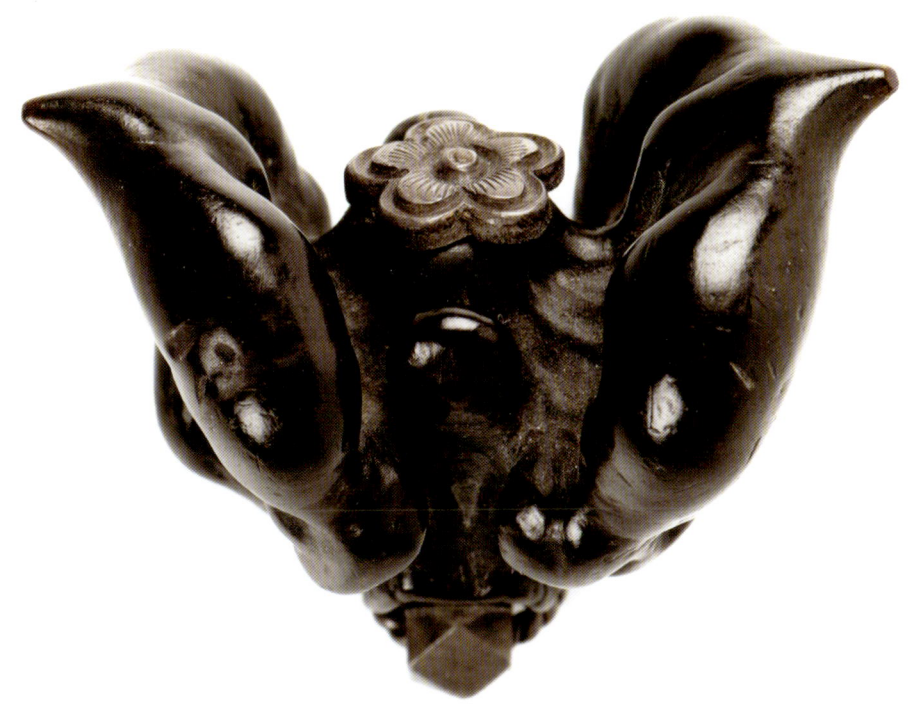

Plate 62

**Toggle made from a water caltrop
decorated with a silver flower**
银花饰菱角坠子

China, c.1700–1940
Water caltrop, silver
28 x 35 x 24 mm
Powerhouse Collection
Gift of Alastair Morrison, 1992
92/481

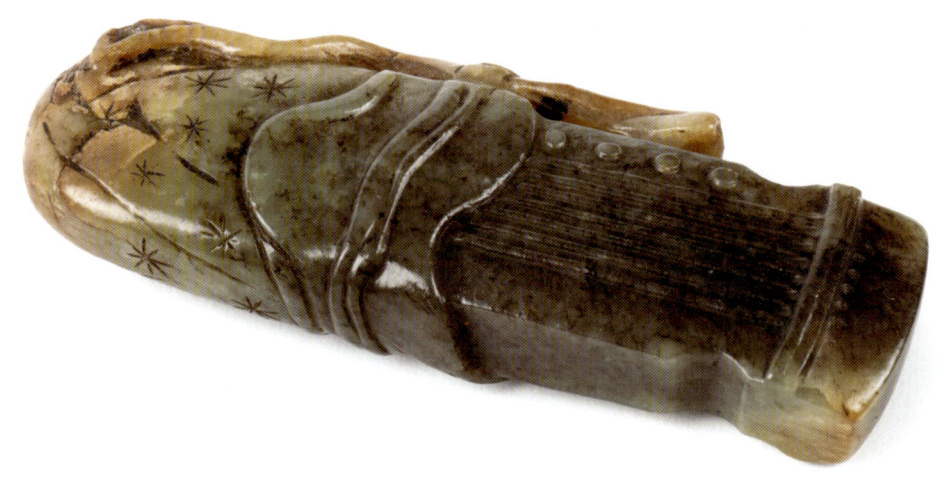

Plate 63

**Toggle in the shape of a zither
covered by cloth**
琴袋覆盖的古琴式坠子

China, c.1700–1940
Jade
31 x 80 x 15 mm
Powerhouse Collection
Gift of Alastair Morrison, 1992

92/486

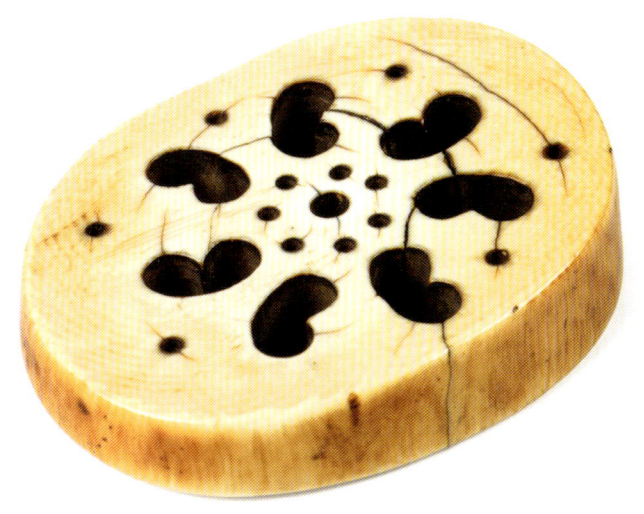

Plate 64

**Toggle in the shape of a slice
of lotus root**
藕片式坠子

China, c.1700–1940
Ivory
52 x 39 x 14 mm
92/623

Plate 65

Toggle in the shape of a lotus root
莲根式坠子

China, c.1700–1940
Soapstone
10 x 65 x 45 mm
92/494

Powerhouse Collection
Gift of Alastair Morrison, 1992

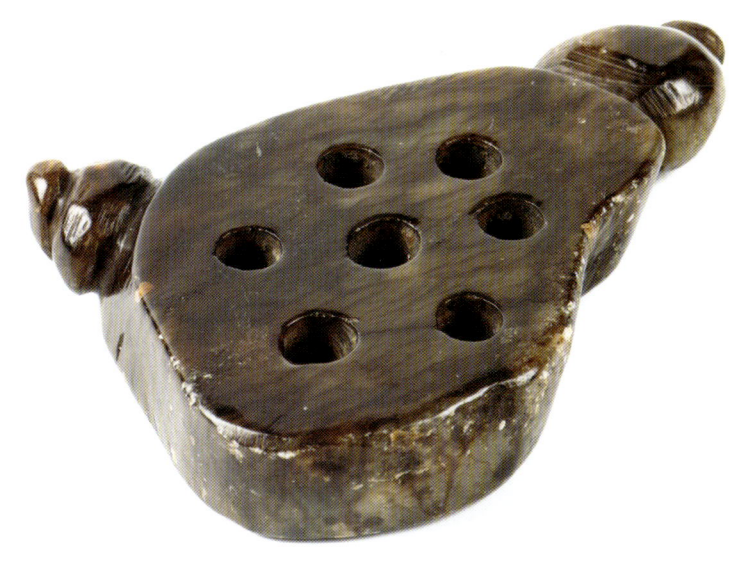

227

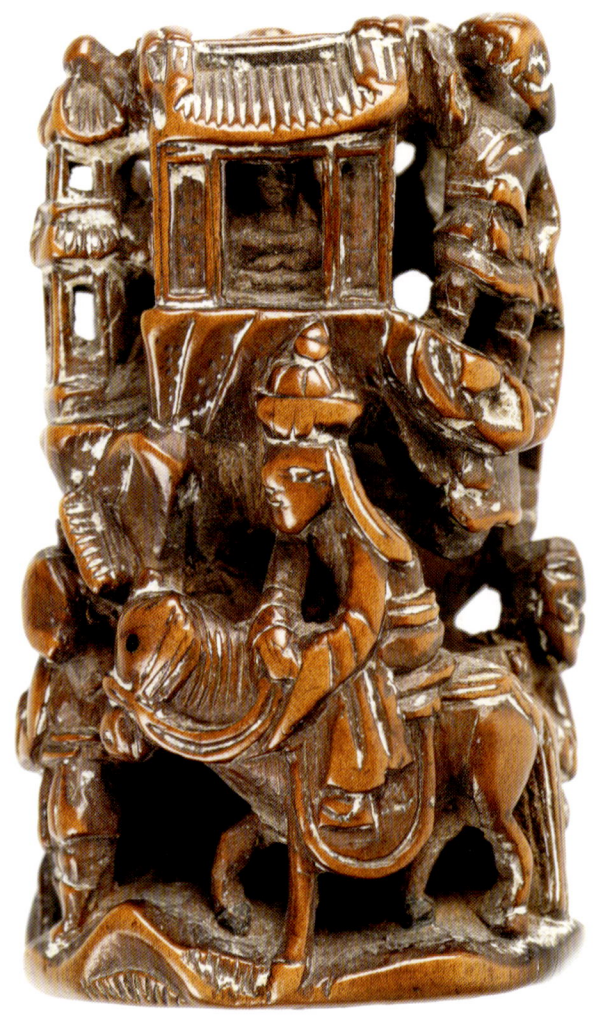

Plate 66

**Toggle depicting a scene
from *Journey to the West***
《西游记》坠子

China, c.1700–1940
Wood
46 x 29 x 20 mm
Powerhouse Collection
Gift of Alastair Morrison, 1992
92/584

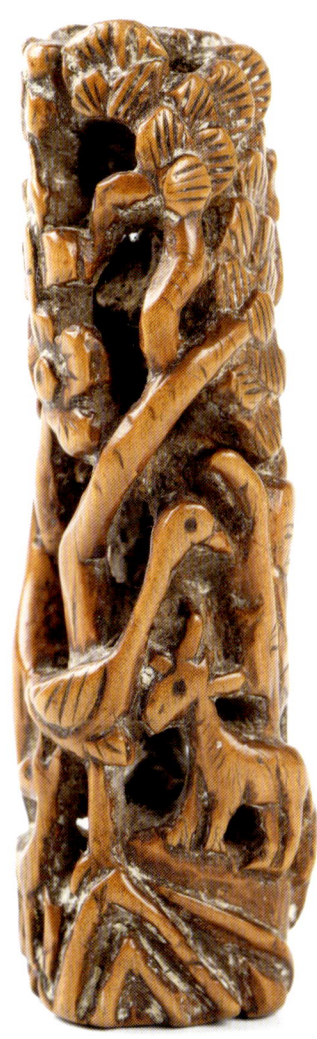

Plate 67

**Seal toggle in the shape of a plum
tree with blossoms and animals**
梅花与瑞兽形图章坠子

China, c.1700–1940
Wood
53 x 17 x 16 mm
Powerhouse Collection
Gift of Alastair Morrison, 1992
92/585

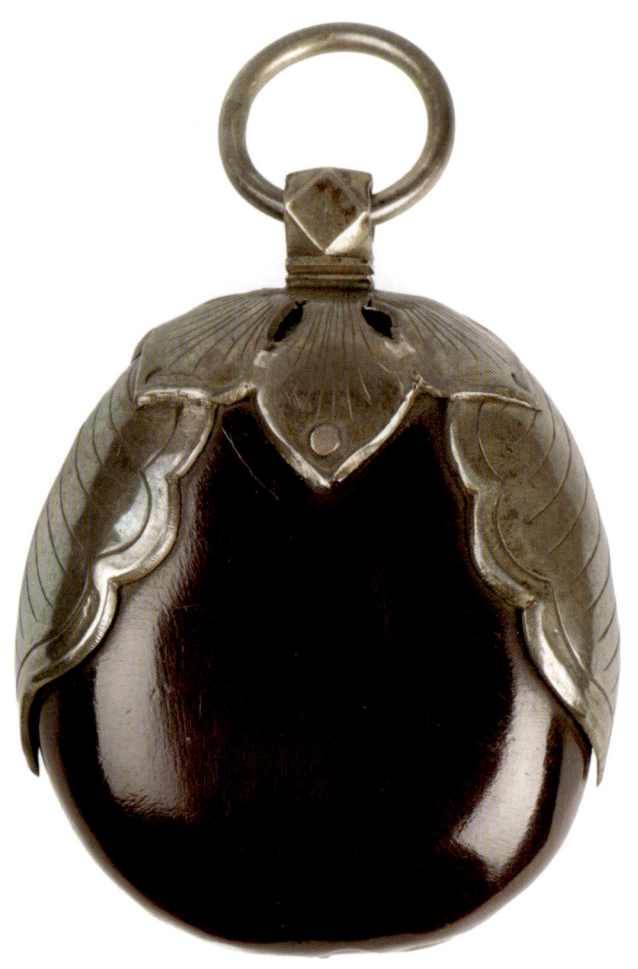

Plate 68

Toggle made of gila bean with a silver mount
楛藤子银托坠子

China, c.1700–1940
Gila bean, silver
20 x 70 x 45 mm
Powerhouse Collection
Gift of Alastair Morrison, 1992
92/476

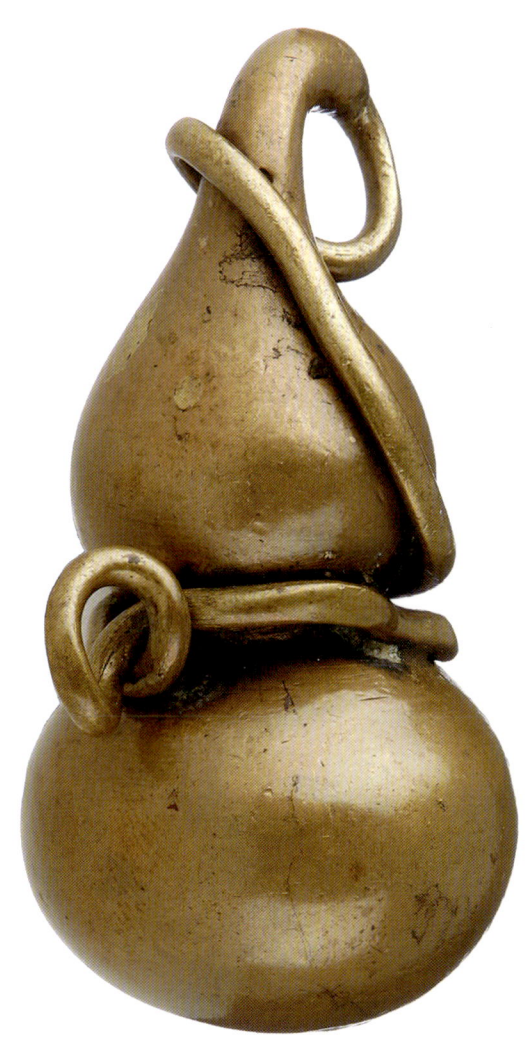

Plate 69

Toggle in the shape of a bottle gourd
葫芦瓶形坠子

China, c.1700–1940
Brass
60 x 37 x 30 mm
Powerhouse Collection
Gift of Alastair Morrison, 1992
92/433

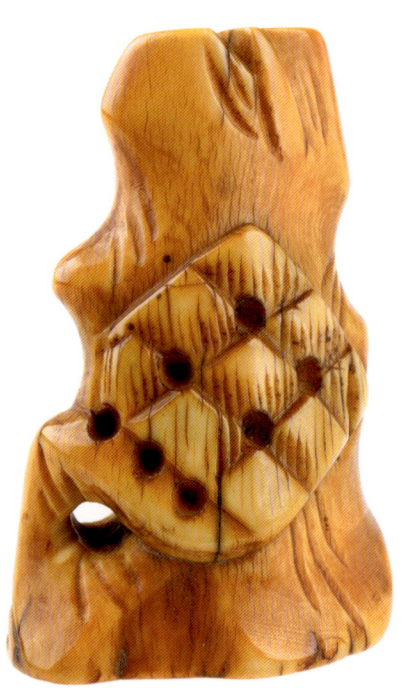
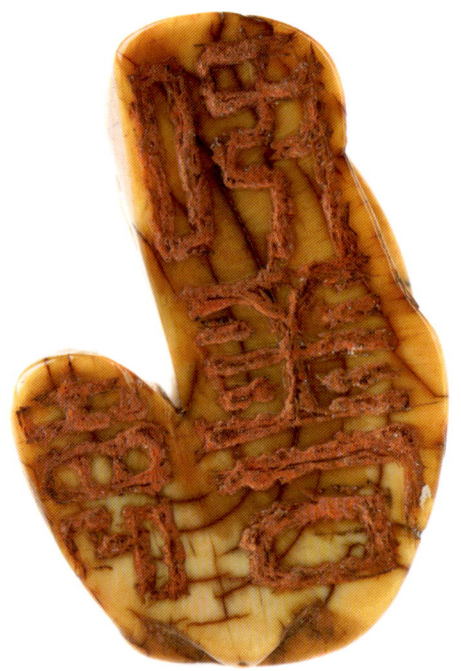

Plate 70

**Seal toggle in the shape of a pine tree,
with Chinese inscription at the bottom**
松树形图章坠子，底部刻有"寿如金石"四字

China, c.1700–1940
Ivory
29 x 44 x 20 mm
Powerhouse Collection
Gift of Alastair Morrison, 1992
92/670

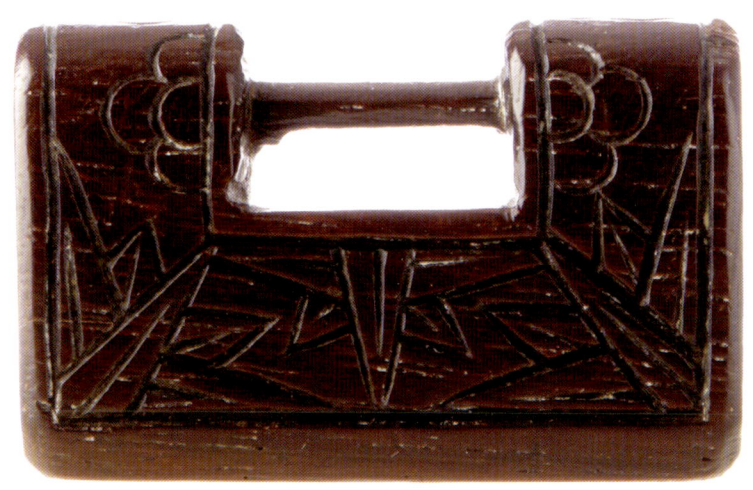

Plate 71

**Toggle in the shape of a padlock
carved with auspicious patterns**
祥纹挂锁式坠子

China, c.1700–1940
Wood
22 x 35 x 28 mm
Powerhouse Collection
Gift of Alastair Morrison, 1992
92/559

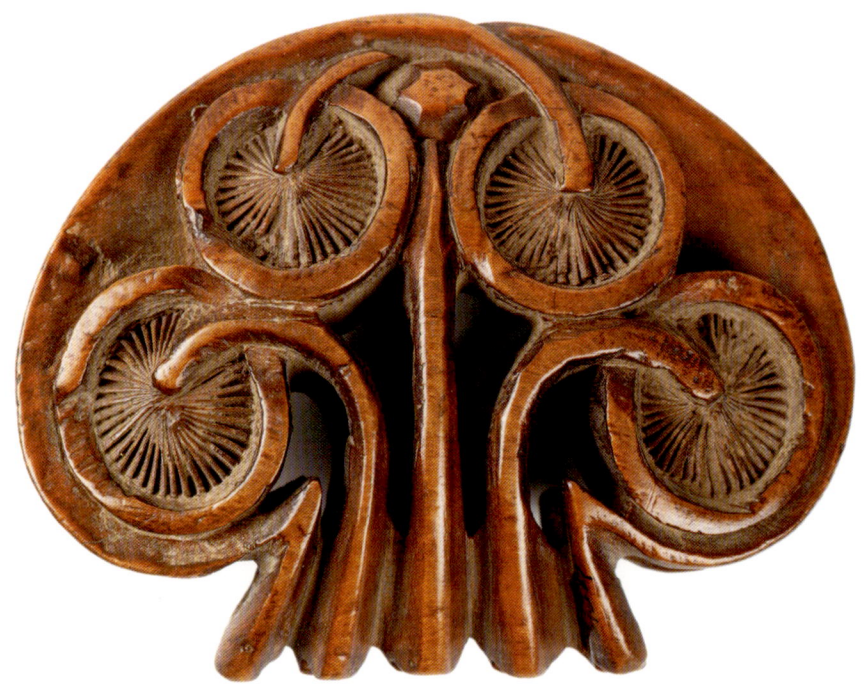

Plate 72

Toggle in the shape of a *lingzhi* fungus
灵芝形坠子

China, c.1700–1940
Wood
48 x 63 x 19 mm
Powerhouse Collection
Gift of Alastair Morrison, 1992

92/517

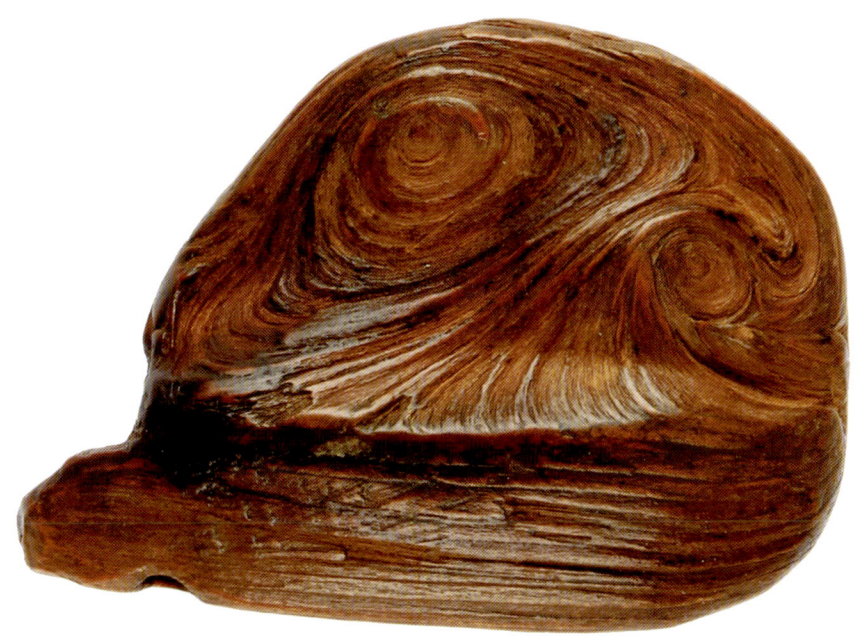

Plate 73

Toggle of grained wood in natural form
自然木纹坠子

China, c.1700–1940
Wood
17 x 35 x 49 mm
Powerhouse Collection
Gift of Alastair Morrison, 1992
92/595

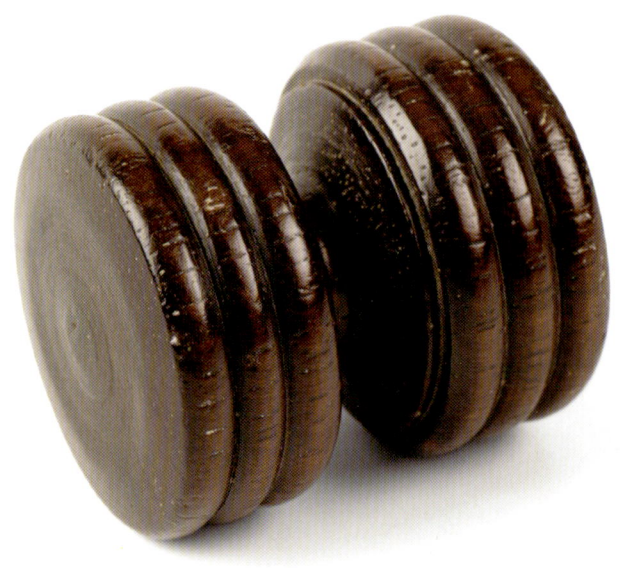

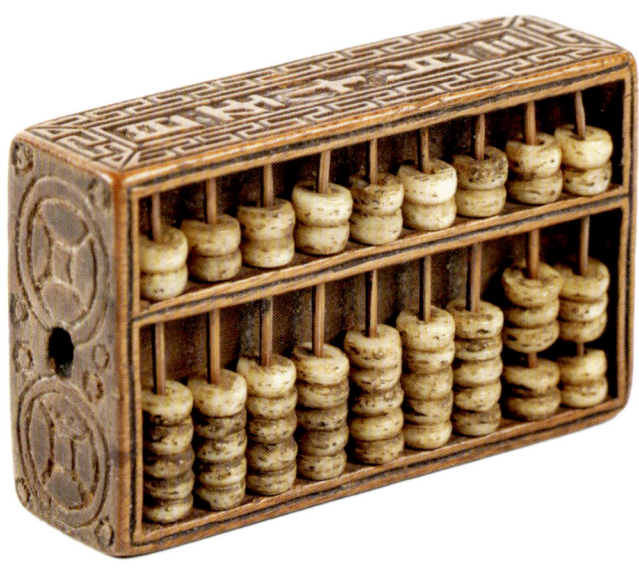

Plate 74

**Toggle in the shape
of a Chinese diabolo**
空竹式坠子

China, c.1700–1940
Wood
30 (diam) x 35 mm
92/549

Plate 75

**Toggle in the shape of
a miniature abacus with
a hidden compartment**
带暗格袖珍算盘坠子

China, c.1700–1940
Wood, bone
11 x 38 x 22 mm
92/494

Powerhouse Collection
Gift of Alastair Morrison, 1992

236

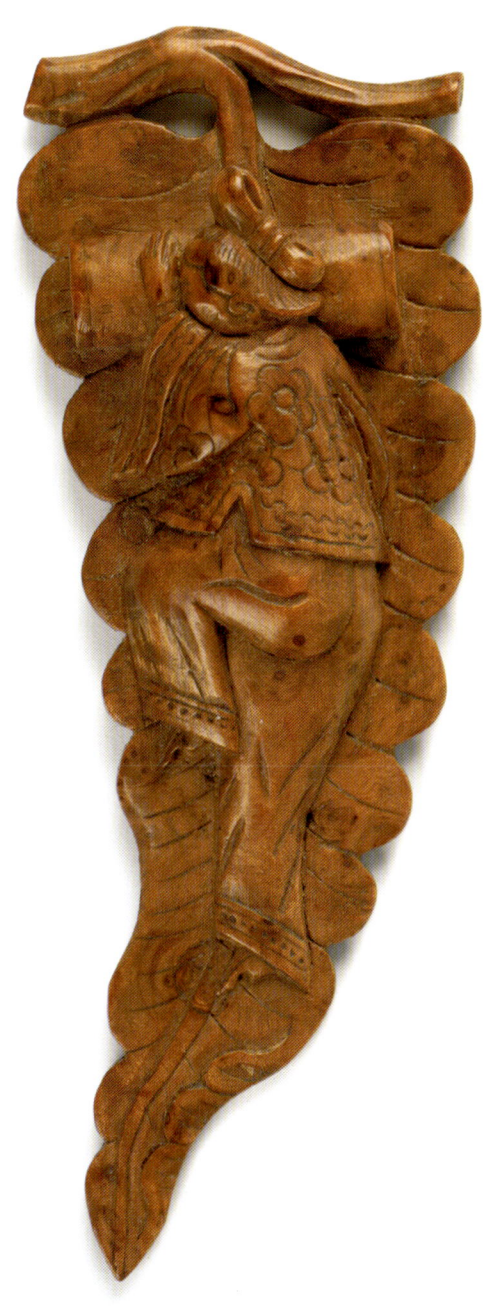

Plate 76

**Toggle in the shape of
a woman lying on a leaf**
女士卧叶形坠子

China, c.1700–1940
Wood
99 × 37 × 13 mm
Powerhouse Collection
Gift of Alastair Morrison, 1992
92/525

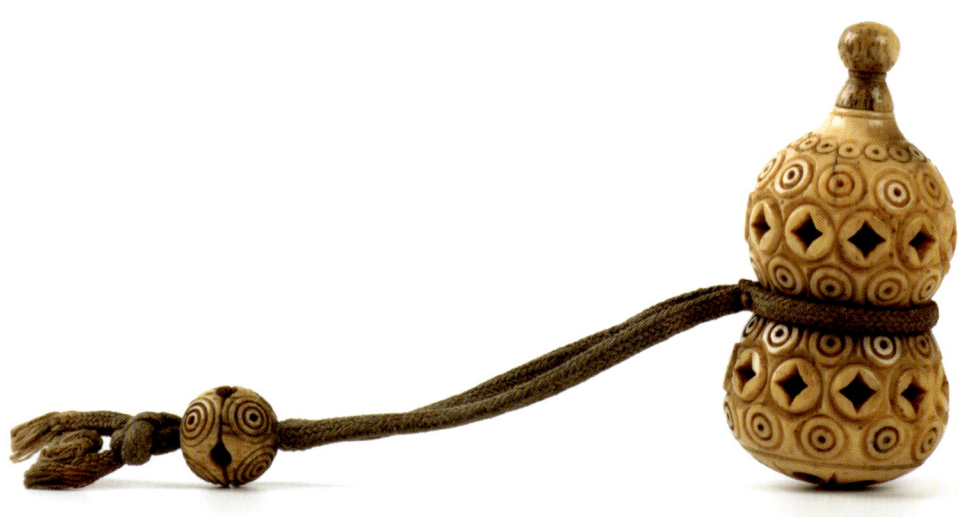

Plate 77

Toggle in the shape of a bottle gourd
葫芦瓶形坠子

China, c.1700–1940
Antler, silk
52 x 115 x 25 mm
Powerhouse Collection
Gift of Alastair Morrison, 1992
92/682

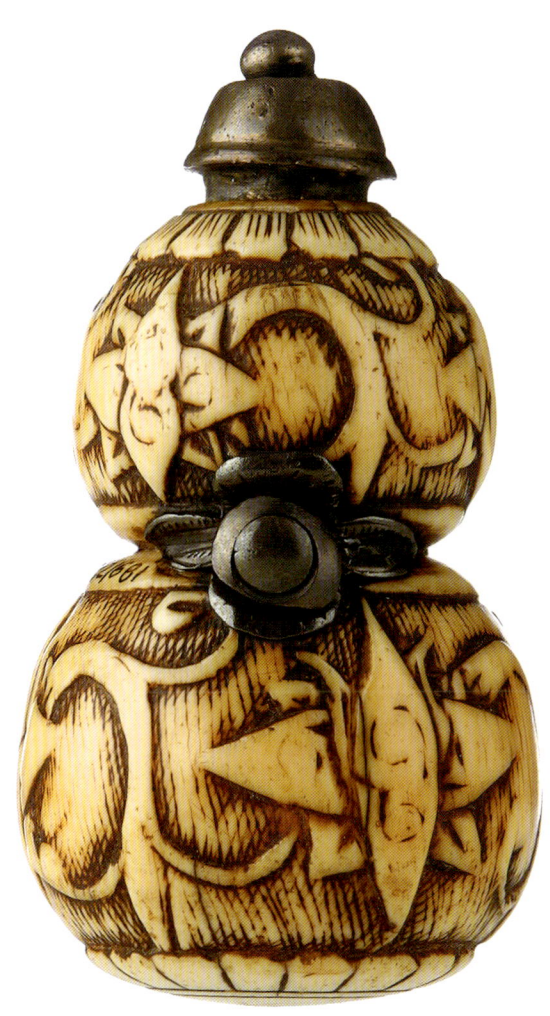

Plate 78

Toggle in the shape of a bottle gourd
葫芦瓶式坠子

China, c.1700–1940
Ivory, metal
55 x 30 x 30 mm
Powerhouse Collection
Gift of Alastair Morrison, 1992
92/681

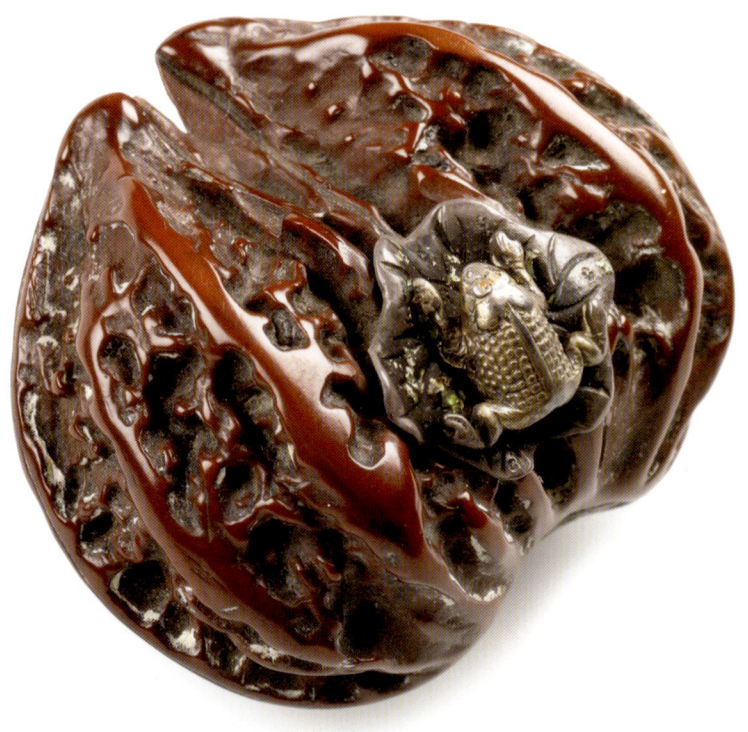

Plate 79
Toggle depicting a frog on a lotus leaf
蛙居莲叶形核桃坠子

China, c.1700–1940
Lacquered walnut, metal, silver alloy
40 x 43 x 33 mm
Powerhouse Collection
Gift of Alastair Morrison, 1992

92/480

Plate 80

Toggle in the shape of a walnut
核桃式坠子

China, c.1700–1940
Ivory, silk
30 x 30 x 20 mm (toggle only)
195 x 30 x 20 mm (with cord)
Powerhouse Collection
Gift of Alastair Morrison, 1992
92/640

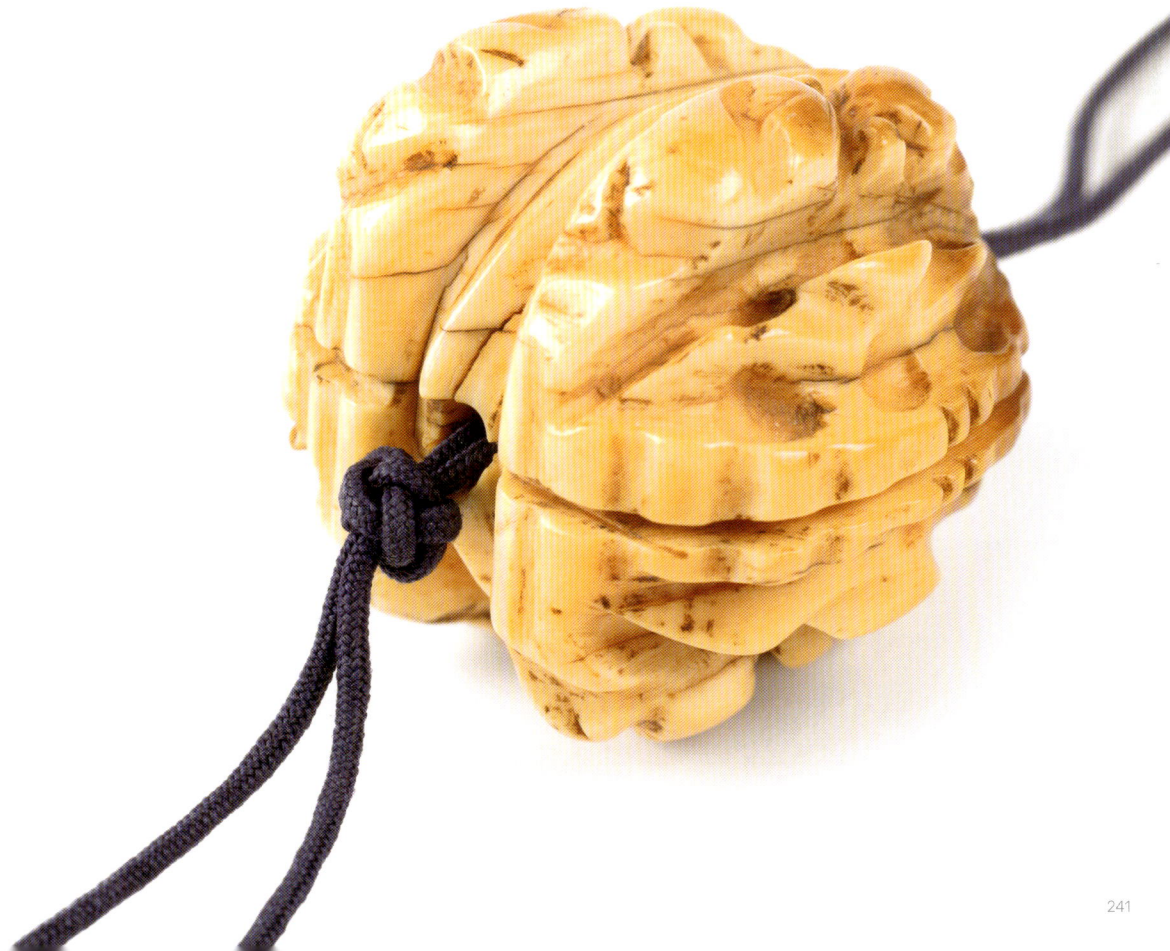

Acknowledgements

Chen Shuxia
Curator, Chau Chak Wing Museum

Min-Jung Kim
Curator, Powerhouse Museum

The Chau Chak Wing Museum and Powerhouse Museum acknowledge the Gadigal people of the Eora Nation as the first and continuing custodians of the lands and waters on which this exhibition and publication were produced. We pay respect to their Elders, past and present.

This book, which accompanies the exhibition of the same title, includes newly commissioned writing by a selection of experts in their fields. We are grateful for their enormous contribution to what has been, until now, an inadequately researched subject. In particular, we would like to thank Dr Elizabeth Carter, Lorraine Leung, Dr Brad Swarbrick and Thérèse Harrison from Sydney Analytical, and Brook Randall, Skye Mitchell and Rebecca Ellis from Powerhouse Museum for their scientific collaboration on this exhibition and publication.

Special thanks to Dr Paul Donnelly, Chau Chak Wing Museum Deputy Director, and Dr Jacqui Strecker, Powerhouse Head of Collection Curatorial, for forging this collaboration and driving it to completion. This endeavour would not have been possible without the enduring support of Michael Dagostino, Director of the Chau Chak Wing Museum, and David Ellis, the previous director. We would like to express our gratitude to the staff at the Chau Chak Wing Museum, including Luke Parker and the talented installation team, together with the collection team: Maree Clutterbuck, Christopher Jones, Emma Conroy, Kerry Head, Julie Taylor, Madeleine Snedden, Kerry Etherington, Aggie Wen-Fen Lu, Virginia Ho and David James, who produced the beautiful exhibition. Chau Chak Wing Museum art curators Dr Ann Stephen and Katrina Liberiou generously helped with the early conceptualisation of this publication. We thank our interns at the Chau Chak Wing Museum, Yimeng Bu and Ruieng Li, for their assistance.

We also extend our sincere gratitude to the Powerhouse Museum for their invaluable support and unwavering commitment to this collaboration. We would like to express special thanks to Lisa Havilah, Chief Executive, whose steadfast support has been instrumental in bringing this project to fruition. Matthew Connell, Director Program, has played a pivotal role in forging this collaboration. We are also deeply grateful to the dedicated team of individuals whose contributions have been indispensable in the creation of both this publication and the accompanying exhibition. Our heartfelt thanks go to Sally Rose, Meredith Freeman, Frances Fitzpatrick, Sue Frost, Bronwyn McKenzie, Chloe Appleby, Kathy Hackett, Harry Ree and Yuan Liu for their meticulous efforts in supporting the production of the exhibition and publication.

We would also like to express our gratitude to Dr Naomi Riddle, Lachlan Thompson, and Marni Williams, our editors at Power Publications, for guiding such an insightful book.

Thanks to exhibition designers Bel Youssofzay and David Hart for their elegant display, to Matt Nix, graphic designer of both the exhibition and this book, and to Dr Diane Fortenberry for her astute copyediting. We are grateful to Zhu Yayun for his graceful translation and to Dr Chen Shuxia for copyediting the Chinese language for the exhibition and part of this publication. Dr Yin Cao, Curator of Chinese art, Art Gallery of New South Wales generously connected us to peers in museums and institutions in China, facilitating our early research on Chinese toggles.

Finally, we would like to acknowledge the generous financial support that has made this volume possible, including grants and gifts from the Pauline and Tim Harding Asian Collection Fund, from David Anstice AO and Ana-Maria Zaugg, and from the Gordon Darling Foundation.

Bibliography

'The Cave of the Silken Web', *The Chinese Mirror: A Journal of Chinese Film History*, https://web.archive.org/web/20131007031150/http://www.chinesemirror.com/index/2011/09/cave-of-the-silken-web-1927.html, (viewed August 2022).

Alexander, William. *The Costume of China, Illustrated in Forty-eight Coloured Engravings*, William Miller, London, 1805.

Allard, Francis, Yan Sun and Katheryn M. Linduff (eds). *Memory and Agency in Ancient China: Shaping the Life History of Objects*, Cambridge University Press, Cambridge, 2018.

Bae, Kiwhan 배기환. 한국의 약용 식물 [*Bibliography of Medicinal Plants in Korea*], 교학사, Daegu, 2000.

Bai, Qianshen. *Fu Shan's World: The Transformation of Chinese Calligraphy in the Seventeenth Century*, Harvard University Press, Boston, 2003.

Barbanson, Adrienne. *Fables in Ivory: Japanese Netsuke and their Legends*, Charles E. Tuttle, Tokyo, 1961.

Barnes, Gina. 'Understanding Chinese Jade in a World Context', *Journal of the British Academy*, vol. 6, no. 1, 2018, pp. 1–63.

Beaumont, Lesley, Nicola Harrington and Candace Richards. 'Play', in *Children in Antiquity: Greece and Egypt*, Sydney University Museums, Sydney, 2015, pp. 8, 14.

琢玉工艺 [*The Art and Craft of Jade Carving*], 1976, film, Beijing Jade Factory 北京玉器厂, The Institute of Archaeology, Chinese Academy of Social Sciences 中国社会科学院考古研究所, Beijing.

Benedict, Carol. *Golden-Silk Smoke: A History of Tobacco in China, 1550–2010*, University of California Press, Berkeley, 2011.

Berna, Beppe. 'The Monkey as a Toggle: Discovering the Unknown World of the Primitive Art of China', *The Journal of Tribal Arts*, vol. 6, no 3, 2000, pp. 96–9.

Bishop, Claire. *Radical Museology: Or, What's Contemporary in Museums of Contemporary Art?*, Koenig Books, New York, 2013.

Bishop, Heber R., Stephen Wootton Bushell, Tadamasa Hayashi, George Frederick Kunz and Robert Lilley. *The Bishop Collection: Investigations and Studies in Jade*, De Vinne Press, New York, 1906.

Brown, Bill. 'Thing Theory', in *Critical Inquiry*, 2001, vol. 28, no.1, pp. 1–22.

Brubaker, David Adam and Wang Chunchen. 'Philosophy of Chinese Ink Art', in *Jizi and His Art in Contemporary China*, Springer, New York, 2015, pp. 59–72.

Cable, Nicholas Matthew. 'Greenstone Distribution Networks in Southern New Zealand', MA thesis. University of Otago, 2006.

Cacchione, Orianna and Wei-Cheng Lin. 'Introduction', in Orianna Cacchione and Wei-Cheng Lin (eds), *The Allure of Matter: Materiality Across Chinese Art*, The University of Chicago Press and Smart Museum of Art, Chicago, 2021, pp. 16–29.

Cammann, Schuyler. 'Chinese Belt Toggles', *Oriental Art*, vol. 8, no. 2, 1962, p. 72–78.

_____. 'Toggles and Toggle-Wearing', *Southwestern Journal of Anthropology*, vol. 16, no. 4, 1960, pp. 463–75.

_____. *Substance and Symbol in Chinese Toggles: Chinese Belt Toggles from the C. F. Bieber Collection*, University of Pennsylvania Press, Philadelphia, 1962.

Chaitae, Apinya, Ronnarit Rittiron, Iain J. Gordon, Helene Marsh, Jane Addison, Suttahatai Pochanagone and Nattakan Suttanon. 'Shining Nir Light on Ivory: A Practical Enforcement Tool for Elephant Ivory Identification', *Conservation Science and Practice*, vol. 3, no. 9, 2021, 486, doi 10.1111/csp2.486.

Chang, Kwang-chih. *The Archaeology of Ancient China*, Yale University Press, Connecticut, 1986.

Chen, Xing 陈性 (ed.). 玉纪 [*The Discipline of Jade*], Yisen gongsi 益森公司, Beijing, 1839.

Cheng, Jihua 程季华, Li Shaobai 李少白 and Xing Zuwen 邢祖文. 中国电影发展史 [*A History of the Development of Chinese Cinema*], China Film Publishing House 中国电影出版社, Beijing, 1998, pp. 86–9.

Field Museum of Natural History. '237 Toggles Boggle Museum Imagination', *Chicago Tribune*, 25 October 1962, Museum File 2780.

Christie's Hong Kong. *Chinese Arts Auction Records*, 26 November 2007, Live auction 2386, Lot 932.

Compilation Committee of Beijing Local Chronicles 北京市地方志编撰委员会 (ed.). 北京志 [*Beijing Chronicle*], Beijing Publishing House 北京出版社, Beijing, 2007.

Cooke Jr., Edward S. Jr. *Global Objects: Toward a Connected Global History*, Princeton University Press, Princeton and Oxford, 2022.

Cordes, Ernest. 'The Chinese Man Who Rubs Walnuts (揉核桃的中国人)', Ling Shuang 凌霜 (transl.), 月报 [*Yue Bao*], vol. 1, no. 1, 1937, pp. 212–5.

Di Cosmo, Nicola and Dalizhabu Bao. 'Introduction: A Brief Survey of Manchu-Mongol Relations Before the Qing Conquest', in *Manchu-Mongol Relations on the Eve of the Qing Conquest: A Documentary History*, Brill, Leiden, 2003, pp. 1–14.

Coutts, Peter. 'Greenstone: The Prehistoric Exploitation of Bowenite from Anita Bay, Milford Sound', T*he Journal of the Polynesian Society*, vol. 80, no. 1, 1971, pp. 42–73.

Creamer, Winifred. 'Mesoamerica as a Concept: An

Archaeological View from Central America', *Latin American Research Review*, vol. 22, no. 1, 1987, pp. 35–62.

de Waal, Edmund. *The Hare with the Amber Eyes: A Hidden Inheritance*, Vintage Books, London, 2010.

Demattè, Paola. 'The Chinese Jade Age: Between Antiquarianism and Archaeology', *Journal of Social Archaeology*, vol. 6, no. 2, 2006, pp. 202–6.

Duda, Margaret. *Traditional Chinese Toggles: Counterweights and Charms*, Editions Didier Millet Pty Ltd, Singapore, 2012.

Duo Limei 多丽梅. '佩玉将将：组玉佩反映的古代礼仪等级制度' ['The Clanking of *Peiyu*: Grouped Jade Pendant and the Ancient Etiquette System'], 原道 [*Yuan Dao*], no. 2, 2015, pp. 159–66.

Eberhard, Wolffram. *A Dictionary of Chinese Symbols: Hidden Symbols in Chinese Life and Thought*, Routledge and Kegan Paul, London, 1986.

Edwards, Howell G. M. and Denis W. Farwell. 'Ivory and Simulated Ivory Artefacts: Fourier Transform Raman Diagnostic Study', *Spectrochimica* Acta Part A: *Molecular and Biomolecular Spectroscopy*, vol. 51, no. 12, 1995, pp. 2073–81.

____, Dennis W. Farwell, T Seddon and Jon K.F. Tait. 'Scrimshaw: Real or fake? A Fourier-Transform

Raman Diagnostic Study', *Journal of Raman Spectroscopy*, vol. 26, no. 8–9, 1995, pp. 623–8.

Childs-Johnson, Elizabeth. 'Jade as Material and Epoch', in R. Solomon (ed.), *China: 5000 Years, Innovation and Transformation in the Arts*, Guggenheim Museum, 1998, pp. 55–68.

Eltringham, S. K. *Elephants*, Blandford Press, Poole, 1982.

Esner, Rachel and Fieke Konijn. 'Curating the Collection', *Stedelijk Studies*, no. 5, 2017, https://stedelijkstudies. com/journal/curating-the-collection/ (viewed January 2022).

Fang, Wenxi 方问溪. '清廷平秘内升署本：盘丝洞' ['Qing Imperial Court Drama *Pingmi Neisheng*: The Cave of Silken Web'], 戏剧月刊 [*The Theatre Monthly*], no. 12, 1932, pp. 178–94.

Gamberi, Valentina. 'Introduction', in *Experiencing Materiality: Museum Perspectives*, Berghahn Books, New York and Oxford, 2021, pp. 1–18.

Gao, Jianping 高建平. 中国艺术的表现性动作：从书法到绘画 [*The Expressive Act in Chinese Art: from Calligraphy to Painting*], Zhang Bing 张冰 (transl.), Anhui Educational Publishing House 安徽教育出版社, Anhui, 2012.

Gao, Qing 高清 and Wang Baoqing 王保青. '浅论文玩核桃的文化品性' ['On Literati Walnuts' Cultural

Characters'], 艺术品鉴 [*Appreciation*], no. 2, 2015, p. 313.

Gu, Fang 古方. '明清时期的苏州玉雕' ['Jade carving in Suzhou During Ming-Qing Period'], 收藏家 [*Collectors*], no. 10, 2021, pp. 239–42.

Gu, Yinghua 顾英华. '历代玉器中闪石玉的材质分析' ['Material Analysis of Amphibole Jade in Ancient Jade Artifacts'], 河南博物院院刊 [*Henan Museum Journal*]. no. 3. 2021, pp. 60–6.

Hansford, S. Howard. *Chinese Jade Carving*, Lund Humphries, London and Bradford, 1950.

Hargreaves, Michael D., N. A. Macleod, Victoria L. Brewster, Tasmin Munshi, Howell G. M. Edwards and Pavel Matousek. 'Application of Portable Raman Spectroscopy and Benchtop Spatially Offset Raman Spectroscopy to Interrogate Concealed Biomaterials', *Journal of Raman Spectroscopy*, vol. 40, no. 12, 2009, pp. 1875–80.

Harlow, George E. and Sorena S. Sorensen. 'Jade (Nephrite and Jadeitite) and Serpentinite: Metasomatic Connections', *International Geology Review*, vol. 47, no. 2, 2005, pp. 113–46.

____, Virginia B. Sisson, Guanghai Shi, 'The Geology of Jade Deposits', in Lee A. Groat (ed.), *The Geology of Gem Deposits, Mineralogical Association*

of Canada Short-Course Series, vol. 44, 2014, pp. 305–74.

Hay, Jonathan. Sensuous Surfaces: The Decorative Object in Early Modern China, University of Hawaii Press, Honolulu, 2010.

He, Song 何松. '中国清代玉器的主要成就 · 艺术特征 · 文化内涵' ['Major Achievement, Art Characteristics and Cultural Connotation of the Jade Carvings of Qing Dynasty of China'], 超硬材料工程 [Superhard Material Engineering], vol. 18, no. 1, 2006, pp. 56–7.

Hölling, Hanna B., Francesca G. Brewer, and Katharina Ammann. 'Material Encounters', in Hanna B. Hölling, Francesca G. Brewer, and Katharina Ammann (eds), The Explicit Material, Brill, Leiden, 2019, pp. 1–14.

Hsieh, I-Yi. 'Nuts: Beijing Folk Art Connoisseurship in the Age of Marketization', Asian Anthropology, vol. 15, no. 1, pp. 59–60.

Hu, Pu-an 胡朴安. 中华全国风俗志 [Gazettes of Chinese Customs], Tai Tat Press 大达图书供应社, Shanghai, 1935.

Hung, Hsiao-Chun, Yoshiyuki Iizuka, Peter Bellwood, Kim Dung Nguyen, Bérénice Bellina, Praon Silapanth, Eusebio Dizon, Rey Santiago, Ipoi Datan, and Jonathan H. Manton. 'Ancient Jades Map 3,000 Years of Prehistoric Exchange in Southeast Asia', Proceedings of the National Academy of Sciences, vol. 104, no. 50, 2007, 1945–50 , doi: 10.1073/pnas.0707304104. Epub 2007 Nov 29. PMID: 18048347; PMCID: PMC2148369.

Jiang, Yonghu 江用虎. '安徽怀宁文物管理所藏明清时期民间佩玉' ['Collection of Everyday Jade Toggles from Ming-Qing Period in Anhui Huaining Cultural Relics Management Office'], 收藏界 [Collection World], no. 12, 2009, pp. 36–8.

Jonas, Fredrick Maurice. Netsuke, Charles E. Tuttle, London and Kobe, 1928.

Katz, David. The World of Touch, Lawrence Erlbaum Associates, New Jersey, 1989.

Kelloway, Sarah, Howell G. M. Edwards, Brad Swarbrick, Elizabeth A. Carter. 'Discrimination of Contraband Ivories Using Long Wavelength Portable Raman Instrumentation', Raman Spectroscopy in Archaeology and Art History, 2018, pp. 123–40.

Krzyszkowska, Olga. Classical Handbook 3: Ivory and Related Materials, British Institute of Classical Studies, London, 1990.

Interview with Alistair Morrison by Claire Roberts. 2006, film, Powerhouse Museum, Canberra, Powerhouse Museum Record Series (Item), MRS/278-218.

Lavine, Steven D. and Ivan Karp (eds), Exhibiting Cultures: The Poetics and Politics of Museum Display, Smithsonian Books, Washington, 1991.

Lederman, Susan J. and Roberta L. Klatzky, 'Hand Movements: A Window into Haptic Object Recognition', Cognitive Psychology, vol. 19, no. 3, 1987, pp. 342–68.

Morrison, Hedda. Letter from Hedda Morrison to Charles Allen, 12 September 1983, Powerhouse Archives, 2021/57/1.

Li, Songling 李松龄 and Qu Chunhai 屈春海. '话说抓周习俗' ['On the Customs of Zhuazhou'], 文史知识 [Chinese Literature and History], no. 10, 1991, pp. 51–5.

Li, Youqian 李有骞 and Yongcai Yang 杨永才. '黑龙江饶河县小南山遗址 2015 年 III 区发掘简报' ['Brief Report on the Excavation of Area III of the Xiaonanshan Site in Raohe County, Heilongjiang in 2015'], 考古 [Kaogu], no. 8, 2019, pp. 3–20.

Lin, Feng 林峰. '试说盘玉' ['On Panyu'], 紫禁城 [Forbidden City], no 1, 2001, pp. 37–9.

Liu, Datong 刘大同. 古玉辨 [Archaic Jade Identification], People's Fine Art Publishing House 上海人民美术出版社, Shanghai, 2018.

Lu, Andong. 'Deciphering the Reclusive Landscape: a Study of Wen Zheng-Ming's 1533 Album of the Garden of the Unsuccessful Politician', Studies in the History of Gardens and Designed Landscapes, vol. 31, no. 1, 2011, pp. 40–59.

Luo, Xingbo. 'Sculpture', in Hua Jueming, Li Jinsong and Wang Lianhai (eds), Chinese Handicrafts, Springer and Elephant Press, Singapore and Zhengzhou, 2022.

Mack, John. The Art of Small Things, Harvard University Press, Cambridge, 2007.

Mao, Xianmin 毛宪民 and Zhang Baozhong 张保中. '清宫揉手核桃' ['The Rubbing Walnuts in Qing Court'], 紫禁城 [Forbidden City], no. 1, 1995, pp. 27, 41–6.

Morrison, Alastair. The Bird Fancier: A Journey to Peking, Pandanus Books, Canberra, 2001.

_____. 'Toggles and Netsuke, a Minor Art from China and Japan,' 24 September 1979, Powerhouse Collection Masterfile, 92/429–92/520.

Morrison, Hedda and Alastair Morrison. 'Chinese Toggles: A Little Known Folk Art', Arts of Asia, vol. 16, no. 2, 1986, pp. 68–75

Morrison, Hedda. A Photographer in Old Peking, Oxford University Press, Hong Kong, 1985.

Ni, Jianlin 倪建林. '战国时代的佩玉——中国古代玉器艺术鉴赏' ['Jade Pendants in the Warring States Period: Appreciating Chinese Ancient Jade'], 中国美术教育 [Chinese Art Education], no. 3, 2003, pp. 50–2.

Ōmura, Seigai 大村西崖. 中国美术史 [Chinese Art

History], Chen Binsu 陈彬苏 (transl.), 商务印书馆 [The Commercial Press], Shanghai, 1930.

Pei, Shuyan, and Chuqiao Yu. 'Exploration on Jade Culture in West Liaohe River Basin in the Neolithic Age', *Advances in Social Science, Education and Humanities Research*, vol. 416, 2020, pp. 557–60.

Power, A .C., J. Chapman, S. Chandra, J. J. Roberts, and D. Cozzolinio, 'Illuminating the Flesh of Bone Identification – an Application of Near Infrared Spectroscopy', *Vibrational Spectroscopy*, vol. 98, 2018, pp. 64–8.

Aisin-Gioro, Puyi 爱新觉罗·溥仪. 我的前半生 [*The First Half of My Life*], Qunzhong Chubanse, Beijing, 1964.

Roberts, Claire. 'Alastair Morrison (1915–2009)', *China Heritage Quarterly*, no. 9, September 2009.

____. 'George E. Morrison's Studio and Library', *Chinese Heritage Quarterly*, no. 13, 2008.

____. *In Her View: The Photographs of Hedda Morrison in China and Sarawak 1933–67*, Powerhouse Publishing, Sydney, 1993.

Sax, Margaret, Nigel D. Meeks, Carol Michaelson and Andrew P. Middleton. 'The Identification of Carving Techniques on Chinese Jade', *Journal of Archaeological Science* no. 31, 2004, pp. 1413–28.

Seok, Ju-Seon 석주선. [*The History of Korean

Costumes*], Bojinjae 보진재, Seoul, 1971.

Shao, Qi, Xiaojing Wen and Paul White., Xiaojing Wen and Paul White. 'Design Thinking under the Qing Dynasty', *A Brief History of Chinese Design Thought*, Shanghai Bookstore Publishing House and Springer, Shanghai and Singapore, 2022.

Stewart, Susan. 'The Miniature', in *On Longing: Narratives of the Miniature, the Gigantic, the Souvenir, the Collection*, Duke University Press, Durham and London, 1993, pp. 37–68.

Sun, Ji 孙机. 汉代物质文化资料图说 [*Illustrated Explanations of the Material Culture of the Han Dynasty*], Shanghai Classics Publishing House 上海古籍出版社, Shanghai, 2008.

_____. '周代的组玉佩' ['On the Group Jade Body Ornament of Zhou Dynasty'], 文物 [*Cultural Relics*], no. 4, 1998, pp. 4–14.

Sun, Shaoyi. 'Fantasy, Vampirism and Genre/ Gender Wars on the Chinese Screen of the Roaring 1920s', in Lin Feng and James Aston (eds.), *Renegotiating Film Genres in East Asian Cinemas and Beyond*, Palgrave Macmillan, Cham, 2020, pp. 99–118.

Sun, Xiaoning 孙小宁. '明、清两代北京的民间儿童游戏' ['Children's Folk Games During Ming and Qing Period'], 体育文史 [*Literature and History of Physical Education*], no. 1, 1990, pp. 20–3.

Swarbrick, Brad. *Multivariate Data Analysis for Dummies*, Wiley, Chichester, 2012.

The Metropolitan Museum of Art. *The Bishop Collection: Investigations and Studies in Jade*, 1906, Met Museum Library, 139.3 N48F.

Van Dyke, Ruth M. 'Materiality in Practice', in *Practising Materiality*, The University of Arizona Press, Tucson, 2015, pp. 3–32.

Wang, Mingying 王铭颖 and Shi Guanghai 施光海. '从宝玉石学角度浅析玉雕俏色艺术' ['A Brief Analysis of the 'Qiaose' Jade from the Perspective of Gemmology'], 美术学 [*Fine Art Research*], no. 3, 2020, pp. 77–8.

____. 'The Evolution of Chinese Jade carving Craftmanship', *Gems & Gemology*, vol. 56, no. 1, 2020, pp. 30–53.

Wang, Rong. 'Progress Review of The Scientific Study of Chinese Ancient Jade', *Archaeometry*, vol. 53, no. 4, 2011, pp. 674–92.

____ and Wei-Shan Zhang. 'Application of Raman Spectroscopy in The Non-Destructive Analyses Of Ancient Chinese Jades', *Journal of Raman Spectroscopy*, vol. 42, no. 6, 2011, pp. 1324–9.

Wang, Shixiang 王世襄 (ed.). 竹刻 [*Bamboo Carving*], People's Fine Art Publishing House 上海人民美术出版社, Beijing, 1991.

Wang, Chunchen. 'Museum Coloniality: Displaying

Asian Art in the Whitened Context', *International Journal of Cultural Policy*, vol. 27, no. 6, 2021, pp. 724–5.

Wang, Yamin 王亚民. '玉器、玉文化及民间藏玉' ['Jade Ware, Jade Culture and Private Jade Collections'], 紫禁城 [*Forbidden City*], no. 5, 2010, pp. 8–17.

Wang, Yuchang 王裕昌. '中国玉文化之管见——兼谈中国的制玉材质' ['Views on Chinese Jade Culture and Jade Materials'], 丝绸之路 [*Silk Road*], no. 8, 2012, pp. 59–63.

Wei, Chenjie 魏晨捷. '透视《盘丝洞》：中国20年代电影与传统印刷媒介的互动' ['The Cave of the Silken Web in Perspectives: The Interaction Between Chinese Cinema and Traditional Print Media in the 1920s'], 当代电影 [*Contemporary Cinema*], no. 2, 2015, pp. 164–5.

Wilson, Frank. *The Hand: How its Use Shapes the Brain, Language, and Human Culture*, Pantheon Books, New York, 1998.

Wu, Dacheng 吴大澂. 古玉图考 [*Illustrations on Archaic Jade*], Chung Hwa Book Company 中华书局, Taipei, 1991.

Wu, Hung 巫鸿. '"材质"与中国艺术的起源' ['Material Quality' and the Origin of Chinese Art'], in Wu Hung 巫鸿 (ed.), 艺术与物性 [*Art and Materiality*], Shanghai Fine Arts Publishing House 上海书画出版社, Shanghai, 2023, pp. 5–32.

_____. '"明器"的理论和实践——战国时期礼仪美术中

的观念化倾向' ['Theory and Practice of Burial Objects: Tendency of Conceptualizing Etiquette Art in the Warring States Period'], 文物 [*Cultural Relics*], no. 6, 2006, pp. 72–81.

Wu, Mo 吴沫. '中国汉代玉器的工艺进步和艺术创新——以安徽出土的汉代玉器为例' ['Technological Progress and Artistic Innovation of Chinese Han Dynasty Jade Wares: Sampling the Han Dynasty Jade Wares Unearthed in Anhui'], 宝石和宝石学杂志 [*Journal of Gems and Gemmology*], vol. 23, no. 3, 2021, pp. 56–7.

Wu, Wenlong 武文龙. '文玩核桃：从产地到古玩圈' ['Play with Walnuts: from Product Place to Antique Circle'], 艺术市场 [*Art Market*], no. 23, 2012, pp. 55–6.

Xu, Lin 徐琳. '切磋琢磨–中国史前至汉代的治玉工艺' ['Cutting, Grinding, Carving and Polishing: Early Jade Craftmanship from Prehistory to the Han Dynasty'], 养德堂珍藏中国古玉器二 [*Chinese Archaic Jades from the Yangdetang Collection PART II*], Christie's, Hong Kong, 2018, pp. 9–10.

Xue, Ning 薛宁. '《盘丝洞》文图史料概况' ['The Historical Articles and Pictures of *Spiders*'], 当代电影 [*Contemporary Cinema*], no. 2, 2019, pp. 73–5.

Yang, Boda 杨伯达. '关于琢玉工具的再探讨' ['Revisiting Jade Carving Tools'], 南阳师范学院学报 [*Journal of Nanyang Normal University (Social Sciences)*], no. 2, 2007, pp. 72–6

Yang, Shengmin 杨圣敏. '多民族在北京地区交往交流交融的历史缩影' ['A Historical Epitome of Multi-ethnic Exchanges in Beijing'], 中国教育新闻网 [*Education News of China*], available at: http://www.jyb.cn/rmtzcg/xwy/wzxw/202201/t20220119_676656.html, (viewed October 2022). Originally published in 中国民族教育 [*Ethnic Education of China*], no. 1, 2022, pp. 61–3.

Yang, Sunny. *Hanbok: The Art of Korean Clothing*, Hollym, Seoul, 1997.

Yu, Haiguang 于海广, '山东龙山文化的大型墓葬分析' ['Analysis of Large-scale Tombs of Shandong Longshan Culture'], 考古 [*Archaeology*], no. 1, 2000, pp. 61–7.

Zhang, Ruixiang 张睿祥, Yang Xiaoping 杨筱平 and Ou Xiuhua 欧秀花. '从神坛走向民间：中国古代玉器的发展历程' ['From the Altar to the Common People: The Development of Ancient Chinese Jade Artifacts'], 文物鉴定与鉴赏 [*Identification and Appreciation of Cultural Relics*], no. 11, 2018, pp. 84–6.

Zhang, Yufu 张玉甫. '明代琢玉大师陆子冈与苏琢史略考' ['Ming Dynasty Jade Carving Master Lu Zigang and Suzhou Jade Carving History'], 中国民族博览 [*Chinese National Expo*], no. 2, 2020, pp. 86–8.

Zhang, Zhang 张章. '清代玉器的纹饰特点与风格研究' ['On the Characteristics and Styles of Jade Products in the Qing Dynasty'], 艺术品鉴 [*Appreciation*], no. 23, 2018, pp. 11–2.

Zhao, Yongkui 赵永魁, Gu Fang古方. '制玉工艺' ['The art and craft of jade-carving'], in Gu Fang 古方 (ed.), 中国古玉器图典 [*The Pictorial Handbook of Ancient Chinese Jades*], The Cultural Relics Publishing House 文物出版社, Beijing, 2007, pp. 27–41.

Zhao, Yulong 赵毓龙 and Feng Wei 冯伟. '舞台蝶变：清宫大戏《昇平宝筏》对《西游记》案头叙事的因与革' ['Butterfly Metamorphosis on Stage: The Inheritance and Reform of Qing Imperial Drama the Precious Raft of Peaceful Times from Closet Drama Journey to the West'], 艺术广角 [*Art Panorama*], no. 5, 2019, pp. 34–41.

Zheng, Jianming 郑建明 and He Yuanqing 何元庆. 中国古代的玉蝉 ['Ancient Jade Cicada in China'], 汉江考古 [*Hanjiang Archaeology*], no. 1, 2006, pp. 44–50.

Zhu, Liangzhi 朱良志. 关于大巧若拙美学观的若干思考 ['Thoughts on the Aesthetics of the Great Artfulness as Clumsiness'], 北京大学学报哲学社会科学版 [*Journal of Peking University Philosophy and Social Sciences*], vol. 43, no. 3, 2006, pp. 33–41.

Zhu, Naicheng 朱乃诚. 汉代玉蝉研究 ['Research on Han Dynasty Jade Cicadas'], 文博学刊 [*Journal of Archaeology and Museology*], no. 1, 2019, pp. 4–16.

Contributors

Elizabeth Carter

Dr Elizabeth Carter is Manager of the Sydney Analytical Vibrational Spectroscopy Facility, a core research facility of The University of Sydney. She is a passionate scientist who has enjoyed working closely with colleagues based in the cultural heritage industry to analyse a range of cultural heritage objects, from ceramics, textiles and pigments to manuscripts and coffins.

Chen Shuxia

Dr Chen Shuxia is a historian and curator of Chinese art and photography. Her research concerns diasporic artistic practice, cultural networks, amateur practice, art collectives and reciprocal relations between people and objects. She has been working on three research projects related to photography from the Sinophone world, including 'A Home for Photography Learning: The Friday Salon, 1977–1980' (2018–23), 'The Grey Zone: Amateur Photography Groups in 1980s Beijing' (2020–), and 'Wayfaring: Photography in 1950s–1980s Taiwan' (with Dr Olivier Krischer, 2021–), each of which comprises an exhibition and scholarly publication. Chen is the State Library of New South Wales David Scott Mitchell Memorial Fellow (2022–23), as well as a grantee of Australian Academy of Humanities' Travelling Fellowship (postponed to 2024). Chen is the inaugural curator of the Chau Chak Wing Museum's China Gallery, and a lecturer in the Master's degree program, Curating and Cultural Leadership, at the University of New South Wales School of Art & Design.

Meredith Freeman

Dr Meredith Freeman is Conservation Manager at Powerhouse Museum (Museum of Applied Arts and Sciences). She has a strong science background, having worked as a pharmacist and conservator. She completed her Masters in Conservation of Cultural Materials at the University of Melbourne and was awarded the inaugural Headley Trust/Crick Smith PhD scholarship at the University of Lincoln, UK. Her doctoral research explores how architectural paint analysis informs the study of material culture and contributes to the revelation and narrative of built heritage. Meredith's research interests include exploring how object-centred analysis generates scientific and practice-informed information, which can be contextualised and interpreted to generate new explicit knowledge.

Paul Donnelly

Dr Paul Donnelly is Deputy Director of the Chau Chak Wing Museum, in charge of curatorial and exhibitions. He came to The University of Sydney in 2015 as Associate Director, leading the development of eighteen opening exhibitions in the new museum, including the China Gallery. Before 2015 he held decorative arts and design curatorial roles for over twenty years at Powerhouse Museum in Sydney. Paul has a BA (Hons) from The University of Sydney, and an MA in Applied History from the University of Technology, Sydney. His PhD from The University of Sydney focused on Middle to Late Bronze Age fine ware of the southern Levant, making extensive use of elemental analyses. In 2017 he attended the Getty Leadership Program in Los Angeles, California. He has published widely in archaeology, and decorative arts and design, has excavated at Pella, Jordan since 1988, and is co-director of The University of Sydney's Zagora Archaeological Project on Andros, Greece.

Gu Fang

Gu Fang is an expert in archaeological research on ancient Chinese jade and Chinese handed-down (*chuanshi*) collections of ancient jade. He is Director, Professional Committee on Collecting, China National Association for the Promotion of Arts and Culture. He previously worked at the Institute of Archaeology, Chinese Academy of Social Sciences (1989–97), and was a visiting scholar at the Metropolitan Museum of Art in New York (1997). Gu has published widely on ancient Chinese jade and Chinese jade collections around the world. He was a Special Editor at China Science Press (1998–2010) and Cultural Relics Press (2010–22). His major publications include *The Complete Collection of Jades Unearthed in China* (15 vols, 2005), *The Pictorial Handbook of Ancient Chinese Jades* (2007), *The Complete Collection of Chinese Handed-Down Jade* (8 vols, 2010), *Ancient Chinese Jades from the Royal Ontario Museum* (with Shen Chen, 2017), *Early Modern Chinese Jadeide: Chinese Jadeide Art from the 17th to the 20th Century* (with Zhong Fumiao, 3 vols, 2021) and T*ranslucent and Pure: Ancient Chinese Jade Culture* (2023).

Thérèse Harrison

Thérèse Harrison is a Professional Officer, Cultural Heritage Analyses, a core research facility at The University of Sydney. She has a background in fine arts and chemistry and specialises in the analysis of cultural heritage across numerous techniques, including vibrational and X-ray spectroscopy. She acts as the liaison between the Chau Chak Wing Museum and Sydney Analytical and offers training and support to internal and external users working in the field of cultural heritage. With an emphasis on non-destructive analysis, Thérèse provides researchers with assistance in the development and application of techniques suitable to different artefacts and materials, using both portable and benchtop instrumentation.

Min-Jung Kim

Min-Jung Kim has been Curator of Asian Arts at Powerhouse Museum (Museum of Applied Arts and Sciences) since 2007. Originally from South Korea, she has dedicated two decades of her career to curating East Asian arts in Australia. Her curatorial expertise spans an extensive range of East Asian exhibitions, covering art forms such as textiles, ceramics, metalworks, woodworks, jewellery, dress and fashion. She has published and lectured widely on curatorial studies, with a particular focus on Asian collections in Western museums. Kim was selected as Plenary Speaker on Asian Art Museums and Collections in the World at the ICOM Kyoto 2019 conference (International Council of Museums, UNESCO), and her exhibition *Spirit of Jang-in* (2011) was honoured with the 2012 ICOM Australia Award for International Relations. Among her many successful exhibitions, a recent example is the highly praised international exhibition, *Five Hundred Arhats of Changnyeongsa Temple* in 2021.

Lorraine Leung

Lorraine Leung has a background in archaeological science and is a Professional Officer, Cultural Heritage, at Sydney Analytical, The University of Sydney. She has worked on a range of archaeological projects in Australia, Cambodia and Hong Kong. She has experience with an array of interdisciplinary projects investigating archaeological, museum and cultural heritage material, using analytical techniques such as vibrational spectroscopy and X-ray fluorescence spectroscopy. Most recently, she published an article on the potential of organic residues on Chinese export porcelain from Angkor Wat, Cambodia (2022). She is currently working on projects involving the scientific analysis of archaeological ceramics, organic residues, paint pigments and ancient Egyptian papyri.

Image credits

Claire Roberts

Claire Roberts is an art historian and curator with an interest in modern and contemporary Chinese art and cultural flows between Australia and Asia. She is Professor of Art History in the School of Culture and Communication at The University of Melbourne and a fellow of the Australian Academy of the Humanities. Her current research explores the international context of modern and contemporary Chinese art. Her publications include *Friendship in Art: Fou Lei and Huang Binhong* (2010), *Photography and China* (2013), *Ian Fairweather: A Life in Letters*, edited with John Thompson (2019) and *Fairweather and China* (2021). She is a former Senior Curator of Asian Arts and Design at Powerhouse Museum (Museum of Applied Arts and Sciences), Sydney (1988–2010).

Brad Swarbrick

Dr Brad Swarbrick is a world recognised expert in the application of near and mid infrared spectroscopy, spectroscopic imaging and chemometrics in a number of industrial sectors, particularly in the pharmaceutical and precision agricultural industries. He is the co-founder of KAX Group, a provider of multivariate data analysis software, and has worked for and with a number of the largest pharmaceutical, biopharmaceutical and medical device companies to implement innovative control strategies using process analytical technology (PAT). He was part of the pioneering Pfizer global PAT group and is currently the pharmaceutical section editor of the *Journal of Near Infrared Spectroscopy*. Brad has a PhD in biospectroscopy and advanced chemometrics from The University of Sydney.

Jules Boag, Ryan Hernandez, Marinco Kojdanovski, and Zan Wimberley, toggle collection photography, Powerhouse Museum: 9, 22, 24–6, 27 (figs 1.5 and 1.6), 32 (figs 1.10 and 1.11), 39, 40 (fig. 1.16), 51, 54 (figs 2.9 and 2.10), 55, 62, 66, 69–71, 76, 83–4, 87, 99, 109–10, 113, 118 (detail), 129 (detail), 132 (detail), 134 (detail), 152, 162–9, 170 (plates 7 and 8), 171–3, 174 (plates 12 and 13), 175–201, 202 (plates 38 and 39), 203–15, 216 (plates 52 and 53), 217 (plates 54 and 55), 218–26, 227 (plates 64 and 65), 228–235, 236 (plates 74 and 75), 237–41

David James, collection photography, Chau Chak Wing Museum: 75 (figs 3.10 and 3.11), 78, 81, 85, 89; installation photography, Chinese Toggles: *Culture in Miniature*, China Gallery, Chau Chak Wing Museum: 12–3, 140–4, 146–7, 149–51, 153, 155–9

Elizabeth A. Carter and Powerhouse Museum, graph, 123 (fig. 6.2)

Jean-François Lanzarone, Powerhouse Museum, 56

Lorraine Leung and Powerhouse Museum, graphs, 135 (figs 6.6, 6.7, and 6.8)

Hedda Morrison, née Hammer, Hedda Morrison Photographs of China, Harvard-Yenching Library: 30, 50, 72, 92; Powerhouse Museum: 46 (fig. 2.4, printed by Jean-François Lanzarone), 49, 116

Brad Swarbrick, graphs, 125 (fig. 6.3), 126 (fig. 6.4), 127 (fig. 6.5); Table, 127 (table 1)

N. Sotoudeh, schematic diagrams, Mucca Design: 121

Susan Wraight, (artwork courtesy of), 40 (fig. 1.17)

Institutional credits, photographers unknown, Academy of Korean Studies, 37 (fig. 1.12); Gansu Provincial Library, 65 (fig. 3.3); Harvard-Yenching Library, 46 (fig. 2.3); National Folk Museum of Korea, 38; National Library of Medicine, United States, 82; National Museum of Korea, 37 (fig. 1.13); Powerhouse Museum, 42, 44, 46 (fig. 2.2, printed by Jean-François Lanzarone), 52 (printed by Jean-François Lanzarone); Taipei Palace Museum, 60

Index

**Chinese Toggles:
Culture in Miniature**
中国坠子：方寸见乾坤

Editors
Chen Shuxia
Min-Jung Kim

Publishing and Production
Paul Donnelly
Naomi Riddle
Lachlan Thompson
Marni Williams

Design
Matt Nix

Copyediting
Diane Fortenberry

Proofreading
Kay Campbell, The Comma
Institute
Chen Shuxia (Chinese text)

Indexing
Miranda Fyfield

Published in association
with the exhibition

*Chinese Toggles:
Culture in Miniature*
中国坠子：方寸见乾坤

Chau Chak Wing Museum and
Powerhouse Museum

29 April 2023 to
4 August 2024

Curators
Chen Shuxia
Min-Jung Kim

Exhibitions
Luke Parker

Translators
Yayun Zhu
Nathan Woolley

Interns
Ruieng Li
Yimeng Bu
Yuan Liu

Exhibition Design
Youssofzay + Hart
Matt Nix

Preparators
Robert Pulie
Lionel Bawden
Szymon Dorabialski
Brendan Van Hek

Mount maker
Kevin Bray

Construction
Art Services NSW
Preset Constructions

Chau Chak Wing Museum

Director
Michael Dagostino

Deputy Director
Paul Donnelly

Curator
Chen Shuxia

Collection Management
Maree Clutterbuck,
Christopher Jones, Emma
Conroy, Kerry Head, Julie
Taylor, Madeleine Snedden,
Kerry Etherington, Aggie
Wen-Fen Lu, Virginia Ho

Museum Photographer
David James

Public Engagement
Craig Barker
Julian Woods

Academic Engagement
Eve Guerry
Jane Thogersen
Liam McGeagh

Marketing
Ben Allison
Robbie Wardhaugh

Media
Jocelyn Prasad
Verity Leatherdale

Alumni and Development
Lilian Nicol-Ford

Powerhouse Museum

Chief Executive
Lisa Havilah

Director, Program (Actg.)
Matthew Connell

Head of Collection Curatorial
Jacqui Strecker

Curator
Min-Jung Kim

Registration
Steve Agius, Talya Aarons,
Bronwyn McKenzie

Conservation
Rebecca Ellis, Frances
Fitzpatrick, Meredith Freeman,
Sue Frost, Skye Mitchell,
Brooke Randall

Publishing
Sally Rose, Nicola Teffer,
Michael Fitzgerald

Photography
Jules Boag, Ryan Hernandez,
Marinco Kojdanovski, Zan
Wimberley

Rights & Permissions Officer
Harry Ree

Photography Librarian
Kathy Hackett

First Published in Australia in
2024 by Power Publications,
in association with the
Chau Chak Wing Museum,
University of Sydney and
Powerhouse Museum, Sydney

Power Publications
Power Institute Foundation
for Art and Visual Culture
University of Sydney
NSW 2006 Australia
powerinstitute.org.au

© 2024 Power Institute
Foundation for Art and Visual
Culture and the individual
authors and artists.

Individual image credits
are listed on page 252

ISBN 978-0-909952-24-2

Front and back cover (details):
*Amber toggle in the shape
of two boys* China c.1700–1940
Amber
Powerhouse Collection
Gift of Alistair Morrison
92/707
Image: Powerhouse

Publication support

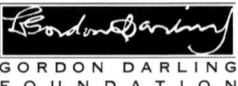

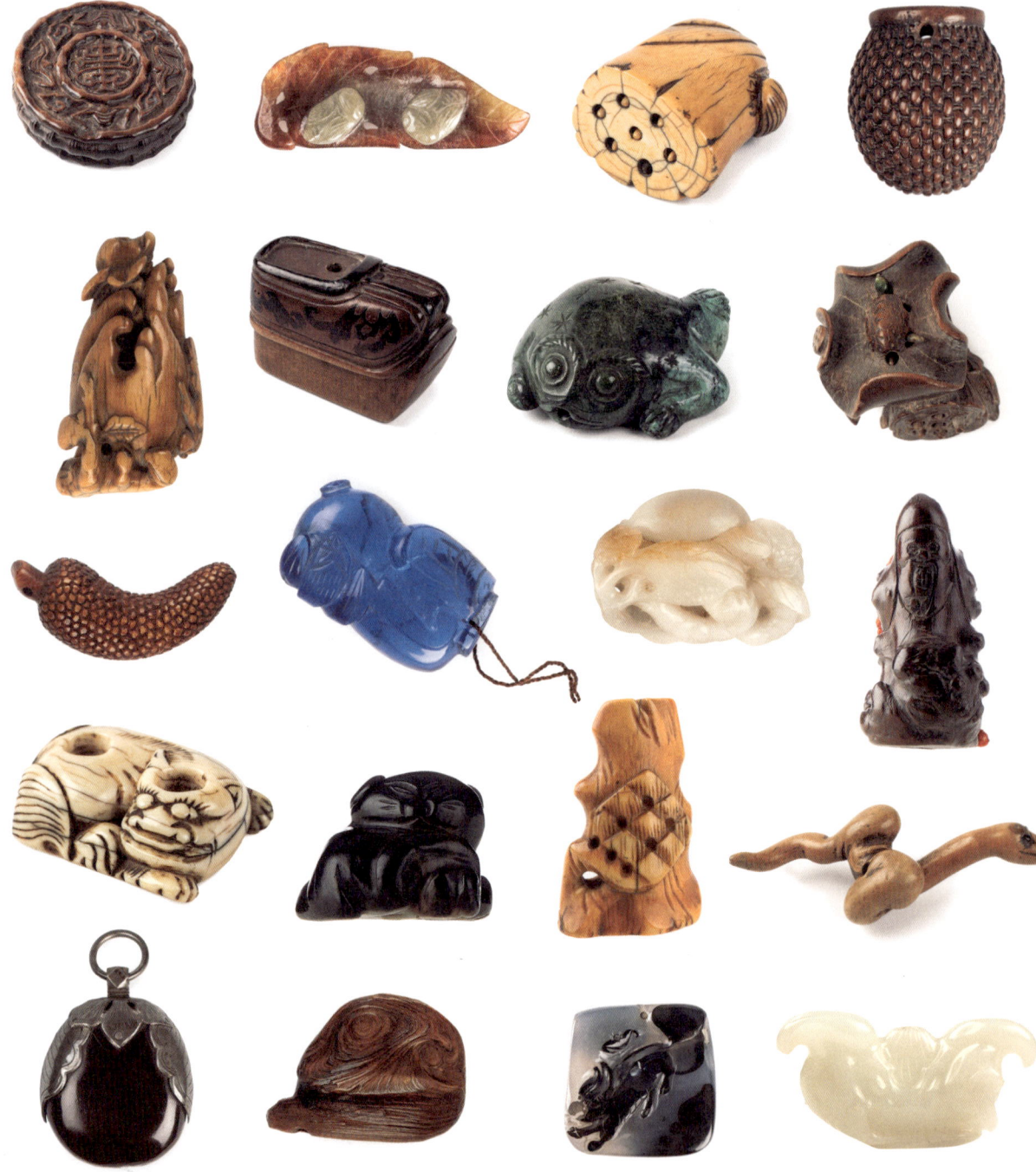